Walking the Camino de Santiago

Bethan Davies
& Ben Cole

Pili Pala Press
www.pilipalapress.com

Walking the Camino de Santiago
Published by Pili Pala Press, 2934 Woodland Drive, Vancouver, BC V5N 3R1 Canada
www.pilipalapress.com

Reprinted in 2004
cover photo: León Cathedral
back cover photo: camino sign, N120 near Astorga
Printed in Canada on 100% post-consumer recycled paper

National Library of Canada Cataloguing in Publication

Davies, Bethan, 1970-
Walking the Camino de Santiago / Bethan Davies & Ben Cole.

Includes index.
ISBN 0-9731698-0-X

1. Christian pilgrims and pilgrimages--Spain--Santiago de Compostela--Guidebooks. 2. Santiago de Compostela (Spain)--Guidebooks. 3. Spain, Northern--Guidebooks. 4. Hiking--Spain, Northern--Guidebooks. I. Cole, Ben, 1970- II. Title.
DP285.D38 2003 914.6'11 C2002-911307-5

About the Authors

Bethan Davies has been dreaming of Spain ever since her first glass of Rioja, and is now marked out as a lunatic supporter of the Spanish national football team (especially Raúl) in bars along the camino. A librarian and former editor, she co-authored Pili Pala Press' *Walking in Portugal* with Ben Cole.

Ben Cole has worked in travel bookshops for longer than he cares to remember, after gaining a degree in archaeology and ancient history. Ben fell in love with Iberia in 1993 while exploring the mountains of Portugal, and a chance encounter with the camino a few years later led to a fascination with the *camino francés*. He finds it hard to start the day without a *café solo, grande*.

Walking the Camino de Santiago

Thank you

Thanks to everyone who helped put *Walking the Camino de Santiago* together.

Our fellow pilgrims, especially Brad, Cesare, François, Frank, Pepe and Rodrigo. The *hospitaleros* along the camino who staff the *albergues* with grace and patience. Marc Stewart for sharing his experiences and getting us excited about the camino.

Bar Fonda, the best bar in the world, for great company, one-eyed football discussions, and for making us a packed lunch. And no, we're not telling you where it is.

Maria de Meynhart for additional information and Spanish lessons, and Eduardo Aragón for checking our *castellano*.

Carmen Mills and Terry Sunderland at Emerald City for answering design questions.

Ann Davies, Kerry Davies, Stuart Davies, Wendy Sokolon, and especially Michael Harling for proofreading; all the mistakes are their fault.

Ed Luciano, Alison Roy and Cudrah.

Tony McCurdy for encouragement, enthusiasm and generous leave-granting.

And to our parents, for love, support and storage.

About Pili Pala Press

Pili Pala Press was founded in 1993 to publish walking guides to the Iberian Peninsula. Pili Pala, for the uninitiated, is Welsh for butterfly (the clue's in the logo). We could say that we chose the name to reflect our love of nature and our restless desire for travel, but really we just like the way it sounds. We donate 4% of the cover price of each book to environmental organizations in Iberia. For updates, photos and more on the camino, see our web site at www.pilipalapress.com. Look out for *Walking in Portugal*, our invaluable guide to this forgotten walking destination.

Trails become overgrown, quiet lanes become main roads, and *albergues* open up and close down. Drop us a line if you find something new or different, and check out our website at www.pilipalapress.com for updates.

Contents

How This Guide Works

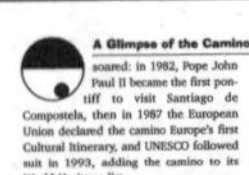

A Glimpse of the Camino

soared: in 1982, Pope John Paul II became the first pontiff to visit Santiago de Compostela, then in 1987 the European Union declared the camino Europe's first Cultural Itinerary, and UNESCO followed suit in 1993, adding the camino to its World Heritage list.

Today's pilgrims rarely make the complete journey from their homes to Santiago and back, and most prefer to follow one of the standard, well-marked routes through Spain or France. Some pilgrims walk the *vía de la plata* from Sevilla or the *camino inglés* from A Coruña, but the vast majority join the *camino francés* at some point between France and Santiago.

Any pilgrim who walks the last 100km to Santiago can apply for a *compostela* (a certificate recognizing the completion of the pilgrimage) from the authorities in Santiago de Compostela. The number of pilgrims travelling the camino peaks during Holy Years: 150,000 people reached Santiago in 1999, and future Holy Years are likely to see even more pilgrims. Even in other years, about 60,000 people follow the camino; more than half are from Spain, and most of the rest are European or from the Americas.

Some pilgrim traditions have survived into the modern era. Many pilgrims walk with the aid of a tall staff and wear a scallop shell attached to their pack or person, mimicking statues of Santiago Peregrino. The beaches of Galicia are awash with scallop shells, and medieval pilgrims would often collect one as a souvenir of their journey; scallop symbols are also ubiquitous along the route, adorning concrete camino markers, churches, and houses along the way.

Even some of the pilgrim songs survive, as does *¡Ultreia!* an exhortation to pilgrims to keep going, which you'll see graffitied on walls and underpasses along the way.

Walking

Hiking is gaining popularity in Spain, particularly amongst certain southern city dwellers who escape to cooler mountain regions like the Picos de Europa on sticky summer weekends. You'll see some signs for day walks along the camino, particularly close to cities like Burgos and Logroño, but most northern urbanites prefer the civilized tradition of the evening stroll, browsing in shop windows, sipping Rioja and nibbling at *tapas*. In places like rural Galicia, walking is an integral part of life, whether heading to work in the fields or making for a post-farming glass of wine, and exercise for exercise's sake can be seen as rather ridiculous.

Of course, the camino's Christian origins make it much more than a multi-week walking holiday, and locals won't consider walking pilgrims the least bit strange. You'll hardly be a curiosity, either, what with hordes of pilgrims streaming towards Santiago. It's not surprising that some locals become fed up with pilgrims tramping past their front door, particularly in Galicia where more and more people join the camino. A smattering of *Castellano* (Spanish) and a willingness to stop and talk will make a big difference to the welcome you receive.

If you decide to continue to Finisterre, the number of pilgrims drops off rapidly,

4

A Glimpse of the Camino

and you'll have far more opportunities to meet and talk to local people.

There's a certain snooty hierarchy amongst pilgrims. Many walkers look down on cyclists, often called *peregrinos descafeinados* (decaffeinated pilgrims), and *albergues* (pilgrim hostels) may refuse to admit cycling pilgrims, or ask them to wait until early evening before deciding if there's room. Self-propelled pilgrims, even non-religious ones, often dismiss car-pilgrims as "tourists." Pilgrims on horses or donkeys are now a rarity: fewer than 1% of pilgrims travel this way.

Trails

The camino heads across Spain on a variety of different surfaces, from narrow paths to wide tracks to tarmac (paved roads). It's mostly easy walking with very few rough or uneven surfaces, although some stone and mud tracks can become slippery after rain. Road walking can be unpleasant, and occasional stretches are dangerous due to narrow shoulders, busy roads, and blind corners. Walk in a group on the left-hand side of the road (facing oncoming traffic) if possible.

Trail marking is generally excellent, and the abundance of yellow arrows makes it difficult to lose your way. Markers vary from concrete bollards marked with scallop shells, to the ever-present yellow arrows painted on everything from pavements to trees to the sides of houses. Navigating through cities can be difficult as new building work or industrial development can obliterate arrows and paths.

On the *meseta* in particular there can be long stretches with very little or no shade. The wind on the plains can be strong and quickly sap your energy; you'll need to eat plenty and drink lots of water, even if it isn't very hot.

Maps

Most pilgrims don't bother with detailed maps, as the camino is generally well-marked and easy to follow. Almost every turn is marked with a yellow arrow or a scallop shell, and people you meet along the way will always be able to direct you to the camino if you should stray from the route — see our language section on page 195 for helpful walking phrases.

Michelin maps 442 and 441 are good for a general overview of the camino, and although they're next to useless for walking, they do mark most of the towns and villages you'll pass through. The sketch maps in this book will give you a general idea of the villages, terrain and sights you'll encounter, along with distances and facilities along the way.

If you're determined to weigh down your backpack with walking maps, the Spanish Instituto Geográfico Nacional (www.mfom.es/ign/) publishes up-to-date 1:25,000 maps, while the Servicio Geográfico del Ejército publishes the most current 1:50,000 maps. Walking maps are difficult to find along the camino, but can be ordered from the UK before you go.

Try Stanfords in London (☎ 020 7836 1321; www.stanfords.co.uk), the Map Centre in Hereford (☎ 01432 266322;

5

Glimpse of the Camino (page 2)

Background information about the camino, walking, geography, food & drink, history and the arts.

Flora (page 16) & Fauna (page 18)

English, Spanish and Latin names of birds, mammals, reptiles, amphibians and trees. Includes detailed identification tips, quirky facts and illustrations.

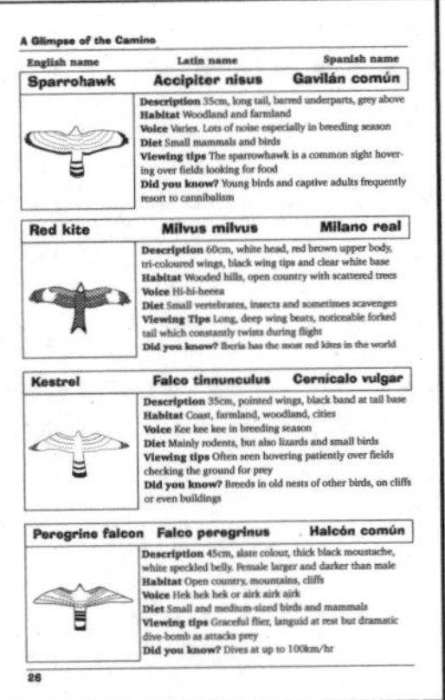

A Glimpse of the Camino

English name	Latin name	Spanish name
Sparrowhawk	Accipiter nisus	Gavilán común

Description 35cm, long tail, barred underparts, grey above
Habitat Woodland and farmland
Voice Varies. Lots of noise especially in breeding season
Diet Small mammals and birds
Viewing tips The sparrowhawk is a common sight hovering over fields looking for food
Did you know? Young birds and captive adults frequently resort to cannibalism

Red kite	Milvus milvus	Milano real

Description 60cm, white head, red brown upper body, tri-coloured wings, black wing tips and clear white base
Habitat Wooded hills, open country with scattered trees
Voice Hi-hi-heeea
Diet Small vertebrates, insects and sometimes scavenges
Viewing Tips Long, deep wing beats, noticeable forked tail which constantly twists during flight
Did you know? Iberia has the most red kites in the world

Kestrel	Falco tinnunculus	Cernícalo vulgar

Description 35cm, pointed wings, black band at tail base
Habitat Coast, farmland, woodland, cities
Voice Kee kee kee in breeding season
Diet Mainly rodents, but also lizards and small birds
Viewing tips Often seen hovering patiently over fields checking the ground for prey
Did you know? Breeds in old nests of other birds, on cliffs or even buildings

Peregrine falcon	Falco peregrinus	Halcón común

Description 45cm, slate colour, thick black moustache, white speckled belly. Female larger and darker than male
Habitat Open country, mountains, cliffs
Voice Hek hek hek or airk airk airk
Diet Small and medium-sized birds and mammals
Viewing tips Graceful flier, languid at rest but dramatic dive-bomb as attacks prey
Did you know? Dives at up to 100km/hr

26

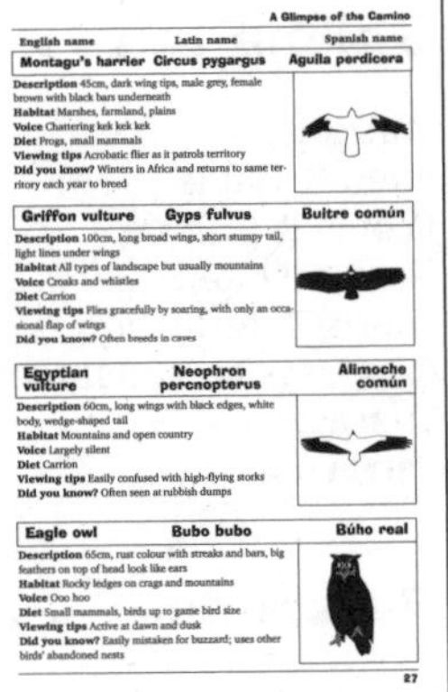

A Glimpse of the Camino

English name	Latin name	Spanish name
Montagu's harrier	Circus pygargus	Aguila perdicera

Description 45cm, dark wing tips, male grey, female brown with black bars underneath
Habitat Marshes, farmland, plains
Voice Chattering kek kek kek
Diet Frogs, small mammals
Viewing tips Acrobatic flier as it patrols territory
Did you know? Winters in Africa and returns to same territory each year to breed

Griffon vulture	Gyps fulvus	Buitre común

Description 100cm, long broad wings, short stumpy tail, light lines under wings
Habitat All types of landscape but usually mountains
Voice Croaks and whistles
Diet Carrion
Viewing tips Flies gracefully by soaring, with only an occasional flap of wings
Did you know? Often breeds in caves

Egyptian vulture	Neophron percnopterus	Alimoche común

Description 60cm, long wings with black edges, white body, wedge-shaped tail
Habitat Mountains and open country
Voice Largely silent
Diet Carrion
Viewing tips Easily confused with high-flying storks
Did you know? Often seen at rubbish dumps

Eagle owl	Bubo bubo	Búho real

Description 65cm, rust colour with streaks and bars, big feathers on top of head look like ears
Habitat Rocky ledges on crags and mountains
Voice Ooo hoo
Diet Small mammals, birds up to game bird size
Viewing tips Active at dawn and dusk
Did you know? Easily mistaken for buzzard; uses other birds' abandoned nests

27

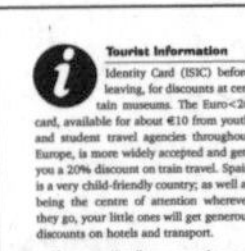

Tourist Information

Identity Card (ISIC) before leaving, for discounts at certain museums. The Euro<26 card, available for about €10 from youth and student travel agencies throughout Europe, is more widely accepted and gets you a 20% discount on train travel. Spain is a very child-friendly country; as well as being the centre of attention wherever they go, your little ones will get generous discounts on hotels and transport.

If you stay in *albergues*, eat the *menu del día* once a day, and picnic on bread and cheese in the meantime, you can get by on €20 a day. To eat all your meals in cafés or restaurants, and to splurge on a hotel every now and then, allow about €40 a day. Exchange rates vary, but as a rough idea, €1=US$1.

How much does it cost?

Albergue	€3–€7
Cheap hotel, double room	€25–€35
Menú (3-course meal)	€6–€9
Cheap bottle of wine	€2–€3

Transport

At some point along the way, you may need to recover from injury, catch up time, or simply miss out a section — some pilgrims skip the *meseta* between Burgos and León, for example. Spanish trains, run by RENFE, are generally good value, and the most useful line for pilgrims is the one from Santiago to Hendaye on the French border, which passes through Ponferrada, Astorga, Léon and Burgos. You can get information and book tickets online at www.renfe.es.

Buses are usually a more flexible option. In smaller places the bus stop can be just a street corner and a café may act as the ticket office; ask a few locals where the bus stops and when it leaves.

Hitching long distances can be a frustrating experience, as foreign visitors are loathe to pick up hitchhikers and locals may only be travelling as far as the next village. For shorter distances, hitching may be a useful option, particularly on weekends when bus services are limited. Hitching does, of course, involve risk, so take care.

Car hire is cheap compared to the rest of Europe, and can be a good way of visiting sites on rest days, or of getting from Santiago to airports like Bilbao and Madrid.

Not all *albergues* allow cyclists to stay, and some will only do so in late evening, after walkers have arrived for the day. This makes for a frustrating wait to find a bed. Road conditions are generally good, and most of the off-road tracks can be ridden on a mountain bike. Most airlines will transport bikes for free, but find out in advance about any restrictions and requirements.

Accommodation

Albergues

Albergues, also known as *refugios*, provide cheap places to stay at regular points along the camino. They are restricted to self-powered pilgrims, and insist on seeing your *credencial* before giving you a bed. While most *albergues* take bicycles, walking pilgrims generally have priority,

30

Tourist Information

and cyclists may have to wait until the evening before being given a space.

No longer simply a roof over your head, modern *albergues* sometimes contain microwave ovens, washing machines and coffee machines. About half the *albergues* along the camino have kitchen facilities, although stoves can work sporadically and pans may be in short supply. Most will provide a sink to wash your clothes and a line to hang them out to dry.

Accommodation is mostly in mixed bunk-bed dormitories, and while blankets are often provided, it's a good idea to bring a thin sleeping bag. Bunk beds are crammed into every available space, and are often laid out side-by-side, letting you have a close relationship with the person in the next bed. Toilets and shower facilities are usually mixed too: if privacy is a big concern, you'll need to stay in a hotel.

Most *albergues* have a 10pm curfew, although some doors stay open until 11pm. Mornings tend to begin early and, even if you fancy a lie-in, the noise of other pilgrims packing up and leaving is likely to wake you up. Earplugs can be an essential piece of equipment, not only to block out early risers, but also to try and get some sleep at night over the noise of *broncadores* (snorers).

Albergues are generally staffed by an *hospitalero*, more often then not a returning pilgrim who works for between a week and a month. In Galicia, *albergues* are minimally staffed and not always well-maintained: invest in some toilet paper. *Albergues* are a wonderful way to meet other pilgrims, share meals and stories, and compare blisters and sore knees. They generally cost from €3 to €7; Galician *albergues* ask for a donation from pilgrims. Some *albergues* stay open year-round, while others close for the winter; all will be packed from June to September.

The Spanish call pilgrim hostels *albergues* or *refugios*; we use *albergue* in this book, and attempt to list every one along the way.

Casas, hotels & paradors

There are places to stay in most villages, and even if there isn't a hotel someone in the village will rent out rooms; local café-bars are generally the best place to ask about somewhere to stay.

At the other end of the price scale, *paradors* are government-run luxury hotels, often in sumptuously converted historic buildings; they're well worth the splurge.

Within each area we include accommodation suggestions for a range of budgets. Accommodation is divided into the price categories given below. The price given is for a double room in high season; rates drop at other times and may be open to negotiation.

$	up to €30
$$	€30–€50
$$$	€50–€75
$$$$	more than €75

Camping

Most campsites are inconveniently located a few kilometres off the camino or a fair way out of town. They often have excellent facilities, but can be noisy on weekends. It may be worth bringing a tent in summer, as packed-out *albergues*

31

Tourist Information (page 28)

Practical information to ease your pilgrimage. What to do before you leave, what to bring, how to get there, where to stay, how much things cost, and what to if things go wrong.

Regional chapters

regional map

weather

regional symbol

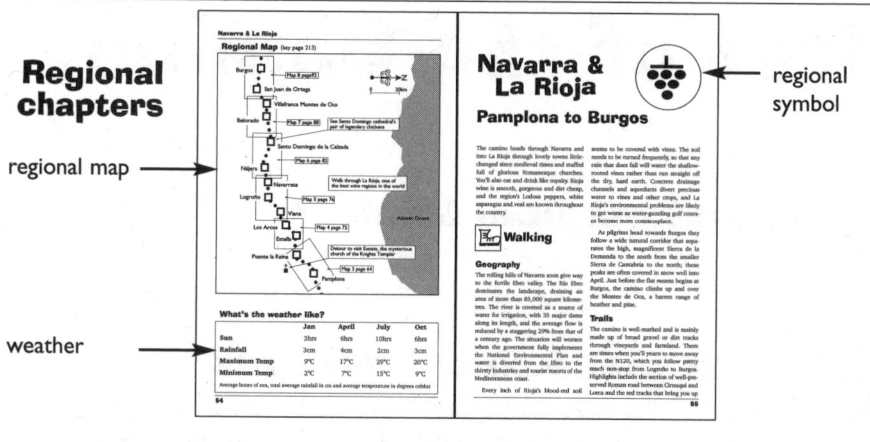

Navarra & La Rioja

Regional Map (key page 213)

What's the weather like?

	Jan	April	July	Oct
Sun	3hrs	6hrs	10hrs	6hrs
Rainfall	3cm	4cm	2cm	3cm
Maximum Temp	9°C	17°C	29°C	20°C
Minimum Temp	2°C	7°C	15°C	9°C

Average hours of sun, total average rainfall in cm and average temperature in degrees celsius

54

Navarra & La Rioja

Pamplona to Burgos

The camino heads through Navarra and into La Rioja through lovely towns little-changed since medieval times and stuffed full of glorious Romanesque churches. You'll also eat and drink like royalty. Rioja wine is smooth, gorgeous and dirt cheap, and the region's Lodosa peppers, white asparagus and veal are known throughout the country.

Walking

Geography

The rolling hills of Navarra soon give way to the fertile Ebro valley. The Río Ebro dominates the landscape, draining an area of more than 85,000 square kilometres. The river is coveted as a source of water for irrigation, with 35 major dams along its length, and the average flow is reduced by a staggering 29% from that of a century ago. The situation will worsen when the government fully implements the National Environmental Plan and water is diverted from the Ebro to the thirsty industries and tourist resorts of the Mediterranean coast.

Every inch of Rioja's blood-red soil seems to be covered with vines. The soil needs to be turned frequently, so that any rain that does fall will water the shallow-rooted vines rather than run straight off the dry, hard earth. Concrete drainage channels and aqueducts divert precious water to vines and other crops, and La Rioja's environmental problems are likely to get worse as water-guzzling golf courses become more commonplace.

As pilgrims head towards Burgos they follow a wide natural corridor that separates the high, magnificent Sierra de la Demanda to the south from the smaller Sierra de Cantabria to the north; these peaks are often covered in snow well into April. Just before the flat meseta begins at Burgos, the camino climbs up and over the Montes de Oca, a barren range of heather and pine.

Trails

The camino is well-marked and is mainly made up of broad gravel or dirt tracks through vineyards and farmland. There are times when you'll yearn to move away from the N120, which you follow pretty much non-stop from Logroño to Burgos. Highlights include the section of well-preserved Roman road between Cirauqui and Lorca and the red tracks that bring you up

55

Regional Information

regional flora & fauna, people & culture, food & drink and tourist information

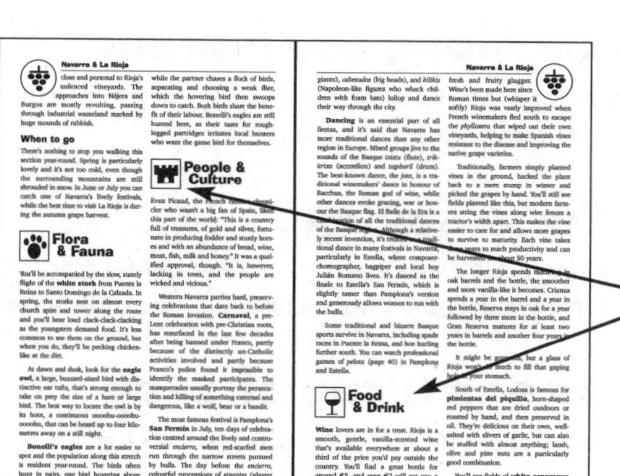

Navarra & La Rioja

close and personal to Rioja's unfenced vineyards. The approaches into Nájera and Burgos are mostly revolting, passing through industrial wasteland marked by huge mounds of rubbish.

When to go

There's nothing to stop you walking this section year-round. Spring is particularly lovely and it's not too cold, even though the surrounding mountains are still shrouded in snow. In June or July you can catch one of Navarra's lively festivals, while the best time to visit La Rioja is during the autumn grape harvest.

Flora & Fauna

You'll be accompanied by the slow, stately flight of the **white stork** from Puente la Reina to Santo Domingo de la Calzada. In spring, the storks nest on almost every church spire and tower along the route and you'll hear loud clack-clack-clacking as the youngsters demand food. It's less common to see them on the ground, but when you do, they'll be pecking chicken-like at the dirt.

At dawn and dusk, look for the **eagle owl**, a large, buzzard-sized bird with distinctive ear tufts, that's strong enough to take on prey the size of a hare or large bird. The best way to locate the owl is by its hoot, a continuous ooooohu-oooohu-oooohu, that can be heard up to four kilometres away on a still night.

Bonelli's eagles are a lot easier to spot and the population along this stretch is resident year-round. The birds often hunt in pairs, one bird hovering above while the partner chases a flock of birds, separating and choosing a weak flier, which the hovering bird then swoops down to catch. Both birds share the benefit of their labour. Bonelli's eagles are still hunted here, as their taste for rough-legged partridges irritates local hunters who want the game bird for themselves.

People & Culture

Even Picaud, the French cleric chronicler who wasn't a big fan of Spain, liked this part of the world: "This is a country full of treasures, of gold and silver, fortunate in producing fodder and sturdy horses and with an abundance of bread, wine, meat, fish, milk and honey." It was a qualified approval, though. "It is, however, lacking in trees, and the people are wicked and vicious."

Western Navarra parties hard, preserving celebrations that date back to before the Roman invasion. **Carnaval**, a pre-Lent celebration with pre-Christian roots, has resurfaced in the last few decades after being banned under Franco, partly because of the distinctly un-Catholic activities involved and partly because Franco's police found it impossible to identify the masked participants. The masquerades usually portray the persecution and killing of something external and dangerous, like a wolf, bear or a bandit.

The most famous festival is Pamplona's **San Fermín** in July, ten days of celebration centred around the lively and controversial *encierro*, when red-scarfed men run through the narrow streets pursued by bulls. The day before the *encierro*, colourful processions of *gigantes* (plaster

56

Navarra & La Rioja

giants), *cabezudos* (big heads), and *kilikis* (Napoleon-like figures who whack children with foam bats) lollop and dance their way through the city.

Dancing is an essential part of all fiestas, and it's said that Navarra has more traditional dances than any other region in Europe. Mixed groups jive to the sounds of the Basque *txistu* (flute), *trikitrixa* (accordion) and *tagbord* (drum). The best-known dance, the *jota*, is a traditional winemakers' dance in honour of Bacchus, the Roman god of wine, while other dances evoke grazing, war or honour the Basque flag. El Baile de la Era is a celebration of all the traditional dances of the Basque region. Although a relatively recent invention, it's treated as a traditional dance in many festivals in Navarra, particularly in Estella, where composer-choreographer, bagpiper and local boy Julián Romano lives. It's danced as the finale to Estella's San Fermín, which is slightly tamer than Pamplona's version and generously allows women to run with the bulls.

Some traditional and bizarre Basque sports survive in Navarra, including spade races in Puente la Reina, and hoe hurling further south. You can watch professional games of pelota (page 40) in Pamplona and Estella.

Food & Drink

Wine lovers are in for a treat. Rioja is a smooth, gentle, vanilla-scented wine that's available everywhere at about a third of the price you'd pay outside the country. You'll find a great bottle for around €5, and even €2 will get you a fresh and fruity glugger. Wine's been made here since Roman times but (whisper it softly) Rioja was vastly improved when French winemakers fled south to escape the *phylloxera* that wiped out their own vineyards, helping to make Spanish vines resistant to the disease and improving the native grape varieties.

Traditionally, farmers simply planted vines in the ground, hacked the plant back to a mere stump in winter and picked the grapes by hand. You'll still see fields planted like this, but modern farmers string the vines along wire fences a tractor's width apart. This makes the vine easier to care for and allows more grapes to survive to maturity. Each vine takes three years to reach productivity and can be harvested for about 50 years.

The longer Rioja spends maturing in oak barrels and the bottle, the smoother and more vanilla-like it becomes. Crianza spends a year in the barrel and a year in the bottle, Reserva stays in oak for a year followed by three more in the bottle, and Gran Reserva matures for at least two years in barrels and another four years in the bottle.

It might be gorgeous, but a glass of Rioja won't do much to fill that gaping hole in your stomach.

South of Estella, Lodosa is famous for **pimientos del piquillo**, horn-shaped red peppers that are dried outdoors or roasted by hand, and then preserved in oil. They're delicious on their own, well-salted with slivers of garlic, but can also be stuffed with almost anything; lamb, olive and pine nuts are a particularly good combination.

You'll see fields of **white asparagus**

57

Walk Description

camino sketch map includes distances & at-a-glance symbols

camino profile chart

camino route description

camino town description includes at-a-glance symbols

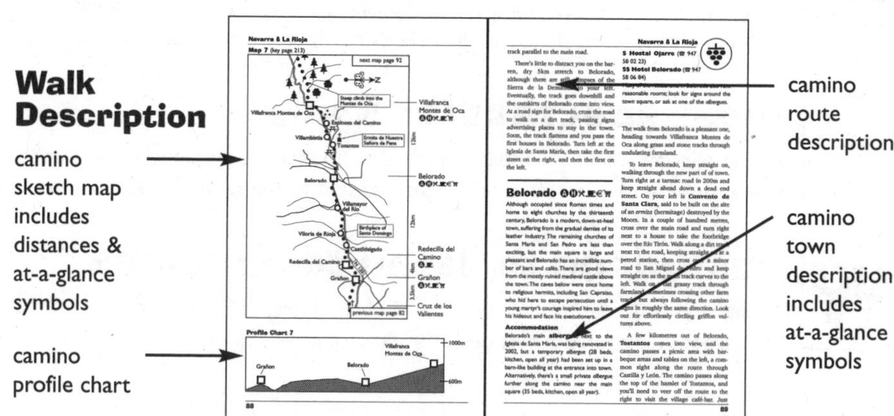

Navarra & La Rioja

Map 7 (key page 213)

Profile Chart 7

88

track parallel to the main road.

There's little to distract you on the barren, dry 5km stretch to Belorado, although there are glimpses of the Sierra de la Demanda to your left. Eventually, the track goes downhill and the outskirts of Belorado come into view. At a road sign for Belorado, cross the road to walk on a dirt track, passing signs advertising places to stay in the town. Soon, the track flattens and you pass the first houses in Belorado. Turn left at the Iglesia de Santa María, then take the first street on the right, and then the first on the left.

Belorado

Although occupied since Roman times and home to eight churches by the thirteenth century, Belorado is a modern, down-at-heel town, suffering from the gradual demise of its leather industry. The remaining churches of Santa María and San Pedro are less than exciting, but the main square is large and pleasant and Belorado has an incredible number of bars and cafés. There are good views from the mostly ruined medieval castle above the town. The caves below were once home to religious hermits, including San Caprasio, who hid here to escape persecution until a young martyr's courage inspired him to leave his hideout and face his executioners.

Accommodation

Belorado's main albergue, next to the Iglesia de Santa María, was being renovated in 2002, but a temporary albergue (28 beds, kitchen, open all year) had been set up in a barn-like building at the entrance into town. Alternatively, there's a small private albergue further along the camino near the main square (35 beds, kitchen, open all year).

Navarra & La Rioja

$ Hostal Ojarre (☎ 947 58 02 23)

$$ Hotel Belorado (☎ 947 58 06 84)

Many of the bars in Belorado also have reasonable rooms; look for signs around the town square, or ask at one of the albergues.

The walk from Belorado is a pleasant one, heading towards Villafranca Montes de Oca along grass and stone tracks through undulating farmland.

To leave Belorado, keep straight on, walking through the new part of of town. Turn right at a tarmac road in 200m and keep straight ahead down a dead end street. On your left is **Convento de Santa Clara**, said to be built on the site of an *ermita* (hermitage) destroyed by the Moors. In a couple of hundred metres, cross over the main road and turn right next to a house to take the footbridge over the Río Tirón. Walk along a dirt track next to the road, keeping straight at a petrol station, then cross over a minor road to San Miguel de Pedroso and keep straight on as the grassy track curves to the left. Walk on the grassy track through farmland, sometimes crossing other farm tracks but always following the camino signs in roughly the same direction. Look out for effortlessly circling griffon vultures above.

A few kilometres out of Belorado, **Tostantos** comes into view, and the camino passes a picnic area with barbeque areas and tables on the left, a common sight along the route through Castilla y León. The camino passes along the top of the hamlet of Tostantos, and you'll need to veer off the route to the right to visit the village café-bar. Just

89

Best of the Camino

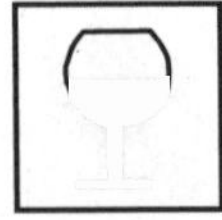

most magical drink

Jesús Jato's *queimada* ritual at the Ave Fenix *albergue* in Villafranca del Bierzo (page 147), where potent *orujo* is set on fire amidst chants and spells.

best place to eat octopus

At Pulpería Ezequiel in Melide (page 171) you'll be served paprika-spiced *pulpo* (octopus) on a wooden platter, washed down with cloudy Ribeiro wine.

oldest person along the camino

Archaeologists at Atapuerca (page 94) discovered an 800,000 year old skeleton, said to be *homo antecessor*, an early ancestor of *homo sapiens*.

best place for a splurge

Save your euros for León (page 120), where you can stay at the Parador San Marcos, one of the world's finest hotels, and graze on *tapas* until the small hours.

best place to see birds of prey

The Pyrenees (page 38) are home to golden eagles, short-toed eagles, griffon vultures and black vultures. If you're lucky, you may catch a glimpse of a lammergeier.

most underrated city

Burgos (page 100) is seen by the rest of Spain as dull and grey, but it's a lively city with don't-miss monuments, particularly its newly spruced-up cathedral.

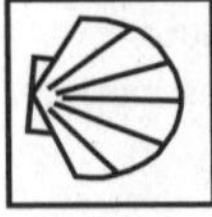

most spectacular Mass

At the pilgrims' Mass in Santiago's cathedral (page 179), the *botafumeiro*, a massive incense burner, is swung across the transept in a huge, head-skimming arc.

best place to listen to bagpipes

Sitting next to a roaring fire in foggy O Cebreiro (page 151), where many of the bars erupt in impromptu sessions of traditional *gallego* music.

best place to get your feet wet

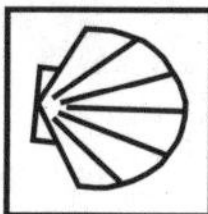

End the camino in feet-soothing style at the sea in Finisterre (page 191), where you can pick up a scallop shell and visit the end of the world.

oddest-looking bird

On the *meseta*, listen out for the pooo-pooo-pooo call of the hoopoe (page 23), and look for its distinctive coral and black mohican.

most eerie landscape

The ruined buildings and empty streets of the abandoned village of Foncedadón (page 138) are at their spookiest in the area's persistent mists and fogs.

best place to be like Hemingway

Ernest Hemingway's favourite weekend retreat was at Burguete (page 48), where he'd stay at the Hostal Burguete and fish for trout in the Río Urrobi.

most spectacular use of glass

León cathedral's acres of stained glass windows (page 121), a riot of blues and reds and greens.

most topsy-turvy dinner

A long, languid *cocido maragato* (page 131), where the meat-laden first course is followed by vegetables and then soup. It's enough to feed the hungriest pilgrim.

best medieval flashback

Set in mountainous isolation, the atmospheric *albergue* at Manjarín (page 139) lacks beds and electricity, and you'll sleep in the same building as the local cows.

most essential equipment

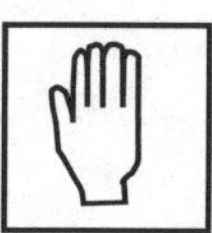

Don't go anywhere without your *credencial* (page 29), the pilgrims' passport that lets you stay in *albergues* along the camino.

best source of up-to-date information on the camino

See our web site at www.pilipalapress.com for photos, updates & links.

Map of the Camino

(key page 213)

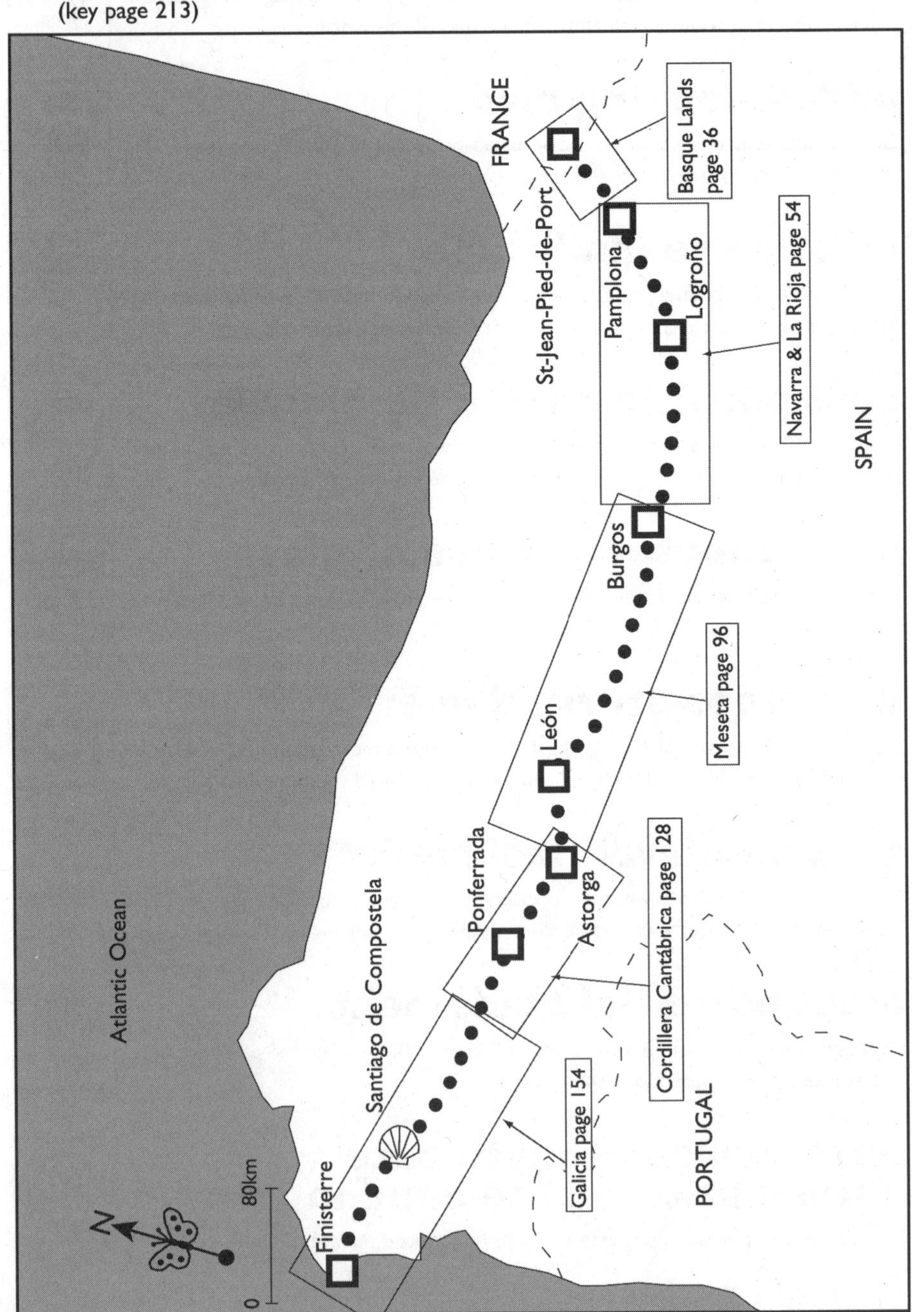

An Introduction to the Camino

The Camino de Santiago (the Way of St James) is a glorious 900km amble across the north of Spain, following an ancient pilgrimage route west to the magnificent cathedral at Santiago de Compostela. Tenth-century pilgrims braved bandits and wolves in their quest to revere the bones of St James, entombed in a silver casket in the cathedral. Ancient star-gazing Celts went this way too, following the Milky Way west towards the setting sun and the solar temple of Ara Solis at Finis Terrae, the end of the earth.

Today, pilgrims walk to Santiago and Finisterre for many different reasons. For some, making a pilgrimage to the Holy City is a lifelong dream borne out of religious faith. Others seek a break from daily routines or want to get back to a simpler way of living, and some want to immerse themselves in Spanish history and culture. You needn't be a hard-core hiker to walk to Santiago, as the trails are well-maintained and ubiquitous yellow arrows make them easy to follow and the journey is made easier and more sociable by a centuries-old infrastructure of *albergues* (pilgrim hostels).

This guide leads you step-by-step along the *camino francés*, from St-Jean-Pied-de-Port in the foothills of the French Pyrenees to Santiago de Compostela and on to Finisterre. On the way, you'll pass through a multitude of Spains. You'll see gorgeous Romanesque churches decorated with grotesque gargoyles and elaborate frescoes, ethereal Gothic cathedrals with airy spires and vast interiors, and tiny *ermitas* (hermitages) tucked into cliff faces. We'll steer you towards colourful, riotous festivals, where you can dance to Galician bagpipes or watch crazy, traditional Basque sports like hoe-hurling. We'll help you choose a great bottle of Rioja, order a cheap and hearty three-course dinner, and try regional specialities from white asparagus to spicy octopus. There's spectacular wildlife, too, from wolves and bears that roam northern Spain's mountain ranges, to peculiar, plain-dwelling birds such as great bustards and hoopoes. And we'll smooth your journey with practical information, from accommodation options to useful phrases in *Castellano* (Spanish) and a smattering of *Galega* (Galician) and *Euskara* (Basque).

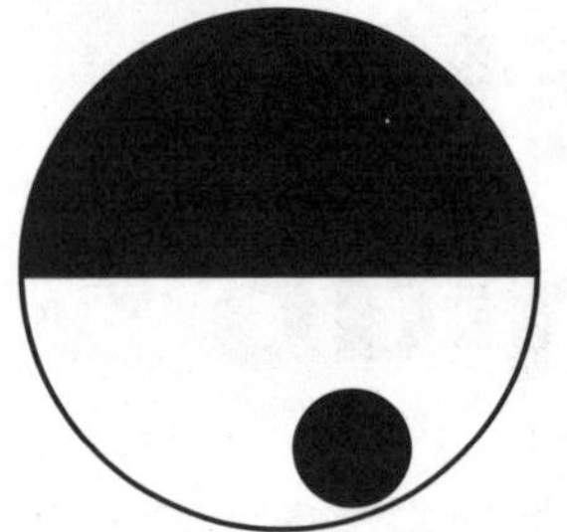

A Glimpse of the Camino

El Camino

The story of Santiago

Quite how Santiago ended up in a remote northwestern corner of Iberia is a strange and marvellous tale.

Santiago, or St James as he's known in English, was one of Jesus' apostles, and after the Crucifixion, he headed to Spain to spread the Gospel. Though he preached as far north as Galicia, he didn't have much luck with the native peoples, and attracted a mere seven converts before turning to head home.

While there's no biblical basis for Santiago's visit to Spain, it is clear that Herod Agrippa had him beheaded in 44AD in Jerusalem, making him the first apostle to be martyred. Santiago's friends managed to sneak his body out from under Herod's nose, and put him on a stone boat headed for northwest Spain without oars, sails or crew. After a week-long journey, the body arrived in Padrón on the Galician coast, where his disciples were waiting. They buried Santiago 20km inland in Compostela, after the local Queen witnessed a series of miracles and converted to Christianity.

Santiago lay forgotten for a good few centuries, while all around him Spain became Christian through rather gradual, more conventional means. The move to Christianity ended abruptly at the start of the eighth century, when Muslim armies crossed over from North Africa, soon conquering most of the Iberian Peninsula and pushing up into central France. Still, pockets of Christianity remained, notably in northwestern Spain.

In 813, a curious Christian hermit followed sweet music and twinkling stars to a remote hillside in Galicia. The bones he found at Campus Stellae (Compostela) were quickly identified as those of Santiago, and the bishop of nearby Iria Flavia sanctified the discovery. Within a few years, Alfonso II, King of Asturias, visited the site, built a chapel and declared Santiago the patron saint of Spain.

Visions of Santiago multiplied, and the saint became instrumental in the fight against the Muslims. His most famous appearance was at the battle of Clavijo, near Logroño, where he rode high above the battle on a white charger, and personally scythed his way through tens of thousands of Moors. This kind of behaviour made him known as Santiago Matamoros (Moor-slayer), to go with his more pacific image as Santiago Peregrino (pilgrim).

The history of the camino

Well before Santiago's time, the ancient Celts had their own version of the camino, following the *via lactea* (Milky Way) towards the sea at Finis Terrae (Finisterre), the end of the known world and as far west as they could travel without getting their feet wet.

By the ninth century, Christian authorities had seized on the pilgrimage to Santiago as a way to drive out Muslim invaders and to prevent the peoples of northern Spain from falling back on their pagan ways. Local churchmen were also keen on the cash flow that a stream of pilgrims would bring, and their promotion of Santiago de Compostela as a pilgrimage destination was a masterful piece of medieval marketing.

The number of pilgrims rose over the next couple of hundred years, particularly after the Turkish capture of the Holy Sepulchre made Jerusalem unsafe for pilgrims. The French were particularly keen, so much so that the main route over the Pyrenees from St-Jean-Pied-de-Port and across Spain is called the *camino francés*.

In 1189, Pope Alexander III declared Santiago de Compostela a Holy City, along with Rome and Jerusalem. Under his edict, pilgrims who arrive during Holy Years (when the Día de Santiago, July 25, falls on a Sunday) can bypass purgatory entirely, while those arriving in other years get half their time off.

It wasn't all voluntary penitence; sometimes people were sentenced to walk to Santiago as punishment for a crime, although wealthy convicts could get around this by paying someone else to walk the pilgrimage. Other pilgrims went on behalf of their villages in an effort to get rid of plagues, floods or locusts, or as an excuse to see the world in the days before package holidays.

Churches and pilgrim hospices sprung up along the camino, often built on the site of miracles. Their walls provided havens from a dangerous and arduous outside world, where wolves and bandits thwarted the faithful.

The stream of pilgrims peaked in the eleventh and twelfth centuries, when about half a million people made the pilgrimage and when many of the towns and cities along the camino were built. French pilgrims of this time may well have been guided by the *Codex Calixtinus*, a twelfth-century travel guide usually attributed to Aymeric Picaud, a cantankerous French monk with bile-filled views about almost all the people he met and most of the land he walked through.

The number of pilgrims dropped off once the Christian reconquest was complete, and had fallen considerably by the time that Domenico Laffi, a seventeenth-century Italian pilgrim, wrote his guide to the *camino francés*. The steady decline continued through the eighteenth and nineteenth centuries, and by the mid-twentieth century only a few hardy souls walked the camino.

The camino today

Although the camino had dropped off the world tourism radar, it wasn't entirely forgotten. Santiago remained the patron saint of Spain, and local people were still able to trace the route of the camino through their villages. In one of these villages in the 1960s, Don Elias Valiña, the parish priest at O Cebreiro, began a meticulous labour of love that eventually became *El Camino de Santiago*, the camino's first modern-day guidebook. By the 1980s, the camino's popularity had soared: in 1982, Pope John Paul II became the first pontiff to visit Santiago de Compostela, then in 1987 the European Union declared the camino Europe's first Cultural Itinerary, and UNESCO followed suit in 1993, adding the camino to its World Heritage list.

Today's pilgrims rarely make the complete journey from their homes to Santiago and back, and most prefer to follow one of the standard, well-marked routes through Spain or France. Some pilgrims walk the *via de la plata* from Sevilla or the *camino inglés* from A Coruña, but the vast majority join the *camino francés* at some point between France and Santiago.

Any pilgrim who walks the last 100km to Santiago can apply for a *compostela* (a certificate recognizing the completion of the pilgrimage) from the authorities in Santiago de Compostela. The number of pilgrims travelling the camino peaks during Holy Years: 150,000 people reached Santiago in 1999, and future Holy Years are likely to see even more pilgrims. Even in other years, about 60,000 people follow the camino; more than half are from Spain, and most of the rest are European or from the Americas.

Some pilgrim traditions have survived into the modern era. Many pilgrims walk with the aid of a tall staff and wear a scallop shell attached to their pack or person, mimicking statues of Santiago Peregrino. The beaches of Galicia are awash with scallop shells, and medieval pilgrims would often collect one as a souvenir of their journey; scallop symbols are also ubiquitous along the route, adorning concrete camino markers, churches, and houses along the way.

Even some of the pilgrim songs survive, as does ¡*Ultreia*! an exhortation to pilgrims to keep going, which you'll see graffitied on walls and underpasses along the way.

Walking

Hiking is gaining popularity in Spain, particularly amongst certain southern city dwellers who escape to cooler mountain regions like the Picos de Europa on sticky summer weekends. You'll see some signs for day walks along the camino, particularly close to cities like Burgos and Logroño, but most northern urbanites prefer the civilized tradition of the evening stroll, browsing in shop windows, sipping Rioja and nibbling at *tapas*. In places like rural Galicia, walking is an integral part of life, whether heading to work in the fields or making for a post-farming glass of wine, and exercise for exercise's sake can be seen as rather ridiculous.

Of course, the camino's Christian origins make it much more than a multi-week walking holiday, and locals won't consider walking pilgrims the least bit strange. You'll hardly be a curiosity, either, what with hordes of pilgrims streaming towards Santiago. It's not surprising that some locals become fed up with pilgrims tramping past their front door, particularly in Galicia where more and more people join the camino. A smattering of *Castellano* (Spanish) and a willingness to stop and talk will make a big difference to the welcome you receive.

If you decide to continue to Finisterre, the number of pilgrims drops off rapidly, and you'll have far more opportunities to meet and talk to local people.

There's a certain snooty hierarchy amongst pilgrims. Many walkers look down on cyclists, often called *peregrinos descafeinados* (decaffeinated pilgrims), and *albergues* (pilgrim hostels) may refuse to admit cycling pilgrims, or ask them to wait until early evening before deciding if there's room. Self-propelled pilgrims, even non-religious ones, often dismiss car-pilgrims as "tourists." Pilgrims on horses or donkeys are now a rarity: fewer than 1% of pilgrims travel this way.

Trails

The camino heads across Spain on a variety of different surfaces, from narrow paths to wide tracks to tarmac (paved roads). It's mostly easy walking with very few rough or uneven surfaces, although some stone and mud tracks can become slippery after rain. Road walking can be unpleasant, and occasional stretches are dangerous due to narrow shoulders, busy roads, and blind corners. Walk in a group on the left-hand side of the road (facing oncoming traffic) if possible.

Trail marking is generally excellent, and the abundance of yellow arrows makes it difficult to lose your way. Markers vary from concrete bollards marked with scallop shells, to the ever-present yellow arrows painted on everything from pavements to trees to the sides of houses. Navigating through cities can be difficult as new building work or industrial development can obliterate arrows and paths.

On the *meseta* in particular there can be long stretches with very little or no shade. The wind on the plains can be strong and quickly sap your energy; you'll need to eat plenty and drink lots of water, even if it isn't very hot.

Maps

Most pilgrims don't bother with detailed maps, as the camino is generally well-marked and easy to follow. Almost every turn is marked with a yellow arrow or a scallop shell, and people you meet along the way will always be able to direct you to the camino if you should stray from the route — see our language section on page 195 for helpful walking phrases.

Michelin maps 442 and 441 are good for a general overview of the camino, and although they're next to useless for walking, they do mark most of the towns and villages you'll pass through. The sketch maps in this book will give you a general idea of the villages, terrain and sights you'll encounter, along with distances and facilities along the way.

If you're determined to weigh down your backpack with walking maps, the Spanish Instituto Geográfico Nacional (www.mfom.es/ign/) publishes up-to-date 1:25,000 maps, while the Servicio Geográfico del Ejército publishes the most current 1:50,000 maps. Walking maps are difficult to find along the camino, but can be ordered from the UK before you go.

Try Stanfords in London (☎ 020 7836 1321; www.stanfords.co.uk), the Map Centre in Hereford (☎ 01432 266322;

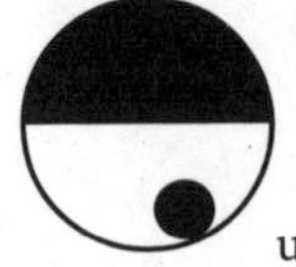

www.themapcentre.com) or the Map Shop in Upton upon Severn, Worcs (☎ 0800 0854080; www.themapshop.co.uk).

Guided Walks

Many tour companies offer guided walks along the camino. Most trips last for about two weeks, taking in a selection of regions from Roncesvalles to Santiago.

Based in A Coruña, **On Foot in Spain**'s (www.onfootinspain.com) small group tours are highly regarded. They're led by José Placer, a native of Santiago and an experienced walker, and Nancy Frey, an American living in Spain, whose *Pilgrim Stories: On and Off the Road to Santiago* (University of California Press, 1998) is one of the best introductions to the camino. **Iberian Adventures** (☎ 920 37 25 44; www.iberianadventures.com), also in Spain, runs nine-day trips between León and Santiago; the company can also arrange custom tours. Based in Oxford, the **Alternative Travel Group** (☎ (01865) 315678; www.atg-oxford.co.uk) runs two-week tours exploring selected stretches of the camino from St-Jean-Pied-de-Port to Santiago.

Many US companies offer camino tours. **Experience Plus** tours (☎ 800 685 4565; www.experienceplus.com) include daily walks of about 10km. **Spanish Steps** (☎ 877 787 WALK; www.spanishsteps.com) organizes a highlights tour from Roncesvalles to Santiago, and is one of the few companies to offer a continuous camino tour, starting at O Cebreiro. **Saranjan Tours** (☎ 800 858 9594; www.saranjantours.com) specialize in tours of Spain and Portugal; their two-week trip includes about seven days of walking, beginning at Burgos.

Geography

One of the most stunning aspects of walking the camino is the gradual unravelling of the landscape in front of you. As the camino snakes its way across the third largest country in Europe, the walker traverses everything from high mountain passes to wide river valleys. Although Spain is the second most mountainous country in Europe (after Switzerland), the camino follows the line of least resistance across gently undulating terrain.

The foothills of the Pyrenees are the first obstacle faced by pilgrims. Created by the collision of the Afro-Iberian and European tectonic plates, these mountains continue to rise fractionally every year. On the other side of the mountains, you'll enter the provinces of Navarra and La Rioja, where grapes grow on rolling hills of sun-baked clay and limestone. The land is dominated by the Río Ebro, which drains the water from a vast area of northeastern Spain, and the camino follows a natural corridor into the heart of Spain between the Sierra de la Demanda to the south and the Sierra de Cantábria to the north. The Montes de Oca are the last major hills before the city of Burgos and the *meseta* beyond.

Many pilgrims expect the *meseta* to be a long flat boring expanse of nothing, but the reality is far more interesting. The 800m-high central plateau dominates central Spain, covering almost two-fifths of the country. Treeless for the most part, the horizon seems to stretch endlessly across yellow wheat fields, broken only by views of the spectacular Cordillera Cantábrica, which dictate the *meseta*'s climate. In winter, a strong, cold wind howls down from their snowy peaks, freezing the land for eight months of the year, while in summer temperatures soar as the same mountains block cool breezes from the ocean and trap the baking heat.

Eventually, the Cordillera Cantábrica must be clambered over, as the mountains curve down towards Portugal, blocking the way to Santiago and marking the end of the *meseta*. Although the western fringe isn't the highest part of the range, it's certainly the wettest section. The Gulf Stream of the Atlantic Ocean brings soggy warm air from the Caribbean that clings to northwestern Spain for weeks on end. The mountains have also protected the indigenous people from successive waves of invaders; consequently, this corner of Spain often seems to have more in common with northern Celtic nations than with the rest of Spain.

Water dominates Galicia—the coastal province gets an average of two metres of rain each year. Deep river valleys have been carved by all that precipitation, and water-loving oak forests cover the land. From Santiago, the lowest point of the camino so far, it's downhill to the ocean at Finisterre, a slim finger of a peninsula that sticks out into the Atlantic towards the setting sun.

Environment

Hunting is a big part of Spanish culture, and Spain gives over much of its land to *reservas nacionales de caza* (hunting reserves). In summer, you'll often hear staccato bursts of noise, although these are just as likely to be from fiesta firecrackers as from hunters' rifles. Since Franco's demise, regional governments have converted many of the *reservas nacionales* into environmentally protected spaces. Hunting has eliminated some of Spain's rarer creatures, and the brown bear, found in the Cordillera Cantábrica, and the lammergeier, a bird of prey that nests in the Pyrenees, are just clinging on to existence. Although the wolf is a protected species, local farmers put their rifles away with gritted teeth, as compensation from the government for lost livestock arrives at glacial speed.

Although it's hard to believe when you're getting soaked by a Galician rainstorm, water is one of Spain's major environmental problems. Not only does the country get less rainfall than it did a few years ago, Spain's per capita water consumption is one of the highest in the world. River flow is decreasing at an alarming rate as water is siphoned off for agricultural irrigation and to satisfy thirsty industries and cities. Tourism, destructive in its own right in Spain's coastal region, is also causing water problems as foreign visitors demand emerald green golf courses even in water-starved areas. Environmentalists are particularly concerned about the National Environmental Plan to further dam and divert the Río Ebro, which rises in the Cordillera Cantábrica and provides La Rioja with a fertile valley, to satisfy the industries and tourist towns of the Mediterranean coast.

As in much of the rest of Europe, modern development has had environmental consequences. Flush with European Union cash, Spain embarked on a frenzy of road building, and there are times along the camino where you'll be surrounded by underused, multi-lane roads. In Galicia, indigenous forests have been torn down to make way for fast-growing eucalyptus. Very few birds and other animals can live in these monocultural stands because the acidic leaves sterilize the soil.

The green movement in Spain is much younger than those of most northern European countries, but it has become much more organized and high-profile in the last few years. For more information about environmental issues in Spain, contact Amigos de la Tierra (www.tierra.org) or Adena, now affiliated with the World Wildlife Fund (www.wwf.es). For more links to environmental organizations, see our web site at www.pilipalapress.com.

When to Go

Pilgrims traditionally timed their journey to arrive in Compostela for the Día de Santiago. Now a Galician holiday, July 25 is still the liveliest time to be in the city, when the Plaza de Obradoiro in front of the Cathedral is illuminated by a magnificent fireworks display.

Summer weather is the most reliable, although it can rain at any time of the year in Galicia, and the *meseta* can be uncomfortably hot from June to August. *Albergues* are crowded throughout the peak season, and hotels may be fully booked in destinations popular with tourists. Many regions along the camino come alive from June onwards with traditional festivals; the Navarrese celebrate with particular gusto in July and August. The end of summer marks the start of the harvest, and food-based fiestas pop up everywhere.

Early autumn is the perfect time for wine buffs, as the grape harvest in La Rioja and Navarra gets into swing. It's also wild mushroom season, and an excellent time to see birds heading south for the winter. The weather is often mild, sometimes wet and windy, and there may be the occasional snow flurry at higher elevations.

The weather worsens through the winter. You'll need to carry more equipment to cope with rain at any time, and to deal with snow and ice on the mountain passes. It can be an inconvenient and chilly time to travel, as churches and tourist sights may also be closed, and those *albergues* and hotels that stay open in the winter months often lack heating. Despite this, travelling the route in winter can be a fabulous, solitary experience, and there's a definite camaraderie amongst the hardy souls who attempt the camino at this time.

Come spring, the weather improves, although there's still a chance of snow at higher elevations and you'll probably be rained on for at least a few days of your trip. Spring is the best time to see wild flowers, which bloom earlier on the warm *meseta* than in chillier, damper Galicia, and it's also the ideal time to spot migrating birds heading north.

The camino is always busier during Holy Years such as 2004 and 2010, when the Día de Santiago falls on a Sunday. Pilgrims who walk the camino in Holy Years get more time off purgatory, and special ceremonies are performed in Santiago and in churches and cathedrals along the way. The number of pilgrims quadrupled in the 1993 and 1999 Holy Years, so space in *albergues* and hotels is obviously at a premium.

How long will it take?

If you're fit and healthy and don't want to stay for more than one night in any of the places along the way, you can walk the camino from St-Jean-Pied-de-Port to Santiago de Compostela in about a month. It's a good idea to allow for extra time in case of any unforseen injuries, an occasional lazy day, or a whimsical decision to linger in one of the lovely towns along the way.

If you have less time, or if you're not used to walking long distances, consider starting somewhere closer to Santiago; you only need to walk the last 100km to Santiago to get a *compostela*. Cities such as Pamplona, Logroño, Burgos, León, Astorga, Ponferrada and Sarria are all popular places to start.

Many pilgrims walk the camino in stages, and returning every year or so to walk another two-week stretch is especially popular with French and Spanish pilgrims.

History

The Iberian peninsula was home to some of the earliest known Europeans, and excavations at Atapuerca, on the camino just before Burgos, have uncovered an 800,000-year-old skeleton. Further north, and a good many years later in 15,000BC, cave dwellers at Altamira created stunning, artistically sophisticated buffalo and deer paintings. Neolithic peoples arrived in Spain in about 5000BC, building some splendid *dolmens* and *menhirs* in Galicia and the Basque country. The Celts came south across the Pyrenees in about 800BC, leaving a string of *castros* along the length of the camino, and much of Galicia's culture and architecture is still heavily influenced by the Celts.

Things were fairly peaceful on the peninsula until the Romans decided to expand their empire in about 200BC. Resistance from the Celtiberian tribes of northern Spain was so strong that it took a couple of centuries for the Romans to control the country and, even then, peoples like the Basques retained their own distinctive cultures. The Romans, as always, chose the shortest, most logical routes for their roads: the camino follows the Via Traiana, the Roman road that linked Bordeaux and Astorga, for much of its length.

As Roman power waned, northern armies poured into Spain. Like the Romans, the Suevi and the Visigoths made little impact on northern Spain, although a couple of lovely Visigothic chapels remain, and others lie buried underneath the foundations of later, grander churches.

In 711, a small force of Moors landed in Gibraltar and quickly moved north, controlling much of the peninsula in a few short years. But just as the Romans and the Visigoths never really got a grip on Spain's unruly northerners, so Muslim strongholds were limited to the south of the country. By the ninth century, while southern Spain was prospering under Muslim rule, pockets of Christian influence were developing in the north.

In 824, the powerful Kingdom of Navarra was formed, becoming strongest during the reign of Sancho el Mayor in the eleventh century, who captured La Rioja and a large chunk of Castilla for the Navarrese Christians. The balance of power was destined to shift west along the camino, however, and by the end of the eleventh century, the kingdom of Castilla was the dominant force in Christian Spain.

The camino's popularity peaked in the Middle Ages, a period that by no coincidence saw the building of some of the grandest and most glorious churches and cathedrals along the route. Meanwhile, Spain's disparate Christian kingdoms were drawing closer together; León, Castilla and Navarra joined forces in 1212 to defeat the Moors at Las Navas de Tolosa, and a more concrete union was cemented in 1479, when Fernando V of Aragón married Isabel I of Castilla.

Fernando and Isabel's reign began a flurry of Spanish exploration and conquest; Columbus discovered the New World in their names and Pizarro set about dominating South America. Back home, the insidious Inquisition was driving almost half a million Jews from the country, and was also systematically rooting out Muslims, gypsies and witches.

Meanwhile, Spain's centre of government was moving south, and Felipe II had set up Court in Madrid by the sixteenth century. The north suffered from its lack of political influence, and many of its towns went into gradual decline.

In 1808, Napoleon crossed over the Pyrenees by the old Camino de Santiago, soon installing his brother on the throne of Spain. The Spanish called for help from the British, who were spectacularly unsuccessful at first, and Sir John Moore's troops trashed towns such as Ponferrada and Villafranca del Bierzo as they speedily retreated to A Coruña on the northern coast. It took Wellington's army to drive the French out of Spain, although his troops were just as apt to destroy the Spanish towns they liberated.

The rest of the nineteenth century is a muddle of coups and counter coups as Spain swung from monarchy to a liberal constitution and back again. While the rest of Europe was experiencing industrial revolution, Spain was gripped by these internal squabbles, and only Bilbao, which became an important port, and Asturias, which developed a significant mining industry, prospered.

By the early twentieth century, politics had splintered into factions, and regionalism, anarchism, communism and fascism all gained ground. Almost inevitably, civil war broke out in 1936. The province of Castilla was firmly on Franco's side, and the Nationalists made Burgos their wartime capital. Galicia was also largely Nationalist, partly because Franco was a local boy from Ferrol, and partly because of the region's inherent conservatism. The Basques sided with the Republicans, becoming increasingly isolated in the Nationalist north, and in 1937 were finally defeated as Nazi planes carpet-bombed Guernica.

When Franco came to power at the end of the civil war in January 1939, he set about rewarding friendly cities like Burgos, which got a ton of money from the dictator for industrial development. The Basques, on the other hand, were punished severely. *Euskara*, the Basque language, was repressed, and the flag and other Basque symbols were banned. Economically, the country suffered from the costly civil war and the isolation of Franco's fascist regime, but an injection of US investment in the 1950s nudged Spain into the industrial age.

Franco finally died in 1975, wielding influence beyond the grave by nominating King Juan Carlos as his successor. Although Spain flirted with dictatorship and military coups in the late 1970s, by 1982 Spain was flinging herself into democracy and capitalism with abandon. Spain's economic development in the last 20 years has been largely due to its enthusiastic membership of the European Union, which it joined in 1986. European money has flooded into the country, leading to industrial development, agricultural modernization and an unstoppable orgy of road building.

In keeping with European Union philosophy, Spain's modern era has seen a devolution of power to the regions, and the Basques and Galicians in particular have been granted a large measure of autonomy.

Spain today

Spain is not so much a single country as a paella of diverse and disparate cultures. Many Galicians and Basques don't even consider themselves Spanish, and even less autonomous regions are intensely proud of their homelands. You'll see *León sin Castilla* (León without Castilla) graffiti in León, and pleas for the Bierzo region to leave Castilla y León and join with Galicia, with which it has much more in common. Having said this, foreign visitors will notice certain things that are distinctly, and often uniquely, Spanish.

Spain might be in the same time zone as many European countries, but the Spanish day is unrecognizable to those from more northern climates. For a start, things happen later in Spain. A lot later in the case of meals, as restaurant lunches aren't usually served until 2pm, and Spaniards rarely eat dinner before 10pm. Nights out in Spain aren't for the fainthearted, nor are they for pilgrims curfew-bound by *albergues*, as bars don't get going until midnight, and clubs rarely open before 4am. It's no wonder that the Spanish need a long siesta, and you'll find that even in the cities, life will grind to a halt from 2pm to 5pm.

Spanish life seems to revolve around eating and drinking. Sunday lunches, in particular, are vast, communal affairs, stretching well into the afternoon and involving all members of the family from the oldest to the youngest. Children are universally adored, and more puritanical northern Europeans may be shocked at the extent to which Spanish kids are heard as well as seen in public. Children are positively welcomed in restaurants, and you'll often see youngsters brought along for a late night stroll or *tapas* crawl.

You won't hear much English spoken along the camino, and even a smattering of *Castellano* (Spanish) will help with communication. Both *Euskara* (Basque) and *Galega* (Galician) are undergoing literary and linguistic revivals. Surprisingly, the noisily nationalistic Basques are less likely to speak their indigenous language than the quieter Galicians, 90% of whom speak some *Galega*.

Spain is an inherently Catholic country, 500 years after the Inquisition drove out Jews and Muslims. Since the 1978 constitution, Spaniards have enjoyed official religious freedom, but there are still fewer than a million non-Catholic souls in the country. In practice, however, secularism is taking hold as church attendance plummets; regular churchgoers are likely to be older, poorer northerners.

The Spanish spend more money than any other Europeans on gambling, and in every town you'll see disabled people patronisingly employed as lotto ticket vendors. The national lottery is hugely popular, and culminates with the Christmas El Gordo (the fat one) draw, thought to be the world's single biggest lottery prize. Each year, about 98% of Spaniards buy a ticket or a share in a ticket and, in 2001, almost €2 billion was gambled on the draw, or €48 for every Spaniard.

You don't pass through any major football towns on the camino, but this scarcely seems to dim support for the beautiful game. Almost all Spanish football fans support either Barcelona or Real Madrid as well as their local club, and matches between the two giants of Spanish football will pack bars everywhere in Spain. Galicians are excited by the recent successes of Deportivo La Coruña, and care much more about the fate of their adopted provincial club than that of the national side.

Arts

The camino is responsible for and replete with gorgeous examples of Romanesque and Gothic architecture. From the stunning Romanesque frescoes of the Basilica de San Isidoro in Léon to the gossamer Gothic spires of Burgos and León cathedrals, you'll be dazzled by the wealth and creativity of medieval Spain. Spain's airy Gothic traditions were both continued and splendidly distorted by Gaudí's fantastical swirling confections, seen at their best in Barcelona, but with examples in León and Astorga.

Spanish art has very few important schools and movements but a few amazing peaks of individual creativity. In the sixteenth and seventeenth centuries, El Greco, a native Greek who lived most of his life in his adopted Spain, painted passionate and deliberate canvasses of elongated figures and intense contrasts of light and colour.

A few decades later, Velázquez painted intricate, life-like portraits and landscapes with meticulous care, so much so that he painted fewer than 200 works.

Goya was contrastingly prolific. He was a late starter who began with fairly conventional paintings before spiralling towards embittered and imaginative works as his health declined and the war with Napoleon sent him into depression.

Picasso is probably Spain's best-known artist, although he spent much of his long life in neighbouring France. After flirting with Toulouse-Lautrec's style in his blue period, Picasso moved on to a rose period, when he was influenced by El Greco and Celtiberian sculpture. With Georges Braque, he developed Cubism, a style also adopted by his countryman, Juan Gris. Politicized by the civil war, Picasso's most famous painting, *Guernica*, portrays the town's decimation by Nazi bombers in 1937. The painting has become a symbol of Basque nationalism, and its presence in

the Museo de Arte Reina Sofia in Madrid really sticks in the collective Basque throat.

Dalí put the fish in surrealism, and was as talented at self-promotion as he was in his bizarre, dream-like art. Alongside him, Spain's other noted surrealist, Joan Miró, seems positively normal.

Spanish film is well-respected internationally, but only a handful of directors are household names. Luis Buñuel and Salvador Dalí made many of their films in France, and Buñuel was forced into exile after the civil war. Carlos Maura's bleak, allegorical films subtly undermined the Franco dictatorship during the 1960s and 1970s. In common with many of Spain's younger generation, Pedro Almodóvar sees the Franco years as irrelevant to his work, instead making quirky, controversial and ultimately successful films about desire and sexuality.

Spain's folk music is firmly regionalised. Even *flamenco*, the closest Spain has to a national music, is firmly rooted in Andalucía and rarely heard outside the south, Madrid and Barcelona. Galician and Basque tunes have much in common with Celtic music from northern Europe, and each culture has its own version of the bagpipes.

Modern musicians have moved away from the rigid traditionalism of folk music under Franco, and are influenced by styles as diverse as *flamenco* and electronica. Basque and Galician musicians also borrow a lot from each other, swapping instruments and styles with creative abandon.

For more about regional culture, see the People & Culture sections in the regional chapters.

Food

The food of Spain is as varied as the country, but as a rule of thumb it's tasty, substantial and lacking in vegetables. It's also very cheap by northern European standards.

Traditionally, the Spaniards have adopted the southern European pattern of a large main meal at lunchtime followed by a much-needed siesta. Although a heavy lunch is becoming less popular with city workers, it's still the norm in rural areas. Sunday lunch is the meal of the week, when the whole day is taken up with the preparation, eating and digestion of the midday meal.

Hungry pilgrims may find it hard to get used to Spanish mealtimes. Restaurants open for lunch at 2pm, and dinner doesn't begin until 9pm or 10pm. The best value comes from the *menú del día*, a three course set meal with bread and wine. Many restaurants along the camino will offer a *menú del peregrino* (pilgrim's menu), an early evening *menú* starting at 8pm, and an excellent deal at between €6 and €9 for three courses and wine.

On most menus there's a choice of dishes for each course. The *primer plato* (first course) can be anything from salad to spaghetti. Soups are fabulous, and often meals in themselves. You shouldn't leave Spain without trying *sopa de ajo*, commonly known as the "soup of the poor", a broth of garlic, bread and water topped with a poached egg. You'll have to wait until Galicia to eat authentic *caldo gallego*, a thick soup made of shredded *gallego* (a dark green cabbage), beans and potatoes. Vegetarians be warned: the soups are usually made using a tasty meat stock, and *caldo gallego* often includes a few slices of *chorizo* (spicy sausage).

Fabada is a hearty dish made from fava beans, *chorizo* and ham — choose this as a starter and you'll barely have room for the main course. The beans are cooked slowly in a stew, soaking up the smoky flavour of the sausage. Salad is a rare treat and tends to come with white asparagus, which is considered a delicacy in Navarra, dropped limply on top.

The *segundo plato* (second course) is a hefty serving of either fried or roasted lumps of meat served with chips or boiled potatoes. Chicken, beef, veal and pork are the most common, although fish, usually trout, may also be on offer.

If you still have room, *postre* (dessert) is mercifully small. Usually you'll be offered a piece of fruit, ice cream or yoghurt served in its plastic container, but *flan* (egg custard) is also a good choice.

Most cafés and bars will serve *bocadillos,* sandwiches made from half a baguette stuffed with a range of fillings. *Bocadillos* are often filled with whatever happens to be in the kitchen, usually cheese, *chorizo* or *jamón serrano* (a *prosciutto*-like ham); one of the most fiendishly tasty and satisfying versions is *tortilla con chorizo* (*chorizo* omelette sandwich). In some cafés you'll also see *sándwiches*; these are usually and disappointingly made from white sliced bread and can be grilled or fried.

Breakfast can be tricky. In summer, early starts mean that pilgrims often begin walking hours before any of the cafés or bars open. Even then, many cafés can't serve food until the bread man has delivered the daily *pan* (bread). To avoid starving, it's best to purchase breakfast the night before and/or to pop into a café or *panadería* (bakery) for a mid-morning refuelling stop. One of the most common breakfasts in Spain is *tortilla*, a deliciously thick omelette made with potatoes, then left to cool and served by the slice with a hunk of bread. Most bars will also have an assortment of usually synthetic packaged pastries (rarely fresh) or a packet of crisps. In larger towns, small rolls with a variety of fillings will also be on offer in the morning.

Vegetarians will have a hard time eating out. The *menú del día* is unlikely to offer a vegetarian option, and your culinary options are probably limited to a *bocadillo con queso* (cheese sandwich), a *tortilla francés* (omelette) or potato-based *tapas* treats like *patatas bravas* and *patatas al alioli*.

The best way to eat well and meet fellow pilgrims is to join in the evening meal at the *albergues*. Most will have a sociable kitchen, where people of different nationalities gather together to cook, generating a fantastic hum as pots boil and bottles of wine are uncorked. There's usually a shop nearby to pick up supplies, and most kitchens are stocked with basics like salt, oil, pots and pans.

When out shopping, look out for staples such as *jamón serrano* (*prosciutto*-like ham) and *chorizo* (smoked sausage) at most *carnicerías* (butchers). Spain's varied climate means that there's a wide selection of fruit and vegetables available year-round. In most shops, you'll need to ask for what you need rather than picking up and squeezing the fruit yourself. Save a fish dinner for short walking days, as

most *pescaderías* (fishmongers) open only in the morning. Try not to get caught short of food on Sundays, when most shops close.

At least once during the camino, head out for an evening of *tapas* grazing. At its most basic, a *tapa* is just a little bite to eat to go with a glass of wine, often offered free by the bartender. In other places, you'll need to order what you like; *pinchos* are small tasters, while *raciones* are bigger portions. The best way to sample the delights of *tapas* is to embark on a *tapeo* (*tapas* crawl) with a large group of friends, hopping from one bar to another. Here, you'll rub shoulders with local bankers and road sweepers sharing a glass of wine and discussing the shortcomings of Real Madrid's latest striker.

For more about regional food, see the regional Food & Drink sections.

Drink

Spanish people spend a lot of time in cafés, and days in Spain rarely begin without a caffeine hit. The coffee's excellent, and even the smallest village café will boast a big, shiny espresso machine. Coffee comes in many variations, but essentially you have two options: the strong and espresso-like *café solo*, or the long and milky *café con leche*.

Tea is just about drinkable, while hot chocolate can be hard to find, and you're more likely to be offered Cola Cao, a sickly, powdery substitute. There's a wide array of soft drinks available, from the usual imports to Spanish sparkling fruity drinks. Fruit juice tends to be sweet and thick, but it's delightfully refreshing when diluted with sparkling water.

Get used to drinking wine with your meal. The Spanish, who have lots of alcoholic proverbs, say, "*comer sin vino es miseria y desatino*" which loosely translates as "a meal without wine is a mean and foolish one." Even teetotal Spaniards will drink wine with food: it's considered such a part of the meal that it's not even thought of as an alcoholic drink.

Foremost among wine regions is La Rioja, the country's most important red-wine-producing area. Its smooth, oak-aged wines are well-known outside Spain, and fans of Rioja will be delighted by the low prices. There are also some great reds from the Navarra and Ribera del Duero regions.

Galicia's cooler climate is ideal for producing white wine. The region's Albariño whites are unoaked and crisp with flavours of peach and apricot, while cloudy Ribeiro wine rarely makes it outside the province; both perfectly complement the region's seafood. For more about regional wines, see the Food & Drink section in the regional chapters.

Spanish beer is rather bland and tasteless, although brands like San Miguel, Cruz Campo and Estrella de Galicia can be refreshing on a hot evening. Ask for a *caña* if you want a small draught beer. As in the rest of the world, Irish and Belgian bars are opening up in larger towns.

Bars and cafés in Spain are mostly interchangeable and you can get a great *café solo* at a late-night bar. It's a bit more of a shock the first time you see locals waking up with a glass of Rioja or a shot of something stronger alongside their morning *café con leche*. Bars are an integral part of Spanish culture, and a 1990s survey found that Spain had 138,200 bars, slightly fewer than the rest of the European Union put together.

Alcohol in bars is very cheap, with wine and beer usually costing less than €1 a glass, although the glasses may be smaller than you're used to. As always in Europe, bars on main squares will be more expensive than those tucked down a side street. It often costs more to drink at a table, particularly one outside, than standing at the bar.

Long, afternoon-consuming lunches aren't complete without a stiff drink. Northern Spain's favourite tipple is *orujo*, a ridiculously strong spirit made, like Italian *grappa*, from grape husks. Despite the pretty bottles, the manufactured version isn't as good as the rough-and-ready homemade version, known as *orujo casero*. Most people you meet will have their own version of *orujo casero*, and you'll see unmarked bottles under the counter in bars, restaurants, and even bakeries. Spanish pilgrims may even have brought their own from home. *Orujo* can be *blanco* (clear, tastes like alcohol) or *hierba* (often green, with more of a flavour from added herbs).

In Navarra, end your meal with *pacharán*, a sweet, pinky-orange drink usually served over ice. Avoid spirits like gin and whisky, which are likely to have been gathering dust on a high shelf for a long while, and stay well away from the dodgy brands of Scotch made for mainland European tastes.

Flora

Spain is one of Europe's richest botanical regions. The mix of Mediterranean, Atlantic and Continental climates makes for a diverse collection of flowers, shrubs and trees. Geographically isolated from the rest of Europe by the Pyrenees, the Iberian peninsula's plant life developed at its own pace, helped by windblown seeds from North Africa. The results are spectacular, with more than 8000 species of flora in the Iberian Peninsula, about a quarter of which are indigenous to the region and occur nowhere else in the world.

Northern Spain was once covered by deciduous forest, dominated by Pyrenean oak and beech. Frequent forest fires and the introduction of faster-growing imported species, such as pine and eucalyptus, are rapidly destroying what little forest survived into the twentieth century.

In the unforested areas that cover much of the central part of the country, the landscape is dominated by dense patches of brambles and wild herbs such as lavender, sage and thyme. At higher altitudes gorse, broom and heather cover the ground and hardy plants such as St Patrick's cabbage, mat grass and sphagnum moss cope with strong winds, deep snow cover and extreme temperature change. In spring and summer, mountain pastures are carpeted with low-growing Pyrenean lilies and irises.

For more about regional flora, see the regional Flora & Fauna sections.

English name	Latin name	Spanish name
Juniper	**Juniperus communis**	**Enebro**

Leaves Needle-like, 1.2cm long, in groups of three; sharp, glossy, green white band on upper surface
Bark Red brown, peels in thin vertical strips
Fruit Berry-like, 6mm-long cone; becomes black when ripe
Habitat Open spaces from coast to mountains
Height Up to 6m
Did you know? Juniper berries give gin its distinctive taste and are used as culinary flavouring

English name	Latin name	Spanish name
Beech	**Fagus sylvatica**	**Haya**

Leaves 4–9cm long, oval, with 7–8 parallel veins, silky hairs underneath
Bark Smooth grey
Fruit Triangular brown nuts
Habitat Farmland
Height Up to 40m
Did you know? Planted for timber because it grows tall and straight without knots

English name	Latin name	Spanish name
Pyrenean oak	**Quercus pyrenaica**	**Roble melojo**

Leaves 20cm long, 10cm across, deep lobes, dark glossy green
Bark Pale grey and craggy
Fruit Acorn 4cm long, two years to mature
Habitat Mountains, particularly in the north
Height 20m
Did you know? Produces very strong lumber, used extensively in construction

English name	Latin name	Spanish name
Olive	**Olea europaea**	**Olivo**

Leaves 2–8 cm long, narrow, grey-green above with delicate silver hairs underneath
Bark Pale grey
Fruit 1–4cm long
Habitat Farmland
Height Up to 15m
Did you know? Fruit is green the first year then turns black when ripe in second year

English name	Latin name	Spanish name
Sweet chestnut	**Castanea sativa**	**Castaño dulce**

Leaves 10–25cm long, oblong with pointed tip and sharp-toothed edges
Bark Grey ridges that seem to spiral around trunk
Fruit Edible chestnut
Habitat Farmland, plains and mixed woodlands
Height Up to 30m
Did you know? Chestnuts are a staple food in parts of Spain, used as a stuffing for meat or to thicken hearty soups

Fauna

Spain is home to an assortment of rare animals. Nooks and crannies hide fire salamanders, genets and wild boar, while large tracts of remote wilderness, especially in Galicia and the Cordillera Cantábrica, offer animals such as the wolf and brown bear the space to roam unhindered. Agricultural underdevelopment in these areas has preserved unique ecosystems that are only now being studied for the first time. Spain is also the main refuelling stop on the north-south bird migration route, and these passages make spring and autumn a great time to visit.

Novice wildlife watchers can greatly increase their chance of seeing animals by going out at dawn and dusk when most animals are active. There's also more chance of spotting animals if you're on the edge of two habitats, like on the fringes of a wood near a river or open woodland. As you walk along, stop every now and then to sit quietly and wait a few minutes. Allow the animals time to get accustomed to your presence and resume their normal routines and you'll gradually see undetected animals emerge before your eyes.

For more about regional fauna, see the regional Flora & Fauna sections.

English name	Latin name	Spanish name
Brown bear	**Ursus arctos**	**Oso pardo**

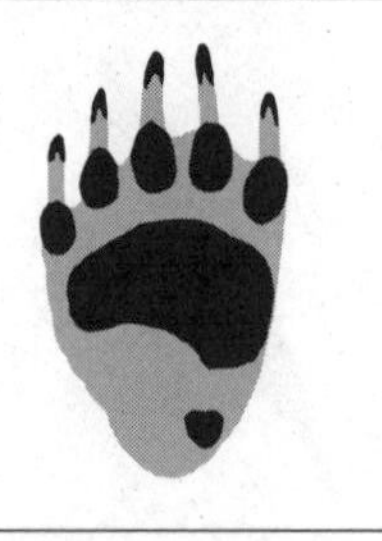

Length 230cm **Tail** 1.5cm **Height** 120cm
Description Very large, heavy build, beige to dark brown
Habitat Mixed woods in the Cordillera Cantábrica
Voice Occasional grunts or howls when angry or frightened
Diet Berries, roots, carrion, insects. Occasionally mammals
Viewing tips Very difficult to see, mainly nocturnal
Did you know? Brown bears have an excellent sense of smell and hearing, but poor eyesight

English name	Latin name	Spanish name
Wolf	**Canis lupus**	**Lobo**

Length 130cm **Tail** 40cm **Height** 80cm
Description Grey, bushy tail, alert ears
Habitat Woods and open country in mountains
Voice Silent when hunting; growls, yelps and long howls
Diet Large and small mammals
Viewing tips Dog-like footprint; visible at dawn and dusk
Did you know? Wolves mate for life. Travel up to 40km per day with a maximum speed of up to 50km per hour

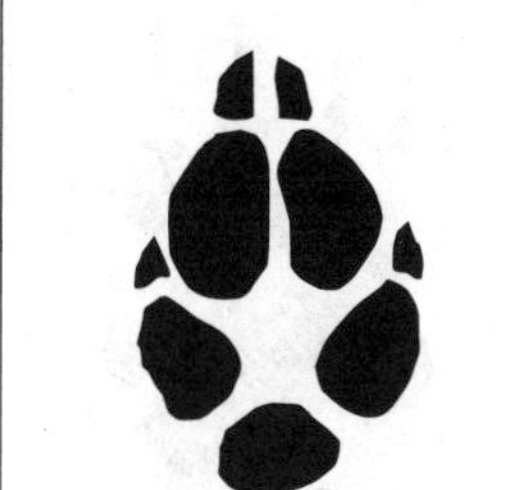

Iberian lynx	**Lynx pardinus**	**Lince Ibérico**

Length 100cm **Tail** 25cm **Height** 70cm
Description Large and small black spots, black tip on tail, distinctive feathery tufts on head
Habitat Pyrenean and holm oak woods in rocky mountains
Voice Hisses and howls
Diet Birds, young deer, fish, small mammals and reptiles
Viewing tips Very rare and difficult to spot; vast territory
Did you know? Most endangered carnivore in Europe

Wild cat	**Felis silvestris**	**Gato montés**

Length 50cm **Tail** 30cm **Height** 35cm
Description Yellow-grey fur with black ringed tail
Habitat Woodland and scrubland
Voice Purrs and meows
Diet Mice, birds, fish and insects
Viewing tips Active in late afternoon, often sunning itself
Did you know? Persecution of cats in medieval times led to spread of black death as rat population exploded

Genet	**Genetta genetta**	**Gineta**

Length 50cm **Tail** 40cm **Height** 20cm
Description Pale fur with defined dark spots & tail rings
Habitat Dark woods close to streams
Voice Purrs loudly
Diet Small birds, mammals, insects
Viewing tips Nocturnal, look for footprints near water
Did you know? Lives up to 21 years. Strong swimmer and climber; found at altitudes up to 2500m

English name	Latin name	Spanish name

Badger | **Meles meles** | **Tejón**

Length 60cm **Tail** 15cm **Height** 30cm
Description Silver-grey back; black & white striped face
Habitat Scrubland, farmland, woods
Voice Growls
Diet Small rodents, reptiles and plants
Viewing tips Nocturnal; listen for the sound of it digging
Did you know? Foxes and birds of prey often follow badgers to catch animals they disturb while digging for food

Wild boar | **Sus scrofa** | **Jabalí**

Length 150cm **Tail** 15cm **Height** 90cm
Description Pale grey to black; tusks up to 30cm
Habitat Mixed, deciduous woodland; scrubland
Voice Snorts. Female barks and chatters teeth when angry
Diet Roots, vegetables, small mammals, insects
Viewing tips Mainly nocturnal but also active in mornings
Did you know? Litters of 4 to 12 piglets common, independent after 6 months and can live up to 25 years

Otter | **Lutra lutra** | **Nutria**

Length 80cm **Tail** 40cm **Height** 30cm
Description Brown fur; long, slender body with short legs
Habitat Rivers, lakes, marshes, estuaries and sea
Voice Clear whistle, sometimes growls
Diet Fish, birds, frogs and aquatic mammals
Viewing tips Look for remains of meals along riverbanks
Did you know? Good climber and jumper, can walk on land for long distances

Greater horseshoe bat | **Rhinolophus ferrum-equinum** | **Murciélago grande de herradura**

Length 6cm **Tail** 4cm **Description** Red-grey back with pale underside
Habitat Woods and scrubland
Voice Loud shrill and squeaks
Diet Insects caught in flight or collected from leaves
Viewing tips Hunts throughout the night, flies close to ground
Did you know? Has only one young at a time, which can fly after four weeks and matures in a year. Lives for 20 years

English name	Latin name	Spanish name
Large mouse -eared bat	**Myotis myotis**	**Murciélago ratonero grande**

Length 7cm **Tail** 5cm **Description** Grey-brown back with grey-white belly
Habitat Open woodland, parks
Voice Chirping and loud shrieks
Diet Insects caught in flight or collected from ground
Viewing tips Hunts after dark; flies straight and silent about 5m off the ground
Did you know? Migrates between summer and winter locations. Large nursing colonies consist of only young and adult females

European tree frog	**Hyla arborea**	**Rana de San Antón**

Length 4cm
Description Usually green but changes to grey or brown as temperature fluctuates
Habitat Marshland, damp meadows, reed beds
Voice Croaks
Diet Insects and spiders
Viewing tips Easily spotted, active by day and twilight
Did you know? Female lays up to 1000 eggs

Natterjack	**Bufo calamita**	**Sapo corredor**

Length 8cm
Description Brown-grey back with huge warts, belly white
Habitat Varied, especially dry sandy soil, up to 1200m
Voice Loud croak
Diet Insects, worms and spiders
Viewing tips Mainly nocturnal, occasionally active in day
Did you know? When the natterjack becomes alarmed, it inflates its body, lowers its head and sticks its bum in the air

Fire salamander	**Salamander salamander**	**Salamandra común**

Length 20cm
Description Shiny black; yellow, orange or red markings
Habitat Damp woodlands, streams, meadows up to 1000m
Diet Insects and worms
Viewing tips Emerges at night or in bad weather
Did you know? Don't touch, as the oily slime that covers the body is poisonous. Can live for up to 42 years

English name	Latin name	Spanish name
Iberian wall lizard	**Podarcis hispanica**	**Lagartija ibérica**

Length 18cm
Description Flat head, long tail, upper parts grey to brown
Habitat Dry, stony places, especially walls and ruins
Diet Small insects and worms
Viewing tips Look and listen for them scuttling away as you approach
Did you know? Lays eggs in holes; lives up to 15 years

Green lizard	**Lacerta viridis**	**Lagarto verde**

Length 40cm
Description Males vivid green with tiny black dots; sky blue throat during mating. Females duller and brownish
Habitat Dry, sunny locations with shrubs, especially near walls and along roads
Diet Insects and fruit
Viewing tips Again, look and listen for scuttling!
Did you know? When threatened opens mouth and bites

White stork	**Ciconia ciconia**	**Cigüeña común**

Description 100cm, long bill and legs, white with black flight feathers, red bill and legs
Habitat Marshes, grassy plains
Voice Hisses and claps bill
Diet Fish, insects
Viewing tips Flies at high altitude, neck straight ahead
Did you know? Nests on buildings and churches along the camino, especially in Navarra, La Rioja and the *meseta*

Black stork	**Ciconia nigra**	**Cigüeña negra**

Description 100cm, black body, white belly, red bill & legs
Habitat Marshy land near forests
Voice Noisy, claps bill, random notes
Diet Fish, insects
Viewing tips Flies like white stork, only more gracefully as less reliant on thermals
Did you know? Nests high in the tops of trees. More solitary than white stork

English name	Latin name	Spanish name
Bee-eater	**Merops apiaster**	**Abejaruco común**

Description 30cm, bright blue belly, yellow throat and shoulders, black eyeband
Habitat Open scrubland with some trees
Voice Prruep prruep prruep
Diet Insects
Viewing tips Sociable, likes to perch & watch the world go by. Good flier, with sudden acceleration and graceful glides
Did you know? Breeds in big groups in holes in the ground

Hoopoe	**Upupa epops**	**Abubilla**

Description 30cm, crest on head, pinkish body, barred white and black wings, long bill
Habitat Farmland, open woodland
Voice Pooo pooo pooo
Diet Insects
Viewing tips Undulating flight as it opens & closes wings
Did you know? One of our favourite birds. Nests in ruins and hollows of old trees

Black woodpecker	**Dryocopus martius**	**Pito negro**

Description 45cm, almost all black, red crown, yellow eyes
Habitat Old coniferous and beech forests
Voice Manic laugh: kwick-wick-wick-wick
Diet Ants and wood-boring beetle larvae, tree sap
Viewing Tips Found in mature forests, listen for call and loud drumming
Did you know? Three separate, isolated populations in Spain

White-backed woodpecker	**Dendrocopos leucotus**	**Pico dorsiblanco**

Description 25cm, white lower back, white bands across wings, pink under tail
Habitat Deciduous forest with lots of rotting logs
Voice tehich
Diet Insects, nuts and seeds
Viewing tips Rare, mainly south-facing Pyrenean slopes
Did you know? Largest spotted woodpecker in Europe

English name	Latin name	Spanish name
Chough	**Pyrrhocorax pyrrhocorax**	**Chova piquirroja**

Description 40cm, red legs and long, thin, curved red bill
Habitat Rolling hills and mountains
Voice High-pitched cheeeaaah and chuff
Diet Mainly insects
Viewing tips Good flier, tumbles and twists during flight, also frequently seen hopping on ground
Did you know? Nest in caves and on crags

Great bustard	**Otis tarda**	**Avutarda**

Description 100cm, pale grey head and upper neck, rufous upper parts. Breeding males have pale fluffy feathers on lower face and fan white tails out in a spectacular display
Habitat Open treeless plains
Voice Not often heard. Low bark in breeding season
Diet Mainly insects
Viewing tips Usually in small flocks on the ground
Did you know? Heaviest bird in Europe

Golden eagle	**Aquila chrysaetos**	**Águila real**

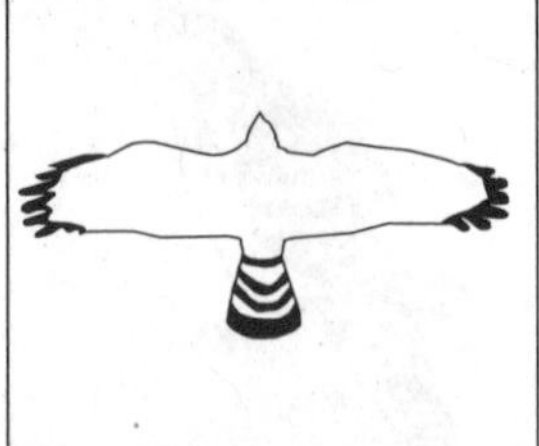

Description 90cm, golden feathers on head, white patches on wings and tail
Habitat Mountains, forests, sea cliffs
Voice Seldom-heard kya
Diet Rabbits, reptiles
Viewing tips Soars with wings in shallow V, solitary
Did you know? The largest eagle in the world

Short-toed eagle	**Circaetus gallicus**	**Culebrera europea**

Description 65cm, long wings and tail, white underneath except for brown chest
Habitat Mountain slopes, plains and coastal dunes
Voice Noisy; jee or peak-oh
Diet Snakes, lizards and frogs
Viewing tips Resembles osprey but without dark stripes
Did you know? Frequently hovers with legs dangling

English name	Latin name	Spanish name
Booted eagle	**Hieraaetus pennatus**	**Águila calzada**

Description 50cm. Two different varieties; can have either dark or white body with black wing edges
Habitat Forest clearings
Voice Keeee
Diet Small birds and reptiles
Viewing tips Always seen near trees; six obvious feathers at end of wings
Did you know? Smallest eagle in Europe

Bonelli's eagle	**Hieraaetus fasciatus**	**Águila perdicera**

Description 70cm, white body underneath, except dark tail band and wing
Habitat Rocky mountains, plains and wetlands
Voice Fast or slow kai kai kai
Diet Rabbits, birds up to heron size
Viewing tips Look for acrobatic courtship display in spring
Did you know? Pairs stay together even when not breeding

Goshawk	**Accipter gentilis**	**Azor**

Description 60cm, barred, grey belly, some white near tail and around eye
Habitat Woods on edge of open country
Voice Pee-lay or kik kik
Diet Wood pigeons and other forest-dwelling birds
Viewing tips Great flier, zooms 2–3m above the ground between and around trees
Did you know? Persistent; chases prey even if ends in crash

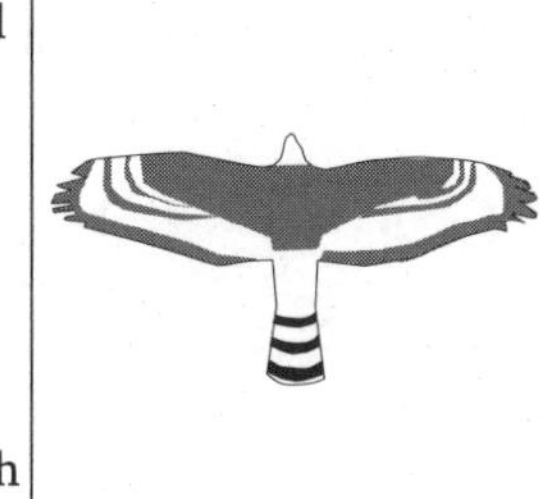

Buzzard	**Buteo buteo**	**Busardo ratonero**

Description 50cm, dark with barred underside, broad wings and fat, round tail
Habitat Mountains, plains, farmland
Voice Peee-aah
Diet Birds, small mammals, insects
Viewing tips Common over most habitats
Did you know? Seen as the laziest raptor, it rarely chases prey and refuses to fly in the rain

English name	Latin name	Spanish name
Sparrohawk	**Accipiter nisus**	**Gavilán común**

Description 35cm, long tail, barred underparts, grey above
Habitat Woodland and farmland
Voice Varies. Lots of noise especially in breeding season
Diet Small mammals and birds
Viewing tips The sparrowhawk is a common sight hovering over fields looking for food
Did you know? Young birds and captive adults frequently resort to cannibalism

Red kite	**Milvus milvus**	**Milano real**

Description 60cm, white head, red brown upper body, tri-coloured wings, black wing tips and clear white base
Habitat Wooded hills, open country with scattered trees
Voice Hi-hi-heeea
Diet Small vertebrates, insects and sometimes scavenges
Viewing Tips Long, deep wing beats, noticeable forked tail which constantly twists during flight
Did you know? Iberia has the most red kites in the world

Kestrel	**Falco tinnunculus**	**Cernícalo vulgar**

Description 35cm, pointed wings, black band at tail base
Habitat Coast, farmland, woodland, cities
Voice Kee kee kee in breeding season
Diet Mainly rodents, but also lizards and small birds
Viewing tips Often seen hovering patiently over fields checking the ground for prey
Did you know? Breeds in old nests of other birds, on cliffs or even buildings

Peregrine falcon	**Falco peregrinus**	**Halcón común**

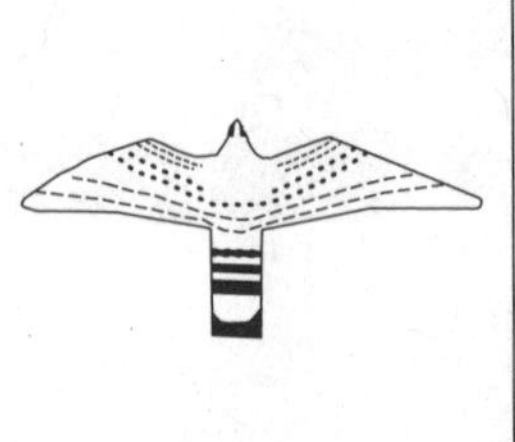

Description 45cm, slate colour, thick black moustache, white speckled belly. Female larger and darker than male
Habitat Open country, mountains, cliffs
Voice Hek hek hek or airk airk airk
Diet Small and medium-sized birds and mammals
Viewing tips Graceful flier, languid at rest but dramatic dive-bomb as attacks prey
Did you know? Dives at up to 100km/hr

English name	Latin name	Spanish name
Montagu's harrier	**Circus pygargus**	**Aguila perdicera**

Description 45cm, dark wing tips, male grey, female brown with black bars underneath
Habitat Marshes, farmland, plains
Voice Chattering kek kek kek
Diet Frogs, small mammals
Viewing tips Acrobatic flier as it patrols territory
Did you know? Winters in Africa and returns to same territory each year to breed

Griffon vulture	**Gyps fulvus**	**Buitre común**

Description 100cm, long broad wings, short stumpy tail, light lines under wings
Habitat All types of landscape but usually mountains
Voice Croaks and whistles
Diet Carrion
Viewing tips Flies gracefully by soaring, with only an occasional flap of wings
Did you know? Often breeds in caves

Egyptian vulture	**Neophron percnopterus**	**Alimoche común**

Description 60cm, long wings with black edges, white body, wedge-shaped tail
Habitat Mountains and open country
Voice Largely silent
Diet Carrion
Viewing tips Easily confused with high-flying storks
Did you know? Often seen at rubbish dumps

Eagle owl	**Bubo bubo**	**Búho real**

Description 65cm, rust colour with streaks and bars, big feathers on top of head look like ears
Habitat Rocky ledges on crags and mountains
Voice Ooo hoo
Diet Small mammals, birds up to game bird size
Viewing tips Active at dawn and dusk
Did you know? Easily mistaken for buzzard; uses other birds' abandoned nests

Tourist Information

Getting There & Back

Many discount airlines fly to various airports in Spain, and the most convenient airport for you will depend on where you choose to begin the camino. Scheduled flights also serve Spain, and both British Airways (www.britishairways.com) and Iberian Airlines (www.iberian.com) offer flights to many destinations, including Santiago de Compostela.

Ryan Air (www.ryanair.com), Air France (www.airfrance.com) and British Airways fly to Biarritz, the most convenient airport for St-Jean-Pied-de-Port. From Biarritz, you'll need to take an airport bus to Bayonne, and then it's a lovely, hour-long train journey to St-Jean. This option may involve an overnight stay in Bayonne, as the late evening train to St-Jean doesn't run every day; see www.sncf.com for up-to-date schedules. You can also reach Bayonne by train from the UK, changing at Paris. It's more difficult to start at Roncesvalles, and although there's a daily bus from Pamplona (except Sundays), it may be easier to get a taxi instead.

Pilgrims from outside Europe will probably land in Madrid, which is also served by dozens of flights daily from the UK, and from where it's easy to get bus or train connections to major centres such as Logroño, Burgos, León, Astorga and Santiago.

Many airlines also visit the newly cool city of Bilbao; it's possible although not particularly convenient to get from there to starting points such as Pamplona, Logroño, Burgos and León. You can also get to Bilbao by ferry from Portsmouth with P&O Ferries (www.poferries.com), or from Plymouth to Santander with Brittany Ferries (www.brittanyferries.com), from where it's a few hours on the bus to Logroño.

International buses and trains will get you from northern Europe to most major towns along the camino. They're unlikely to be any cheaper than flying, however, and will take considerably more time. For UK bus fares and schedules, contact Eurolines (www.eurolines.co.uk), and for selected train schedules, visit SNCF's web site at www.raileurope.co.uk.

Getting back

Iberian airlines offer a 50% pilgrim discount on one way tickets out of Santiago. There are a few trains a day from Santiago to Madrid, and there's also a daily train from Santiago to the French border at Hendaye; change in Vitoria for Bilbao. If you're heading back to Biarritz, you'll need to stay overnight in Hendaye before making the short hop by train to

Bayonne in the morning. It's also possible to rent a car in Santiago and drop it off in Madrid, Bilbao, or another airport; car hire rates are cheaper in Spain than in most of the rest of Europe.

Red Tape

EU nationals can stay in Spain indefinitely, and you don't need a visa if you're from Australia, Canada, USA, or New Zealand and you stay for less then 90 days.

EU nationals are covered by reciprocal health care arrangements; UK residents should pick up an E111 form at a post office before they leave. Travel insurance will give you extra health protection and also cover your baggage. Be sure to read the fine print, as some policies classify walking as a dangerous activity.

In order to stay at an *albergue* (pilgrim hostel), you must show a *credencial*, a pilgrim passport which gets stamped with a *sello* (stamp) each night by the *hospitalero* (person who runs the *albergue*). You can also get *sellos* in churches, monasteries and even cafés. You can get a *credencial* from your local Camino de Santiago organization before you go (see page 192 for a list of these), or simply pick one up at the *albergues* in St-Jean-Pied-de-Port, Roncesvalles, and elsewhere along the camino. The stamping of *credenciales* is a slow, methodical process that usually involves recording details about the country of origin, starting point, and means of transportation of each pilgrim in a huge ledger. It can be therapeutic and comfortingly ritualistic or frustratingly time-consuming, depending on your state of mind and feet when you've finished walking for the day, but there's nothing you can do to speed the process along.

To qualify for the *compostela* (certificate of completing the camino), you must show your stamped *credencial* to prove that you have walked the last 100km or cycled the last 200km to Santiago.

Money & Costs

Spain is a member of the European Monetary Union, and like the other members its currency is the euro (€). You'll still occasionally see prices marked in pesetas, mostly for cars, houses and other items costing large amounts of money.

The most convenient way to get cash is to use your debit or credit card in a cashpoint or ATM. Banks charge high commission fees on travellers' cheques and cash exchanges and often close for the day at 2pm in smaller towns, and *bureau de change* rates are generally unfavourable. We list bank and cashpoint locations at the beginning of each regional chapter. Cashpoints frequently dispense €50 notes, which can be hard to change in small towns and villages. Try to break bigger notes in supermarkets and restaurants, or get smaller denominations from banks—this may or may not be possible, depending on how much cash is in the bank! Visa and Mastercard are widely accepted in restaurants, hotels and larger shops; American Express is less common.

Your cultural and transport costs can go down significantly if you're under 26, over 60 or a student. If you're a student, be sure to get an International Student

Identity Card (ISIC) before leaving, for discounts at certain museums. The Euro<26 card, available for about €10 from youth and student travel agencies throughout Europe, is more widely accepted and gets you a 20% discount on train travel. Spain is a very child-friendly country; as well as being the centre of attention wherever they go, your little ones will get generous discounts on hotels and transport.

If you stay in *albergues*, eat the *menu del día* once a day, and picnic on bread and cheese in the meantime, you can get by on €20 a day. To eat all your meals in cafés or restaurants, and to splurge on a hotel every now and then, allow about €40 a day. Exchange rates vary, but as a rough idea, €1=US$1.

How much does it cost?

Albergue	€3–€7
Cheap hotel, double room	€25–€35
Menú (3-course meal)	€6–€9
Cheap bottle of wine	€2–€3

Transport

At some point along the way, you may need to recover from injury, catch up time, or simply miss out a section — some pilgrims skip the *meseta* between Burgos and León, for example. Spanish trains, run by RENFE, are generally good value, and the most useful line for pilgrims is the one from Santiago to Hendaye on the French border, which passes through Ponferrada, Astorga, Léon and Burgos. You can get information and book tickets online at www.renfe.es.

Buses are usually a more flexible option. In smaller places the bus stop can be just a street corner and a café may act as the ticket office; ask a few locals where the bus stops and when it leaves.

Hitching long distances can be a frustrating experience, as foreign visitors are loathe to pick up hitchhikers and locals may only be travelling as far as the next village. For shorter distances, hitching may be a useful option, particularly on weekends when bus services are limited. Hitching does, of course, involve risk, so take care.

Car hire is cheap compared to the rest of Europe, and can be a good way of visiting sites on rest days, or of getting from Santiago to airports like Bilbao and Madrid.

Not all *albergues* allow cyclists to stay, and some will only do so in late evening, after walkers have arrived for the day. This makes for a frustrating wait to find a bed. Road conditions are generally good, and most of the off-road tracks can be ridden on a mountain bike. Most airlines will transport bikes for free, but find out in advance about any restrictions and requirements.

Accommodation

Albergues

Albergues, also known as *refugios*, provide cheap places to stay at regular points along the camino. They are restricted to self-powered pilgrims, and insist on seeing your *credencial* before giving you a bed. While most *albergues* take bicycles, walking pilgrims generally have priority, and cyclists may have to wait until the evening before being given a space.

No longer simply a roof over your head, modern *albergues* sometimes contain microwave ovens, washing machines and coffee machines. About half the *albergues* along the camino have kitchen facilities, although stoves can work sporadically and pans may be in short supply. Most will provide a sink to wash your clothes and a line to hang them out to dry.

Accommodation is mostly in mixed bunk-bed dormitories, and while blankets are often provided, it's a good idea to bring a thin sleeping bag. Bunk beds are crammed into every available space, and are often laid out side-by-side, letting you have a close relationship with the person in the next bed. Toilets and shower facilities are usually mixed too: if privacy is a big concern, you'll need to stay in a hotel.

Most *albergues* have a 10pm curfew, although some doors stay open until 11pm. Mornings tend to begin early and, even if you fancy a lie-in, the noise of other pilgrims packing up and leaving is likely to wake you up. Earplugs can be an essential piece of equipment, not only to block out early risers, but also to try and get some sleep at night over the noise of *broncadores* (snorers).

Albergues are generally staffed by an *hospitalero,* more often then not a returning pilgrim who works for between a week and a month. In Galicia, *albergues* are minimally staffed and not always well-maintained: invest in some toilet paper. *Albergues* are a wonderful way to meet other pilgrims, share meals and stories, and compare blisters and sore knees. They generally cost from €3 to €7; Galician *albergues* ask for a donation from pilgrims. Some *albergues* stay open year-round, while others close for the winter; all will be packed from June to September.

The Spanish call pilgrim hostels *albergues* or *refugios*; we use *albergue* in this book, and attempt to list every one along the way.

Casas, hotels & paradors

There are places to stay in most villages, and even if there isn't a hotel someone in the village will rent out rooms; local café-bars are generally the best place to ask about somewhere to stay.

At the other end of the price scale, *paradors* are government-run luxury hotels, often in sumptuously converted historic buildings; they're well worth the splurge.

Within each area we include accommodation suggestions for a range of budgets. Accommodation is divided into the price categories given below. The price given is for a double room in high season; rates drop at other times and may be open to negotiation.

$	up to €30
$$	€30–€50
$$$	€50–€75
$$$$	more than €75

Camping

Most campsites are inconveniently located a few kilometres off the camino or a fair way out of town. They often have excellent facilities, but can be noisy on weekends. It may be worth bringing a tent in summer, as packed-out *albergues*

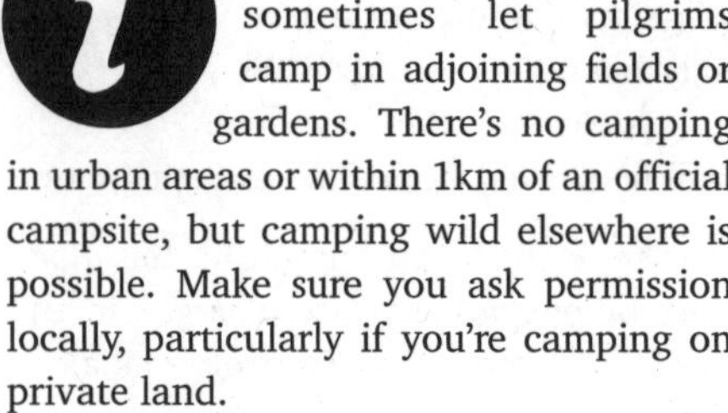

sometimes let pilgrims camp in adjoining fields or gardens. There's no camping in urban areas or within 1km of an official campsite, but camping wild elsewhere is possible. Make sure you ask permission locally, particularly if you're camping on private land.

Equipment

Bring as little as possible. Spain is a modern European country and the camino passes through many towns and cities where you can shop to your heart's content. Remember that you'll need to carry everything you bring, and every luxury in your backpack leaves you more vulnerable to blisters and other injuries. Once you start walking, it's easy enough to ditch non-essentials and send them on to Santiago or post them home.

Good walking shoes are the best bet for your feet. Walking boots are probably overkill on the camino's good tracks and can be uncomfortable in hot weather, though you may be glad of them in winter. Take a pair of sandals or other shoes to pad about towns, villages and *albergues* in the evening.

Even in summer, it's a good idea to bring rain gear. A good quality rain poncho will keep you and your equipment dry; avoid the cheap versions found in supermarkets as these can shred in high winds. Lightweight waterproofs will be fine for summer rain, but bring something more substantial to protect against winter downpours.

Other clothes should be comfortable and fast-drying—bring lightweight layers rather than bulky sweaters. You'll be washing clothes most nights, so pack some laundry soap or travel wash and bring a few pegs or safety pins to hang things out to dry.

Bring a sun hat, sunglasses and sunscreen from spring to autumn, and a warm hat and gloves from autumn to spring. It's important to drink fluid throughout the year, and a collapsible bladder holds more water for long, dry stretches and takes up less room than a rigid water bottle.

A lightweight sleeping bag can make your stay in *albergues* more comfortable. Not all *albergues* provide blankets and some, especially those in monasteries, can be chilly at night. A small torch can be useful at night and for poking around churches, and an alarm clock can get you up in the morning, although unless you're a very heavy sleeper you'll be woken up by the rustling of other pilgrims. To join in the rustling, bring lots of plastic bags, which are also useful for keeping clothes and other equipment dry. Keep toiletries and first aid to a minimum, but bring something for blisters, and consider packing earplugs to block out the *roncadores* (snorers) in the *albergues*.

A phrasebook can help you communicate with people you'll meet along the way; choose one with a menu reader to avoid nasty surprises while eating out. Binoculars can help you identify soaring birds of prey; they're also ideal for looking at lofty cathedral ceilings and windows.

A walking stick is a matter of personal choice; some pilgrims swear by them, while others find them awkward. Unless you bring a telescopic hiking pole, it's best to pick up a stick in Spain, as airlines are wary of carrying weapon-like objects. Many pilgrims hang a scallop shell from their packs or round their necks to distinguish themselves from ordinary tourists. If you're starting the camino before Ponferrada, you should also bring a small stone from home to place on the pile at Cruz de Hierro (see page 139).

Health & Safety

Pharmacies are generally open from 9am to 2pm and from 5pm to 8pm. There should be at least one pharmacy open outside these times too; look at the notice posted outside each one. Pharmacists will often speak English, offer more medical advice than in other European countries and be able to prescribe some drugs without a doctor's prescription.

In an emergency, dial 091 or ask for Cruz Roja (Red Cross), who run a national ambulance service. EU nationals are covered by reciprocal health care arrangements; UK residents should pick up an E111 form at a post office before they leave, although it's often a good idea to supplement this coverage with private insurance.

Walking Hazards

Although the pilgrimage presents few natural hazards, walking every day will inevitably take a toll on your body—see Training & Fitness overleaf for more information. Read the description of your day's route before setting out each morning and make sure you are equipped to deal with any problems that may arise.

Ask at the *albergue* or elsewhere about the weather forecast before heading over the mountain passes, and be prepared to delay your start or to detour via an easier route in case of fog or snow. On uninhabited stretches, make sure that you have enough warm and waterproof clothes, and always take more food and water than you'll need.

Route-finding is easy along the camino and there will usually be someone around to point you in the right direction but, if you do get lost, take the time to look around you for any obvious natural or man-made landmarks and use these to pinpoint your whereabouts. Better still, return to the last yellow arrow or camino marker that you passed. If you're not sure where you are, if it's getting dark or if visibility is poor, stay put.

Specific health risks

Blisters are the most common health problem you'll encounter. You're more likely to get blisters if your feet are hot, wet or tired, so be sensible about the distance you cover and the speed you walk at. Vaseline may help prevent blisters, and sheep's wool can help cushion sore feet. If you do get blisters, try the following treatment: sterilize a needle and thread (or use dental floss), poke it through the blister, leaving the string in place, then cover the pierced blister with a non-padded plaster or band-aid.

Other common problems are related to the heat. Wear a wide-brimmed sun hat, take good sunglasses and use plenty of suntan lotion with a high sun protection factor. Treat mild sunburn with cold water, ice or calamine lotion, and consult a doctor in more serious cases.

Drink lots of fluid and acclimatize

gradually to hot conditions to stave off heat exhaustion and the more serious heatstroke. Rest often and take things slowly until your body is used to the heat. The Spanish siesta for a reason: it can be uncomfortably hot in the afternoon, and many pilgrims choose to finish their day by 2pm. Symptoms of heat exhaustion include cold and clammy skin, nausea and dizziness. Try to get to a cool place, and be sure to sip plenty of water. With heatstroke, there may be some early sensation of feeling unwell, but the symptoms of flushed skin, dizziness, lack of sweating and restlessness usually occur suddenly. Move the sufferer to a cool place, cover them with wet clothes, and fan constantly. Get medical advice immediately, as the condition can be fatal.

Water from local springs is delicious and most villages have drinkable water in the village fountain; use your common sense about drinking water from streams and purify or boil it if there are villages or farms nearby.

Most Spanish snakes are harmless, but there are a couple of venomous vipers and adders. Avoid poking around in holes or sitting on piles of rocks, and make slow, deliberate movements if you spot a snake. If someone does get bitten, secure and support the affected limb. Seek medical help, armed with a description of the snake, if possible.

Training & Fitness

The most important thing you can do is to wear comfortable, sturdy shoes and walk them in thoroughly before leaving home. A couple of months before you leave, start walking. If you can, try to walk every day, even if it's only for a short while, as this mimics the feeling of the camino and will help you to get used to daily walking. Gradually build up the distance walked over the next few weeks, then once you start to get fitter, take your pack along with you. A few times before you leave, pack everything you plan to take and go for a long walk; you'll get used to carrying a load, and perhaps leave non-essentials behind.

If you've left things until the last minute, or if you plan to get fit along the way, don't make your first day too tough. Begin at Roncesvalles or Pamplona to avoid the climb over the Pyrenees from St-Jean-Pied-de-Port, or start at León or Triacastela rather than Villafranca del Bierzo or Rabanal del Camino.

Be sensible distance-wise for the first few days, and walk at a gentle pace. Even after you've been walking for a while, there will be days when you'll be lacking in energy. Try to be flexible about how far you travel each day, and be prepared to stop if you're flagging. Consider doing shorter days in wet weather, as you're more likely to get tired if you're soaking, and you'll also give your pack and shoes more time to dry out.

Communication

Post Offices

Correos (post offices) in smaller towns often close at 2pm, while city *correos* reopen after the siesta from 5pm to 8pm. It's faster and more convenient to buy stamps at *estancos*, state-run tobacconists.

It's easy to send packages overseas, but if you're simply trying to lighten your load, then it's cheaper to send items on to Santiago. Label the package with your name (surname first and in capitals), and address it to *Lista de Correos*, Santiago, Galicia. At the post office, if nothing's found under your last name, ask the staff to check under any other names too.

Phones

Most public phones will take both coins and *tarjetas de telefónica* (phonecards). If a phone booth posts international dialling codes, then you can make overseas calls: dial 00, then the country code (44 for UK; 1 for Canada and USA; 61 for Australia; 64 for New Zealand). It costs about €2 to make a short call across Europe or to North America. Mobile phones are ubiquitous on the camino as many companies provide Europe-wide coverage, and often the *albergue* bathroom will be sacrilegiously crowded with recharging phones.

Internet

Internet cafés are springing up in cities and bigger towns all along the camino. They're frequently open late into the evening, and are a sociable place to hang out and check e-mail. Most charge very low hourly rates; ask at the *turismo* (tourist office) for a list. Don't forget to check out www.pilipalapress.com for up-to-date information and useful links.

Opening Hours & Public Holidays

The Spanish take the siesta seriously. Most shops, banks and post offices open at 10am, firmly close their doors at 2pm, then open for the evening from 5pm to 8pm. Museums often stay open through the siesta and close for the day at 4pm; most also close on Mondays. Mealtimes are later than in northern Europe. Lunch starts at 2pm, while the evening meal is eaten from 10pm. Along the camino, restaurants often cater to pilgrim schedules, serving a set menu at 8pm. For more on Spanish eating habits, see the Food and Drink sections earlier in the book.

Public Holidays

Most shops and banks close on public holidays, and public transport is limited. Restaurants and café-bars usually stay open, and there'll be a packed, holiday atmosphere inside. If you're low on cash, take some out a few days before the holiday, as bank machines can empty fast. The following public holidays are celebrated in most of Spain. For regional festivals and holidays, see the Events & Festivals section in each regional chapter.

January 1	*Año Nuevo* (New Year's Day)
January 6	*Día de los Reyes* (Epiphany)
March/April	*Jueves Santo, Viernes Santo* (Maundy Thursday, Good Friday)
May 1	*Fiesta del Trabajo* (May Day)
August 15	*Asunción* (Feast of the Assumption)
October 12	*Día de la Hispanidad* (National Day)
November 1	*Todos Santos* (All Saints' Day)
December 6	*Dia de la Constitución* (Constitution Day)
December 8	*Inmaculada Concepción* (Immaculate Conception)
December 25	*Navidad* (Christmas Day)

Regional Map (key page 213)

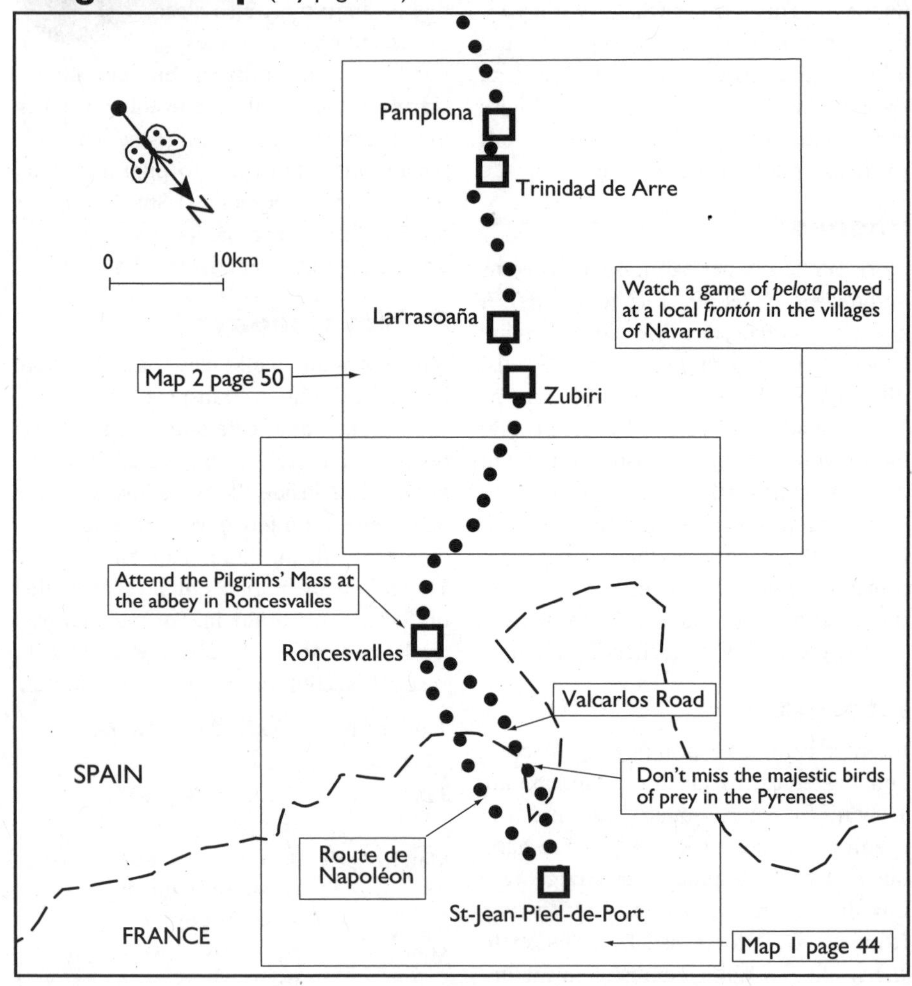

What's the weather like?

	Jan	April	July	Oct
Sun	3hrs	6hrs	10hrs	5hrs
Rainfall	15cm	10cm	5cm	12cm
Maximum Temp	8°C	15°C	28°C	19°C
Minimum Temp	1°C	5°C	14°C	8°C

Average hours of sun, total average rainfall in cm and average temperature in degrees celsius

Basque Lands

St-Jean-Pied-de-Port to Pamplona

The Basques are thought to be the original Europeans, passed over by successive waves of invaders and content to remain in and fight to protect this beautiful region. The route over the Pyrenees from St-Jean to Roncesvalles is one of the most dramatic of the camino, climbing steeply and soared over by eagles, buzzards and kestrels. As the Pyrenees peter out, you'll pass traditional villages of beautiful whitewashed stone houses with ornate rafters, and walk alongside trout-filled rivers lined with beech trees.

Walking

Geography

Although it may not feel like it when you're huffing and puffing uphill, the pass at the Col de Lepoeder is on the lower, western fringes of the Pyrenees as they taper off into the Atlantic. This chain of mountains stretches for 435km marking the border between France and Spain; the highest peak is Picos de Aneto (3404m), some 200km southeast of the pilgrim crossing point. The Pyrenees were formed when the Afro-Iberian tectonic plate collided with the European plate and the mountains still grow by fractions of a millimetre every year.

The lofty peaks of the Pyrenees attract clouds like a magnet, and it sometimes seems that any storm that comes into the Bay of Biscay is drawn relentlessly to them. The resulting high winds can bring snow at almost any time of the year: if crossing outside the summer months, beware of avalanches caused by the build up of loose snow pockets that can be released without warning, carrying the hapless pilgrim with them. When the weather is fine the views are fantastic and the mountains' harsh reputation seems overplayed.

The Pyrenees recede reluctantly as the pilgrim heads west into pretty, undulating countryside with wooded hillsides and farmed valleys.

Trails

The camino climbs over the Pyrenees along a paved narrow mountain road, then veers off the road along a wide dirt track. It's an exposed route in bad weather, easy to get lost in fog or caught in snow, and almost every year pilgrims get into trouble along this stretch. Start early from St-Jean, take things slowly, and be prepared to take the alternative Valcarlos route in bad weather. After Roncesvalles the camino follows dirt farm tracks or purpose-built, blister-inducing paved stretches, laid out by the Navarran government.

When to go

The weather in the Pyrenees can be unpredictable at any time of year, and in winter the pass may be snowbound, although it's rarely impassable for long periods of time. Even if there's no snow, fog, high winds and cold can make walking miserable. In the foothills, the weather's changeable in spring and autumn; summers are more settled and the region comes alive with festivals at this time, although the *albergues* will be more crowded.

Flora & Fauna

There's a good chance you'll see **birds of prey** in the Pyrenees. The mountains are home to hundreds of griffon vultures, languidly circling the lower peaks and valleys, often in fairly large groups. There are also black vultures and Egyptian vultures here, as well as golden and short-toed eagles, kestrels and buzzards. The **lammergeier**, called *quebrantahuesos* in Spanish (he who breaks bones) after its habit of dropping animal bones from a great height to smash them and get at the marrow within, is mainly found in the eastern Pyrenees, but occasionally ventures this way. Equally difficult to see are the bouncy chamois, an agile member of the antelope family, and the marmot, occasionally seen amongst rocks but more commonly heard whistling. Rocky terrain is also a favourite of the blue rock thrush, ptarmigan and rock bunting, while the solid, fan-tailed capercaille prefers pine forests. Around 160 plants are indigenous and unique to the Pyrenees; look for gentians, orchids and splendid, carnivorous sundews.

On your way down the mountain into Roncesvalles, you skirt the edge of the **Bosque de Irati**, a beech haven for wildlife that once stretched across the Basque lands to form one of the biggest forests in Spain. The loveliest parts of Irati are further east (see Rest Days & Detours), but along the camino you may see genet, beech marten, wild boar and red, roe and fallow deer. The forest teems with bird life: listen out for the tap-tap-tapping of woodpeckers, and look for golden orioles, treecreepers, woodcock and ptarmigans.

The valley bottoms from Roncesvalles to Pamplona have been heavily farmed but willow, poplar, ash and maple stands provide refuge for many songbirds.

People & Culture

Although the camino from St-Jean-Pied-de-Port to Pamplona nominally begins in France and soon enters Spain, many locals insist that it travels through just one country, Euskedi, or the **Basque** lands. The Basque people's fierce independence has helped to preserve unique folk cultures like the *trikitnixa*, a whirling dervish of accordion music, but has also aroused suspicion from Spaniards and other foreigners.

Aymeric Picaud, a twelfth-century pilgrim who wrote the *Codex Calixtinus*, was particularly uncomplimentary:

> "This is a barbarous people, different from all other people in customs and in race, malignant, dark in colour, ugly of face, debauched, perverse, faithless, dishonourable, corrupt, lustful, drunken, skilled in all forms of violence, fierce and savage, dishonest and false, impious and coarse, cruel and quarrelsome, incapable of any good impulses, past masters of all vices and iniquities."

Picaud's book was widely circulated in France and did much to sully the reputation of the Basques, culminating in a call for their excommunication by the French church in 1179.

Spanish authorities continued to find the Basque people a little weird. The **Inquisition**, notorious for its decimation of Spain's Jewish population and persecution of other religions, also worked to rid Navarra of the scourge of witchcraft. In a rash of accusations and confessions, stories surfaced of initiation ceremonies run by a toad, along with vampirism, cannibalism, and having sex with the devil. By 1611, the Inquisition had uncovered almost 2000 witches in Navarra. Even after the Inquisition died down, many Spaniards continued to believe that the region's women were prone to witchcraft, a natural consequence of their fondness for apples, Eve's forbidden fruit.

Euskara, the Basque language, is the oldest living European language, and has no linguistic relative; its origins aren't even Indo-European. About half a million Basques speak the language in Spain, with more *Euskara*-speakers across the Pyrenees in France. Under Franco, spoken *Euskara* was forbidden, and Basque-language publications were forced underground. Furious at the censorship of Basque symbols, and frustrated with an older generation who seemed content to wait for Franco to die before taking action, a group of young Basque Nationalists formed an organization in the 1950s that became known as Euskadi ta Astatasuna (**ETA**).

Begun as an intellectual movement, primarily promoting *Euskara*, ETA's initial activities were largely peaceful. Activists daubed pro-ETA graffiti on walls and statues, and derailed a train carrying people to San Sebastián where a celebration of Franco's 1936 victory was to take place. By the late 1960s, however, ETA attacks and Spanish reprisals (or Spanish attacks and ETA reprisals, depending on your point of view) had escalated into murder.

While there's widespread condemnation of ETA violence among the Basques, there's also some support for the group's independence aims. And although human rights groups like Amnesty International have protested political arrests and torture of Basque nationalists, the Spanish government and western media continue to portray the complex Basque problem as a one-sided terrorist campaign.

Post-Franco, the Basques have gained some measure of independence, and there's been a revival of interest in traditional Basque culture, with increased attendance at and participation in sports such as goat racing, stone lifting and wood chopping.

The most popular Basque sport by far is *jai alai* or **pelota**, a game where two or four players smack a rock-hard ball with their bare hands against high walls. The village *frontón* (*pelota* court) is as ubiquitous as the village church, and you'll see the high-sided concrete courts in almost every inhabited place between the French border and Pamplona. The palm-bruising balls are made from tightly wound rubber tape covered in wool and cotton yarn, all of which is enclosed in goatskin. The monopoly on production is held by a single family-run factory near Bilbao, and managers of local clubs order fast, slow or bouncing balls to suit local courts and supporters. Once a folksy, machismo pastime, the sport has moved away from its village origins and is now unromantically reliant on TV money.

The camino between the Pyrenees and Pamplona is rife with tales of the exploits of the French king, **Charlemagne**, and his heroic knight, **Roland**, laid out in the epic French tale, the *Chanson du Roland*. According to the story, Charlemagne rode into Spain with his army, determined to win back the Muslim-dominated lands for Christianity. His seven-year-long operation was going pretty well until he reached Zaragoza, where Ganelon, an evil and cowardly knight determined to exact revenge on his nephew Roland, persuaded Charlemagne to accept Muslim peace terms instead of sacking the city. Satisfied with a job well done, Charlemagne headed back to France, but the rearguard of his army was ambushed by a Muslim army, killing Roland and many other brave knights.

It seems more likely that Charlemagne was heading back home after sacking Pamplona in 778, part of a brief campaign to extend French territory, when his army was attacked and defeated by the understandably furious Basques. The battle of Roncesvalles was never actually recorded by Charlemagne, as his only defeat represented a blight on an otherwise victorious military career. The French may even have appropriated the legend of Errolan, a Basque giant of great strength, in creating the figure of Roland. Nevertheless, the *Chanson du Roland* provides some of the more colourful legends of the region.

Food & Drink

Meals in Navarra centre around roast meat, game, trout and *jamón serrano*, a *prosciutto*-like cured ham. The woods provide pheasant, wood pigeon and woodcock, a rare delicacy, while the rivers are home to a seemingly endless supply of trout. Try *trucha a la Navarra*, Pyrenean trout wrapped in *jamón serrano* and then baked, or *chilindrón de cordero*, a delicious and spicy lamb stew made with local peppers.

Navarra **wine** suffers in comparison with its more famous Riojan neighbour. The wines are similar, and like Rioja, the more robust Navarra depends heavily on the tempranillo grape, usually mixed with garnacha or some other variety. Now being widely exported as a cheaper alternative to Rioja, Navarra wine has been produced locally in vast quantities since the Romans first arrived. Legend has it that when the church in Mendigorría, a few kilometres south of Puente la Reina, was built, the builders used wine instead of water to mix the cement.

Wine not your thing? Try the local tipple, **pacharán**, a deep pinky-orange fortified liqueur made from sloes, anise and sugar. *Pacharán* is usually drunk cold over ice, either neat or with water in a long glass. Often served as an aperitif, and said to aid digestion, it's sweet and tastes dangerously non-alcoholic.

Cheese is made in many places in the Pyrenean foothills. The most famous is the *queso de Roncal*, made from unpasteurized sheep's milk in the western Pyrenees. It's a compact, cylindrical cheese, ivory-coloured or very pale yellow, with a straw-coloured thin rind and a distinctive, creamy flavour.

Tourist Information

Tourist Offices

There are *turismos* in St-Jean-Pied-de-Port and Roncesvalles. Contact information for the *turismos* is under individual towns.

Transport

There's one bus a day between Pamplona and Burguete, and sporadic buses on to Roncesvalles; taxis may be more reliable. A quaint, two-carriage train links St-Jean-Pied-de-Port and Bayonne a few times a day, and it's a gorgeous, relaxing one-hour trip alongside the Rivière Nive.

Money

Banks machines in St-Jean-Pied-de-Port, Burguete, Zubiri, and Trinidad de Arre.

Accommodation

The *albergues* are small and evenly-spaced, so you'll keep bumping into the same pilgrims and a great sense of camararderie develops. There are few hotels and those that do exist are inevitably small, family-run *casas* or *pensiones*. Pamplona's *albergues* are always changing, so it's a good idea to stay in Trinidad de Arre or in Cizur Menor instead.

Shopping

Stock up in St-Jean-Pied-de-Port on supplies as once you leave there are no shops until after Roncesvalles; the changeable mountain weather makes carrying extra food over the heights of the first day a good idea anyway. If you're lucky enough to be in St-Jean-Pied-de-Port on a Monday, it's hard to miss the food market.

Events & Festivals

Navarra catches alight for the Noche de San Juan on June 21, a summer solstice festival of bonfires and festivities held in almost all the local villages. In Burguete's version, the whole village dances the *trebolé* and the *torralba del río*, symbolising the capture of Juan Lobo, a legendary medieval bandit. From May to mid-June, there's a *romería* (religious procession) in Roncesvalles every Sunday, involving costumed locals from nearby village, and penitents shouldering huge crosses.

Rest Days & Detours

It's well worth spending the night in **St-Jean-Pied-de-Port**. There are enough things to do to fill the day, you can stock up on food, and then set off fully rested early the next morning.

Although not quite a rest from exertion,

the **Bosque de Irati**, just west of Roncesvalles, has some of the best birdwatching in all of Spain, including all seven species of European woodpecker.

Hemingway's favourite mini-break when he was tired of running from bulls in Pamplona was a relaxed weekend in **Burguete**, trout fishing on the Río Urrobi.

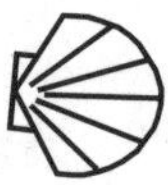

St-Jean-Pied-de-Port

Ⓐ Ⓗ ✗ ☕ € ⓘ 🛒

St-Jean-Pied-de-Port is a pretty walled town, attractively located in the French Pyrenean foothills. The town's tourist highlights lie along a single cobbled street, Rue de la Citadelle, which is crowded on both sides with distinctive wooden buildings and uniform souvenir shops.

From the top of Rue de la Citadelle, walk downhill to the gothic **Prison des Evêques**, the Bishop's Prison that housed thieves and conmen and other good-for-nothings, many of whose victims were hapless pilgrims. Further down the street, the elegantly plain fourteenth-century **Eglise de Nôtre Dame** butts against the Porte Notre Dame, an imposing town gate with a statue of Santiago Peregrino. There's a scallop shell decorated fountain in front of the church. The street changes its name to Rue d'Espagne here, then crosses the Rivière Nive over a gently rounded bridge, leading past lots of trinket shops towards the Porte d'Espagne, the gateway to the camino.

Above the town, at the top of Rue de la Citadelle, you can still visit the lower ramparts of the seventeenth-century **citadel**, built on the orders of Cardinal Richelieu and now converted into a college.

It's worth coming to St-Jean-Pied-de-Port on a Monday, when the lively Basque open-air market takes over the town.

Turismo Place du Général-de-Gaulle 14 (☎ 05 59 37 03 57). Ask here about rooms at nearby *gîtes d'étape*.

Accommodation

Albergue 55 rue de la Citadelle, towards the top of town (18 beds, kitchen, open all year). You can pick up a *credencial* here, and get advice on walking and weather conditions between St-Jean and Roncesvalles.

$$ Hôtel Itzalpea, 5 Place du Trinquet (☎ 05 59 37 03 66)

$$ Hôtel des Remparts, 16 Place Floquet (☎ 05 59 37 13 79)

$$$ Hôtel Ramuntcho, 1 Rue de France (☎ 05 59 37 03 91)

$$$$ Hôtel de Pyrénées, 19 Place Général de Gaulle (☎ 05 59 37 01 01)

The claustrophobic cobbled streets and tourist bustle of St-Jean-Pied-de-Port are left abruptly behind at the imposing Porte d'Espagne. Almost immediately, you're confronted with a signpost and there's a decision to be made.

There are two routes to Roncesvalles: the Route de Napoléon, which climbs gloriously high and steep over the Pyrenean foothills, and the lower road route via Valcarlos. In medieval times, the Route de

Napoléon was considered the safer bet, as pilgrims were less likely to be ambushed in the high mountains. On the Valcarlos route, according to Aymeric Picaud,

> "they come out to meet pilgrims with two or three cudgels to exact tribute by improper use of force; and if any traveller refuses to give the money they demand they strike him with their cudgels and take the money, abusing him and rummaging in his very breeches."

Nowadays, there are fewer vagabonds to worry about, and your choice of routes will be dictated mainly by the weather. The Route de Napoléon is exposed and isolated, it can be subject to snow as late as May, and cold winds and rain at any time of year. In bad weather, particularly if snow or fog are forecast, choose the low road.

The Route de Napoléon also makes for a very strenuous first day. Consider going via Valcarlos if you're worried about your fitness level or, alternatively, stay at Honto, a tiny village 5km outside St-Jean. There's almost no water along the way and nowhere to buy food, so bring enough provisions for a long day.

Valcarlos route to Roncesvalles

The route via Valcarlos is well-marked and initially follows the Rivière Petit Nive close to the C135 road. At the border at **Arneguy**, you can stop for a coffee before joining the road and following the N135 to the town of **Valcarlos**, 1km away. The town's Iglesia de Santiago has a life-size statute of Santiago Matamoros (St James the Moorslayer) inside; outside, there's a sculpture of prematurely exhausted pilgrims. If you need to stay, try the **Hotel Maitena** (**$$**, ☎ 948 79 02 10) or the **Casa Etxezuria** (**$$**, ☎ 948 79 00 11); there are also a fair few souvenir shops here. Continue along the N135 for another 8km or so, then begin a steep climb uphill to the Alto Ibañeta, avoiding the road's long switchbacks. The route meets up with the Route de Napoléon at **Ibañeta** (page 46).

Route de Napoléon to Roncesvalles

The more dramatic Route de Napoléon offers fabulous views of the Pyrenees, and great wildlife watching: look for eagles, vultures, fox and deer. Although the route is loosely named after Napoleon, his crossing of the Pyrenees into Spain was hardly groundbreaking — the Roman Via Traiana, which you'll follow for much of the next few weeks, went this way, linking Burdegala (Bordeaux) with Asturica Augusta (Astorga). The route mostly follows very quiet minor roads, although there are a couple of sections on tracks, and the turn offs for these can be difficult to see in bad weather.

From the Porte d'Espagne, walk down the main road, then turn right in a few hundred metres down a minor road, following the sign for Chemin St Jacques de Compostelle. The camino here follows the French long-distance GR65 footpath, and you'll see red and white horizontal markers alongside the traditional yellow arrows of the camino. The route heads uphill immediately, although the initial climbing is mostly gradual. A few kilometres after St-Jean-Pied-de-Port, pass a farm and follow the signs to Ferme

Map 1 (key page 213)

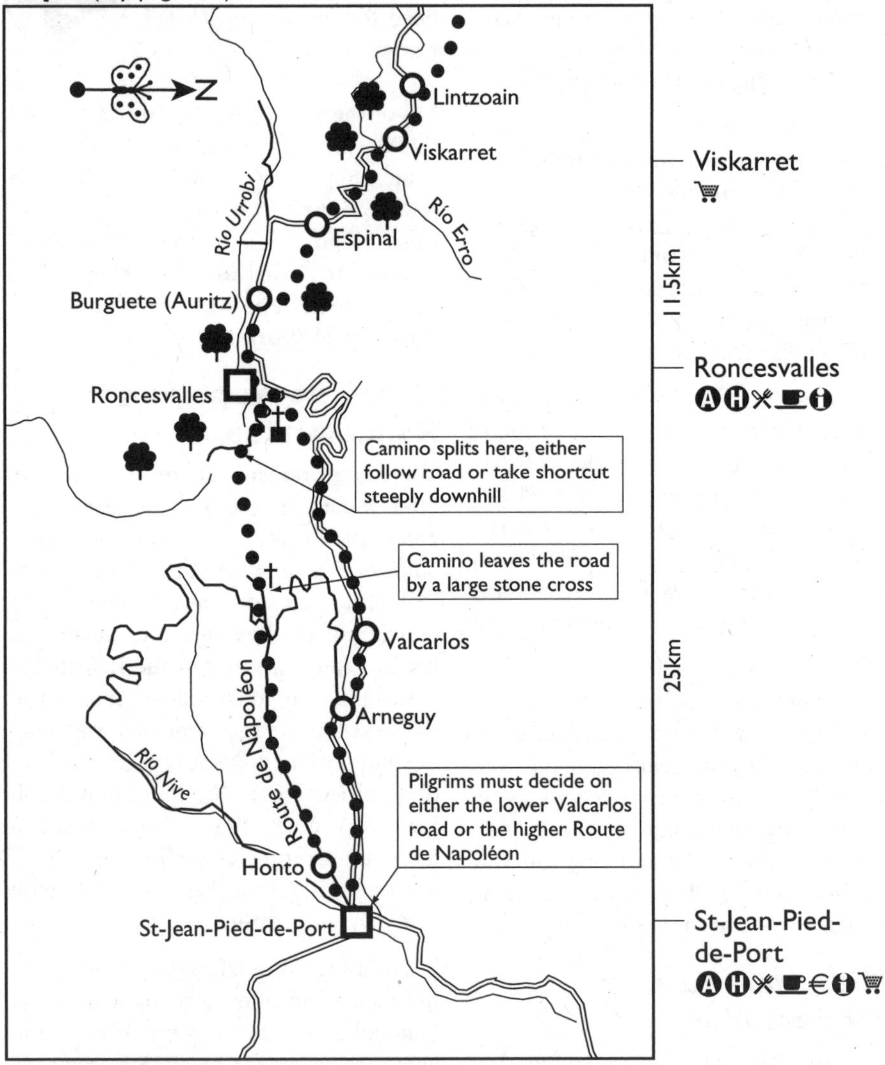

Z

Lintzoain

Viskarret

Río Erro

Río Urrobi

Espinal

Burguete (Auritz)

Roncesvalles

Camino splits here, either follow road or take shortcut steeply downhill

Camino leaves the road by a large stone cross

Valcarlos

Arneguy

Route de Napoléon

Río Nive

Pilgrims must decide on either the lower Valcarlos road or the higher Route de Napoléon

Honto

St-Jean-Pied-de-Port

Viskarret

11.5km

Roncesvalles

25km

St-Jean-Pied-de-Port

Profile Chart 1

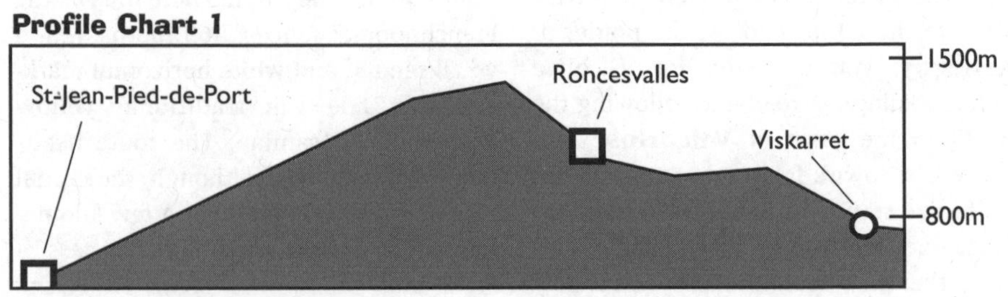

Ithurburia. Look out for lizards in the undergrowth at the side of the road and in walls; listen for rustling sounds to try and spot them.

In another couple of kilometres, the road begins to climb much more steeply, and shortly after a sharp hairpin to the left, you'll arrive at **Ferme Ithurburia** (**$**, ☎ 05 59 37 11 17), a *gîte* that does bed and breakfast in the village of **Honto** (no sign).

The route here is very steep, but there are increasingly dramatic views of the Pyrenees to the east, often snow-capped well into the summer. Behind you, St-Jean-Pied-de-Port and the surrounding valley are strikingly visible. Immediately after Honto, the road curves round to the right and flattens out a little. Turn left here along a track, next to a GR65 post giving times to the Col de Bentarte and Roncesvalles, then follow the track to the right 100m later. The steep, zig-zag trail is lined with gorse, and can be mucky after rain; you can stay on the road to avoid this section. The mountains here are more barren and the only agriculture is the occasional sheep grazing.

In a little while, the track rejoins the road. Turn left here; you'll soon pass a fountain on your right and a fascinating map on your left, which names towns, peaks and camino routes. Although you're still climbing, the route becomes less steep now and the views of the Pyrenees just keep getting more spectacular. This is also one of the best parts of the camino for birds of prey, particularly in spring and autumn when numbers are swelled by migratory birds. Gangs of griffon vultures are fairly common, but you may also see red kites, golden eagles, Egyptian vultures and the rare lammergeier.

The road is edged with a soft grass verge: use it and save your knees for the downhill stretch to Roncesvalles. You also start to see distinctive concrete camino bollards marked with a scallop shell, and these will become more common as you continue the camino. Although the route is less strenuous now, it's a long slog (about 6km from Honto) until you reach the next major landmark, the **Vierge d'Orisson**. The statue of the Virgin Mary here is just off the main route to the left, and is said to have been brought here from Lourdes. Any loneliness she might feel in such an isolated spot must be more than made up for by the glorious views she has of the Pyrenees.

Continue along the road, much less steep now, following the signs for Urkulu. In a few kilometres, keep a look out for a large memorial cross on the right-hand side of the road, surrounded by other, plainer crosses left by pilgrims. Here, the camino leaves the road up a wide grassy track, headed for the peaks you've been able to see from the road for a while. If you're lucky, you may also bump into a kindly Frenchman who spends much of his retirement driving up to this point with buckets of water for thirsty pilgrims. Hapless medieval pilgrims were not so lucky. Picaud's medieval guide warns,

> "On this mountain, before Christianity was fully established in Spain, the impious Navarrese and the Basques were accustomed not only to rob pilgrims going to St James, but to ride them like asses and kill them."

Climb up the grassy track to a pass between two small peaks with great views into the valley below. The trail veers to

the left at the pass, along a mostly flat track that can be clogged with tar-black mud after rain or snowmelt. Follow the signs to the Fontaine de Roland, a disappointing concrete fountain you'll get to in about 2km. Almost immediately afterwards, cross over a cattle grid, where a concrete sign welcomes you to Spain. In 150m, the GR11 route (which traverses the Spanish Pyrenees) joins up with the camino for a few kilometres. The route winds through beech forest with a spectacular drop to your right into the lovely valley below.

In a couple of kilometres, the camino passes some farm buildings, and the track begins to get wider and stonier. A few hundred metres after the farm buildings, keep straight on, following the yellow arrows and ignoring a track that heads right downhill then, 100m later, go straight on at another fork, ignoring the left-hand track going downhill. After a short steep stretch, the track heads around a corner and there are more stunning Pyrenean views. Join a road at the **Col de Lepoeder**, from where you'll be able to see the grey-roofed Roncesvalles monastery in the valley below.

In medieval times, this was the site of Charlemagne's Cross, a monument marking the spot where Charlemagne supposedly gave thanks for his army's safe crossing of the Pyrenees and prayed to Santiago for help in his battles with the Moors. The fact that Charlemagne's campaigns in Spain took place at the end of the eighth century and that Santiago's bones weren't discovered until 813 didn't deter medieval pilgrims, who would stop here to plant their own wooden crosses and pray to Santiago for a safe journey.

From the Col de Lepoeder, there are two routes to the abbey.

Roman route to Roncesvalles

The old Roman road is more direct but very steep: you'll need energy, good knees and a friend or two to help find the occasionally obscured yellow markers. From the Col de Lepoeder, follow the signs to the left for the GR65, cross over the minor road and keep straight ahead through a beech forest. It's a lovely spot, particularly in spring when it's filled with songbirds and bluebells. The beech forests around Roncesvalles are the only sites in Europe where you can see all seven species of European woodpecker. Look in particular for the black woodpecker and the white-backed woodpecker, but also keep an eye out for the red-backed shrike and the tiny crested tit.

As you near the abbey, the path gets wider and clearer. At the bottom of the hill, about 4km after the Col de Lepoeder, turn right at the minor NA43 road, pass through a green gate, cross the stream via a concrete bridge, then climb up some steps to emerge at Charlemagne's Silo, just in front of the Abbey.

Puerta de Ibañeta Route to Roncesvalles

The second route from the Col de Lepoeder is longer but less steep, and goes via the Puerta de Ibañeta, the spot where Charlemagne heard Roland's horn, asking for help in his rearguard battle against the Moors. At the Col de Lepoeder, follow the signs to the right for the GR11, skirting the minor road until you reach the **Puerta de Ibañeta** in about 3km. The *Chanson du Roland* tells of a great battle between the rearguard of Charlemagne's army, led by Roland and local troops (probably Basque but often described as Moorish infidels). Roland was told to blow his horn, Olifant, if he got into trouble, but he left it until the last minute, and in any case Charlemagne, who heard Roland's cry from his camp in Puerta de Ibañeta, was persuaded that the sound was a false alarm. Nowadays, it's a pleasant 2km walk from the Puerta de Ibañeta downhill to the abbey at Roncesvalles.

Roncesvalles

Roncesvalles (Orreaga) is a small hamlet, utterly dominated by its imposing abbey. Pilgrims' Mass is held at 8pm each evening and, as part of the service, the nationality of each pilgrim is read out and pilgrims are invited to go to the front of the church. The moving ceremony and the communal meals that follow in the hamlet's two restaurants make your stay in Roncesvalles feel like the beginning of an important journey. Having said that, the abbey's strange zinc roof and its location in a sun-starved valley can make Roncesvalles seem rather bleak and grey.

Roncesvalles' attractions are generally related either to Roland and Charlemagne, or to Sancho El Fuerte (the strong), a Navarran king famed for his defeat of the Muslim army at Las Navas de Tolosa in 1212, which marked a turning point in the Christian *reconquista*. Sancho ordered the construction of the Gothic **Real Colegiata**, and his tomb, alongside that of his wife, Doña Clemencia, can be seen in the fourteenth-century chapter house that's annexed to the Colegiata's Cloister. At the foot of his massive tomb (Sancho was said to be well over 2m tall) are the chains of Christian prisoners freed at Las Navas. In the church of the Real Colegiata is a silver-covered wooden statue of the Virgen de Roncesvalles, who was made patroness of Navarra in 1960.

Legend has it that Charlemagne's soldiers, including Roland, were buried in the Capilla de Sancti Spiritus, a simple twelfth-century ossuary in front of the monastery, better known as the Silo de Charlemagne. Whatever the truth of the legend, the ossuary also contains the bones of medieval pilgrims who died trying to make it across the Pyrenees. The monastery's museum includes treasures such as Roland's carved ivory horn, Olifant, with which he tried in vain to summon Charlemagne, and Roland's maces, which may or may not be on display. Charlemagne's chessboard, also in the museum, is actually an intricate fourteenth-century reliquary containing the bones of 32 saints and nothing at all to do with the Frenchman.

There's not much in Roncesvalles apart from the abbey; the closest shops are in Burguete, a couple of kilometres away. The **turismo** is in the old windmill (☎ 948 76 03 01).

Accommodation

Albergue Basic but well-maintained facilities, can be very cold (40 beds, open all year). No kitchen, but both hotels serve pilgrim *menús*. Obtain a *sello*, and a *credencial* if necessary, at the entrance to the abbey.

$ youth hostel in the monastery (☎ 948 76 03 07)

$$ Hotel La Posada (☎ 948 76 02 25)

$$ Hostal Casa Sabina (☎ 948 76 00 12)

The route from Roncesvalles to Zubiri wanders along varied surfaces (paved tracks, farm tracks and narrow paths) through rolling woodland and farmland.

Basque Lands

The camino passes through lovely Basque villages where *frontones*, on which the popular Basque sport of *pelota* is played, are as commonplace as churches.

To leave Roncesvalles, turn left and walk down the road. In 200m, just before the **Cruz de Peregrinos** (a fourteenth-century cross depicting Sancho el Fuerte on the base), turn right down a track marked with yellow arrows and an informative map of the camino to Zubiri. The flat track runs parallel to the road, through holly and beech trees.

After a few hundred metres, there's an alternative route to the right signposted *Camino Canonicus*. Ignore this option and keep straight on, arriving in a couple of kilometres at some fairly new buildings. At these buildings, turn left on to a minor road, then turn right in 100m just past a police station, and walk into Burguete, passing picnic tables on your left.

Burguete

Burguete (Auritz) is a lovely village of shuttered houses made famous as Hemingway's trout-fishing base in *The Sun Also Rises*. While here, he wrote to F. Scott Fitzgerald that, "heaven would be a big bull ring with me holding two *barrera* seats and a trout stream outside that no one else was allowed to fish in." The writer's presence is less noticeable than camino symbolism such as the house railings decorated with scallop shells and the pilgrim fountain in front of the Iglesia de San Nicolás de Bari. Burguete has an excellent café-*panadería* (bakery).

Accommodation

$ Hostal Juandeaburre (☎ 948 76 00 78)

$$ Hostal Burguete (☎ 948 76 00 05)

$$$ Hotel Loizu (☎ 948 76 00 08)

In Burguete, turn right 50m after San Nicolás de Bari church, although you'll need to keep straight on here to detour to the bakery and Burguete's other practical attractions. Walk through a farmyard, then cross a stream over a wooden bridge, and join a wide dirt track on the other side. From this broad, flat valley, there are good views of the nearby, beech-clad hills.

After a few hundred metres, walk through a gate, then cross first one, then another stream in quick succession. The track narrows to a path, and the GR11 splits off soon afterwards to the right. Keep straight on, crossing another stream, then climb steeply uphill. At the top of the hill, go straight over a clearing and head down a path on other side. Pass through a gap in a wall, and soon reach **Espinal** (), a small town with distinctive decorative railings, a bar, restaurant, *panadería* and shop. There are a couple of *casas rurales* in the village: ask for details at the shop. In Espinal, turn right at the main road, then turn left in a couple of hundred metres, following the yellow arrows down a broad, semi-paved track.

In about 500m, turn right up a smaller path, following the yellow arrows. After a steep burst of about 100m, the path curves round to the right. Walk along a short, narrow section that can be muddy after rain, then pass through a gate and the track soon widens. Cross over a road in a few hundred metres, following the clear signs and ignoring the smaller path to the right. You're now walking through a beautiful, peaceful beech wood on a wide, gravel path, which soon narrows as the road drops steeply away to the left.

The wood is home to bullfinches, coal tits, and robins, and to the more elusive fox. There's some erosion here and exposed roots in places, but the path is generally good and the route is obvious.

In a kilometre or so, pass through a gate, then follow a wide, rocky path going downhill. The camino almost reaches the road at a tight left-hand bend, but then veers away to the right, heading uphill on a shady, stony path. After 300m, turn left to walk along a grey paved track. The government of Navarra is busy "improving" the camino by paving over some of the paths along the route. Although this may help with erosion problems and is great for cyclists, walkers may find the surface hard on the feet. The track again veers close to the road at a stream, and you may need to use the road bridge if the water level is high. Keep straight on at the other side of the stream, walking uphill on the same paved track, and you'll soon see Viskarret ahead.

You'll emerge in Viskarret's outskirts on a minor road. Turn right here, then follow the road as it curves around to the left and cross over the main road into the centre of the village. **Viskarret** (🛒) is a fascinating village with a distinctive and uniform architecture; look out for wooden balconies, huge wooden roof joists, and stone doorways carved with crosses. The stone church has a big bell tower and is a mix of Romanesque and Gothic styles. Just as prominent is the village *frontón*, where the Basque sport of *pelota* is played. You'll see these large concrete courts in almost every village you'll pass between here and Pamplona.

Follow the road through Viskarret. At the end of the village, there's a shop on your left. Turn left here, just before the main road, to walk downhill and ford a stream via concrete stepping-stones. After a few hundred metres, pass a cemetery, then curve to left and walk downhill on the centre of three narrow paths, pretty with shade and a great place to see and hear songbirds. After a few hundred metres, the path curves round to the right and reaches the main road. Turn left on to the road, then almost immediately turn right down a concrete track that changes to gravel.

You'll soon reach the quiet hamlet of **Lintzoain**. Walk through the village, past the roofed *frontón*, and turn right to walk under a wooden bridge that links the upper storey of one of the hamlet's gorgeous stone houses with a high-walled garden on the other side of the street. The camino becomes a dirt track at the top of the village and begins to climb steeply uphill. It's a hot climb in summer, with very little shade initially, but the main track is well signposted. After a couple of kilometres, the track flattens out a bit. Look out for a very low, yellow-painted rock just to the right of the trail; this insignificant-looking monument is said to mark the length of Roland's huge stride.

The path begins to go downhill here, then passes a radio tower and crosses a road next to a disused well. The trail undulates for a kilometre or so before reaching the pass at **Alto de Erro**, where the ruins of a pilgrims' inn are now home to local cows, and the nearby fields are a good place for a picnic. In autumn, there's a feast of mushrooms in the local woods; make sure you ask for local advice before eating anything you don't recognize. The splendid crossbill is a year-round resident, but easiest to see in the winter months

Map 2 (key page 213)

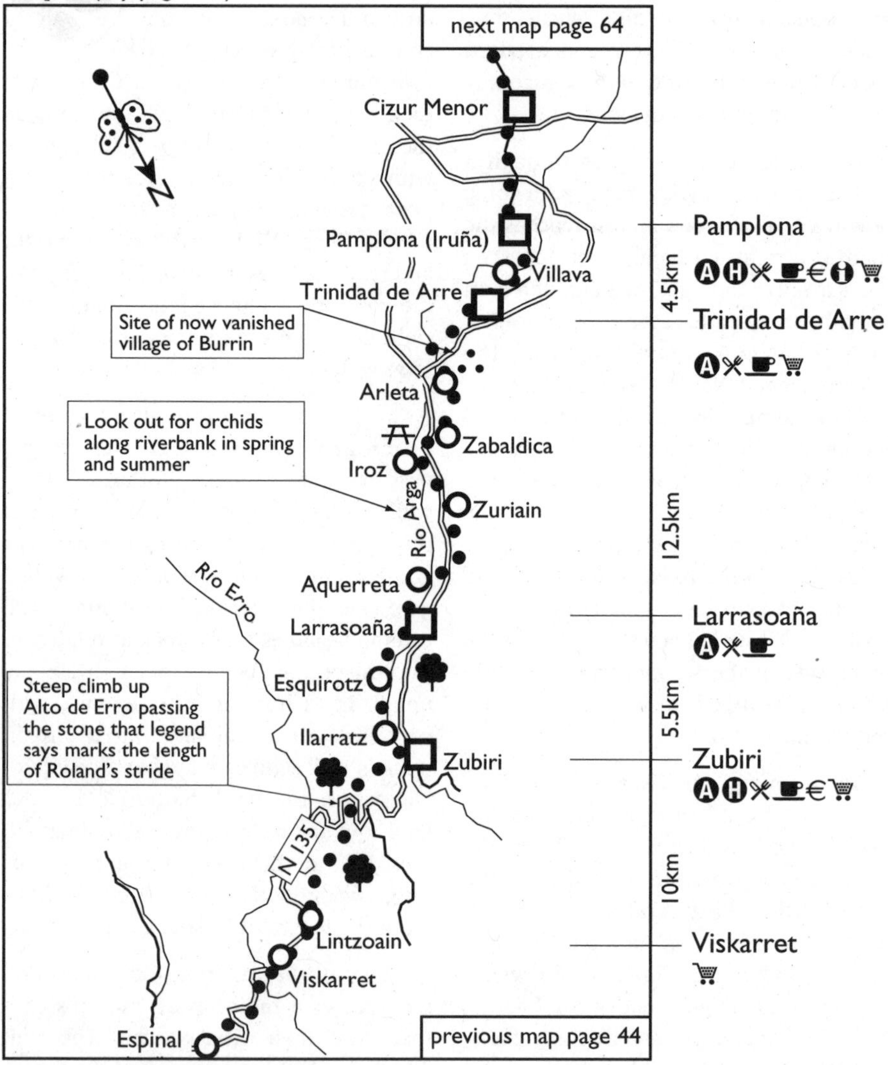

next map page 64
Cizur Menor
Pamplona (Iruña)
Villava
Trinidad de Arre
Site of now vanished village of Burrin
Arleta
Look out for orchids along riverbank in spring and summer
Zabaldica
Iroz
Zuriain
Río Arga
Río Erro
Aquerreta
Larrasoaña
Esquirotz
Steep climb up Alto de Erro passing the stone that legend says marks the length of Roland's stride
Ilarratz
Zubiri
N 135
Lintzoain
Viskarret
Espinal
previous map page 44
Pamplona
4.5km
Trinidad de Arre
12.5km
Larrasoaña
5.5km
Zubiri
10km
Viskarret

Profile Chart 2

Zubiri
Larrasoaña
Trinidad de Arre
Pamplona
900m
400m

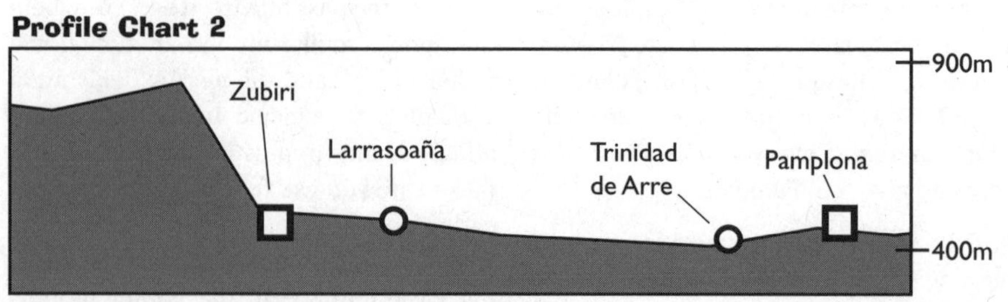

when it feeds closer to the ground. From here onwards, it's downhill to Zubiri, about 4km away along a well-marked track. As Zubiri comes into view, the path becomes steeper: watch your footing on the occasional smooth rock sections.

On reaching the first houses in Zubiri, turn right and cross the bridge to go to the shop and the *albergue*; turn left to continue the camino towards Larrosoaña.

Zubiri Ⓐ Ⓗ ✗ ☕ € 🛒

Even if you choose not to stay in Zubiri, it's a good place for a picnic and a siesta on sunny days. The town's lovely Gothic bridge, the Puente de la Rabia, crosses the Río Arga to the main part of town. It's said that if cattle are driven around the bridge's central pillar three times, they will be cured of rabies.

Accommodation

Albergue (46 beds, no kitchen, open all year)
$$ Hostería de Zubiri (☎ 948 30 43 29)
$$ Hostal Gau Txori (☎ 948 30 40 76)

Climb steeply out of Zubiri, pass between two houses and take the well-signed right-hand fork. Cross a small stream via a concrete bridge, walking on fairly flat ground through farmland. Walk downhill and cross a stream on wobbly stepping stones, then 30m later, join a gravel road, and turn right.

You're now heading towards a huge factory that produces magnesite, a compound used in fertilizers, cement, ceramic tiles and synthetic rubber. After a long stretch of farmland punctuated by quiet, traditional villages that seem to have changed little in centuries, the factory is an ugly, jarring reminder that you're now in the twenty-first century.

After about 400m, turn left at a minor road, passing alongside the factory. As the factory buildings end, turn right off the road on to a gravel track, then follow yellow arrows and a camino marker down some steps. Cross a stream via a bridge, and start walking on crazy paving as the factory ends and fields reappear.

Head uphill towards the village of **Ilarratz**, where there's a fountain and some shade. Turn right opposite the fountain to follow a minor road, passing a dilapidated former church with a satellite dish on top. At a hairpin bend in the road, take the left-hand track signposted **Esquirotz**. You'll reach the hamlet, which has a sporadically working fountain, in about 500m. Walk through Esquirotz and continue on the other side on a grassy stone track. Walk past some modern farm buildings, then follow the track as it widens and then crosses a road. From here, you can see Larrasoaña up ahead on the right.

After a few hundred metres, and just as it seems that you have missed the village, you reach a track and a camino map. Turn left to continue the camino, or turn right for Larrasoaña, entering the village via the Gothic, fourteenth-century Puente de los Bandidos, a camino bottleneck where opportunistic bandits would lie in wait for medieval pilgrims.

Larrasoaña Ⓐ ✗ ☕

Although the layout of Larrasoaña's main street dates from the twelfth century, the

grand houses which line it were mostly built in the fifteenth and sixteenth centuries. Nothing remains of the village's two hospices, but the Clavería de Roncesvalles, the long low building opposite the thirteenth-century Iglesia de San Nicolás de Bari may have been a monastery warehouse. The village's small bar has a nightly pilgrim *menú*, and sells basic provisions. Larrosoaña's mayor runs the **albergue** (53 beds, kitchen, open all year) with a gentle, caring officiousness.

The section between Larrasoaña and Arleta is a lovely one; look out for orchids in spring and early summer along the riverbanks. From the map of the camino on the far side of the Puente de los Bandidos, head uphill along a gravel track towards the village of **Aquerreta**, which you can see perched on a spur above you. You'll soon reach the village, its three-storey houses typical of the region's rural architecture, with the ground floor for animals, the first floor for people, and the shallow top storey reserved for pigeons, kept for food and fertilizer. Once in the village, turn right downhill through a cattle gate, then walk along a narrow gravel path with stone walls and hedgerows on either side.

After a few hundred metres, pass through another gate before the path widens as it meets the main road (N135). Cross straight over the road to the path on the other side marked with a camino sign. The path is now a wide, well-marked gravel track passing through pine forest and descending via some stairs towards the Río Arga. Slowly, the pine forest gives way to farmland as you approach the village of **Zuriain** on the other side of the river, whose medieval Iglesia de San Millán was restored in the sixteenth and seventeenth centuries.

The trail emerges at a modern bridge, which you cross before heading up to the main road. Turn left to walk along the road, taking care as there's not much of a shoulder. In about 500m, turn left down a minor road and re-cross the Río Arga. Cross another modern bridge and leave the main road by taking the lane straight ahead, marked with a camino post.

The road soon becomes a gravel lane, then starts to climb slowly before zig-zagging around some houses. Follow the well-marked, level route as it heads into pine forest, ignoring the tracks that lead down to the fields by the river. The trail narrows before curving to the left and leading into the village of **Iroz**. On entering the village, take the paved path right downhill, reaching a fountain in 50m and the village church a little later on.

Follow the road out of Iroz, crossing the humpback bridge. Immediately after the bridge, ignore the first lane which goes straight down to the river on the left, and instead take the next single track on the left. This stretch of the Río Arga is a popular fishing spot with both locals and sparrowhawks. The path is lined with orchids in spring and summer, although the pastoral scene is spoiled by the huge clearcuts on the hills opposite, created to feed the nearby sawmill. Walk straight through the village of **Zabaldica**, looking out for the Romanesque twelfth-century Iglesia de San Esteban.

The track eventually rejoins the main road. Cross the road, heading towards a picnic site, then head over a small wooden bridge and climb briefly and steeply uphill. The trail is very dramatic as you walk high above the river with the valley spread out before you. Soon, the camino arrives at the tiny hamlet of **Arleta**, where there's a graceful manor house and the lovely Iglesia de Santa Marina.

The path climbs around to the right and leads in a kilometre or so through the now vanished village of **Burrin**, which disappeared in the fourteenth century. Look out for songbirds and birds of prey here. The trail soon heads towards a road and passes underneath it via a grubby tunnel. Once on the other side of the road, the camino changes from a dirt lane to a small paved road and heads downhill. From here, you can turn around and see your route from Larrasoaña along the Río Arga. At the bottom of the hill, cross over the Romanesque bridge to walk into Trinidad de Arre.

Trinidad de Arre

Trinidad de Arre has been a strategic town since Roman times, and the town has a long camino history. The end of the bridge is dramatically marked by the Basilica de la Trinidad de Arre, where there's a monastery, an *albergue*, and the remains of an old hospice. Trinidad de Arre's sixteenth-century bylaws, which required each local to provide the pilgrim hospice with half a pound of bread a year, have long since been repealed, but luckily for hungry pilgrims, the main street is now lined with delicious *panaderías*.

Albergue 34 beds, kitchen, open all year.

Turn left at the end of the bridge and head down Calle Mayor. Trinidad de Arre leads seamlessly into **Villava**, famous as the birthplace of Spain's famous cycling hero, Miguel Induraín. Both villages were swallowed up long ago by suburban Pamplona, and it's a fair way into town through these suburbs. As city approaches go, however, it's surprisingly non-industrial, and there's a pleasant mix of old and new buildings crunched up on either side of the road.

Keep following the pleasant, tree-lined street. Just before the road crosses the river, turn right down Calle la Larrainzar, passing a school on your right. Cross over a main road and walk down a quiet side street, following the camino sign on the first house on your left. As the sidewalk turns into a riverside park, follow the road straight on, from where you'll get your first view of Pamplona and its cathedral, looming above you behind the city's impressive walls. Look out for the Casa de los Conchas, which is covered with scallop shells embedded in concrete.

The street ends at the Río Arga. Turn right here, then turn left to cross the river over the fourteenth-century Puente de Magdalena, decorated with stone statues and a stone cross donated by Santiago de Compostela in the 1960s. Nothing remains of the leper hospital that once stood at this spot, safely and superstitiously outside the city walls.

Pass a fountain on the far side of the bridge, then cross a main road and head towards Pamplona's imposing town walls. Walk over a drawbridge and pass through the first town gate, then head through the inner walls via a second town gate and enter Pamplona's old town.

Regional Map (key page 213)

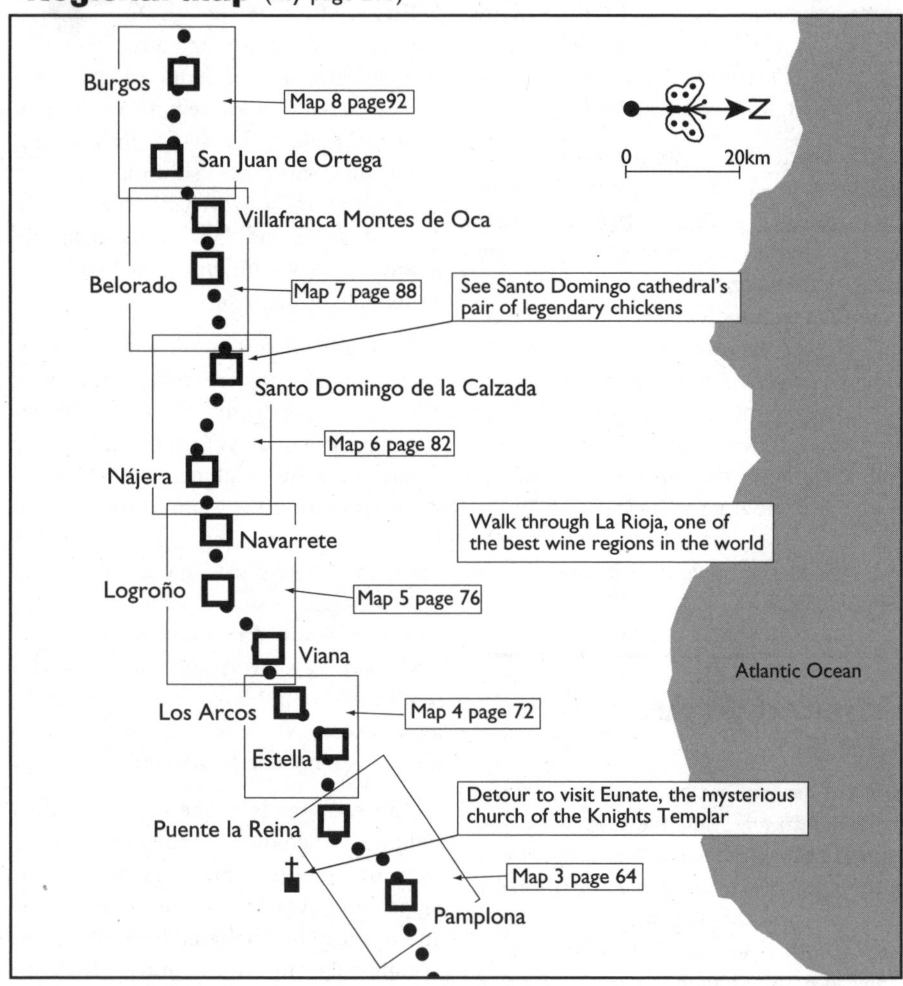

What's the weather like?

	Jan	April	July	Oct
Sun	3hrs	6hrs	10hrs	6hrs
Rainfall	3cm	4cm	2cm	3cm
Maximum Temp	9°C	17°C	29°C	20°C
Minimum Temp	2°C	7°C	15°C	9°C

Average hours of sun, total average rainfall in cm and average temperature in degrees celsius

Navarra & La Rioja

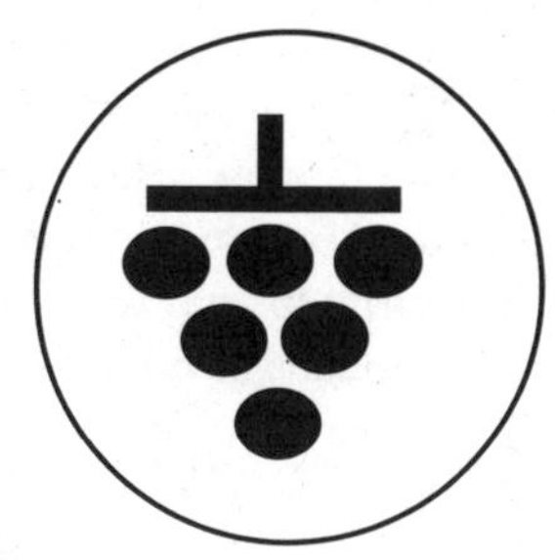

Pamplona to Burgos

The camino heads through Navarra and into La Rioja through lovely towns little-changed since medieval times and stuffed full of glorious Romanesque churches. You'll also eat and drink like royalty. Rioja wine is smooth, gorgeous and dirt cheap, and the region's Lodosa peppers, white asparagus and veal are known throughout the country.

Walking

Geography

The rolling hills of Navarra soon give way to the fertile Ebro valley. The Río Ebro dominates the landscape, draining an area of more than 85,000 square kilometres. The river is coveted as a source of water for irrigation, with 35 major dams along its length, and the average flow is reduced by a staggering 29% from that of a century ago. The situation will worsen when the government fully implements the National Environmental Plan and water is diverted from the Ebro to the thirsty industries and tourist resorts of the Mediterranean coast.

Every inch of Rioja's blood-red soil seems to be covered with vines. The soil needs to be turned frequently, so that any rain that does fall will water the shallow-rooted vines rather than run straight off the dry, hard earth. Concrete drainage channels and aqueducts divert precious water to vines and other crops, and La Rioja's environmental problems are likely to get worse as water-guzzling golf courses become more commonplace.

As pilgrims head towards Burgos they follow a wide natural corridor that separates the high, magnificent Sierra de la Demanda to the south from the smaller Sierra de Cantabria to the north; these peaks are often covered in snow well into April. Just before the flat *meseta* begins at Burgos, the camino climbs up and over the Montes de Oca, a barren range of heather and pine.

Trails

The camino is well-marked and is mainly made up of broad gravel or dirt tracks through vineyards and farmland. There are times when you'll yearn to move away from the N120, which you follow pretty much non-stop from Logroño to Burgos. Highlights include the section of well-preserved Roman road between Cirauqui and Lorca and the red tracks that bring you up

close and personal to Rioja's unfenced vineyards. The approaches into Nájera and Burgos are mostly revolting, passing through industrial wasteland marked by huge mounds of rubbish.

When to go

There's nothing to stop you walking this section year-round. Spring is particularly lovely and it's not too cold, even though the surrounding mountains are still shrouded in snow. In June or July you can catch one of Navarra's lively festivals, while the best time to visit La Rioja is during the autumn grape harvest.

Flora & Fauna

You'll be accompanied by the slow, stately flight of the **white stork** from Puente la Reina to Santo Domingo de la Calzada. In spring, the storks nest on almost every church spire and tower along the route and you'll hear loud clack-clack-clacking as the youngsters demand food. It's less common to see them on the ground, but when you do, they'll be pecking chicken-like at the dirt.

At dawn and dusk, look for the **eagle owl**, a large, buzzard-sized bird with distinctive ear tufts, that's strong enough to take on prey the size of a hare or large bird. The best way to locate the owl is by its hoot, a continuous oooohu-oooohu-oooohu, that can be heard up to four kilometres away on a still night.

Bonelli's eagles are a lot easier to spot and the population along this stretch is resident year-round. The birds often hunt in pairs, one bird hovering above while the partner chases a flock of birds, separating and choosing a weak flier, which the hovering bird then swoops down to catch. Both birds share the benefit of their labour. Bonelli's eagles are still hunted here, as their taste for rough-legged partridges irritates local hunters who want the game bird for themselves.

People & Culture

Even Picaud, the French camino chronicler who wasn't a big fan of Spain, liked this part of the world: "This is a country full of treasures, of gold and silver, fortunate in producing fodder and sturdy horses and with an abundance of bread, wine, meat, fish, milk and honey." It was a qualified approval, though. "It is, however, lacking in trees, and the people are wicked and vicious."

Western Navarra parties hard, preserving celebrations that date back to before the Roman invasion. **Carnaval**, a pre-Lent celebration with pre-Christian roots, has resurfaced in the last few decades after being banned under Franco, partly because of the distinctly un-Catholic activities involved and partly because Franco's police found it impossible to identify the masked participants. The masquerades usually portray the persecution and killing of something external and dangerous, like a wolf, bear or a bandit.

The most famous festival is Pamplona's **San Fermín** in July, ten days of celebration centred around the lively and controversial *encierro*, when red-scarfed men run through the narrow streets pursued by bulls. The day before the *encierro*, colourful processions of *gigantes* (plaster giants), *cabezudos* (big heads), and *kilikis* (Napoleon-like figures who whack children with foam bats) lollop and dance their way through the city.

Dancing is an essential part of all fiestas, and it's said that Navarra has more traditional dances than any other region in Europe. Mixed groups jive to the sounds of the Basque *txistu* (flute), *trikitrixa* (accordion) and *tamboril* (drum). The best-known dance, the *jota*, is a traditional winemakers' dance in honour of Bacchus, the Roman god of wine, while other dances evoke grazing, war or honour the Basque flag. El Baile de la Era is a combination of all the traditional dances of the Basque region. Although a relatively recent invention, it's treated as a traditional dance in many festivals in Navarra, particularly in Estella, where composer-choreographer, bagpiper and local boy Julián Romano lives. It's danced as the finale to Estella's San Fermín, which is slightly tamer than Pamplona's version and generously allows women to run with the bulls.

Some traditional and bizarre Basque sports survive in Navarra, including spade races in Puente la Reina, and hoe hurling further south. You can watch professional games of *pelota* (page 40) in Pamplona and Estella.

Food & Drink

Wine lovers are in for a treat. Rioja is a smooth, gentle, vanilla-scented wine that's available everywhere at about a third of the price you'd pay outside the country. You'll find a great bottle for around €5, and even €2 will get you a fresh and fruity glugger. Wine's been made here since Roman times but (whisper it softly) Rioja was vastly improved when French winemakers fled south to escape the *phylloxera* that wiped out their own vineyards, helping to make Spanish vines resistant to the disease and improving the native grape varieties.

Traditionally, farmers simply planted vines in the ground, hacked the plant back to a mere stump in winter and picked the grapes by hand. You'll still see fields planted like this, but modern farmers string the vines along wire fences a tractor's width apart. This makes the vine easier to care for and allows more grapes to survive to maturity. Each vine takes three years to reach productivity and can be harvested for about 50 years.

The longer Rioja spends maturing in oak barrels and the bottle, the smoother and more vanilla-like it becomes. Crianza spends a year in the barrel and a year in the bottle, Reserva stays in oak for a year followed by three more in the bottle, and Gran Reserva matures for at least two years in barrels and another four years in the bottle.

It might be gorgeous, but a glass of Rioja won't do much to fill that gaping hole in your stomach.

South of Estella, Lodosa is famous for **pimientas del piquillo**, horn-shaped red peppers that are dried outdoors or roasted by hand, and then preserved in oil. They're delicious on their own, well-salted with slivers of garlic, but can also be stuffed with almost anything; lamb, olive and pine nuts are a particularly good combination.

You'll see fields of **white asparagus**

along the camino, particularly between Pamplona and Puente la Reina. As the asparagus grows under black, light-blocking plastic, soil is gradually piled up around the stems. The government has designated the Valle del Ebro in Navarra, around Logroño, as the *denominación* (official region) for *espárrago de Navarra*. Cooked asparagus is most often seen pickled in jars, and is frequently served in restaurants as an anaemic-looking starter, smothered in mayonnaise.

The people of Navarra and Rioja eat a lot of meat. Veal from Navarra is known throughout the country, and Pamplonan *chorizo* is also very good. Fiestas are a great excuse to spit roast pig, kid or lamb, while more economical dishes like *patatas con chorizo* (potato with *chorizo* stew) and *los caparrones* (red bean stew with *chorizo* and scrag ends of meat) help to eke out the meat a little longer.

Tourist Information

Tourist Offices

You'll find helpful tourist offices in Pamplona, Puente la Reina, Estella, Los Arcos, Viana, Logroño, Nájera and Santo Domingo de la Calzada. Contact information for the *turismos* is under individual towns.

Transport

It's easy to get around by bus and there are frequent services between Pamplona and Estella, Estella and Logroño, and Logroño and Burgos, stopping at sizeable places in between.

Money

There are cash machines in Pamplona, Puenta la Reina, Mañeru, Estella, Los Arcos, Viana, Logroño, Navarrete, Nájera, Santo Domingo de la Calzada, Grañón, Belorado, and Villafría.

Accommodation

Albergues are well maintained and tend to be fully equipped with kitchens, ideal for cooking the local *chorizo, pimientas del piquillo* and sampling a glass or two of Rioja. If you fancy a break from the *broncadores* (snorers), splurge at the *parador* in Santo Domingo de la Calzada, a splendidly opulent hotel just across the square from the cathedral.

Shopping

Estella's Thursday market has been in place since the fifteenth century, and other historic markets are resprouting as younger generations revive local traditions. It's mostly easy to pick up supplies and stop for a mid-morning coffee, although there are stretches like the Montes de Oca with no facilites.

Events & Festivals

The people of Nájera take to the streets for the Fiestas de San Juan y San Pedro at the end of June, singing and dancing to catchy, militaristic music said to have originated with soldiers in the Carlist wars. Pamplona's famous San Fermín explodes into action on the July 6, while Estella's marginally calmer version takes place on the first Friday in August. At the end of September, Logroño livens up for the week-long Fiesta de San Mateo, worth visiting for the grape-crushing ceremonies in the Paséo del Espolón.

Rest Days & Detours

Just south of Nájera, a trip into the Sierra de la Demanda to visit the two monasteries of **San Millán de Cogolla**, designated as UNESCO World Heritage Sites, will add about fifteen kilometres or so to your route towards Santo Domingo de la Calzada. Since it's difficult to find somewhere to stay along the way, it may be easier to visit on a day trip from Nájera.

The serene monastery at **Suso**, just above the village, was established in the seventh century and incorporates the hermit caves of San Millán and Santa Oria. Expanded in the tenth century to a pre-Romanesque church, the monastery was rebuilt in the eleventh century in a mix of Mozarabic, Romanesque and Gothic styles. The cloister-like front porch holds the gruesome, headless remains of the seven Infantes de Lara, princes betrayed by their uncle to the Muslims, who decapitated the Infantes and brought their heads to their father for identification.

Inside, the central cave contains San Millán's lovely twelfth-century tomb. Lower down, the village is dominated by **San Millán de Yuso**, a sixteenth-century Renaissance monastery. The statue on the façade might look like Santiago Matamoros, but is in fact San Millán, complete with horse and sword. Plaques in the Salon de los Reyes record the first written use of *Castellano* (Spanish) and Basque in the tenth century.

If it's wine you're after, head to **Haro**, 40km northwest of Logroño, particularly in the last week of June during the fiestas de San Juan, San Felices and San Pedro, when the *bodegas* fill the plaza with free samples and bottles at knock-down prices. On June 29, the wine flows even more freely when villagers drench each other with Rioja's finest in the *batalla del vino* (wine battle).

About 20km south of Logroño is **Clavijo**, the eighth-century scene of Santiago Matamoros' first appearance in battle, resplendent on his white charger. Apart from the ruined castle above the hamlet, there's not much to see here. Further southwest, and a good few thousand years earlier, **dinosaurs** roamed the boggy ground around **Arnedillo**, leaving massive prints when the mud hardened to stone. In the Middle Ages, the footprints were said to be those of giant chickens that lived during the times of the Moors, or the hoof marks of Santiago's horse. If you want to learn more, nearby Enciso has a Centro Paleontológico; once you've finished, you can relax at Arnedillo's spa.

About 10km northwest of Los Arcos, the church in the village of **Sorlada** holds the sacred bones of San Gregório, a bishop who rid the surrounding area of a plague of locusts in the eleventh century. On May 9 each year, the anniversary of his death, church officials pour water over his saintly bones, and villagers collect this blessed water to use on their fields.

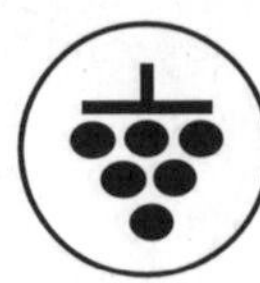

Pamplona

Ⓐ Ⓗ ✂ ☕ € ⓘ 🛒

Pamplona (Iruña) is a compact city, its narrow cobbled streets seemingly squashed together to fit within its commanding walls. There's very little modern building in the centre of the city, although there's a fair bit of pro- and anti-ETA graffiti to remind you of current Basque concerns. Pamplona was founded by Pompey and the city's Cathedral is said to be built on the spot of the Roman capitol. Excavations of the cloister have discovered a market, forum, houses and baths, and an archaeological dig at the Plaza del Castillo is continuing to uncover more of Pamplona's Roman past. Charlemagne razed Pamplona in 778, which goes a long way to explain the rout of his army and the death of Roland at the hands of the understandably annoyed Basques.

Pamplona's Gothic **cathedral** was begun in the late fourteenth century after the earlier Romanesque building collapsed in 1390. The present cathedral's late-eighteenth-century façade stretches up in thick, solid, grey columns more in keeping with a grand mausoleum than a church. The façade is almost universally hated, although it's actually quite impressive in a morose kind of way. Among the cathedral's highlights are the delicate, fifteenth-century alabaster tombs of Carlos III el Noble and his wife Leonor, and the intricate Gothic cloister, with its glorious, appropriately named Puerta Preciosa (precious door). The kings of Navarra, many of whom were crowned in the cathedral, swore their oaths of allegiance to the laws of the land in front of the Romanesque, silver-covered Virgen del Sagrario, which is now in the main altar. The cathedral's Museo Diocesano is worth a visit, particularly for the exquisite twelfth-century French reliquary. On a more prosaic note, you can also add to your *sello* collection in the cathedral by asking the priest to stamp your *credencial*.

The **Museo de Navarra**, just east of the cathedral on Calle Santo Domingo, is housed in a magnificent former hospice and contains a wealth of information about Pamplona's history, including intricate Roman mosaics and Romanesque capitals from the cathedral.

Pamplona loses its head at the annual **San Fermín** festival from July 6 to 14, and if you've seen pictures of the city before you arrive, it's likely to be of the world-famous *encierro*, the running of the bulls that forms part of this festival. Each year, local men and male tourists race through Pamplona's narrow streets pursued by drugged-to-the-eyeballs bulls; it's a dangerous event in which tourists seem to be disproportionately among the gored. If you're a woman, you'll have to wait until the mixed Estella event on the first weekend in August for your slice of insanity. San Fermín, a 700-year tradition, is a week and a half of processions, music, dancing, fireworks, and drinking: apparently, three million litres of alcohol are consumed each year. Procession participants include *gigantes* (giant plaster puppets) and *cabezudos*, big-headed figures who attack onlookers with rubber sticks.

Pamplona's a large city, with some excellent restaurants and plenty of bars, shops and banks. The **turismo** is at Calle Eslava 1, Plaza San Francisco (☎ 948 20 65 40).

Accommodation

Albergues in Pamplona are notoriously impermanent, and extremely busy in summer. It's a good idea to stay either in Trinidad de Arre (5km east), or Cizur Menor (5km west). Recently, there's been an *albergue* in the Iglesia de San Saturnino (20 beds, kitchen, open April to October), and a summer-only *albergue* in the *colegio público*. If you decide to stay in Pamplona, check with the *turismo* on the current state of the *albergues*.

$ Casa Santa Cecilia, Calle Navarrería 17 (☎ 948 22 22 30)

$$ Hostal Otano, Calle San Nicolás 5 (☎ 948 22 50 95)

$$$ Europa, Calle Espoz y Mina 11 (☎ 948 22 18 00)

$$$$ Iruña Palace Los Tres Reyes, Jardines de la Taconera (☎ 948 22 66 00)

There are only sporadically open café-bars between here and Obanos, 20km away, so make sure you have enough food and water before leaving Pamplona.

The camino through Pamplona takes you past the cathedral, then down the narrow Calle Curia to the tiny Plaza Consistorial. Go past the thirteenth-century church of San Saturnino, then walk down Calle Mayor, which changes its name to Avenida Pío XII and arrives at the park that surrounds Pamplona's *ciudadela* (citadel), a star-shaped fort surrounded by lovely gardens. Walk through the park on a broad path, then turn right off this path to walk along Calle Fuente de Hierro.

This street soon leads to the university district. Walk under an overpass, then pass the university and its park-like grounds, where students wander and you can get yet another *sello* for your *credencial*.

On the hills up ahead, you can see a line of modern windmills on the Alto de Perdón, which provide some of the region's electricity; you'll pass these later on the camino.

Head downhill and cross a small wooden bridge next to an older stone bridge. Further along, the wide concrete path ends at a junction and the camino follows a minor road with no shoulder. Walk over a small bridge, but be careful as it's very narrow and too small to accommodate both a car and a pilgrim. After another 100m, cross the road, taking a small road to the right past some buildings.

You're now outside Pamplona and back in farmland. At some railway tracks, the yellow arrows lead you up and over the railway on concrete stairs, although locals just carry straight on over the railway tracks. The climb up to Cizur Menor is along a broad sidewalk, popular with promenaders in the evenings and on weekends. Trees have been planted here, but it will be a few years before they provide much summer shade.

Cizur Menor Ⓐ

The thirteenth-century church of San Miguel, to the right of the main road, is worth a quick look for its Romanesque-Gothic door. It was recently restored, having been used for more than a century as a grain warehouse. More impressive is the church of San Andrés in Cizur Mayor, 2km away up this road.

Accommodation

Cizur Menor's small **albergue** (35 beds, kitchen, open all year), just off the main road to the right, is run by the *grande dame* of the village and located in the grounds of her beautiful home. There's also a second *albergue* nearby (27 beds, kitchen, open June to September).

From Cizur Menor, it's a steep climb with stunning views to the windmill-topped Alto de Perdón. Go straight down the main road, turning right in about 100m at a *frontón*, then walk downhill past a housing estate to your right. In 2002, this was a construction site, so there may well be more houses here by now. In a few hundred metres, turn right at a tarmac road, then keep straight on 200m later, ignoring the right-hand junction. In 100m, turn left just after some electricity pylons down a dirt track through farmland, following yellow arrows.

This stretch of the walk marks a transition between the green, rolling hills of the Pyrenean foothills and the wider, more arid wine-growing regions of Navarra and La Rioja. Cross over a tarmac road and keep on the same track. Look out for linnets, greenfinches and other songbirds here.

The camino continues through farmland, bypassing the small hamlet of Galar. The main track curves left in a kilometre or so towards Galar, but the camino carries straight on along a smaller track; the junction is well-marked. Cross a stream via an old bridge, pass a small reservoir on your left almost immediately afterwards, then keep straight on 100m later at a crossroads, where the yellow arrow is difficult to see. To your right is the dilapidated hamlet of **Guenduláin**, which once housed a pilgrim hospice but is now mostly abandoned.

You're still heading up towards the line of windmills on the Alto de Perdón, and there are great views of Pamplona behind you. Keep straight on at a crossroads of tracks, then at the top of a short climb, you arrive at **Zariquiegui**. Decimated in the fourteenth century by an outbreak of bubonic plague, most of the houses in the village date from a century or two later. The impressive crests on a few of the houses are worth a look, as are their solid carved doors. Zariquiegui's Romanesque church of San Andrés is on your right as you enter the village, and there's a fountain here, too.

A few hundred metres from the last house in the village, the path curves to the left and becomes narrower and steeper as it heads up to the Alto del Perdón. The low, eerie sound that you can hear is from the regimental line of windmills, built to catch the strong winds at the top of the ridge.

Just before the summit, you pass the dry **Fuente Reniega** (fountain of denial). Legend tells of a parched and tired pilgrim who was offered water by the Devil, disguised as a fellow pilgrim, if he renounced his faith. The pilgrim refused, and Santiago appeared to reveal a spring, quenching the pilgrim's thirst from his handy scallop shell. Almost immediately after the fountain, you arrive at the **Alto de Perdón** ridge, home to a pilgrim hospice until the early nineteenth century and now decorated with a cast-iron pilgrim silhouette statue. Cross a minor road at the top of the ridge and follow the stony track on the other side. From here you can see your next destinations: Uterga, Muruzábal and Obanos are clearly visible ahead, and Puente la Reina is just in view to the west of the ridge behind Obanos. At the southeast end of the ridge, look for a trail leading down to a circle of pine trees, which hides the octagonal church of Eunate.

The route downhill is stony and steep, and can be slippery in wet weather. Pass through a gate in about 100m, down a path lined with wild hyacinth and orchids in spring. After a few hundred metres, the track curves left, and then at the end of a steep section, you pass through a gate scrawled with ¡*Ultreia*! (a word of encouragement amongst pilgrims, which roughly translates as "Onward!"). The trail becomes broader, and flattens considerably. The landscape is much greener and more fertile here too, and you can see a collection of beehives to your right.

In a few hundred metres, join a track, then turn left to cross a small bridge 100m later. In spring, there are long, low tunnels of black plastic in many of the surrounding fields; these are used to grow white asparagus, a regional delicacy which requires careful cultivation to halt photosynthesis. After climbing a slight rise, **Uterga** (Ⓐ) comes into view. Uterga's *albergue* has just four beds, no kitchen and is open year round. There are no other facilities in this lovely stone village, apart from a drinks machine. Turn right just after the village square, home to a couple of impressive mansions, to visit the church of La Asunción and the village fountain but otherwise, carry straight on.

At the end of Uterga, as the road curves to the right, go left down a paved road, following the camino sign. This road also curves right, and soon becomes a track. Keep straight on at a crossroads 100m later, then turn right in another few hundred metres to climb up to a small ridge with great views. There are wildflowers and olive groves heavy with huge fruit on either side of the shadeless track, and it's an ideal place to see hovering kites and kestrels.

In a little over a kilometre from Uterga, the track becomes paved as you pass the first houses in **Muruzábal**. The olive grove on your right is a glorious mass of orchids in spring. Pass a football field, then join the main road 20m later at a road sign. Pass a *frontón* and the large, high-walled church of San Esteban, which contains an impressive, colourful sixteenth-century *retablo*. A sign here points towards Eunate, a unique Romanesque church with a tiny *albergue* next door, well worth the 4km round-trip detour.

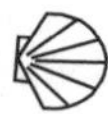

Detour to Eunate

To detour to Eunate, turn left following the sign, walk through Muruzábal's village square, and keep straight on past a fountain. Go downhill on a tarmac road, then take the right-hand narrow tarmac road at a fork in a few hundred metres, which soon becomes a dirt track. Just before a whitewashed building soon afterwards, turn right down a track, and then turn left on reaching the main road 500m later. Walk along this busy road for a few hundred metres, then turn right down a narrow side road that leads to **Eunate** (Ⓐ). This incongrously located church (usually closed Mondays and for December), surrounded on all its eight sides by dusty fields, is one of the most stunning you'll see on the camino. Eunate's origins are unknown. Its shape suggests a link with the Knights Templar, one of the earliest religious military

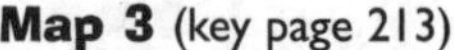

Map 3 (key page 213)

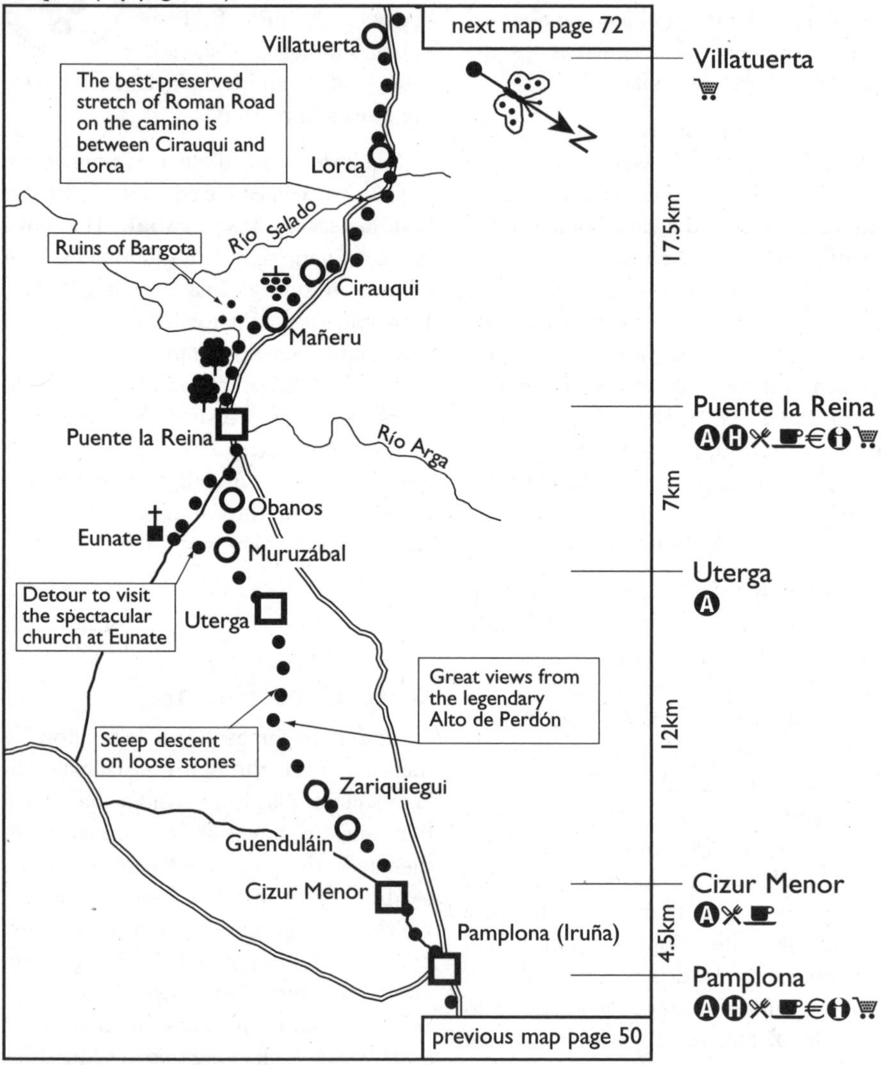

next map page 72
Villatuerta
The best-preserved stretch of Roman Road on the camino is between Cirauqui and Lorca
Lorca
Río Salado
Ruins of Bargota
Cirauqui
Mañeru
Puente la Reina
Río Arga
Obanos
Eunate
Muruzábal
Detour to visit the spectacular church at Eunate
Uterga
Great views from the legendary Alto de Perdón
Steep descent on loose stones
Zariquiegui
Guenduláin
Cizur Menor
Pamplona (Iruña)
previous map page 50
17.5km
7km
12km
4.5km
Villatuerta
Puente la Reina
Uterga
Cizur Menor
Pamplona

Profile Chart 3

Pamplona
Cizur Menor
Alto de Perdón
Puente la Reina
Villatuerta
800m
300m

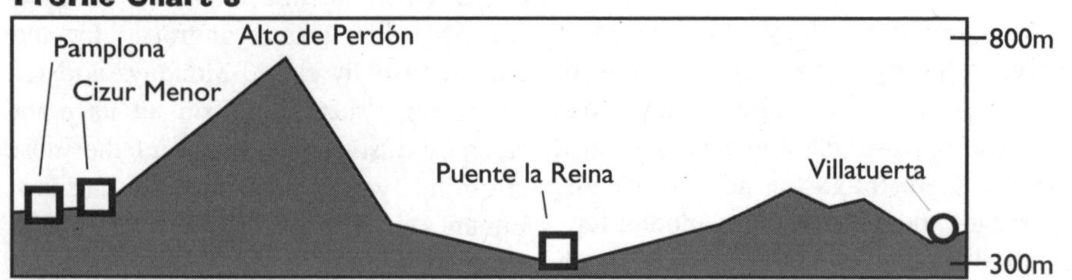

orders, who often built octagonal churches in the style of the Church of the Holy Sepulchre in Jerusalem. It could also be a major funerary chapel on the camino de Santiago, as graves containing scallop shells, presumably those of pilgrims, have been discovered between the church and the outside walls.

Inside, the church is breathtakingly serene. Marble windows let in a gentle light and floor-to-ceiling pillars buttress each octagonal angle, stretching upwards to support an eight-angled roof. Although the simple interior is spartan, you can spend hours outside looking at the gargoyles and faces carved on the church façade and on the arcaded wall that surrounds it. Binoculars will bring monsters, musicians, and stonemasons' marks into focus, and let you puzzle over capitals carved with men whose beards twist around their ears like ram's horns.

Next to the church is a tiny **albergue** (4 beds, no kitchen, open all year), as Eunate lies on the branch of the camino that leads from Sangüesa to Puente la Reina. From Eunate, you can return the way you came, or miss out Obanos by following the *camino aragonés* along the Río Robo into Puente la Reina (page 66).

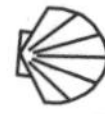

If you decide not to visit Eunate, keep heading straight along the road, then take the right-hand track at a metal cross at the end of Muruzábal. Walking along this grassy, sometimes shady track, you can see Obanos up ahead. In a couple of hundred metres, turn right on meeting a dirt track, then at the top of a short climb, take the right-hand fork and enter Obanos. Once in town, turn right down Calle San Juan, right again down Calle Julian Gayarre, then left soon afterwards to arrive at a roundabout in front of the Iglesia de San Juan Bautista.

Obanos

Obanos is a pretty, restful village, and many of its lovely houses are graced by elegant iron balconies. Yet the place is best-known for its legend of sibling love and murder.

Felicia, the sister of Guillermo, Duke of Aquitaine, was so moved by a pilgrimage to Santiago that she decided to live the life of a hermit in northern Navarra rather than return to the French court. Livid, and unsuccessful in persuading Felicia to return to a life of nobility, Guillermo killed her. Overcome with remorse, Guillermo went to Santiago himself and, on his return, decided to spend the rest of his life mourning his sister. Both siblings were beatified, and Guillermo's silver-covered skull now lies in Obanos' neo-Gothic church, where it is used each *Jueves Santo* (Maundy Thursday, the day before Good Friday) to bless wine that is then ceremonially served to villagers.

Near the church, there's a good shop and an excellent butcher.

In Obanos, take the right-hand road off the roundabout, through the arch. At the *frontón* in 20m, cross the road and walk diagonally left along a concrete path, following the yellow arrow. Soon after passing the Ermita de San Salvador on the left, the road becomes a dirt track. Head downhill, forking left, and you'll soon see Puente la Reina ahead as you walk through fields and vineyards.

Reach a main road in a few hundred metres and cross straight over on to a dirt track to walk parallel to the road. Turn left on reaching a minor road, then turn left again 30m later at the N111, where a modern statue of Santiago Peregrino marks the meeting point of the *camino francés* and the *camino aragonés*. Look out for nesting storks on top of the brick chimney to your left, then in about 300m, turn left down Carretera Pamplona just as you reach Puente la Reina. The *albergue* is the first building on the left (on the corner), opposite the Iglesia del Crucifijo.

Puente la Reina

Ⓐ Ⓗ ✂ ☕ € ⓘ 🛒

Puente la Reina exists, like many other towns you pass through, solely because of the camino. In the eleventh century, there was no single place to cross the Arga, and unscrupulous ferry captains charged high prices to carry pilgrims to the other side. It's not known whether the farsighted queen who commissioned the **bridge** and gave her name to the town was Doña Mayor, wife of Sancho el Fuerte, or her successor, Doña Estefania, wife of Don García de Nájera. Whichever queen was responsible, the result is a gorgeous, six-arched bridge that's a wonderful place to see the sun set.

Puente la Reina lacks the open squares of other towns and villages in Navarra but its pedestrianized main street is a giant meeting place, where children, mothers and grandmothers gather in the early evening. Most of Puente la Reina is found along this Calle Mayor, a canyon-like street of tall buildings whose balconies drip with geraniums: don't walk below them at plant-watering time!

The soothingly simple **Iglesia del Crucifijo**, at the beginning of town, was founded in the twelfth century by the Knights Templar. A second nave was added a couple of hundred years later to display a remarkable, Y-shaped crucifix brought here by a German pilgrim. A restored arch, providing a graceful, intimate entrance into Puente la Reina, joins the church to the monastery that stands opposite on the site of a pilgrim hospice. Further towards the river, on Calle Mayor, the **Iglesia de Santiago** shows Moorish influences in its south portal, which is carved with saints, sins and grotesque, hell-guarding monsters. Inside, the flamboyant Baroque *retablo* shows scenes from the life and martyrdom of Santiago, and the left aisle contains a famous Gothic statue of Santiago Peregrino, known in Basque as Santiago Beltza (black Santiago).

Puente la Reina is fully equipped with banks, pharmacies, and shops. The **turismo** (☎ 948 34 08 45) is beneath the town hall.

Accommodation

There are two **albergues** here: one at the far end of town over the bridge (100 beds, no kitchen, open May to October), and the other just as you enter Puente la Reina, on Carretera Pamplona. This second *albergue* is modern and well-equipped with small dormitories (80 beds, kitchen, open all year). There's a doctor available for pilgrims in the early evening.

$$ Hotel Rural Bidean (☎ 948 34 04 57)

$$$ Hotel Jakue (☎ 948 34 10 17)

$$$ Mesón del Peregrino (☎ 948 34 00 75)

Walk down Calle Mayor, and leave Puente la Reina via the medieval bridge. Turn left at the end of the bridge, then cross the main road 30m later to a minor road on the other side. Pass a convent, then at an iron cross marked with a scallop shell in a couple of hundred metres, turn left down a dirt track.

This broad, flat track follows the river, filled with fish, lined with poppies in season, and home to vivid kingfishers and dragonflies. After about a kilometre, pass to the left of a factory, then turn right 100m later up a narrow path. This is the last you'll see of the Río Arga, a river you've followed and criss-crossed since Zubiri. At the top of a steep stretch, join a broader track and turn right.

In a little while, a small sign at the top of a rise marks the site of the former priory and hospital of **Bargota**, which looked after pilgrims from the early thirteenth century onwards. Take the path off to the left to explore the weed-choked remains of the priory walls and a deep well.

Back on the track, pass some beehives on your right then, shortly after the ruins, a short, sharp climb brings you close to the road near the top of a hill. From here, you can see the hilltop village of Cirauqui in the distance. As you approach Mañeru, join a side road then keep straight on when you reach a sixteenth-century crucifix, following the yellow arrows into the village over a small bridge.

Mañeru is a maze of narrow, angular streets graced with grand houses, stone balconies and imposing stone crests. Turn right to visit the neoclassical Iglesia de San Pedro, otherwise keep straight on to continue the camino, turning left at the Casa Consistorial, then immediately right to leave the village on a narrow tarmac road. This road soon changes to a dirt track, and passes a graveyard on the left. It's a pretty stretch along a flower-lined track through olive groves and vineyards. Up ahead, you can see the pale grey limestone cliffs of the Sierra de Urbasa in the distance that have been visible since the Alto de Perdón.

After a short downhill stretch, keep straight on at a crossroads. The camino is now a narrow path flanked by stone walls — look out for Iberian wall lizards here. Keep straight on at another crossroads a few hundred metres later, and arrive in Cirauqui via a farmyard.

Cirauqui

Built on a distinctive rocky hill, Cirauqui is a beautiful medieval village that's a great place to linger over a *café con leche*. Narrow, cobbled streets lead you uphill to the oldest part of the village, where you'll be struck by the **Iglesia de San Román**, a twelfth-century Romanesque church with impressive capitals and a portal resembling the one at the Iglesia de Santiago in Puente la Reina.

Cirauqui has a couple of bars, a shop, and a produce market at the top of the hill.

The camino heads through Cirauqui's walls via a Gothic arch, and the steep, winding route to the top of the village is clearly marked with yellow arrows. At the top, the camino peculiarly passes through a building, where there's a self-serve *sello* for your *credencial*.

The route out of Cirauqui soon becomes a dirt track, then joins up with a Roman road. The section of Roman road from Cirauqui to Lorca is one of the best preserved of the entire camino. Cross the river over a dilapidated Roman bridge, then walk uphill to cross the main road (watch out for fast cars) and join a dirt track on the other side. You're now walking over rolling, arid hills, and traces of the Roman road disappear and reappear beneath a wide farm track. Walk downhill to a medieval bridge, now being restored.

At the top of a short, sharp climb, keep straight on as the farm track curves to the right. Make sure you take the right-hand of two parallel tracks here, as this is the best remaining example of Roman road. You can clearly see the road's central divide, and the drainage channels which slice across it every 50m or so. A couple of hundred metres after the Roman road appears, keep straight on at a crossroads, and do the same at another crossroads 200m later. Cross a stream over a wooden bridge, keep straight on at a crossroads 100m later, then fork left soon afterwards to skirt an abandoned building.

The track leads down to the main road. Turn right down a side road 20m later, pass under a sky-high aqueduct, then turn left 50m later down a well-marked track. There's a medieval bridge across the **Río Salado** here, noisy with frogs in spring, and the undergrowth alongside the river hides grey Cetti's warblers, although you're more likely to hear a loud, brief burst of song than see the birds. This spot is also the setting for one of Aymeric Picaud's more distressing camino experiences. The twelfth-century guidebook writer warned:

> "At a place called Lorca, to the east, there flows a stream known as the Salt River. Beware of drinking from it or of watering your horse in it, for this river brings death. On its banks, while we were going to St James, we found two Navarrese sitting there sharpening their knives; for they are accustomed to flay pilgrims' horses which die after drinking the water. In answer to our question they lied, saying that the water was good and drinkable. Accordingly we watered our horses in the river, and at once two of them died and were forthwith skinned by the two men."

Once safely across the bridge, pass under the road via a tunnel, turning immediately right down a narrow tarmac road, then turn left 30m later and see Lorca ahead. Keep straight on at a crossroads, turning around to look at the great views behind you, then turn left at a tarmac road almost immediately, entering the town. In **Lorca** (✂☕), there's a pleasant square with a fountain on the left, and a bar/restaurant on the main road, slightly off the camino.

Keep straight on past the square, following line of the town's retro street lamps. Turn left on joining the N111, but instead of following it, turn left down a track then immediately right to walk along a narrow path that winds through fields next to the busy main road.

In a few kilometres, Villatuerta comes into view. Walk under the N111 via a tunnel, then cross a modern bridge and enter the outskirts of town. Turn left after 200m and walk past some modern houses. Turn right in about 200m past a bizarre, mostly concrete park, then turn left at the end of the park to walk past a school. Cross an arched, Romanesque bridge, turning left at the end of it to walk up Calle Rúa Nueva and into **Villatuerta** (✂☕🛒), which has bars, shops, and the restored, twelfth-century Iglesia de la Asuncíon, reached at the top of Calle Rúa Nueva. This is a shady spot for a rest; there's a statue of Santiago Peregrino at the front of the church and drinkable water around the back.

Follow the Camino de Estella, a narrow tarmac road, out of town. In a couple of hundred metres, cross a road and take a track on the other side. The track curves left to the Ermita de San Miguel, of which little remains; keep straight on to continue the camino. The track soon narrows to a path, and then heads down some stone steps to a picnic area. Cross a road to a well-marked path on the other side, looking out for orchids in spring. Curve around a field, over a water channel, then cross a stream over a modern wooden footbridge.

On the other side of the bridge, follow a track to the left of a stone building, now a stable. There are glorious flowers at this spot in spring — the fields near the river are full of irises and poppies. Up ahead, turn right next to a factory on to a tarmac road, and pass the first houses of Estella. Walk past the Iglesia del Santo Sepulcro, keep straight on under a road bridge, and the *albergue* is on your left, just after the Puente de los Peregrinos.

Estella

Estella (Lizarra) is a graceful, compact town, rich in Romanesque monuments, and attractively located on both sides of the Río Ega. While the Basque town of Lizarra had existed for some time on the north side of the river, Estella really got going in the late eleventh century, when Sancho I founded a new town on the opposite bank, at a spot where shooting stars had earlier revealed a statue of the Virgin Mary hidden in a cave. Even Picaud, the hard-to-please twelfth-century author of the *Codex Calixtinus*, thought the city, "fertile in good bread and excellent wine and meat and fish and full of all delights."

Estella is a lively place to visit at the end of May, when the Baile de la Era, a festival of traditional dances, comes to town. It all gets a little crazy on the first weekend in August, when Estella is taken over by bull-running, processions and dances for the annual San Fermín festival, only slightly less over-the-top than the famous version in Pamplona.

Estella's clear architectural highlight is the **Palacio de los Reyes de Navarra**, a rare example of civic Romanesque building, with a capital depicting Roland's fight with the giant Ferragut. The Palacio's museum is home to the works of Gustavo de Maeztú, a famous early twentieth-century Navarrese painter. Estella's rulers didn't skimp on religious buildings, either; the city boasts no fewer than nine churches, which are generally open only for the half hour before Mass.

Just above the Palacio de los Reyes de Navarra, the fortified **Iglesia de San Pedro de la Rúa** looms above Estella. Although damaged in 1572 when Felipe II blew up the nearby castle so that it couldn't be used against him, the remains of the cloister contain masterful Romanesque capitals depicting biblical scenes and monsters. The church's Capilla de San Andrés is said to house St Andrew's shoulder bone, brought here by the Greek Bishop of Patras, who fell ill and died in Estella on his way to Santiago.

Most of Estella's bars, shops and banks lie on the opposite bank of the Río Ega. The **Iglesia de San Miguel** looks grandly

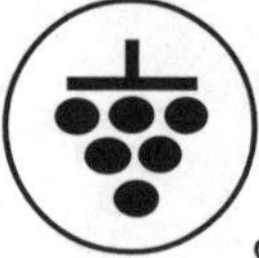

down on such practicalities from its site above the Puente de los Peregrinos. The portal, which dates from the twelfth century, is an incredible example of Romanesque sculpture, and its depiction of the Last Judgment includes fantastic goat-demons and monkey-musicians.

Cross back over the Río Ega via the delicate, single-arched Puente de los Peregrinos, watching your footing on the slippery cobbles, and turn left to visit the **Iglesia de Santo Sepulcro**. The thick façade, added a couple of hundred years after the twelfth-century church was built, is the first sight that greets pilgrims at the entrance to Estella, and it's a suitably dramatic introduction. Bring your binoculars to get a close look at fantastic carvings of the Crucifixion, the Last Supper, and hundreds of quirky beasts, saints, mortals and monsters.

The **turismo** (☎ 948 55 63 01) is in the same building as the Palacio de los Reyes.

Accommodation

Estella's **albergue** has an excellent kitchen, 114 beds, a pretty courtyard and limited bathroom space. It's open all year, although the doors don't open until 3pm.

$ Fonda Izarra, Calle Caldería (☎ 948 55 06 78)

$$ Hostal Cristina, Calle Baja Navarra 1 (☎ 948 55 04 50)

$$ Pensión San Andrés, Calle Mayor 1 (☎ 948 55 41 58)

$$ Hotel Yerri, Avenida Yerri 35 (☎ 948 54 60 34)

Keep straight on along the lovely, antique-shop-lined cobbled road in Estella. Walk across the Plaza San Martín, passing the Palacio de los Reyes on your right. At the end of the cobbled lane, leave the old part of town via a gate with a carved representation of the Crucifixion.

Cross the main road at a roundabout and keep straight on past a garage on the left, following the road sign for Logroño. At a second roundabout, decorated with a large sculpture of a star, cross a minor road and then walk uphill along a dirt road. Note that suburban Estella is encroaching here, and the route may have changed to accommodate new housing. Climb slowly, keeping straight on as you pass behind a large supermarket on the left. The road becomes paved as you enter a modern housing development in the suburb of **Ayegui**.

At the top of a hill, just before a playground, turn left to head towards the Monasterio de Irache. Yellow arrows lead the way, but also point right towards the village of Azqueta, which you'll pass through whichever option you choose. Head downhill, past a cross on the right, then turn right and cross over the main road to veer left down a lane.

You'll soon reach the **Fuente del Vino**, a tap of free wine (and another of water) provided by the Bodegas de Irache to fortify thirsty pilgrims on the way to Santiago. From here, you can wave at technophile friends back home via the webcam (www.irache.com) opposite the fountain. Just uphill from the fountain, the grand, imposing, twelfth-century **Monasterio de Irache** contains a simple Romanesque church and Plateresque cloister.

Pass through the Plaza de Irache, which has some useful benches for those who need to sit down after the joys of the wine fountain. A gravel road lined with vines takes you towards a modern housing development. Just before you reach the houses, turn right to meet up with the main road, then cross over it to walk down a side road behind the **Hotel Irache ($$$, ☎ 948 55 11 50)**. The new houses you pass come as a bit of a jolt after the uniformly quaint villages of the rest of the camino, where even modern houses were sympathetically designed to fit in with the existing local architecture.

Up ahead, perched high on a hill, you can see the Ermita de San Esteban, which was built from the stones of Monjardín castle. Pass through a tunnel underneath the main road, and emerge to walk alongside fields and woodland. The well-marked dirt track heads downhill until you eventually pass through a gate and cross straight over a paved road, where there's a white building and a fountain. Keep following the track downhill before it zigzags to join up with a larger gravel road that takes you up to the village of **Azqueta**. Walk through Azqueta, and just before joining the main road take the lane off to the right through a farm, turning left at a T-junction as the farm ends.

Halfway up a hill, keep straight on up a narrow path as the lane curves sharply to the right. Walk through a gap in a wall and keep to the edge of a field, slowly making your way towards Villamayor de Monjardín, whose church tower you can see poking above the ridge.

At the top of the climb, and just before the village, you reach the **Fuente de Moros**, an interesting Gothic cistern, recently restored and thought to date back to Islamic Spain. Pass the metallic Castillo de Monjardín winery, and enter Villamayor de Monjardín along the well-signposted street.

Villamayor de Monjardín

Ⓐ ☕

Sancho Garcés took the castle above the town from the Moors in the tenth century, although French revisionists claimed that it was captured by **Charlemagne**. In the French version, Charlemagne asked God before the battle which of his soldiers would be killed, and the doomed troops were conveniently marked with an illuminated cross on their backs. Determined to save his men, Charlemagne went into battle without the marked soldiers, leaving them to guard his camp instead. When he returned from the victorious battle, he found them all dead. More recently, the castle was used in the Spanish civil war to control the valley below.

The **Iglesia de San Andrés** is worth a stop for its solidly beautiful Romanesque entrance and seventeenth-century Baroque tower. On the off-chance that it's unlocked, pop inside to see the exquisite silverwork of the Romanesque processional cross.

There's a new, comfortable **albergue** in Villamayor, (12 beds, kitchen, open April to October), with a small café attached and a fountain nearby.

Follow the road out of Villamayor and at the first bend take a trail downhill through vineyards. In a few hundred metres, veer right as the trail meets up with the gravel road again. The rest of the route to Los Arcos slowly winds its way through a wide, shadeless valley along red-dirt tracks. Pass some underground wine cellars on your right, topped by a statue of a Roman goddess. The track heads slightly downhill as it makes its way to the main road. Cross straight over

Map 4 (key page 213)

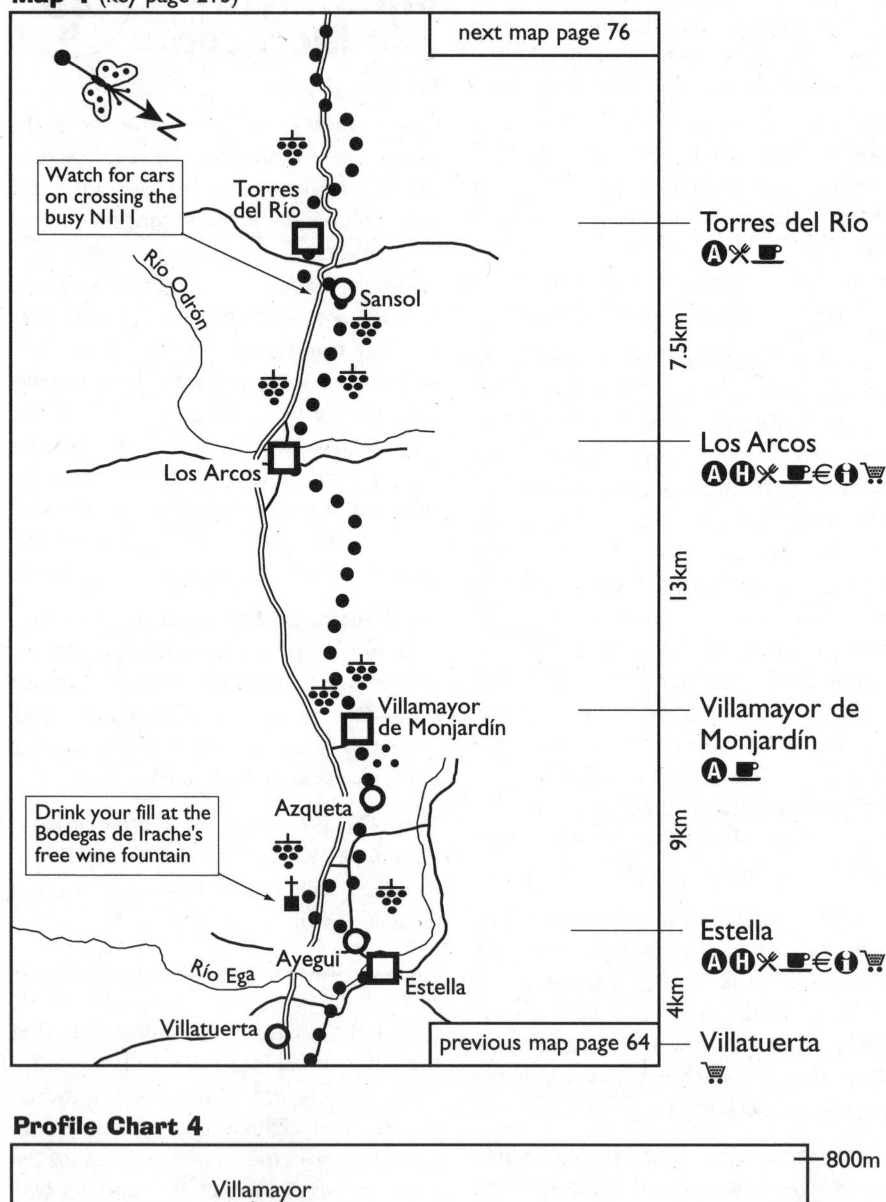

Profile Chart 4

800m
Villamayor
Estella
Torres del Río
Los Arcos
400m

the road next to a fountain, your last water for 10km; fill up, as there's little shade between here and Los Arcos.

For about 5km, follow the gravel road along the valley bottom, passing some ruins and taking a shortcut around the back of a field, before the camino leaves the main track at a left-hand turn and heads downhill to the hills to your left.

Watch out here for vultures circling high above you looking for food, a disturbing sight when you're on your last legs on a hot day. There are good views of the Basilica de San Gregorio a few kilometres away to the right, and of the windmills on the distant hills straight ahead. As you near the small hills, the camino leaves the gravel road and heads left, lined by drought-hardy pine trees, before following a stream along a smaller valley.

The camino rejoins the gravel road and climbs slightly. Take a right-hand fork, then come over a rise and see Los Arcos in front of you. There's a fountain at the edge of town for thirsty pilgrims; take the left-hand fork soon afterwards, and follow the Calle Mayor into Los Arcos.

Los Arcos

Los Arcos is a small town, dominated by the somewhat dour-looking **Iglesia de Santa María de la Asunción**. Inside, the church explodes in a riot of Baroque, and the main, walnut retablo is one of the finest and most ornate on the camino; the Gothic cloister is soothing in comparison. Immediately after Mass, pilgrims can climb to the top of the church's Renaissance bell tower.

Self-catering is a good option in Los Arcos, as there's an excellent butcher and fishmonger (open mornings only). The **turismo** is at Plaza Fueros (☎ 948 64 00 77).

Accommodation

Los Arcos has three **albergues**. The first is a newer place on Calle Mayor as you come into town (28 beds, kitchen, open all year), and there's also a smaller one in the old town (17 beds, no kitchen, open all year). It's worth walking a little further (past the church, through the gate and across the bridge) to the friendly Albergue Isaac Santiago (70 beds, kitchen, open May to October). The *albergue* is well-equipped and comfortable, marred only by rubber sheeting on the beds, and *hospitaleros* can arrange for a massage therapist to visit from Logroño, if pilgrims are willing to pay.

$$ Hostal Ezequiel (☎ 948 64 02 96)
$$ Hotel Mónaco, Plaza del Coso 22 (☎ 948 64 00 00)

In Los Arcos, walk past the church, through the archway and across the Río Odrón. Aymeric Picaud, the twelfth-century pilgrim who seems to have had something against rivers, said, "through the town known as Los Arcos there flows a deadly river." Assuming you make it across in one piece, keep straight on out of town, passing a camino sign and a graveyard on your right. The route to Sansol and Torres del Río is a pleasant one, through farmland and vineyards. If you're lucky, you may see a hovering red kite or kestrel and hear musical bursts of song from a solitary skylark or woodlark.

The road becomes a broad, dirt track and climbs a slight rise, passing over a crossroads next to a power station. Soon, you'll see Sansol ahead, with Viana in the distance behind. After a few kilometres, turn right off the main track, following the yellow arrow painted on a stone hut, then turn left in another kilometre or so along a narrow tarmac road and walk into the village.

Sansol has some lovely Baroque architecture, including grand houses decorated with coats of arms, and the simple Iglesia de San Zoilo, from where there are marvellous views to Torres del Río below. In the village, turn right up Calle Mayor, then left down Calle Real (keep straight on to visit the church), following the yellow arrows and walking steeply downhill to meet a tarmac road. Turn right to follow this road downhill, carefully crossing to the left-hand side to face the speedy oncoming traffic, and again seeing Torres del Río below. Ignore the left-hand road to Lazagurri in 100m, but take the next left almost immediately afterwards down a tarmac road, and then turn left again to walk into Torres del Río, passing a fountain on the right.

Torres del Río Ⓐ✕☕

Torres del Río lies tucked into the steep Río Liñares valley, a strategically dubious location for a town that's survived Muslim and Christian battles. The striking, octagonal **Iglesia del Santo Sepulcro** is thought to be Templar in origin, although its function is obscure. As in Eunate, excavations around the church have revealed a number of tombs, so it may have been a funeral chapel, an explanation that seems more likely than the one that suggests Torres del Río's lantern vault acted as a beacon to guide pilgrims, as the town is all but invisible from the surrounding countryside. The church's design echoes that of the mosques of southern Spain, particularly the altar niche and the cupola's crossed arches. If the church is locked, ask for the key in the village, or hang around outside looking pilgrim-like if your Spanish isn't up to asking questions.

There's an **albergue** at the top of town (32 beds, kitchen, open all year), and opposite the church there's a bizarre, Templar-themed bar that serves food.

Walk up the road around the church, and at the top of town turn left for the *albergue*, or right to continue the camino. Heading out of town, you pass a graveyard on your left as the road becomes a dirt track. In a short while, you start to head downhill; take the left-hand track as you skirt the road. Follow the yellow arrows, staying fairly close to the road, then walk down a few stone steps to cross a tarmac road, then turn left after 20m to walk along a dirt track. Behind you, there are fabulous views of the route from Los Arcos, and of the surrounding mountains. After a couple of hundred metres, cross over a broad dirt track just before a stone building, then walk down a flight of stone steps and head back towards the road.

Turn right here to walk around a big, left-hand bend, then turn right down a well-signposted track 100m later, soon heading left uphill. As you climb, Logroño comes into view up ahead, and the Sierra de la Demanda appear dramatically in the distance. At the top of a ridge, turn left at a tarmac road, then right in 30m to walk down a dusty track. Almost immediately, take the right-hand track at a fork, and zigzag downhill through arid farmland.

At the bottom of the hill, turn left to

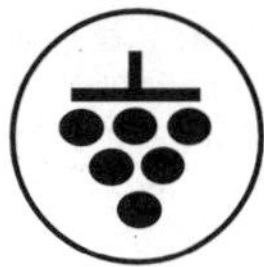

join a wide dirt track through scrubland, then follow the camino signs through a maze of tracks. You can see where water has eroded deep ravines in the arid landscape, but after a while, the land becomes more fertile as fields replace the scrub, and the route is occasionally shaded.

Walk past a couple of farm buildings, then turn left at a track and go left again 200m later at a shady spot under some trees. Keep straight on at a crossroads soon afterwards next to a pile of large rocks. Follow a line of telegraph poles past a house on the right — the site of a Roman villa known as Cornara — then keep straight on at a crossroads soon afterwards. You'll soon join the road again. Turn left here, then turn left again in 100m down a grassy stone track, and then 200m later keep straight on at a crossroads. There are trees planted alongside the camino, too small to provide any shade now, but a wonderful boon for future pilgrims.

The path soon ends, leaving you walking along the side of the N111, with only the occasional shoulder. After about a kilometre, at a "no overtaking" sign, turn left on to a small path that runs parallel to the road. Watch out for kites hovering over the fields and scrubland. Walk downhill, then turn right on meeting a track near a ruined house, and turn left 50m later. In a few hundred metres, turn left to walk down the main road for just 30m, before taking a right-hand track just after the sign for Viana.

Keep straight on as the track becomes a tarmac road, passing an abstract mural of the camino painted in splendidly garish colours on the side of a building. Follow the camino uphill through town, walking up Calle Algorrada through an arch in Viana's town walls, then walk up Rúa de Santa María into the middle of town.

Viana

An attractive town, Viana is circled by high walls and filled with imposing, family-crest-decorated mansions. Like many towns in Navarra, Viana was founded in the thirteenth century by Sancho el Fuerte, but its best-known hero is the infamous Cesare Borgia.

Although Borgia's political machinations largely took place in his native Italy, he found himself imprisoned in Spain at the beginning of the sixteenth century. Escaping from prison and universally unloved in Italy, Borgia headed for Navarra, where he fought for the King of Navarra at the siege of Viana. He died in a chaotic blaze of glory, rushing out of Viana to single-handedly take on the enemy rearguard, while the rest of the town held back, struggling to understand what was happening.

The **Iglesia de Santa María** no longer holds Borgia's grand mausoleum, as it was desecrated by vandals in the seventeenth century and replaced with a simple tomb in front of the church. It's difficult to spot the tomb, mostly because your attention is inevitably drawn to the glorious Renaissance façade, combining biblical themes with Greek legends and peculiar animals. Inside, there's a beautiful Gothic interior and a Baroque *retablo*.

The church takes up one side of the lovely Plaza de los Fueros, a café-lined square with a fountain in the middle. Viana has a **turismo** (☎ 948 44 63 02) and is well-equipped with restaurants and shops.

Accommodation

Albergue 54 beds, kitchen, open all year

Map 5 (key page 213)

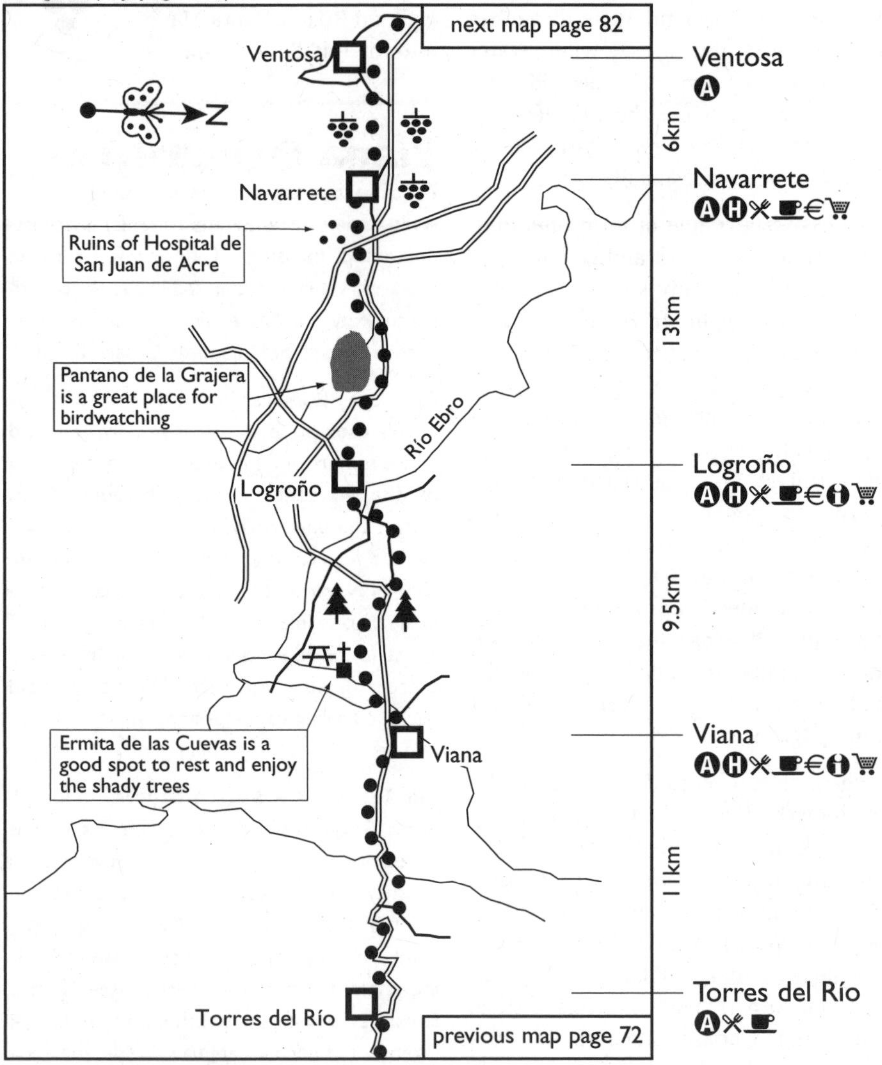

next map page 82

Ventosa

Navarrete

Ruins of Hospital de San Juan de Acre

Pantano de la Grajera is a great place for birdwatching

Río Ebro

Logroño

Ermita de las Cuevas is a good spot to rest and enjoy the shady trees

Viana

Torres del Río

previous map page 72

Ventosa

6km

Navarrete

13km

Logroño

9.5km

Viana

11km

Torres del Río

Profile Chart 5

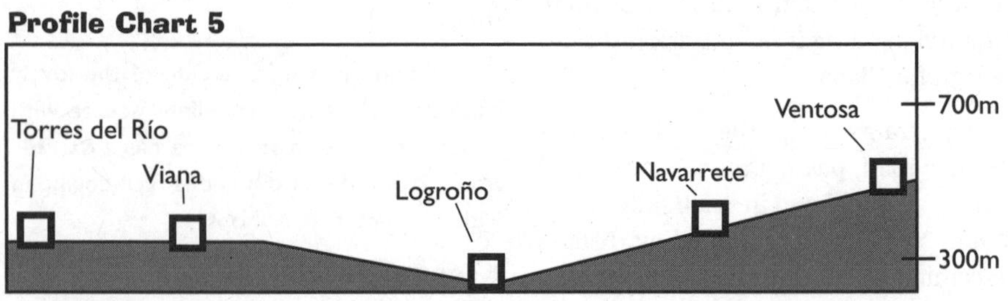

$$ Casa Pitu (☎ 948 64 59 27)
$$$ La Granja (☎ 948 64 50 78)
$$$$ Borgia (☎ 948 64 57 81)

To leave Viana, keep straight on at the Plaza de los Fueros, then pass the ruined Iglesia de San Pedro and leave town under the Portal de San Felices. Turn left down Calle la Rueda, then first right. Keep heading downhill out of town, following the yellow arrows.

For the next couple of kilometres, the camino passes through fields and beside houses, criss-crossing roads. As you pass a school on the left, the road changes to a wide track. Pass a couple of allotments and buildings, then in a couple of hundred metres cross a minor road to keep walking on a wide dirt track. After a few hundred metres, cross a road, watching for fast cars, then turn left at a side road 50m later, and right down another minor road in 100m or so.

A few kilometres after Viana, the camino reaches the **Ermita de las Cuevas**, a former hermitage that's now a shady spot for a picnic. At the end of the picnic area, take the middle of three tracks, then turn right 20m later. A kilometre or so away, the artificial Laguna de las Cañas is an important birdwatching area that's home to breeding pairs of purple herons, night herons and bitterns. The dirt track approaches a small pine wood; turn right here then, on reaching the road 100m later, cross over and walk along a track. Stay low to skirt around to the left of a hillock, all the time walking parallel to the road.

Join the main road at the Papelera del Ebro, and then cross over a wooden bridge to walk past the factory on a red paved road. This paving will be the rather soul-destroying (or at least blister-inducing) surface that you'll follow all the way to Logroño. You've now also crossed unceremoniously into the province of La Rioja, and while you'll be hard-pressed to notice any difference, medieval pilgrims were suddenly confronted with an entirely different culture, people and currency.

Pass an unhelpful abstract map of the camino, and walk through a couple of tunnels daubed with pilgrim graffiti. As you walk uphill, there are bad smells from the KUPSA factory on your right. Keep straight on across a tarmac road parallel to the end of the factory. Skirt around a flat-topped hill, which contains prehistoric, Roman and medieval ruins, and see Logroño up ahead. Walk past a couple of ramshackle houses, where a local woman offers *sellos* and sells expensive cold drinks.

The camino joins the road in another half a kilometre. Turn right here, walking alongside a cemetery, then cross the road at the end of the cemetery. The yellow arrows direct you to an unattractive riverside track, which you can avoid by staying on the road. In a few hundred metres, turn left to cross the Puente de Piedra over the Río Ebro. At the end of the bridge, take the second right at a small roundabout to walk down Rúa Vieja. Logroño's *albergue* is about 100m down this road, on the left.

Logroño Ⓐ Ⓗ ✗ ☕ € ⓘ 🛒

Although Logroño is the biggest town in La Rioja and the centre of its wine industry, most tourists skip the city in favour of the province's grape-growing centres. A city with a no-nonsense, working feel, Logroño's distinct personalities bump up against each other in its large centre. The airy Plaza del Mercado is home to attractive cafés, and dominated by the stork-nest-topped towers of Logroño's cathedral, the **Iglesia de Santa María la Redonda**. High-class clothes shops line pedestrianised streets in the smarter end of the city around the pleasant Paséo del Espolón, while closer to the Río Ebro, the cocooned, older part of the city around the Rúa Vieja is grimier and grittier (the *albergue* is opposite a police station).

The Gothic **Iglesia de Santiago** lies directly on the camino at the end of the Rúa Vieja. The church takes its name seriously and oozes monuments to the saint: the humble Santiago Peregrino and the impressive, war-mongering Santiago Matamaros that guard the entrance only hint at the plethora of Santiago carvings you'll see inside. The present building stands on the site of a ninth-century church built to honour the battle of Clavijo, when Santiago Matamoros' timely intervention helped to defeat the Moors. In front of the church is the sixteenth-century Fuente de los Peregrinos, and on the ground is a large painted mosaic, the Juego de la Oca. This version of a popular, snakes-and-ladders-like board game is full of camino motifs: the board represents the pilgrimage, the squares are the different places and people met along the way, and passing pilgrims are, of course, counters to be moved from square to square.

At the end of September, Logroño livens up for the **Fiesta de San Mateo**, worth visiting for the grape-crushing ceremonies in the Paséo del Espolón.

The **turismo** is in a modern building in the Paséo del Espolón (☎ 941 29 12 60).

Accommodation

Logroño's **albergue** has a bright and spacious first-floor kitchen and a couple of huge, stuffy rooms crammed with 88 bunk beds. It's open all year.

$$ Hostal La Numantina, Calle Sagasta 4 (☎ 941 25 14 11)

$$ Hotel Isasa, Calle Doctores Castroviejo 13 (☎ 941 25 65 99)

$$$ Hostal Marqués de Vallejo, Marqués de Vallejo 8 (☎ 941 24 83 33)

$$$$ Carlton Rioja, Gran Via del Rey Juan Carlos I 5 (☎ 941 24 21 00)

Walk through Logroño along the Rúa Vieja, passing the giant board game in front of the Iglesia de Santiago, then turn right to pass through an arch in the town walls. Bear left here, following the road signs to Burgos at the roundabout. It can feel as if you'll never leave Logroño as you walk along this bustling road lined with banks and shops, and yellow arrows can be difficult to spot. After a few hundred metres, cross the road at Calle del Marques de Nájera and continue walking on the other side.

After a little over a kilometre, turn left on Calle de Prado Vieja, then turn right 200m later to walk along a broad dirt road. Go straight on at a roundabout. This area was a construction zone in 2002, and will most likely be a housing estate by now, so watch out for yellow arrows as the route may have varied. Walk down a dirt track, then under an underpass, and the camino soon becomes a paved track alongside a road. The track then veers away from the road to walk through La Grajera park, popular with joggers and dog walkers, and the paved tracks ends at

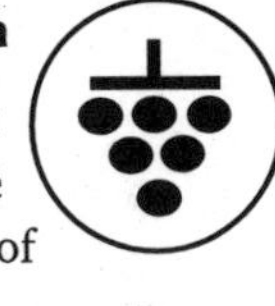

the Pantano de la Grajera. This reservoir is an ideal spot for birdwatching, particularly in the early morning. Look for herons, rails, ducks and grebes in the water, and woodpeckers, flycatchers, larks and goldfinches in the trees nearby.

Turn right at the reservoir to walk along a wide gravel track that curves around the water. Pass a shady picnic area on your right, then a birdwatching hide on your left. As the track moves away from the reservoir, there's a fountain. Turn right at a narrow tarmac road, then left 100m later on to another tarmac road that soon changes to a dirt track as it heads through farmland and grapevines.

Walk uphill for a short stretch, turning around for good views of the reservoir as the path becomes paved and leads high above and parallel to the main road. This is a dull stretch, enlivened by a large metal outline of a bull and the rustic wooden crosses stuck by pilgrims in the wire fence to the right of the track. At the end of the tarmac stretch, turn left down a side road, seeing Navarrete up ahead, then take the right-hand track off this road in a couple of hundred metres. The track winds through vineyards, and the fields of vines stretch towards the horizon in all directions. In a kilometre or so, cross the motorway via a pedestrian bridge and arrive almost immediately at the ruined **Hospital de San Juan de Acre**.

Founded in the late twelfth century, the church and hospice of Hospital de San Juan de Acre served pilgrims for four centuries. The site has been recently excavated, and although some of the restoration work is clumsy, there's a clear picture of how the hospice was set up. Pass the Don Jacobo winery, walk along a farm track, and then up some stone steps to cross a busy road. Follow the street on the opposite side of the road uphill into the centre of Navarrete.

Navarrete Ⓐ Ⓗ ✕ ☕ € 🛒

Navarrete is a pretty, fortified hillside town where every street corner seems to be daubed with a yellow arrow. The hill itself is pocketed with small caves, used to store Navarrete's plentiful harvests of mushrooms and wine in cool, dark conditions.

The **Iglesia de la Asunción**, near the top of town, is dominated by a Baroque *retablo* of dazzling extravagance, possibly the finest in the country. It may have dazzled the church's other architects and builders too: the church tower was begun in the fifteenth century and not completed until 300 years later.

There's a grocery store opposite the *albergue*, and a fabulous *panadería* close by on Travesa Mayor Alta.

Accommodation

Navarrete's **albergue** is at the beginning of town, its entrance hidden in the pretty arcades of the Calle Mayor (40 beds, kitchen, open all year).

$ Hostal La Carioca (☎ 941 44 00 06).

In Navarrete, turn right up Calle La Cruz to reach the Iglesia de la Asunción. Turn left at the church down Calle Mayor Alta, then keep straight on past a couple of fountains. Make sure you fill up with water, as it's a long, fountain-less stretch between here and Nájera.

Leave town along the main road, reaching the town cemetery about 300m.

Although the cemetery was built fairly recently, its stately façade is thirteenth-century Romanesque, brought here from the Hospital de San Juan de Acre on the other side of Navarrete. The marvellous capitals depict great battles, such as Roland's defeat of the giant Ferragut and St George killing the dragon, but also portray gentle, mundane scenes of camino life such as pilgrims eating a meal together and washing each other's hair.

The camino now follows a wide gravel track that runs parallel to the road. Take a look at the huge pots made in the ceramic factory across the road: Navarrete's potters are renowned for their great use of the region's distinctive red clay soil.

The camino between here and Nájera winds through vineyards and the occasional olive grove, veering right and left to walk around fields lined with cornflowers and poppies in spring, but always staying close to the road. It's a fairly dull walk, made worse in hot weather by a complete lack of shade, although it's interesting to see the different vine-growing techniques used by local farmers.

After about a kilometre, curve to the right and cross the road towards a lurid peach-coloured winery. Follow the yellow arrows as the route alternates between narrow paved road and farm track, always shadowing the main road. About 5km after the winery, signs and yellow arrows point to the **Albergue de San Saturnín** (24 beds, kitchen, open all year) in **Ventosa** (Ⓐ), about 500m off the main route. Turn left at the minor road to visit the *albergue*, or keep straight on to continue the camino. Can't make up your mind? Don't worry, there's another turning to Ventosa a kilometre further on.

Soon after this junction, the camino leaves the roadside for a while, heading uphill on a grass farm track. Pass a collection of shepherd stones left by pilgrims, then keep heading uphill as the path narrows towards the **Alto de San Antón**. From the top of the hill there are views of Nájera, its urban sprawl splayed out to meet nearby villages, and to the right, the ruins of the monastery and pilgrim hospice of San Antón.

At the bottom of the hill, the track meets the main road once more. Turn left here, then turn right off the road just 50m later, walk down some concrete steps and turn left to follow a track. Walk along this level, red-dirt track through vineyards. A few kilometres after crossing the main road, the track leads to the right of a flat hillock topped with radio masts, known as the **Poyo de Roldán**.

According to one legend, the region around Nájera was the home of Ferragut, a giant who was descended from Goliath. Charlemagne sent many brave knights to defeat Ferragut, but all were unsuccessful. It's not clear whether Roland was sent by Charlemagne to fight the giant or if the knight just happened to be passing through but, in any case, Roland reputedly hurled a huge rock at Ferragut, knocking him dead. It's said that the Poyo de Roldán itself is the rock that Roland threw.

The romance surrounding the legend is quickly stifled by the route through semi-industrial Nájera, possibly the most horrible town approach of the whole camino. In the distance, you can just about make out Nájera's factories through the polluted haze as you pass piles of rubbish on your left. Head downhill towards a cement factory and turn right at a minor road to curve around the factory buildings. Turn left down a track 200m later, then turn left soon afterwards to go down some concrete steps and cross a rickety wooden bridge.

Pass pilgrim songs and poems scrawled in Spanish and German on the factory wall on the left of the camino, and a few lonely looking picnic tables to your right. To relieve the industrial monotony, look left towards the Sierra de la Demanda, a dramatic line of mountains rising to more than 2000m. Up ahead, the vegetation on the slopes of the conical, cross-topped Pico de Nájera has been trimmed to form a dove of peace.

Take the bridge over a small canal, then walk over a road and soon reach the outskirts of Nájera. Turn right at a main road a few hundred metres later, following the yellow arrows and the signs to Centro Urbano. The tall, ugly buildings of modern Nájera soon give way to the grimier yet far more attractive old town. The sidewalks here are so narrow that you may have to leap into traffic if you meet an oncoming pedestrian.

Turn right to cross a bridge over the Río Najerilla, which is lined with manicured grass verges and picnic benches. Turn left at the end of the bridge down the pedestrianized Calle Mayor, ignoring the yellow arrows that direct cyclists the long way round, then turn right down Calle Garran to reach the Monasterio de Santa María and the *albergue*.

Nájera

Nájera's attractive old town sits squashed between the Río Najerilla and the cliffs behind it, its largely pedestrianised streets home to traditional butchers, bakeries and *pastelarías*. The town's heyday came in the tenth and eleventh centuries, when the Navarrese court moved here en masse after its capital, Pamplona, was destroyed and Sancho III diverted the camino through the new capital.

The old town seems to grow organically from the pink cliffs that rise up behind it, living up to its Arabic name, "the place between the rocks." The **Monasterio de Santa María de Real** is literally built into the cliffs, and its lovely Gothic buildings surround a simple, natural cave where the church's history began. In 1004, García III was hunting partridge along the banks of the Río Najerilla. He sent his hawk after one bird, and followed the hawk as it chased the partridge into the cave. Inside the cave, he was startled to see a beautiful statue of the Virgin Mary, with a vase of lilies, a burning lamp, and a bell at her feet. Close by, the hawk and the partridge were sitting together, at peace.

García saw the miracle as a blessing for the *reconquista*, and spent part of the treasure he captured from the Moors on building a chapel in honour of Santa María. The statue now occupies pride of place in the church's Baroque *retablo*; an early replica and a vase of fresh lilies grace the simple cave. Missing from the *retablo* is the statue's original crown, which was stolen in the fourteenth century and its jewels divvied up: Pedro the Cruel gave Edward the Black Prince a particularly fine stone, and the **Black Prince Ruby** now gleams from the front of the English Coronation Crown.

Flanking the entrance to the cave is the **Panteón Real**, where a sombre line of Renaissance tombs hold the remains of a Who's Who of Navarra royalty from the tenth to twelfth centuries, including the monastery's founder, García III. To the left of

Map 6 (key page 213)

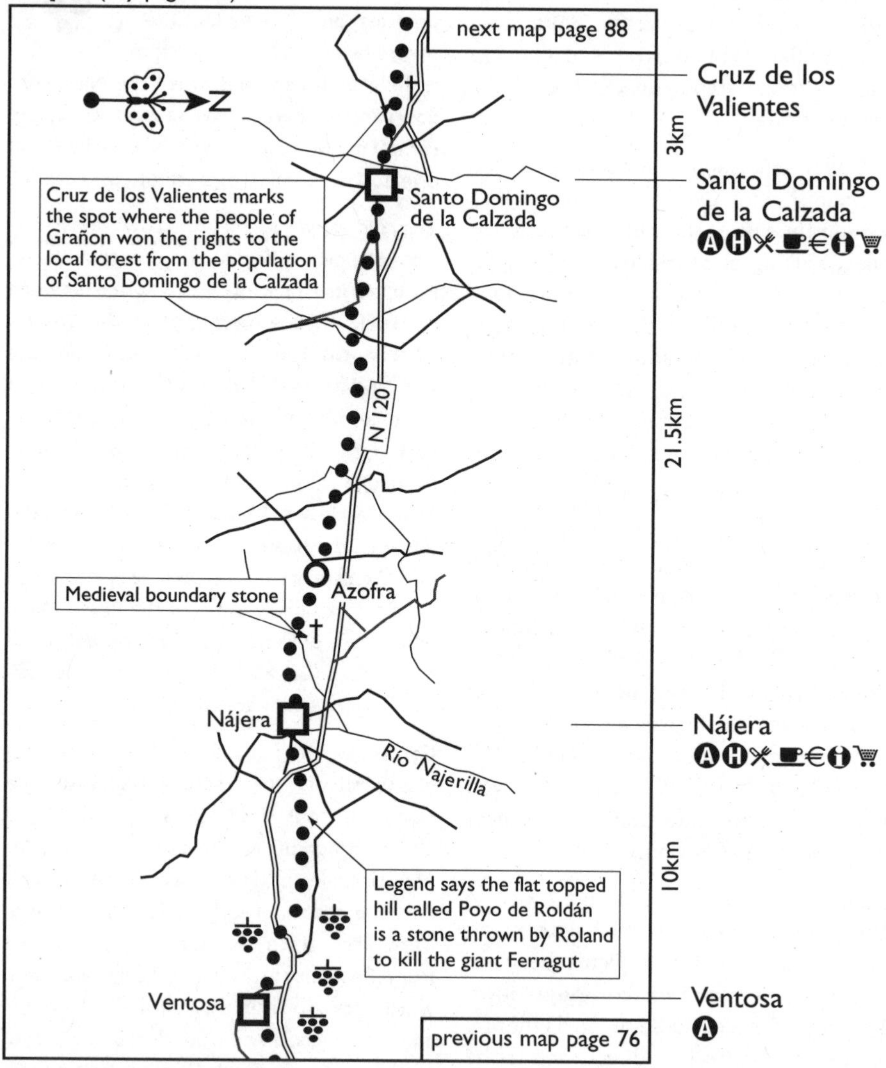

next map page 88
Z
Cruz de los Valientes
3km
Cruz de los Valientes marks the spot where the people of Grañon won the rights to the local forest from the population of Santo Domingo de la Calzada
Santo Domingo de la Calzada
Santo Domingo de la Calzada
N 120
21.5km
Azofra
Medieval boundary stone
Nájera
Nájera
Río Najerilla
10km
Legend says the flat topped hill called Poyo de Roldán is a stone thrown by Roland to kill the giant Ferragut
Ventosa
Ventosa
previous map page 76

Profile Chart 6

Nájera
Santo Domingo de la Calzada
700m
400m

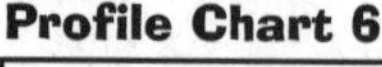

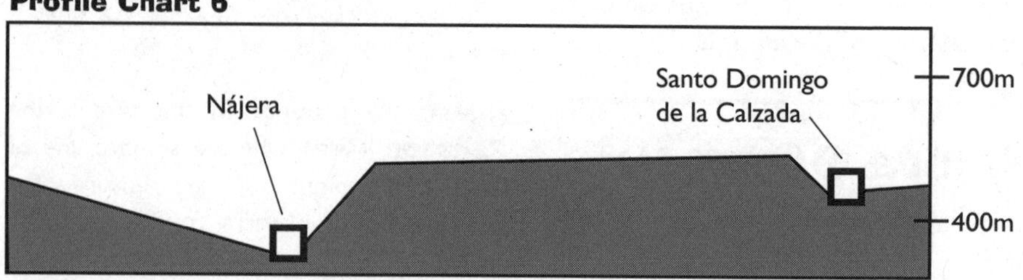

the cave, set apart from the rest, is the glorious Romanesque tomb of Sancho III's young wife, Doña Blanca, carved with biblical scenes and images of the dying queen and her grieving family. Upstairs, the graceful wooden choir-stalls date from the 1490s. The intricate detail of the Gothic carving can be overwhelming, and every surface is covered with monsters, fantastical animals or strange geometric shapes. The sponsor and director of the work were apparently proud of what they had accomplished: both Andrés Amutio and Pablo Martínez de Uruñuela, Nájera's first abbot, are buried beneath lower row seats. Outside the church, reached through a carved walnut Plateresque door, is the peaceful Claustro de los Caballeros, where yet more tombs lie amongst delicate Gothic archways.

The people of Nájera take to the streets for the Fiestas de San Juan y San Pedro at the end of June, singing and dancing to catchy, regimental music said to have originated with soldiers in the Carlist wars.

Turismo Calle Garran 8 (☎ 941 34 12 30)

Accommodation

The **albergue** (60 beds, open all year) is in a restored part of the monastery, with a good kitchen, long, communal dining tables and best of all, nightly visits from a local "foot doctor" who patiently lances blisters while surrounded by fascinated, if slightly disgusted, pilgrims.

$$ Hotel Hispano II, Calles Duques de Nájera 2 (☎ 941 36 29 57)

$$ Hostal Hispano, La Cepa 2 (☎ 941 36 36 15)

$$ Pensión El Moro, Calle Mártires 21 (☎ 941 36 00 52)

$$$ Hotel San Fernando, Paseo San Julián 1 (☎ 941 36 37 00)

The route from Nájera continues along the dirt farm tracks and through the vineyards and vivid red soil so characteristic of the camino in La Rioja.

Walk past the Monasterio de Santa María de Real and turn right uphill past some modern houses. At a bend in the road after a couple of hundred metres, turn right at a large boulder up a dirt track through pine trees. As you come to the top of a rise, the trees end and you can clearly see the route ahead. Pass a farm on the right, walking through scrubland, then turn right about 200m later at a second farm down a paved road, as the landscape becomes more fertile and vines reappear.

Eventually, you meet up with a busier paved road that joins from the right, and soon see the village of Azofra poking up from behind a small mound. As you approach the village, look out for intricately engineered, gravity-powered water channels, which pass under the road and around fields and vineyards. Since the region is dry and grapevine roots are very shallow, getting water to the plants in this way is an essential part of local farming.

Once you get to **Azofra** (Ⓐ✕☕🛒), take the right-hand fork to walk down Calle Mayor. In Azofra, look out for the Iglesia de Nuestra Señora de los Angeles, which includes a carving of Santiago Peregrino; the village also has an **albergue** (16 beds, kitchen, open all year).

At the far side of the village, there's a modern shrine to the Virgen de Valvanera in a small park, next to the Fuente de los Romeros, a pilgrims' fountain. Turn right at the road here, then left 50m later to walk up a gravel track past small farms.

On the right is a stone pillar, a weathered medieval cross that marked the boundary between the villages of Azofra and Alesanco. Keep straight on at a crossroads 100m later, then zigzag down to the main road and turn left. Even though you're next to the main road, the walking is made pleasant by a small stream that attracts lots of birds.

At a minor road about 1km later, keep straight on. The camino moves away from the main road, and you can see your route winding through fields and climbing up the ridge ahead of you. The track gets steeper here, but the views from the top of the ridge make the climb worthwhile. Sadly, these views may be reserved for golfers in the near future, as this plateau is the future home of the Rioja Alta Golf Club. It's not clear what effect a golf course will have on the local economy and environment nor on the future direction of the camino, but an awful lot of water will be needed to transform the barren scrubland into verdant golf greens.

The camino marches straight across the plateau, bypassing **Cirueña** to the left, and **Cirińuela** to the right. Both villages are tiny, and seem on their last legs: Cirueña's only bar closed a few years back from lack of business. Turn right at a minor road, then take the dirt track on the left after a bend in the road. In the distance, you'll see the dramatic peaks of the Sierra de la Demanda, and the area is a great place to spot grey wagtails, stonechats and other songbirds.

Ignore minor junctions, walk down and then up a large bowl, and emerge at the top of a hill to your first views of Santo Domingo de la Calzada in the valley below. Look out for kestrels overhead, helpfully hoovering up crop-destroying locusts and grasshoppers for the local farmers. After a few more kilometres, pass some factories on your right and meet the road into Santo Domingo. Keep straight on at a roundabout with a stone cross, then bear right at a fork just afterwards. The outskirts of town are a bit drab and run down, but you soon enter the attractive, compact old town, passing a modern statute of a pilgrim. Walk down Calle Mayor, where you'll pass the *albergue* and the cathedral.

Santo Domingo de la Calzada ⒶⒽ✗☕€ⓘ🛒

Santo Domingo de la Calzada is a pretty, bustling town, largely established by the tireless work of its founder and namesake, and given its place in camino legend and on the tourist trail by a couple of chickens.

Santo Domingo was a poor shepherd from nearby Viloria who wanted to be a monk, but did so badly at his studies that he was rejected by the nearby monasteries. Still, Domingo decided to pursue the religious life, becoming a hermit in the woods around the Río Oja, and for the rest of his life he helped pilgrims by building bridges and improving the camino road, often helped by his disciple, San Juan de Ortega. Domingo used a heavy sickle to cut a pilgrim road through the forests between Nájera and Redecilla del Camino, and legend has it that when he stopped to pray, angels miraculously continued to cut a path through the trees.

The town has some grand old sixteenth-century buildings and tranquil squares, but its undoubted highlight is the **cathedral**. Little remains of Santo Domingo's original church as it was largely rebuilt in Gothic style a century or so after the saint died.

Most visitors to the cathedral head straight for the **live cock and hen** housed in a Gothic cage on the east side. The legend behind these birds is told in various guises throughout Europe, and even the Santo Domingo miracle has many versions. In the fourteenth century, a young German pilgrim travelling with his parents spurned the advances of a maid. Furious, the jilted maid planted a silver goblet in the youth's bag, and the youth was caught and hanged for the theft. His distraught parents continued their pilgrimage to Santiago, and on their return were shocked to discover that their son, still dangling from the gallows, was alive. The parents rushed to the *corregidor* (the village's chief magistrate) to tell him of the miracle, but he scornfully replied that their son was as alive as the pair of roast chickens he was about to tuck into for his dinner. The cock and hen miraculously jumped from the plate and began to crow and the German pilgrim was released. The live chickens are replaced each month, and any pilgrim who hears them crow will have luck on the journey to Santiago.

Below the chickens, in the crypt, is the tomb of Santo Domingo, a simple Romanesque statue covered by an ornate Gothic temple. The Romanesque pillars that separate the Gothic ambulatory from the main altar are beautifully carved with biblical scenes, including the Wise and Foolish Virgins, the former smugly holding upright lamps, and the latter holding their lamps upside down and hanging their heads in shame. The main altar itself is dominated by the ornate *retablo*, carved in alabaster and walnut by Damíen Forment in the early sixteenth century, and painted in gaudy, gorgeous, Renaissance style by Andrés de Melgar.

If your knees are up to it, it's well worth climbing the stone steps up to the roof, from where you get a great view of the town and the cathedral's 70m-high **bell tower**. The Baroque tower, completely detached from the rest of cathedral, was built after lightning destroyed the first tower and the second was torn down to prevent its imminent collapse.

Santo Domingo is both a working town and a big tourist destination, so you'll find modern, air-conditioned bars serving delicate *tapas* alongside no-nonsense bars with no seats and a day's layer of peanuts and sugar sachets covering the floor.

Next to the cathedral, the town's opulent *parador* is housed in a converted pilgrim hospice originally built by Santo Domingo. Before he built the hospice, Santo Domingo fed passing pilgrims at a long table next to the river, known as the *mesa del santo*.

Santo Domingo has a couple of small supermarkets, some banks and a smattering of restaurants. The **turismo** is at Calle Mayor 72 (☎ 941 34 12 30).

Accommodation

There are two **albergues** in town. The first is in the Casa de la Cofradía del Santo, a beautiful old building often visited by tourists, with single beds rather than bunks (70 beds, kitchen, open all year). The other is the Albergue del Abadía Cisterciense Nuestra Sra de la Anunciación (32 beds, kitchen, open all year).

$ Hostal del Río (☎ 941 34 00 85)
$$ Pensión Miguel (☎ 941 34 32 52)
$$$ Hospederia Cisterciense (☎ 941 34 07 00)
$$$$ El Parador (☎ 941 34 03 00)

In Santo Domingo, walk past the cathedral down Calle Mayor. There aren't many

yellow arrows in town, so keep a look out for subtle carved stone scallop shells in the middle of the street. Keep straight on after crossing a tarmac road to leave the old town, then turn right 100m later to cross the Río Oja over Santo Domingo's original bridge, now mostly hidden by concrete additions.

Turn right straight after the bridge down a track, then turn immediately left to walk parallel to the road, passing storks-nest-topped brick chimneys to the left. After 200m, cross the road and take the track to the right, then turn left at a T-junction with another track a few hundred metres later.

The countryside here is mostly flat, the surrounding fields irrigated by concrete water channels and La Rioja's ubiquitous vineyards being gradually replaced by more diverse crops. Cross a road, then after half a kilometre or so, turn right then immediately left; the track soon changes to tarmac. At the top of a slight ridge, the tarmac changes to gravel and you can see Grañon up ahead.

To the left of the road is the **Cruz de los Valientes**, which marks the spot where two men fought over some woodland on behalf of the towns of Santo Domingo and Grañon, believing that God would protect whoever was in the right. Martín García of Grañon won the fight, and an extra *Padre Nuestro* (Our Father) was recited at Mass there until the 1950s.

Shortly after the track changes to tarmac, you have a choice of routes at a T-junction. If you're in a rush, turn right to walk along the road, but it's much more pleasant to turn left here and continue walking through rolling farmland. Turn right down a track, passing some stone benches on your left and turning round for good views of Santo Domingo and the surrounding mountains. The conical hill to your right was an important strategic location, and Celtiberian burials have been discovered there.

At a crossroads just before Grañon, a camino concrete pillar directs you right towards the road. Ignore it, and keep straight on instead — you'll soon meet the yellow arrows again. Pass a graveyard on your left, then just past a couple of buildings follow the signs to the right into Grañon, walking downhill to the church on a paved road. You can detour to avoid Grañon, but it's an attractive old village, well worth a visit.

Grañon Ⓐ✕☕€🛒

At one time, Grañon boasted two monasteries and a medieval pilgrims' hospice, and in the Middle Ages, it was a walled town with an important castle. Nowadays, its only monument is the **Iglesia de San Juan Bautista**, built over a former monastery and with a gorgeous sixteenth-century Baroque *retablo*.

The old church bell tower houses the town's **albergue**, and its communal meals and beautiful surroundings make it a wonderfully relaxing place to stay (16 beds, kitchen, open all year). There are a couple of shops and cafés here, too.

To leave Grañon, curve around the church, then pass a fountain and walk up the main street. Turn right near the top of the street, then turn left down a track almost immediately. Turn right a couple

of hundred metres later, following a metal arrow, then turn left at the second of two crossroads 300m later, where another metal arrow shows the way.

At the top of a rise, a stone map marks the border of La Rioja and Castilla y Léon. Walk along a wide dirt track, from where there are good views of Grañon behind, Redecilla del Camino in front, and occasional glimpses of the Sierra de la Demanda to the left. On the outskirts of Redecilla, turn right and pass another stone map, then cross the main road and turn left at a fountain and a stone cross to walk down the main street, the Camino de Santiago.

Redecilla del Camino Ⓐ

Redecilla is yet another one-street village that grew up with the camino in the eleventh century. Its Iglesia de Nuestra Señora de la Calle contains a massive Romanesque baptismal font, the most impressive of the whole camino. A serpent circles the font's base, while the solid bowl is decorated with a city of tall, multi-storeyed buildings, probably a representation of celestial Jerusalem.

Redecilla's **albergue** (50 beds, kitchen, open all year), which stands on the site of the Hospital de San Lázaro, the town's old pilgrim hospice, is a great place to pick up leaflets and gather information about the camino in Castilla y Léon. There's also a bar here which does a great breakfast.

To leave Redecilla, walk down the Camino de Santiago past the church, then cross back over the main road in 100m as the village ends to walk along a track. Cross a stream via concrete stepping stones and you'll see **Castildelgado** (Ⓗ) ahead, which you reach in a couple of kilometres. Although the village contained a monastery and hospice at one time, there's little to detain you nowadays apart from a bar, a *panadería*, and the modern **Hostal El Chocolatero** (**$$**, ☎ 947 58 80 63).

Walk through Castildelgado on Calle Mayor, passing a fountain on the right and the Iglesia de San Pedro on the left. At the end of the village, the camino snakes down to join a track at the side of the main road. Turn left after a few hundred metres to go up the tarmac road towards **Viloria de Rioja**, the birthplace of Santo Domingo. Pass a dilapidated church on the left, which still contains the Romanesque font in which Domingo was baptised, although the house where he was born has recently been demolished. The whole village is less picturesque than others in the region, but it has a certain charm as well as fantastic views. All in all, a fairly auspicious start to a saint's life.

Walk out of the village on a minor road, then turn left just before the main road about half a kilometre later to walk once more on a wide dirt track. The track, which is beginning to feel like a pilgrim highway, parallels the main road between here and Belorado. Look out for grey and yellow wagtails along the track. A little over a kilometre later, cross a tarmac side road and see **Villamayor del Río** ahead. Turn left up Calle Mayor into Villamayor, walk past the fountain (non-drinkable water) in the square, then head up Calle Real. You soon leave Villamayor behind and resume walking on a dirt

Map 7 (key page 213)

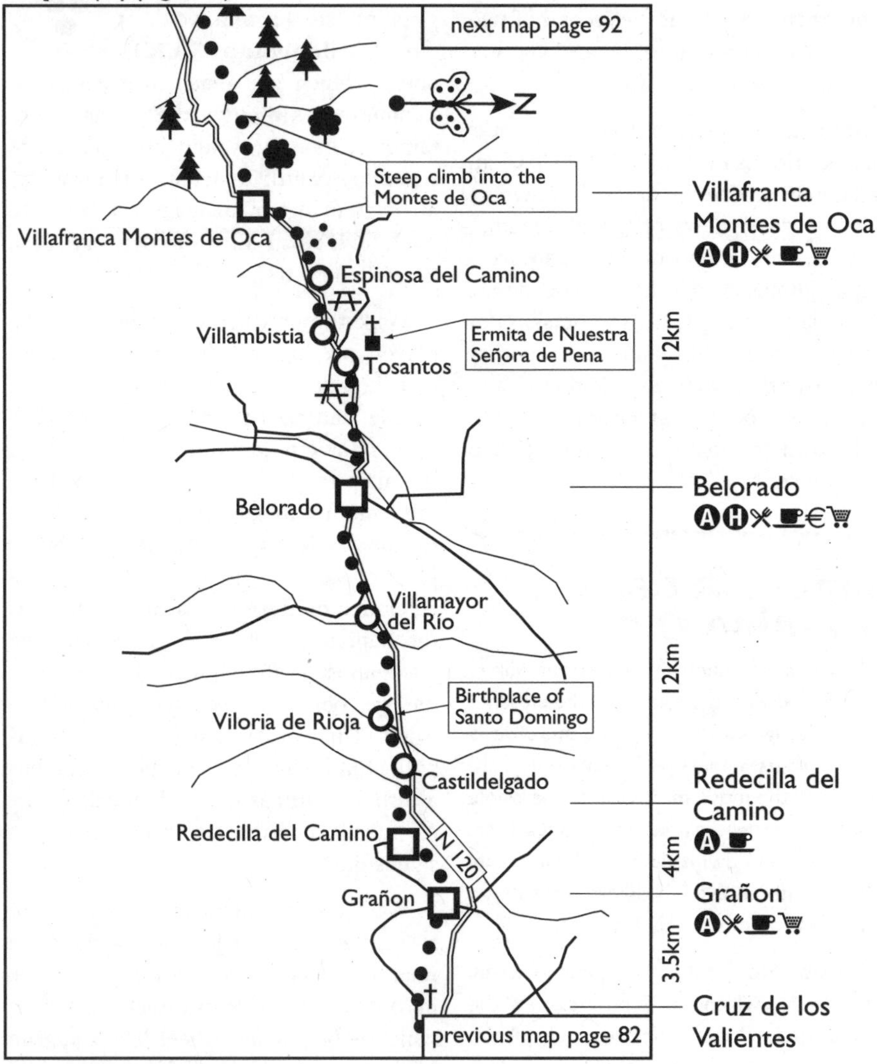

next map page 92

Z

Steep climb into the Montes de Oca

Villafranca Montes de Oca

Espinosa del Camino

Villambistia

Tosantos

Ermita de Nuestra Señora de Pena

Belorado

Villamayor del Río

Birthplace of Santo Domingo

Viloria de Rioja

Castildelgado

Redecilla del Camino

N 120

Grañon

previous map page 82

Villafranca Montes de Oca

12km

Belorado
€

12km

Redecilla del Camino

4km

Grañon

3.5km

Cruz de los Valientes

Profile Chart 7

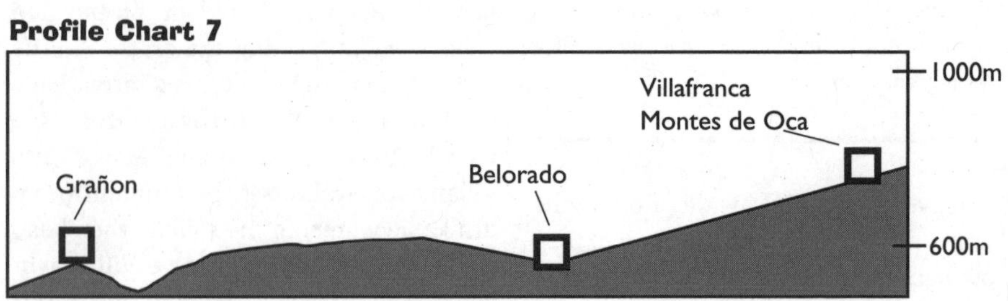

track parallel to the main road.

There's little to distract you on the barren, dry 5km stretch to Belorado, although there are still glimpses of the Sierra de la Demanda to your left. Eventually, the track goes downhill and the outskirts of Belorado come into view. At a road sign for Belorado, cross the road to walk on a dirt track, passing signs advertising places to stay in the town. Soon, the track flattens and you pass the first houses in Belorado. Turn left at the Iglesia de Santa María, then take the first street on the right, and then the first on the left.

Belorado Ⓐ Ⓗ ✕ ☕ € 🛒

Although occupied since Roman times and home to eight churches by the thirteenth century, Belorado is a modern, down-at-heel town, suffering from the gradual demise of its leather industry. The remaining churches of Santa María and San Pedro are less than exciting, but the main square is large and pleasant and Belorado has an incredible number of bars and cafés. There are good views from the mostly ruined medieval castle above the town. The caves below were once home to religious hermits, including San Capraiso, who hid here to escape persecution until a young martyr's courage inspired him to leave his hideout and face his executioners.

Accommodation

Belorado's main **albergue**, next to the Iglesia de Santa María, was being renovated in 2002, but a temporary *albergue* (28 beds, kitchen, open all year) had been set up in a barn-like building at the entrance into town. Alternatively, there's a small private *albergue* further along the camino near the main square (35 beds, kitchen, open all year).

$ Hostal Ojarre (☎ 947 58 02 23)

$$ Hotel Belorado (☎ 947 58 06 84)

Many of the restaurants in Belorado also rent reasonable rooms; look for signs around the town square, or ask at one of the *albergues*.

The walk from Belorado is a pleasant one, heading towards Villafranca Montes de Oca along grass and stone tracks through undulating farmland.

To leave Belorado, keep straight on, walking through the new part of of town. Turn right at a tarmac road in 200m and keep straight ahead down a dead end street. On your left is **Convento de Santa Clara**, said to be built on the site of an *ermita* (hermitage) destroyed by the Moors. In a couple of hundred metres, cross over the main road and turn right next to a house to take the footbridge over the Río Tirón. Walk along a dirt track next to the road, keeping straight on at a petrol station, then cross over a minor road to San Miguel de Pedro and keep straight on as the main track curves to the left. Walk on a flat grassy track through farmland, sometimes crossing other farm tracks but always following the camino signs in roughly the same direction. Look out for effortlessly circling griffon vultures above.

A few kilometres out of Belorado, **Tostantos** comes into view, and the camino passes a picnic area with barbeque areas and tables on the left, a common sight along the route through Castilla y León. The camino passes along the top of the hamlet of Tostantos, and you'll need to veer off the route to the right to visit the village café-bar. Just

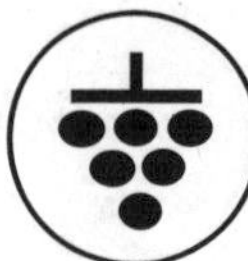

before Tostantos peters out, turn left up a dirt farm track, clearly signed. As you climb slightly, look out for the **Ermita de Nuestra Señora de Pena** to your right, built directly into the hill and looking as if it's organically part of the landscape.

Many of the plants on either side of the track will be covered in fine tunnel-like webs in spring and summer. These webs are home to tent caterpillars, voracious insects that strip leaves from trees and shrubs. Local farmers often spray the plants with toxic pesticides, but the caterpillars can also controlled by destroying the tents with a well-aimed stick.

In under 2km, the camino passes through the hamlet of **Villambistia**, where there's not a lot to see, and where the modern church, built from large stone blocks, has seen better days. Take the left-hand fork at the church as the path becomes paved. Keep straight on through the village, passing a fountain and a cattle water trough. The route soon becomes a farm track once more, and Espinosa del Camino soon comes into view. Pass another picnic table on the right, then cross over the main road 100m later, keeping a look out for fast traffic. Turn left down the main road, then take the right-hand path 20m further on.

Walk through **Espinosa del Camino**, just 2km from Villambistia, past a bar on the left and a fountain on the right. Head down Calle Santa Cecilia, then turn left at the track at the end of the village. Walk uphill through rolling, green countryside, and keep straight on as you walk under electricity pylons at the top of a rise, from where you can see Villafranca Montes de Oca ahead. Descend a little, then pass the ruined **Monasterío San Felices** on your right. Although only a single arch remains of this once-important ninth-century Mozarabic monastery, it's an interesting place to poke around in. The ruins hold the bones of Diego Porcelos, who founded Burgos after recapturing it from the Moors.

In another half a kilometre, the track curves left to meet the main road. Turn right to walk along the road, cross the Río Oca and pass the sign into Villafranca Montes de Oca.

Villafranca Montes de Oca Ⓐ Ⓗ

Villafranca's beautiful location in a sheltered valley at the foot of the Montes de Oca has attracted settlers for almost 3000 years. Nearby, there's evidence of an Iron Age settlement from 700 BC, while the town's name comes partly from Auca, a large Roman town that once stood here, and partly from the Franks who resettled the area as the camino became popular.

The fourteenth-century **Hospital de San Antonio Abad**, also known as the Hospital de la Reina in honour of its founder, Queen Juana Manuel, sheltered up to 18,000 pilgrims a year in the sixteenth century and has now been converted back into an **albergue** (23 beds, kitchen, open all year). Visit the massive, eighteenth-century Iglesia de Santiago to see the altar's Santiago Peregrino statue and a baptismal font made from a giant Philippine shell.

There are rooms in **El Pájaro** (**$**, ☎ 947 58 20 29), a couple of bars, and a *panadería* on your right as you enter the village. There's another shop further down the main road, just off the camino route, your last chance to buy anything at all for about 20km and the last place before Burgos with a well equipped shop.

In Villafranca, turn right off the main road to walk past a fountain and the church. From here to San Juan de Ortega, it's a steep initial climb followed by a lovely ridge walk through swathes of heather, and ending in a long, dull stretch through pine forest. The road quickly changes to a dirt path and heads very steeply uphill. Soon, the climb becomes less steep and the track passes through woodland.

Pass a picnic area on the left at the Fuente de Mojapán and see an oak wood up ahead. In spring, there are primroses and songbirds here, but your eye is inevitably drawn to the endless, spectacular stretches of pink and purple heather. In autumn, look out for mushrooms, which in seventeenth-century pilgrim Domenico Laffi's words were once "of unbelievable size, as big as a straw hat." Luckily for Laffi, who got lost here, they were also plentiful.

As you climb higher, the trees get noticeably shorter and the landscape changes to scrubland. There are great views from here, and the track is well-marked. Things were not so easy in medieval times, when the Montes de Oca's steep, rugged terrain, dense forest, wolves, thieves and murderers made it one of the most difficult stretches of the camino. If you're here early in the morning, you may be lucky enough to see fox, wild boar or roe deer.

The track veers close to a road, then heads past the Monumento de los Caidos, a memorial to Spanish civil war victims. Keep straight on, walking downhill for a short stretch to cross the Río Peroja, then climb briefly up the other side.

At a pine wood a little under a kilometre later, turn right at a T-junction on to a wide dirt track. You'll be following this track all the way to San Juan de Ortega, crossing scrub and heather and passing through occasional pine woods. There's not much to see along the final, pine-edged stretch, and this tedious part of the walk seems to last forever.

Finally, the track starts to descend and soon emerges from the trees at a pastoral countryside setting with the monastery of San Juan de Ortega in the distance. The deciduous trees, fields and flowers are a jolt to the senses after all that pine, and the scene is so pretty and old-fashioned that it seems straight out of an English hymn. Cross a stream and enter the tiny hamlet of San Juan de Ortega.

San Juan de Ortega

Just like Santo Domingo de la Calzada, the hamlet of San Juan de Ortega is the work of a single man. Juan was a disciple of Santo Domingo, and like his mentor, he improved the pilgrim road and built bridges, hospices and cathedrals. Disaster almost befell Juan as he returned from a pilgrimage to Jerusalem when his boat was shipwrecked in stormy seas, but he prayed to San Nicolás de Barí and was spared to continue his pilgrim work. On his return, Juan dedicated a hospice in the Montes de Oca wilderness to San Nicolás, calling the place Ortega, after the Spanish word for nettle.

Map 8 (key page 213)

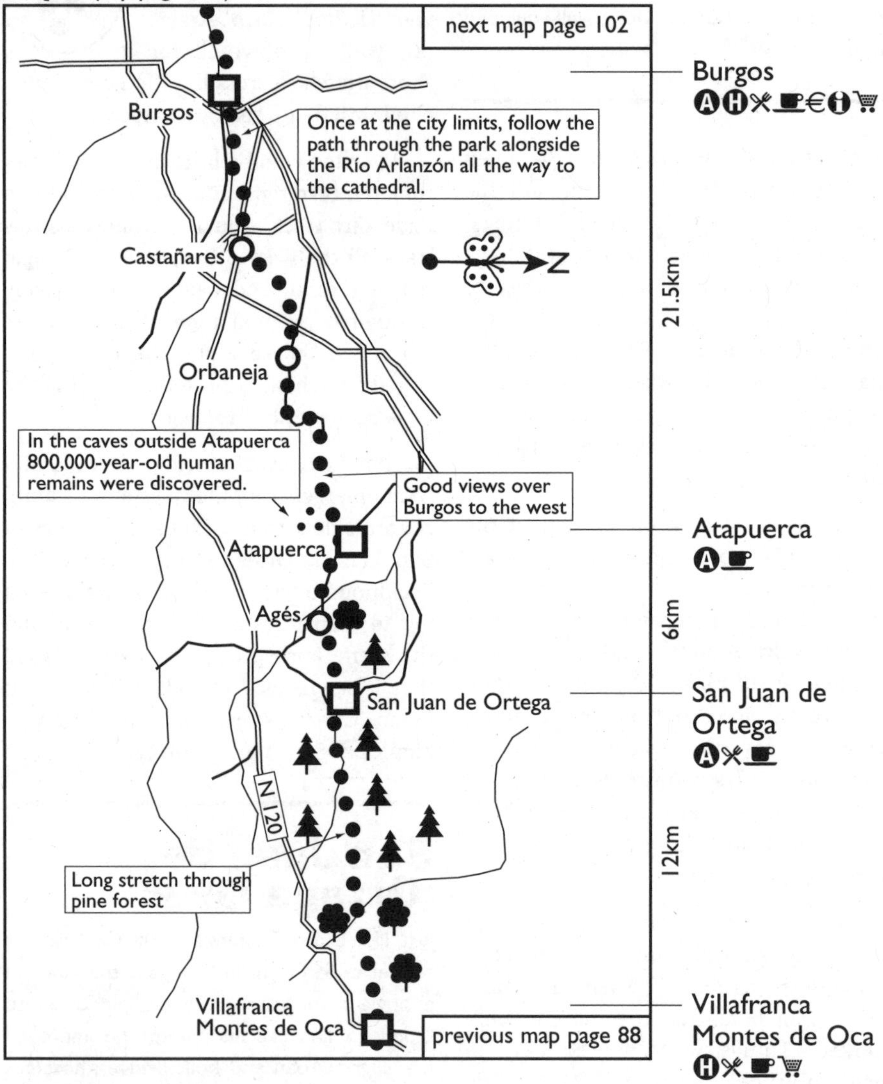

next map page 102
Burgos
Once at the city limits, follow the path through the park alongside the Río Arlanzón all the way to the cathedral.
Castañares
Z
21.5km
Orbaneja
In the caves outside Atapuerca 800,000-year-old human remains were discovered.
Good views over Burgos to the west
Atapuerca
Agés
6km
San Juan de Ortega
N 120
12km
Long stretch through pine forest
Villafranca Montes de Oca
previous map page 88
Burgos
Atapuerca
San Juan de Ortega
Villafranca Montes de Oca

Profile Chart 8

1200m
San Juan de Ortega
Atapuerca
Burgos
800m

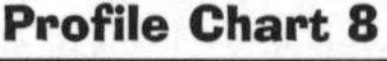

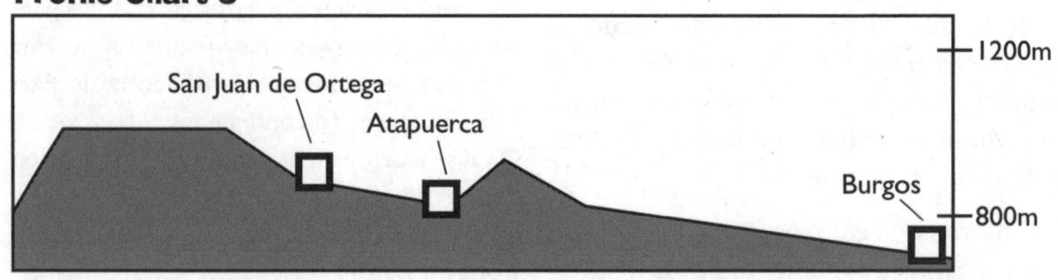

San Juan also founded a monasterial order here and built a church, currently being restored. The **Iglesia de San Juan de Ortega**'s twelfth-century apses are said to have been built by the saint himself, and the church is still laid out according to its original Romanesque plan. The church and monastery soon fell into disrepair, but were expanded in the fifteenth century thanks to an injection of cash and the efforts of the bishop of Burgos.

Meanwhile, San Juan garnered a reputation as a patron of fertility after his tomb was opened and a swarm of white bees flew out, surrounded by a beautiful smell. The bees were seen as the souls of unborn children, kept safe by the saint until they could be placed in suitable Christian wombs. Hearing of this, the long-childless Isabel la Católica visited, determined to produce an heir for the Kingdom of Castilla. When she gave birth to a son, she named him Juan, and when her son died early, Isabel returned to ask for the saint's help once more, this time conceiving a daughter, who she called Juana. Grateful, Isabel ordered the rebuilding of the chapel of San Nicolás de Bari, and commissioned a Gothic baldachin to ornament San Juan's tomb. The alabaster tomb itself is carved with scenes from San Juan's life, including the legend of the bees and the appearance of San Nicolás at sea.

Above you, there's a Romanesque capital showing the battle between Roland and the giant Ferragut, and a magnificent triple capital depicting the Annunciation, the Visitation, the dream of Joseph and the Nativity. Impressive at any time, the capitals literally shine at the time of the Milagro de la Luz, when a shaft of sunlight illuminates the womb of the Virgin of the Annunciation in the late afternoon at the spring and autumn equinox.

Part of the monastery is reserved for the use of pilgrims, and is now an authentic, atmospheric but decidedly chilly **albergue** (58 beds, no kitchen, open all year). The *albergue* is famous for its delicious garlic soup, served to pilgrims at a long, communal table each night after Mass.

The tiny hamlet also has a bar, and a fountain that doubles as the *albergue*'s clothes washing facilites, but watch out for Ortega's namesake nettles here.

Walk down the road out of San Juan de Ortega. At a bend in the road after 200m, take the well-signposted right-hand track through a pine wood. The pines soon clear and you're walking through less dense oak wood: listen for birds, especially cuckoos, in spring.

The landscape here is much flatter, breaking you in gradually for the *meseta* proper in the long stretch from Burgos to Astorga. You'll soon reach a flat-topped pasture, which is criss-crossed by many paths, although yellow arrows clearly show the way.

Up ahead is the village of **Agés** (☕), and the track heads downhill towards it. The remains of García de Nájera, who was killed near here by his brother Fernando I of Castilla, were originally entombed at the Iglesia de Santa Eulalia before they were moved to Nájera's Panteón Real.

Keep straight on through the village, walking on a narrow paved road that will take you to Atapuerca, a couple of kilometres away. Look out for standing stones on either side of the road — these are modern but were raised using prehistoric means by archaeologists and villagers of nearby Atapuerca. Walk into Atapuerca

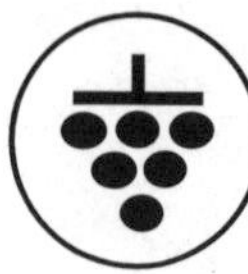

along the road, passing a water pump to the left of the road.

Atapuerca Ⓐ

Although Atapuerca was one of the first towns wrestled from Muslim control in the *reconquista*, it was a minor stop along the camino with nothing much of interest before archaeologists dug up prehistoric human remains in the nearby hills. Caves were discovered in the Atapuercan massif in the nineteenth century, but it wasn't until the mid-1970s that excavations began in earnest.

These excavations have uncovered some of the best-preserved early human remains ever found. In 1997, archaeologists at the site identified the 800,000-year-old bones as a new species, *homo antecessor*. The site is now a UNESCO World Heritage Site.

There's limited information in the village; many of the site's finds are now in the Burgos archaeological museum, and there's also a museum in the nearby village of Ibeas de Jarros, from where guided tours can sometimes be arranged (see www.atapuerca.net). There's a café-bar in Atapuerca, and an **albergue** (32 beds, kitchen, open all year) 3km away in Olmos de Atapuerca: follow the Camino A signs in Atapuerca to reach it.

The camino to Burgos splits here, taking different routes over or around the Sierra de Atapuerca. In the village, a sign for Camino A points right. Follow this option if you want to stay at the *albergue* in Olmos de Atapuerca, otherwise keep straight on.

Turn left soon afterwards to walk diagonally across a football pitch, then turn left at a track, passing a picnic table on your right. Head uphill, taking a right-hand fork a few hundred metres later. In spring, look out for wild hyacinths and other flowers as you climb. Head towards a cross on the flat-topped summit, from where you get views of Burgos and of the immense, flat *meseta* that stretches west from the city. Head to the left of the radio towers towards a clump of trees, then walk downhill along a grassy track, passing a quarry on the right. Just past the edge of the quarry, turn left to walk along a dirt road, then follow a web of tracks along a small ridge.

There's little shade here, and no trees or posts to paint yellow arrows on, so look out for markings on low stones instead. Veer right at a junction in 200m, then left along a grassy track in another 200m, and left again about half a kilometre later. There are some crops here, but it's mostly stony pasture dotted with wildflowers. To the left, you can get your final glimpse of the Sierra de la Demanda.

Eventually, the route heads downhill towards the village of **Orbaneja**. Turn left at a junction with a tarmac road in front of a small hillock and keep straight on 50m later. In Orbaneja, turn left for the village bar, but turn right to continue the camino on a tarmac road which soon crosses the busy A1 via a bridge. Turn left in 100m to circle around an abandoned building, possibly a former military barracks. You're walking on a dirt track through fields that get progressively uglier and more barren. On the plus side, Burgos' sprawling modern outskirts disappear from view for a while.

At a wire fence in about a kilometre, turn left at a T-junction, then turn right 100m later. The track winds around the back of an airport and the little agriculture that remains is dwarfed by wasteland. After a few hundred metres, turn left at the end of some garbage piles, aiming for the suburbs of Castañares and La Ventilla, just to the right of a shiny factory, and reaching the N120 in a kilometre or so.

Turn left to detour to a couple of cafés, and right just before the main road at a fountain to continue the camino, which soon joins the N120, heading along a gravel track on its right-hand side. Watch out for cars at busy junctions, then in a little over a kilometre, just before a large camino road sign, turn left to make a kamikaze crossing of the N120 (there are no signs or lights here). If you're safely across, turn right to follow a dirt road towards the outskirts of Burgos. Pass the San Miguel brewery away to your right, then keep straight on through an industrial area and walk under the railway via a tunnel.

Here, yellow arrows lead you straight on, past some apartments and along an endless industrial-suburban grind into the centre of Burgos. It's a much better idea to ignore the camino signs and instead approach the city centre via the attractive path alongside the Río Arlanzón. To do this, turn left at the road, then as the road bends to the right, turn left to cross the river on a pedestrianized bridge. At the end of the bridge, turn right, following a pretty path popular with joggers, dog walkers and afternoon strollers, and dotted with shady rest spots and benches. The track passes over and under a couple of bridges, then arrives in a few kilometres in the centre of Burgos. Up ahead you can see the cathedral on your right and the castle on the hill behind.

Keep straight on past the Puente de San Pablo, a beautiful bridge guarded by a statue of El Cid on horseback, to walk along a wide, tree-lined boulevard. At the next bridge, the Puente de Santa María, turn right to cross the river. Turn immediately left to continue the camino or keep straight ahead through the gate to reach the cathedral in 100m or so. Continue walking alongside the Río Arlanzón, now on your left, for about a kilometre, then cross over a stone bridge, following the first yellow arrow you've seen since the outskirts of Burgos. Cross a road, then veer right to walk through a pretty park, reaching the *albergue* in a couple of hundred metres.

Regional Map (key page 213)

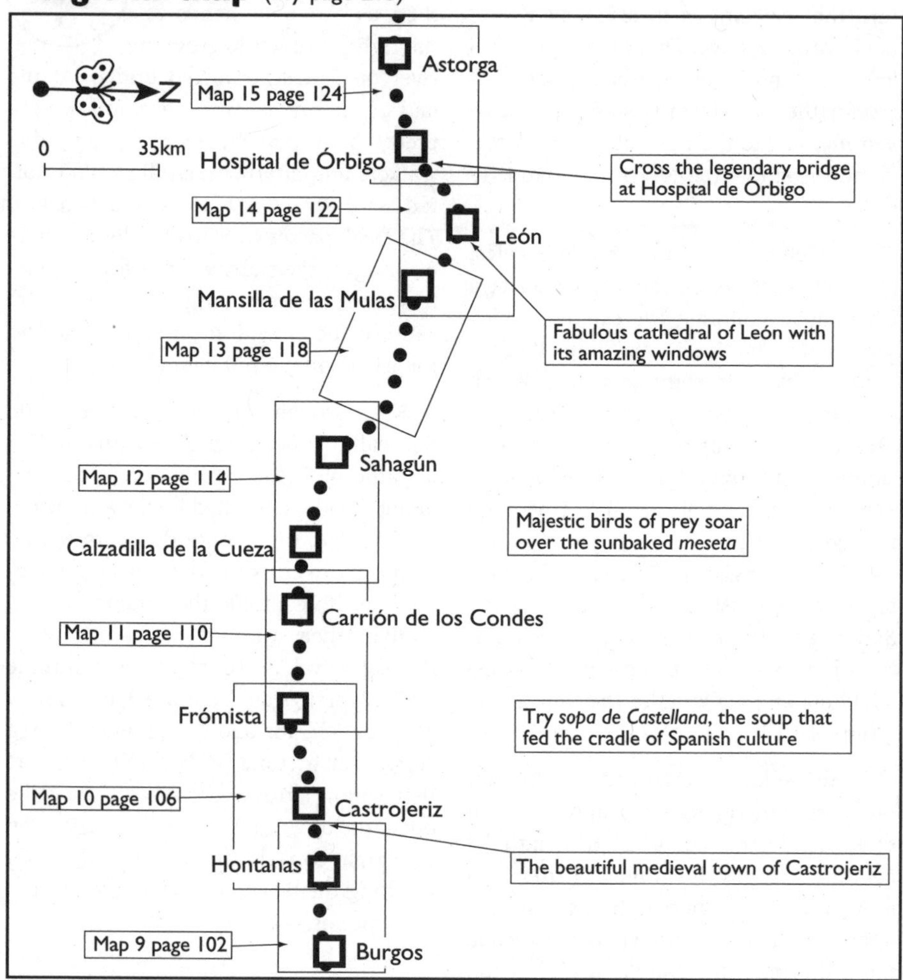

What's the weather like?

	Jan	April	July	Oct
Sun	4hrs	8hrs	12hrs	6hrs
Rainfall	6cm	5cm	2cm	5cm
Maximum Temp	7°C	15°C	28°C	18°C
Minimum Temp	-1°C	3°C	11°C	6°C

Average hours of sun, total average rainfall in cm and average temperature in degrees celsius

Meseta

Burgos to Astorga

The *meseta* has a bad reputation. Flat, desolate, and the section most likely to be missed out by pilgrims running short of time, the plains can also be hauntingly beautiful. And it's not all desolate wilderness: Burgos and León, the camino's liveliest cities, offer sophisticated restaurants and stunning cultural attractions.

Walking

Geography

The vast expanse and huge skies of the *meseta* are striking and strange, swinging from depressingly monotonous to exhilaratingly infinite in the space of a kilometre. The Cordillera Cantábrica in the north will provide some distraction, but mostly your senses will be overloaded by an endless flatness.

From Burgos, the camino climbs to a flat tableland dented with inhabited valleys and depressions. Towards Frómista, canals drain into poppy-lined wheat fields in a fertile region known as the breadbasket of northern Spain. It's stiflingly hot on summer days, with sudden drops in temperature at night that produce condensation, essential moisture for the rain-starved *meseta*. Winters are long and bitingly cold, as strength-sapping winds whip off the snow-covered mountains.

Trails

The walking is generally good, although the camino often follows purpose-built gravel tracks alongside the main road, which can seem like a dismal, never-ending camino highway. There are a couple of stretches, notably around Calzadilla de los Hermanillos, when you move away from civilization and crunch along thyme-scented tracks with the desolate, sparsely inhabited *meseta* all to yourself.

When to go

Summers are hot, winters are cold, and while the brief spring and autumn seasons are more bearable, the wind can still be bone-chilling. Start early in summer and you'll miss the worst of the heat and catch a wonderful dawn chorus. Wrap up warm in winter to enjoy crisp, cloudless days that make for wonderful walking.

Flora & Fauna

The wheat fields and scrubland of the *meseta* initially seem lifeless and deserted, but if you stop for a while and leave the camino treadmill, you'll hear and see a stunning array of birds.

One of the most distinctive is the **great bustard**, a stocky, Canada-goose-sized bird that loves the *meseta*'s wide open spaces. In spring, the males coquettishly rustle their tails in a dramatic courtship display; their size and fluffy white feathers make a group of males indistinguishable from a flock of sheep at a distance. Intensive cultivation and tree planting are eroding the bustard's habitat, while a hunting ban may ironically reduce numbers further, as landowners now have no incentive to conserve territory for the former game bird.

Up above, the skies are a bonanza of aerial hunters. You can see kestrels, peregrine falcons, Egyptian vultures, hen harriers and Bonelli's eagles. It takes more patience to look for birds that live low to the ground in fields or scrubland, and at first you're more likely to hear the melodic songs of the *meseta*'s many **larks** — there are short-toed, Dupont's, crested, and calandra larks here — than to see the well-camouflaged birds. Much easier to spot is the bold, coral-coloured crest of the **hoopoe**, which also has distinctive black and white bars on its tail and wings, and flies in such an ungainly, undulating style that it seems to fall from the sky with each wingbeat.

The lack of rain on the *meseta* means that flowers either burst quickly into life in the rains of spring and autumn, or conserve moisture and heat in tubers and bulbs. Orchids, cornflowers, vetch and corn poppies are a riot of colour among the endless, straw-coloured fields, while moisture-loving plants crowd rivers, streams and ponds.

People & Culture

Castilla y León can justly claim to be the cradle of Spanish culture. One of the first regions to be won back by the Christians after the Muslim invasion, Spain is so entwined with **Castilla** that the Spanish even call their language *castellano* (Castilian). As the southern regions came back under Christian control, the power base of the country moved south, leaving the cities of Burgos and León to their glorious Gothic cathedrals.

Burgos' second brief moment in the spotlight came during the civil war, when Franco made the firmly Nationalist city his capital. Just as in the *reconquista*, however, as soon as the southern cities came under Franco's control after the war, the capital moved south to Madrid, although Franco rewarded the northern city with generous investment in industry.

There's not much stone around in the *meseta*, so locals have had to use alternative building materials. Inspired by Muslim architects, intricate **brick** churches were built in many towns, notably in Sahagún, where the recently restored Iglesia de San Tirso is a highlight.

More modest folk have been equally creative. In many *meseta* villages, notably Calzadilla de los Hermanillos, houses are made from adobe, a logical choice in a bone-dry climate, cheap to build and repaired by simply patching the walls with more straw and mud. Hobbit-like underground **cellars** are a common sight on the outskirts of villages and towns, providing cool storage for wine and other produce. The round- or horseshoe-shaped buildings that sit plum in the middle of fields are **palomares** (dovecotes). Pigeon droppings are a valuable source of nitrogen-rich fertilizer, and the game birds also make their way to the dinner table.

Food & Drink

Castilla y León is known for its **pork**, particularly the suckling pig, traditionally roasted in a baker's oven with pine branches, broom, rosemary and thyme. Pork is also a main ingredient of the region's heavy stews, padded out with pulses and rice-blood sausage. Most famous of these is Burgos' unappetisingly named *olla podrida* (putrid pot), a hearty one-pot meal made with chickpeas and various types of meat.

Keep vampires away with Castilla's famous **sopa de ajo** or *sopa de castellana*, a soup made by frying bread in paprika and lots of garlic, pouring on stock and cracking an egg on top. A staple food in hard times, *sopa de ajo* is now appearing in the finest restaurants.

You'll see plenty of **caracoles** (snails) along the trail, and occasionally spot locals collecting them by the bucketful. *Caracoles* are normally boiled for a few hours with onion, garlic and parsley, a bit of *chorizo* and *jamón*, a splash of white wine, and served in a shallow earthenware dish. Delicious! Soft, fresh Burgos cheese is a fine end to a meal, usually served with quince jelly or honeyed nuts.

Ribera del Duero **wines** are a recent introduction to the international scene, and the Duero basin in the south of Castilla y León is now attracting almost as much attention as its more famous Riojan cousin. The deep burgundy wines have more acidity than Rioja or Navarra wines due to the extreme temperature fluctuations in the region.

Tourist Information

Tourist Offices

You'll find tourist offices in Burgos, Frómista (summer only), and León. Contact information for the *turismos* is under individual towns.

Transport

There are regular buses and trains between Burgos and León, via Sahagún.

Money

There are cash machines and banks in Burgos, Tardajos, Castrojeriz, Frómista, Carrión de los Condes, Sahagún, Mansilla de las Mulas, Puente de Villarente, León, and Hospital de Órbigo. Banks in smaller places may have limited opening hours.

Accommodation

Albergues vary wildly in quality, space and facilities, from the crammed bunk beds but beautiful setting of Burgos to the spacious, quiet *albergue* in Calzadilla de los Hermanillos. There are plenty of hotels in both Burgos and León if you want to dally in either of those cities, and the Parador de San Marcos in León is one of the best hotels in Spain.

Shopping

Burgos and León are modern cities, with

everything a pilgrim could need. In between, supplies and opening hours can be limited, and there are no facilities at all between Calzadilla de los Hermanillos and Mansilla de las Mulas.

Events & Festivals

Hospital de Órbigo recreates a medieval **jousting** competition at the beginning of June each year to honour Don Suero de Quiñones, a knight who defended the bridge at Hospital from all-comers after being rejected by his lady love.

Burgos sheds its dour image during the Fiestas de San Pedro y San Pablo at the end of June. In mid-August, young girls dance through **León**, led by a veiled woman in a turban, celebrating the end of a Moorish law that demanded a sacrifice of 100 maidens from local villages.

Rest Days & Detours

The logical places to take a break are Burgos and León, pleasant cities to wander around, visit spectacular monuments or simply rest sore feet.

Further off the camino, the Gregorian monastery at **Santo Domingo de Silos**, some 70km southwest of Burgos, is well worth a visit. The double-decked Romanesque cloister is breathtaking, with beautifully carved capitals and a gorgeous restored Mudejár ceiling. The monks have an internationally renowned choir school, and their Gregorian chants broke into the pop charts in the 1990s.

At **Quintanilla de las Viñas**, reached along the N234 on the way to Santo Domingo de Silos, you can see the lovely seventh-century Visigothic church of Nuestra Señora de las Viñas.

North of Frómista, around **Aguilar de Campóo**, you'll find what is said to be the highest concentration of Romanesque churches in Europe. The simple, elegant churches are mostly unrestored, and remain unadorned and untainted by Gothic or Baroque flourishes.

Just south of Calzadilla de La Cueza is the Villa Romana de Tejada, an excavated Roman villa with mosaic-floor remains.

Burgos

Burgos comes as a bit of a culture shock after the mellow, timeless feel of the camino so far. It's a sizeable city with traffic jams, nightlife and noise, and so chock-full of monuments that it's worth staying an extra day or two to see them all. Despite this, the rest of Spain sees Burgos as less than cosmopolitan.

Thanks to famous sons such as El Cid and Fernando III, reconquerer of southern Spain, Burgos had a reputation as a centre of staid military might before the civil war. The city's Nationalist ties during the war and throughout the Franco era simply reinforced the city's image as a bastion of conservative Catholicism. In democratic Spain, the city is trying to cast aside its tarnished reputation: literally so, in the case of Burgos' talismanic cathedral, whose blackened exterior has been polished to gleaming white.

The massive Gothic **cathedral** sits right in the middle of Burgos, and is a natural place to begin a tour of the city. Begun by Fernando III at the beginning of the thirteenth century, it was completed in just 22 years, and although there were additions over the next few hundred years, the cathedral retains its Gothic style. It's almost impossible to get a complete picture of the cathedral from the outside: there's simply no vantage point in Burgos from where you can take in the delicate, air-filled spires, the monumental doorways and arches and the tall, solid towers. The cathedral was made a UNESCO World Heritage site in 1984.

Inside, there's an overwhelming array of stunning sculpture and artwork. The octagonal walls of the late-fifteenth-century **Capilla del Condestable** rise up towards an elegant, star-vaulted dome, whose geometrical carvings show a Muslim influence. The Gothic-Renaissance chapel contains stunning fourteenth-century *retablos* and a beautifully carved marble tomb, replete with realistic details.

The **Capilla del Santo Cristo** contains a frankly disturbing statue of its namesake. The statue's hair and fingernails were said to be real and in need of regular trimming, and although the skin was also said to be human, it's now been identified as buffalo hide. The Capilla de Santa Tecla contains Burgos' famous **Papamoscas**, a fifteenth-century mechanical clock that springs into action on the quarter hour.

Back in the main body of the cathedral, you can peer into the caged choir to see a gilded Mudéjar lantern vault. You'll also be dazzled by the staggeringly shiny Plateresque Escalera Dorada, which rises from the ground floor of the cathedral to meet the Puerta Alta, some 30m above. El Cid is buried beneath the choir, in a simple tomb brought to Burgos in the 1920s.

Of Burgos' many smaller churches, the **Iglesia de San Nicolás de Barí**, on Calle Fernán Gonzalez near the cathedral , is worth visiting for its stunning, massive alabaster *retablo*.

Across the Río Arlanzón in the Casa de Miranda, the **Museo de Burgos** has a good prehistoric archaeology section, boosted considerably by finds from Atapuerca. Above the town, there's not much left of Burgos' castle, destroyed by successive invaders, including Napoleon, who blew it up in 1813, shattering the cathedral's stained glass windows in the process.

The twelfth-century **Monasterio de las Huelgas Reales**, on the western outskirts of Burgos, close to the *albergue*, was made famous and powerful by Fernando III, who was knighted into the Order of Santiago here, starting a trend. The statue of Santiago Matamoros used in these ceremonies has a jointed arm so that the saintly sword can be moved up and down. The convent is the final resting place of a good proportion of Castilian royalty, and although the tombs were damaged by plunderers, they contained some beautiful textiles inspired by Islamic designs, which are now displayed in Las Huelgas' Museo de Ricas Telas. Nearby, little remains of the **Hospital del Rey**, which provided food and lodgings for pilgrims from the twelfth century onwards, but it's worth taking in the sixteenth-century gateway.

Map 9 (key page 213)

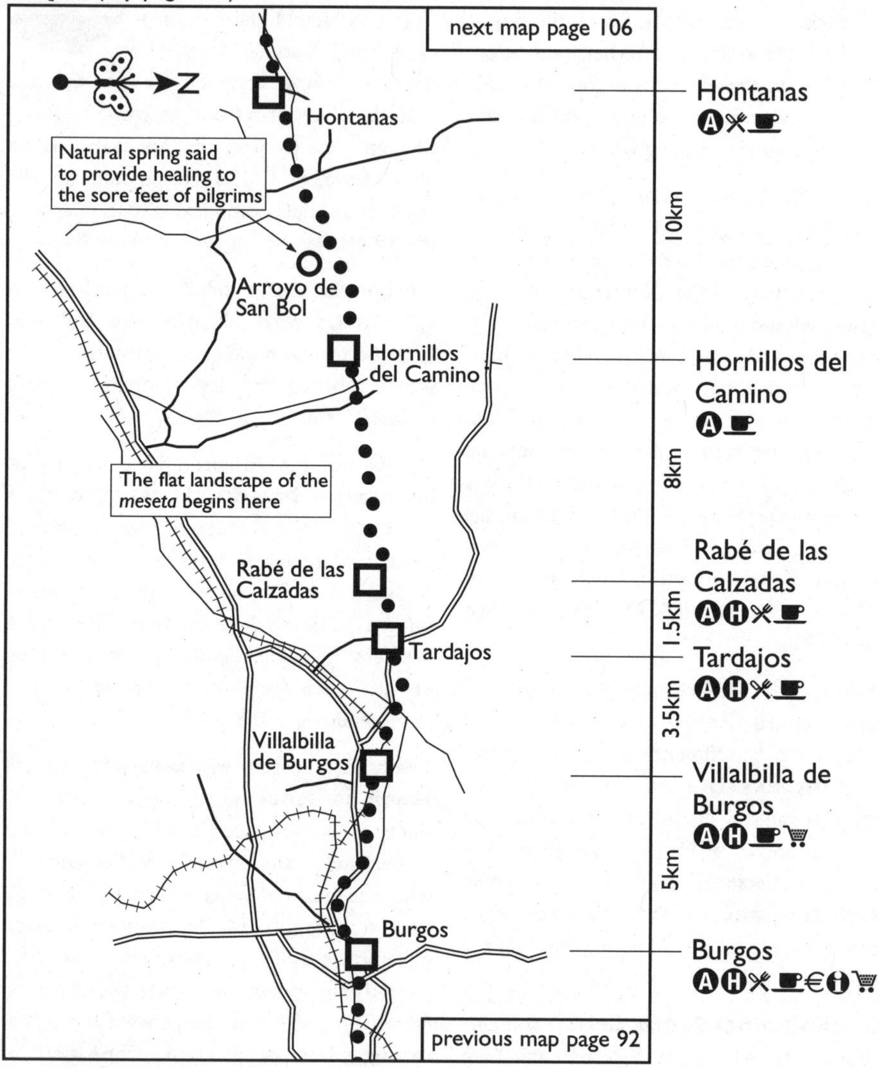

next map page 106
Z
Hontanas
Natural spring said to provide healing to the sore feet of pilgrims
Arroyo de San Bol
Hornillos del Camino
The flat landscape of the *meseta* begins here
Rabé de las Calzadas
Tardajos
Villalbilla de Burgos
Burgos
previous map page 92
Hontanas
10km
Hornillos del Camino
8km
Rabé de las Calzadas
1.5km
Tardajos
3.5km
Villalbilla de Burgos
5km
Burgos

Profile Chart 9

900m
Burgos
Hornillos del Camino
Arroyo de San Bol
Hontanas
500m

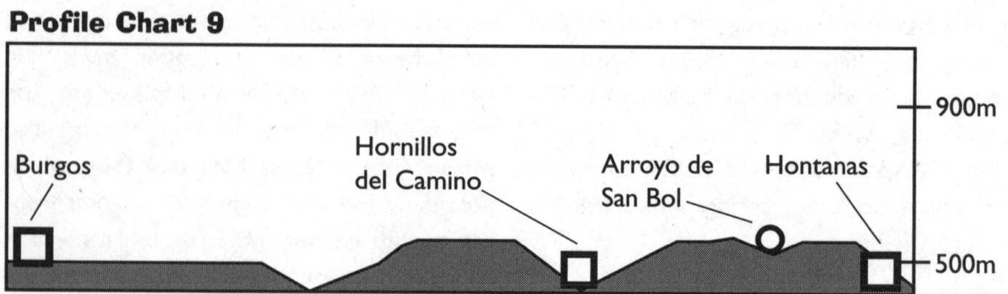

At the other end of the city, the **Cartuja de Miraflores** stands serenely in beautiful parkland, not far from the riverside path you followed into Burgos. The fifteenth-century church — the only part of the still-working monastery open to the public — is stamped with the artistic skills of Gil de Siloé and the patronage of Isabel la Católica. The alabaster tombs of Isabel's parents, Juan II and Isabel de Portugal, took four years to complete and are among the most detailed and intricate ever carved; the wall tomb of Alfonso, Isabel's brother, is crafted in similar style. Gil de Siloé's magnificent, overpowering wooden *retablo* is gilded with gold brought back from America by Columbus in the 1490s.

Burgos casts aside its pious image at the end of June during the two-week Fiestas de San Pedro y San Pablo, with bullfighting, feasts, music, and street parades with *gigantillos*.

Burgos is a large city with all facilities, including some very good restaurants. The **turismo** is on Plaza Alonso Martínez 7 (☎ 947 20 31 25).

Accommodation

Although Burgos' **albergue** (96 beds, no kitchen, open all year) is attractively located in a park near the university, the crowded dormitories can be stifling in summer.

$ Pensión Peña, Calle Puebla 18 (☎ 947 27 65 74)

$$ Hostal San Juan, Calle de Bernabe Perez Ortiz 1 (☎ 947 20 51 34)

$$$ Norte y Londres, Plaza Alonso Martinez 10 (☎ 947 36 41 25)

$$$$ Del Cid, Plaza Santa María 8 (☎ 947 20 87 15)

From Burgos' *albergue*, keep straight on through the park, turn right at the gate at the end of the park, then turn left at a cross 50m later on to the main road. Walk down the road, pass under a railway bridge, then ignore the two huge neon yellow arrows painted on a couple of trees that direct you left at a roundabout. About 100m after the roundabout, turn right down a narrow paved road that soon changes to a dirt track.

In no time at all, you've left the city and, as the camino passes through a deciduous wood, you can glimpse the jail that held political prisoners during Franco's time on your right. The camino wanders through flat farmland and soon passes near **Villalbilla de Burgos** (ⒶⒽ☕🛒), where you can stay at the **albergue** (18 beds, no kitchen, open all year) or the **Hostal San Roque** (**$**, ☎ 947 29 12 29).

Cross an aqueduct and walk alongside a railway as the dirt track becomes tarmac. Turn right at an abandoned train station, then turn left down a dirt track in about 200m as the road curves to the right and crosses a stream via a stone bridge. The well-marked route snakes through fields and gardens, then in a little under a kilometre, it turns right at a road and follows the track on the left-hand side. Note that ongoing road construction may change the route pattern here.

Cross the Río Arlanzón and walk into **Tardajos** (ⒶⒽ🍴☕) along the N120, passing an eighteenth-century stone cross that marks the site of an old pilgrim hospital. There's a bar and a *panadería* on the right-hand side of road, and an **albergue** (22 beds, no kitchen, open all year) in the village. There are rooms available in the **Restaurante Ruiz** (**$**, ☎ 947 45 11 25).

Meseta

Follow the camino as it goes left down the Calle de la Magdalena, then winds through a pretty stretch of older terraced houses, small squares and fountains. In a little over a kilometre, cross the Río Urbel, where there's good fishing, and veer left on a minor tarmac road, keeping an eye out for larks and magpies. Pass some modern houses on the right and enter **Rabé de las Calzadas** (Ⓐ), passing the **albergue** (22 beds, kitchen, open all year) on the right as the village ends.

At the end of Rabé, take the right-hand fork at the cemetery. The road changes to a dirt track at the end of the village, and passes through fields and pasture, heading uphill. Black poplars and willows line the streams. There are many farm tracks here, but the route is always well marked. You'll pass a fountain on the right with picnic tables and barbecue areas.

At the top of the rise, the scenery is jaw droppingly, never endingly flat. Welcome to the *meseta*, treeless, stunningly beautiful, and loud with wind, birdsong and crickets. Calandra larks are difficult to see, except in early spring, when males perform a melodious song flight, wings held stiffly and showing distinctive black wing undersides and a pale belly.

After a few kilometres of flatness, the camino arrives at Hornillos del Camino, hidden from the elements in a hollow and approached by way of a steep downhill track. As the track flattens, turn left at a T-junction, cross a tarmac road, and enter Hornillos over a bridge across the Río Hornazuela.

There's not much action in **Hornillos del Camino** (Ⓐ☕), an ancient, single-street town of pale, local stone. The **albergue** (32 beds, kitchen, open all year) is on the right, next to a Gothic church built on the site of an Iron Age *castro*, and the Fuente del Gallo, a strange cockerel-topped fountain. The bar on the right on the way out of the village serves good *bocadillos*.

At the end of the village, fork right then, about 500m later, fork left at a well-signposted junction. Look out for the dovecote to the right of the route. The terrain between Burgos and Hontanas is surprisingly hilly, the flat *meseta* dented with shallow, inhabited valleys. Woodlarks and buzzards are common here, and you may also see Bonelli's eagles, kestrels and kites.

At the next valley, about 5km after Hornillos, is the **Arroyo San Bol** (Ⓐ), a natural spring just off the camino. Pilgrims who wash their feet in the spring are said to have no foot problems from here to Santiago. The spring marks the site of San Baudillo, a village mysteriously abandoned in 1503, possibly due to disease or possibly related to the expulsion of the Jews from Spain. There's a basic, summer-only **albergue** here (20 beds, kitchen, open all year).

From San Bol onwards, it's a long, flat stretch through fields, a wonderful area for watching birds of prey and listening to noisy choruses of songbirds hidden in wheat fields. Seventeenth-century pilgrims were more concerned about bigger animals: Laffi was warned to only cross the *meseta* in the middle of the day, when shepherds and their dogs provided some protection against marauding packs of wolves. Shepherds still guard against wolves, but they're uncommon now and you'd be very lucky to see one.

After a few kilometres of *meseta* walking, the sudden view of Hontanas, tucked into a valley and named after the large number of local springs, is astonishing. There are gorgeous views of Hontanas' timeless medieval rooftops as you walk steeply downhill, passing dovecotes on the right.

Hontanas

Hontanas is a tiny, one-street village, dominated by the lovely, looming fourteenth-century Iglesia de la Inmaculada Concepción.

In the village, there's a couple of café-bars and a gorgeous new **albergue** (20 beds, kitchen, open all year), located in the beautifully restored Mesón de los Franceses, a former pilgrim hospice. There are two other **albergues** tucked in the village: El Viejo (14 beds, kitchen, open all year) and La Escuela (16 beds, no kitchen, open all year).

On the far side of Hontanas, cross over the main road and head down a track on the left. Turn left again 100m later, following a path that leads along a very dry hillside just above the valley floor, where poplars line the river's edge. Pass the curious ruined hamlet of San Miguel in the field on the right, then follow the grassy track gradually downhill towards the road that runs along the valley bottom. Turn right at the road, following it towards the spectacular ruins of the Gothic **Convento de San Antón**, whose dramatic arch spans the camino. The Orden de los Antonianos rose out of a miraculous cure of San Antón's fire, a burning disease similar to leprosy that was rampant in the Middle Ages. Hospices like this one were set up all along the camino, treating diseased pilgrims with exercise and red wine as well as the divine hand of San Antón. Locked-out latecomers could sleep in the porch and eat food that the monks left in niches. The niches, visible on the right-hand side of the road, now contain messages scribbled by pilgrims on scraps of paper and held in place by small stones.

Laffi, the seventeenth-century pilgrim chronicler, bemoaned the locusts along this part of the camino: "It moves one to pity to see how people are dying of hunger, and the beasts too, as their pastures are devoured by these insects."

Soon after passing San Antón, the dramatic fortress perched above Castrojeriz comes into view. In a couple of kilometres, at a sign describing the town's attractions, turn right, walk past the Iglesia de Nuestra Señora del Manzano, then follow the camino signs along the long approach into the centre of Castrojeriz.

Castrojeriz

Castrojeriz is a beautiful town with surprisingly stylish bars and restaurants. The town has been inhabited since Celtiberian times, if not earlier, and it didn't take much imagination to see this spot as an ideal place for a settlement, near a river and ably defended by a hill with views for miles around. The Romans used its glorious vantage point to guard the route to their valuable gold mines near Astorga and, by the Middle Ages, the town's long main street was packed with hospices and churches. Unusually, the town's tenth-century *fuero* (charter) gave Christians and Jews equal rights, and a murderer of a

Map 10 (key page 213)

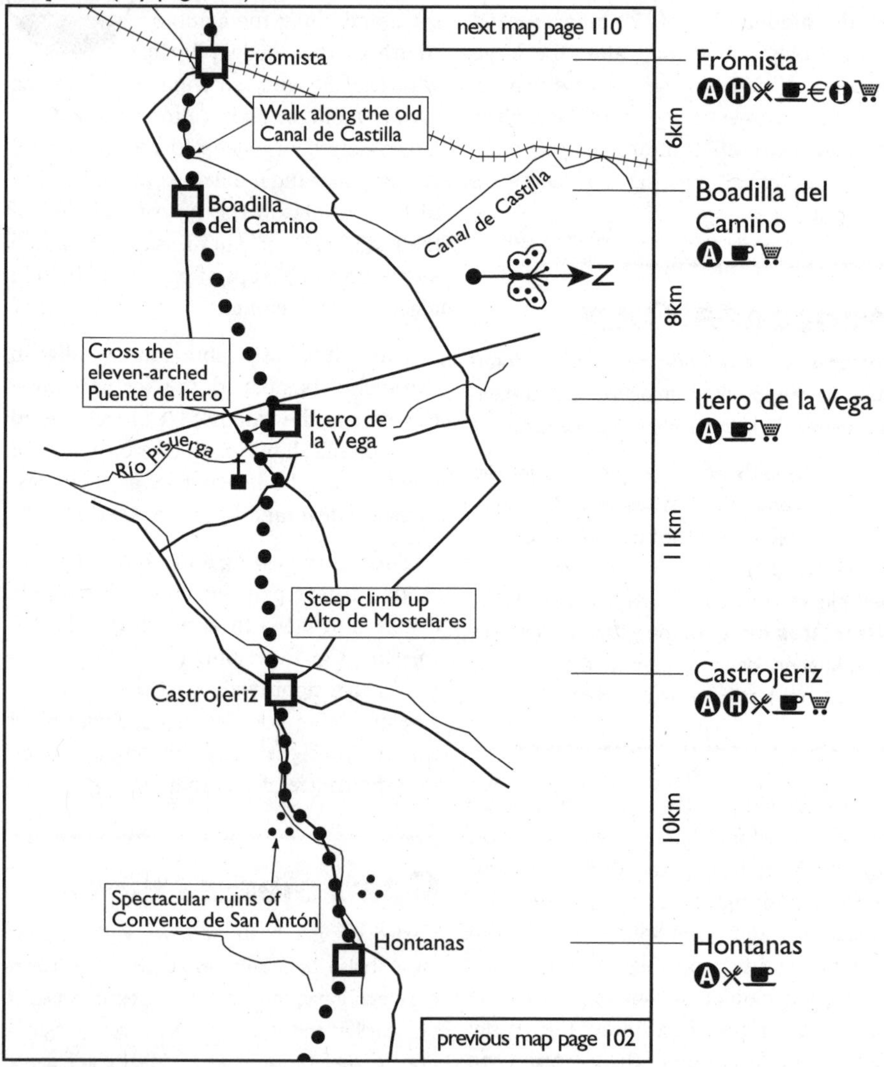

next map page 110
Frómista
Walk along the old Canal de Castilla
Boadilla del Camino
Canal de Castilla
Z
Cross the eleven-arched Puente de Itero
Itero de la Vega
Río Pisuerga
Steep climb up Alto de Mostelares
Castrojeriz
Spectacular ruins of Convento de San Antón
Hontanas
previous map page 102
6km
8km
11km
10km
Frómista
Boadilla del Camino
Itero de la Vega
Castrojeriz
Hontanas

Profile Chart 10

Castrojeriz
Alto de Mostelares
Boadilla del Camino
Frómista
900m
500m

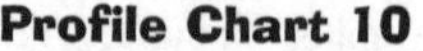

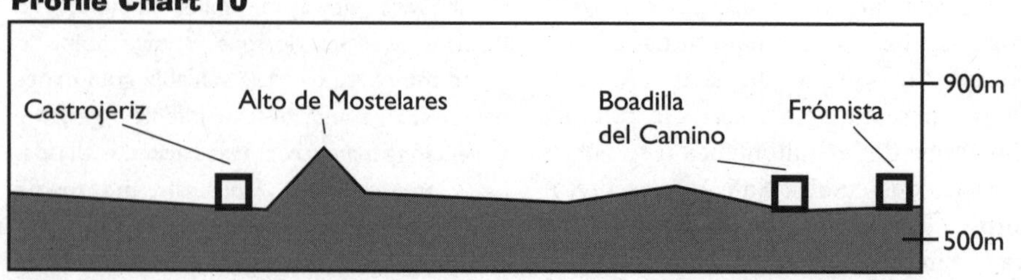

Jewish resident was to be treated identically to one who killed a Christian.

At the entrance into town, the **Iglesia de Santa María del Manzano** marks the spot of a camino miracle. Coming into town, Santiago was so excited to see an image of the Virgin in an apple tree that he leapt heavily on to his horse, leaving behind hoofprints that are embedded in a rock at the church entrance. The Gothic church, largely remodelled in the eighteenth century, includes a fine *retablo*, and the thirteenth-century Virgen del Manzano, made famous by miracles ascribed to her in Cántigas, the Galician-language poems written by Alfonso X.

The **Iglesia de Santo Domingo** is decorated on the outside with scary skulls and inside with seventeenth-century tapestries based on Rubens cartoons, while the thirteenth-century **Iglesia de San Juan de los Caballeros** has lovely Mudéjar ceilings, particularly in the semi-ruined cloister.

For the best views in Castrojeriz, climb the hill to the **castle**. Although legend claims that it was founded by either Caesar or Pompey, archaeology dates the castle much earlier. The castle changed hands frequently over the centuries from Visigoths to Muslims to Christians, finally ending up as a private residence a few centuries later. The hill beneath is honeycombed with *bodegas*, built to keep locally produced wine cool and linked to each other by tunnels. Castrojeriz has some very good, lively restaurants and bars, and a couple of shops that sell basic food.

Accommodation

There are two **albergues** in Castrojeriz: San Esteban is towards the top of town near the Plaza Mayor (25 beds, no kitchen, open April to October) and Refugio de Castrojeriz (32 beds, no kitchen, open all year, better kept but with stricter rules). This *albergue*, in the lower part of town, is reached by turning right at the foot of the steps next to the town monument.

$$ Hotel La Cachava (☎ 947 37 85 47)
$$ Méson de Castrojeriz (☎ 947 37 74 00)
$$$ Hotel la Posada (☎ 947 37 86 10)

Follow the main road through Castrojeriz. At the far side of town there's a fountain on the right-hand side just off the road; the camino heads left here past an industrial building along a gravel road. The route up the Alto de Mostelares is clearly visible straight ahead. About 1km outside town, you come to a wonderfully restored section of raised Roman road, built as a solid route across the boggy Odrilla valley floor. Cross the Río Odrilla by a low medieval bridge, then fork right uphill 100m later. The river is usually fairly dry, although the marshy ground is ideal for bulrushes and reeds, used by craftspeople to make baskets and chairs.

At the start of the climb look to the right to see the remains of old Roman mines; higher up, you'll see the seams of mica more clearly. Take the time to enjoy the view and notice how the Río Odrilla has slowly carved out the valley from the *meseta*. From this angle it's easy to see how a change in the river's direction thousands of years ago left a pillar of the *meseta* uneroded, leaving Castrojeriz with enviable defensive attributes. Higher up, the old terraced slopes have been planted with pine trees and you may see one of the many rabbits that inhabit the area.

At the top of the stiff climb, weary pilgrims are rewarded with fantastic views,

blasts of wind and a marvellous interpretative eco-garden, highlighting some of the plants found on the *meseta*.

Walk across the flat top of the **Alto de Mostelares**, heading steeply downhill along the same track 300m later. Look west and you can see the camino stretching off into the western horizon towards Puente Fitero, Itero de la Vega and Boadilla del Camino. Once at the bottom of the hill, follow a dirt track through fields, ignoring turnings to the left and right. The camino follows the valley bottom until it reaches the small nose of a ridge where there's a rest area with benches, trees and a fountain. Just afterwards, turn right on to a paved road and climb up a small rise, then turn left down a dirt track 500m later as the views open up ahead. The massive, open sky is staggering, competing for attention with the spiky church steeples of nearby villages.

In a few kilometres, the camino takes you past the thirteenth-century **Hospital de San Miguel** (Ⓐ), which is now a lovely, old-fashioned **albergue** (12 beds, no kitchen, open end of June to September) run by an Italian confraternity. There's no electricity and meals are provided under lamp light. Cross the **Puente de Itero**, a lovely, eleven-arch bridge built on the orders of Alfonso VI. The Río Pisuerga is a tranquil, wide river, a great spot for fishing, birdwatching and paddling. Look out for goldfinches and greenfinches amongst the poplars.

On the far side of the bridge, a stone marker indicates the border between the provinces of Burgos and Palencia. Just after this marker, turn right along a dirt road that initially follows the river before it curves around into the village of **Itero de la Vega** (Ⓐ☕🛒). As you enter the village, look for the thirteenth-century Ermita de la Piedad, which contains a statue of Santiago Peregrino. There's an **albergue** here (20 beds, no kitchen, open all year) as well as a shop, a couple of café-bars and a fountain.

Walk out of the village, then go straight ahead at a crossroads, passing the first vines you've seen for a few days. Keep straight on, past the road to the hamlet of **Bodegas**, then start to climb slowly towards the bumpy ridge ahead. On reaching the top, the views are fantastic in all directions. Along this stretch of the camino, ornate dovecotes of all shapes and sizes are a distinctive feature of the landscape; now used mainly as a source of fertilizer, doves and pigeons are also a useful supplement to the local diet.

A few kilometres after the ridge, the camino arrives at the village of **Boadilla del Camino** (Ⓐ☕🛒), where there's a rest area with benches and a fountain. The **albergue** (12 beds, no kitchen, open all year) is on the left next to the sixteenth-century Iglesia de Sana María de la Asuncíon and close to a fifteenth-century village cross decorated with scallop shells. There's also a newer **albergue** (48 beds, kitchen, open March to October) in the village.

Follow the well-marked route through Boadillo, then at the far side of the village, turn left at a fork to follow a tree-lined dirt track. The barley fields are home to finches, skylarks and woodlarks, all inviting prey for the Montagu's harrier. In a kilometre or so, the route runs parallel to the **Canal de Castilla**, a feat of eighteenth-century engineering that's home to lots of water birds. Although the

canal was originally designed to move goods, it was quickly overtaken by the new-fangled railways, and now the canal mainly provides irrigation and electricity for the region's many wheat fields and factories.

After a couple of kilometres, walk over a canal lock at the entrance to Frómista, where the town's rail, road and water transportation links criss-cross next to a picnic spot.

Follow the road into Frómista, passing under a railway bridge, then walk up the modern street to a crossroads with a small, sporadically open *turismo*. Keep straight on here for the *albergue*, or turn left to continue the camino.

Frómista Ⓐ Ⓗ ✂ ☕ € ℹ 🛒

Frómista sits proudly in the middle of a rich agricultural region. Known as the breadbasket of the Roman Empire, its name possibly comes from *frumentum*, Latin for cereal. Later, Frómista was an important Visigothic town destroyed by the Moors, who chose not to settle in this flat, indefensible position.

The eleventh-century **Iglesia de San Martín** was once part of the Benedictine monastery built as the town flourished after the defeat of the Muslim armies. Nothing remains of the monastery, and the now-deconsecrated church stands solidly alone in the centre of Frómista. The church was heavily restored around 1900 to much criticism, but although the painted frescoes are gone, the gorgeous Romanesque capitals remain, carved with religious and agricultural motifs.

In the same square, pop in to the **Museo de Queso** to look at antique cheese presses and paddles made of gorgeous worn wood, and stop to sample the cheese over a glass of wine in the adjoining upscale bar.

Frómista's summer-only **turismo** is near the Iglesia de San Martín on Plaza del Tui 11 (☎ 979 81 01 13).

Accommodation

The **albergue** (55 beds, no kitchen, open all year) is also in Plaza del Tui and has excellent facilities, although the well-equipped kitchen is off-limits to pilgrims.

$ Pensión Marisa, Plaza San Martín (☎ 979 81 00 23)

$$ Hostal San Telmo, Calle Martín Veña 8 (☎ 979 81 10 28)

$$ Hotel San Martín, Plaza San Martín (☎ 979 81 00 00)

$$$$ Hostería de Los Palmeros, Plaza San Telmo (☎ 979 81 00 67)

To leave Frómista, walk down the Paseo de Julio Senador, then veer on to the purpose-built gravel pilgrim track that runs alongside the main road to Carrión de los Condes. After almost 4km, the route joins the road and passes the thirteenth-century Ermita de San Miguel on the left, just before the village of **Población de Campos** (Ⓐ). Turn right down a side road, following the signs to the **albergue** (18 beds, kitchen, open all year), which you'll soon reach. The village street curves around to rejoin the main road. Just before it does, you'll pass the exquisite **Ermita de La Virgen de la Socorro**, a tiny church reached via a set of stone steps. Look for Gothic arches, grooves and tombs in the floor, and a stone sarcophagus.

From here, there's a choice of routes to Villalcázar de Sirga. The gravel pilgrim

Map 11 (key page 213)

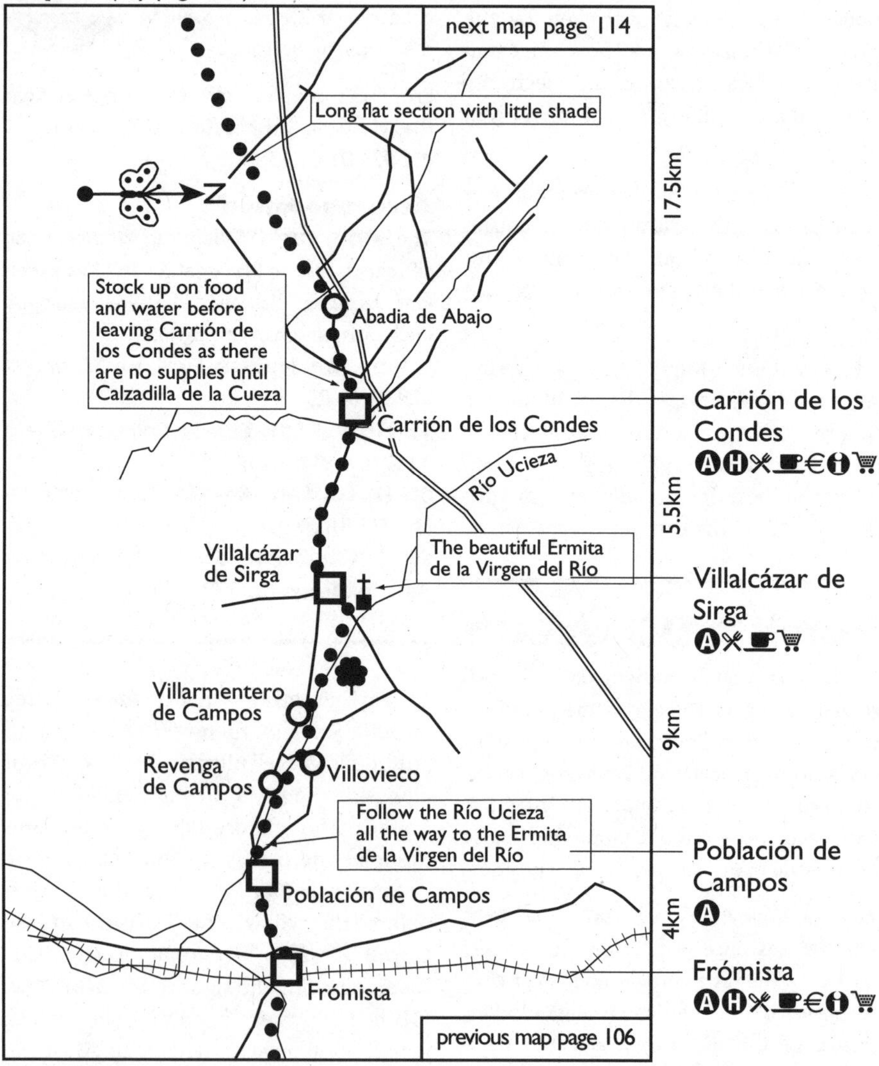

next map page 114
Long flat section with little shade
N
17.5km
Stock up on food and water before leaving Carrión de los Condes as there are no supplies until Calzadilla de la Cueza
Abadia de Abajo
Carrión de los Condes
Carrión de los Condes
Río Ucieza
5.5km
Villalcázar de Sirga
The beautiful Ermita de la Virgen del Río
Villalcázar de Sirga
Villarmentero de Campos
9km
Revenga de Campos
Villovieco
Follow the Río Ucieza all the way to the Ermita de la Virgen del Río
Población de Campos
Población de Campos
4km
Frómista
Frómista
previous map page 106

Profile Chart 11

900m
500m
Frómista
Villalcázar de Sirga
Carrión de los Condes

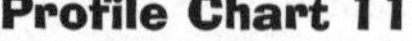

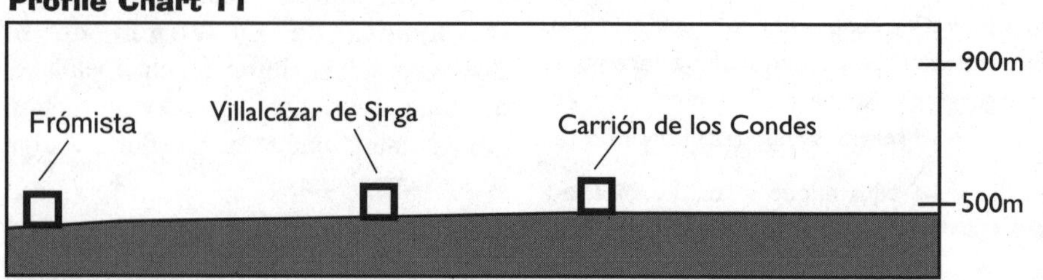

highway shadows the main road all the way to Carrión de los Condes, a quick if dull, exhaust-filled route to follow. It's far nicer to veer away from the road towards the village of Villovieco, which most pilgrims get to via a farm track. Instead of following this track, we describe a pretty route alongside the river, offering great birdwatching, particularly in the early morning.

From La Virgen de la Socorro, follow the raised grassy track to the right-hand side of the river, walking towards a clump of trees. Follow the track as it heads through the trees, broadens out then curves right, still shadowing the river. Shortly after the bend, ignore the bridge to the left, which leads to Revenga de Campos and the road route, and keep walking along the riverbank. In a few hundred metres, turn left at a gravel track to head into **Villovieco**, where the yellow arrows reassuringly reappear. Turn left at the start of the village, then left again 200m later to cross an arched stone bridge over the Río Ucieza.

Turn right at the end of the bridge to follow a dirt track along the left bank of the river. Keep straight on at a concrete bridge a few hundred metres later, or turn left to detour to Villarmentero de Campos, where the Iglesia de San Martín de Tours has some fine Mudéjar touches. This is a very flat stretch of the camino, still winding alongside the tree-lined river, with occasional dips to cross tributary water channels: these can be slippery after rain. This isolated, tranquil walk feels authentically medieval, particularly when you get your first glimpse of the **Ermita de la Virgen del Río** through the trees ahead.

Turn left at a brick and stone arched bridge to walk along a paved road, soon passing the *ermita* on your right. The *ermita* contains an alabaster image of Santiago Peregrino as well as a statue of its namesake, which is said to have swam up the Río Ucieza during a flood and stopped at this site. Follow the road into Villalcázar de Sigar, passing some caves in a small hill on the right and a concrete cross commemorating the 1999 Holy Year. Keep straight on, skirting the village, then turn right just before the main road, following the yellow arrows to the *albergue* and the Iglesia de Santa María la Blanca.

Villalcázar de Sirga

The various alternative routes from Frómista converge at Villalcazar de Sirga, a town with Templar connections that's dominated by the monumental Iglesia de Santa María la Blanca. The camino was re-routed via Villasirgar, as it's commonly known, mainly due to Alfonso X's persistent mention of the Virgen Blanca's miracles in his thirteenth-century *Cántigas*. Her achievements include restoring the sight of a blind pilgrim, helping a nobleman recover his favourite hunting falcon, and saving a crew of Italian pilgrims from a storm at sea after their frantic prayers had been ignored by a succession of saints, including Santiago. The chalice they were taking to Santiago is now in Villasirgar's church treasury.

The Romanesque-Gothic **Iglesia de Santa María la Blanca** is thought to have been built by the Knights Templar, and although their presence in the town was likely short-lived, tacky Templar signs are displayed throughout the village. The enormous church was once even bigger: the west end

was damaged in the 1755 earthquake that flattened Lisbon, and finished off by Napoleon's troop half a century later. The huge, high porch remains, modelled on the Monasterio de Las Huelgas in Burgos. Inside, the Capilla de Santiago's *retablo* shows detailed scenes from the Saint's life and holds the statue of the Virgen Blanca, in squat Romanesque style with a headless Jesus.

Also in the Capilla are the tombs of Don Felipe, Alfonso X's brother, Doña Leonor, Felipe's wife, and a Templar tomb, which is unusual as the knights were generally buried simply, face-down in the earth. Felipe and Alfonso didn't exactly get on: Felipe's first wife was a Norwegian princess promised to and then discarded by Alfonso. Their rivalry eventually spiralled into all-out war, which continued until Felipe died in 1274, possibly murdered by Alfonso's hand.

Villasirgar has an **albergue** (20 beds, kitchen, open all year), and the bar opposite the church makes excellent *tortillas*. Ask at the bar about rooms in the village.

To leave Villasirgar, cross the Plaza Mayor, where there's a fountain, and join up with the roadside track. Head slightly uphill towards Carrión de los Condes — there's a great view of the Cordillera Cantábrica ahead to the right, particularly beautiful when they're dusted with snow.

In about 5km, on reaching the outskirts of Carrión de los Condes, turn left to cross the road and walk past a church decorated with a large mosaic of Jesus. The yellow arrows fork after a few hundred metres; turn left to visit the Monasterio de Santa Clara and the Iglesia de San Francisco, or turn right on to head into Carríon de los Condes, arriving at the Iglesia de Santa María del Camino, where there's an *albergue*.

Carrión de los Condes

Carrión de los Condes was an important medieval town, home to 10,000 people and described by Aymeric Picaud in the tenth century as "an industrious and prosperous town, rich in bread and wine and meat and all fruitfulness." It was also the centre of disputes between Castilla and León, particularly after Alfonso VI of León murdered his brother, Sancho II of Castilla, much to the annoyance of El Cid.

The pro-Castilian epic poem, *El Cantar de mío Cid* recounts the tale of Castilian nobles from Carrión who married El Cid's daughters, took their fortune, and then tied them to oak trees and beat them. El Cid murdered the counts, who gave the town the name *de los Condes*, and who are buried in the **Monasterio de San Zoilo**. This lovely monastery, on the far side of town, contains a beautiful Renaissance cloister with a splendidly carved ceiling.

The **Iglesia de Santa María del Camino** celebrates victory over the Moors in a legendary battle on this site. The local Christian Spanish were understandably annoyed at the annual tribute of 100 virgins demanded by their Moorish rulers, and prayed for deliverance. Santa María obliged, sending a herd of bulls to attack the Moors and drive them away, and her Romanesque statue is one of the highlights of the church's interior.

Although the lovely frieze over the **Iglesia de Santiago**'s twelfth-century façade remains, the church's recent restoration is unsympathetic and critics claim that the renovation did as much damage as Napoleon's troops, who blew up the church in the nineteenth century.

The **Monasterio de Santa Clara**, at the entrance into Carrión de los Condes, sheltered St Francis of Assisi on his pilgrimage to Santiago. It now has a small museum.

Carrión has plenty of shops, restaurants and cafés and some banks. Stock up now, as there are few chances to buy food between Carrión de los Condes and Sahagún, almost 40km away.

The **turismo** is in the Plaza Santa María (☎ 979 88 09 32).

Accommodation

There are two **albergues** in town; one as you come into Carrión in the **Monasterio de Santa Clara** (30 beds, kitchen, open all year) and the other on the way out of Carrión in the **Monasterio San Zoilo** (58 beds, kitchen, open all year).

$ El Resbalón, Calle Marqués de Santillana (☎ 979 88 00 11)

$$ Hostal La Corte, Calle Santa María 34 (☎ 979 88 01 38)

$$$ Hotel Real Monasterio San Zoilo (☎ 979 88 01 38)

It's a dull, shadeless treadmill of a route from Carrión to Calzadilla de la Cueza, about four hours away, with the single, glorious distraction of the Cordillera Cantábrica far away to the right.

Follow the well-marked route through town, turning left to cross the Río Carrión over a sixteenth-century bridge, from where there's a striking view of the distinctive triangular modern bridge to your right. Once on the other side, pass the Monasterio de San Zoilo on your left, opposite some picnic tables and an unhelpful abstract map of the camino.

Cross the C615 and keep straight on the paved road, then in a few hundred metres cross over the busy N120 road. You're now walking on a minor, quiet road through farmland, its unswerving straightness a clue to its Roman origins as the camino once more follows the route of the *Via Traiana* from Burgundy to Astorga. After about 4km, pass the **Abadía de Abajo**, behind which are the ruins of the Abadía de Santa María de Benevívere. Cross a bridge here, then turn right to walk along a stone track built over the old Roman road.

There are great chances to see birds of prey in these skies: look for hen harriers and buzzards in particular. The occasional marshy sections and man-made ponds on either side of the track are home to herons, mallards and coots. If you're lucky, you may see the big, dramatic great bustard, once common in continental Europe but now restricted to the Iberian meseta. Along the long, occasionally tree-lined route into Calzadilla de la Cueza there are also fabulous, endless views, particularly of the Cordillera Cantábrica to the right.

After crossing a road and walking up a slight rise, you spot Calzadilla's church tower from a long way off, and eventually reach the small village. **Calzadilla de la Cueza** (ⒶⒽ✕☕) is a tiny, one-street village tucked into a depression in the *meseta*. The **albergue** (60 beds, kitchen, open all year) is on the left at the entrance to the village, and there's also a good bar-restaurant that has a few rooms.

Map 12 (key page 213)

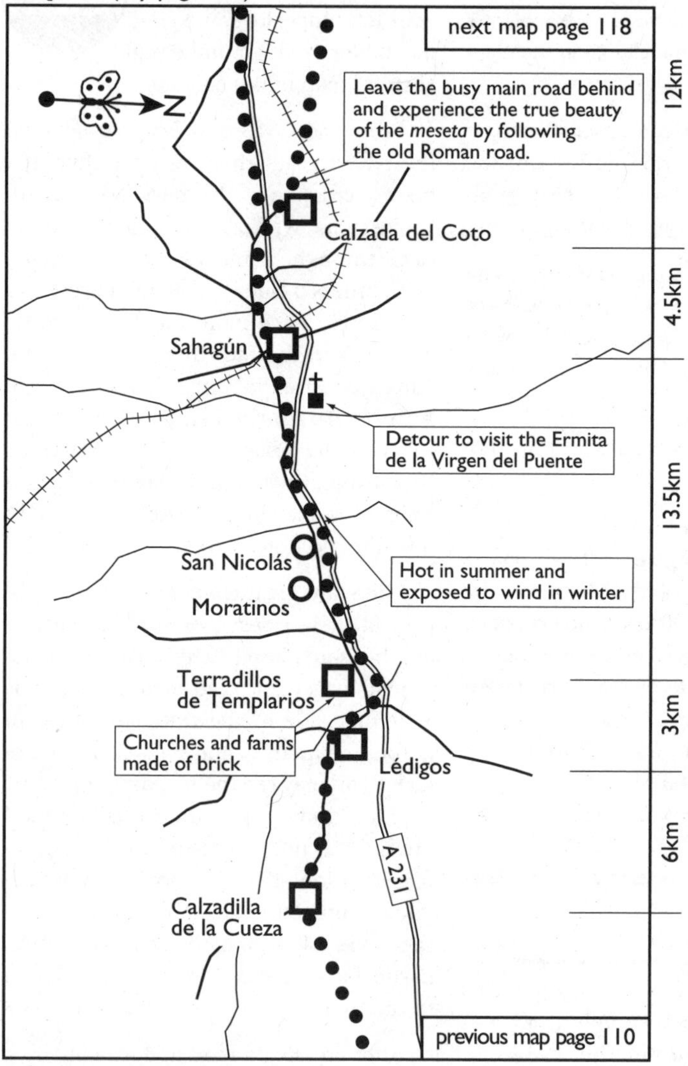

next map page 118
Leave the busy main road behind and experience the true beauty of the *meseta* by following the old Roman road.
12km
Calzada del Coto
4.5km
Sahagún
Detour to visit the Ermita de la Virgen del Puente
13.5km
San Nicolás
Moratinos
Hot in summer and exposed to wind in winter
Terradillos de Templarios
3km
Churches and farms made of brick
Lédigos
6km
A 231
Calzadilla de la Cueza
previous map page 110

Calzada del Coto

Sahagún

Terradillos de Templarios

Lédigos

Calzadilla de la Cueza

Profile Chart 12

900m
Calzadilla de la Cueza
Terradillos de Templarios
Sahagún
500m

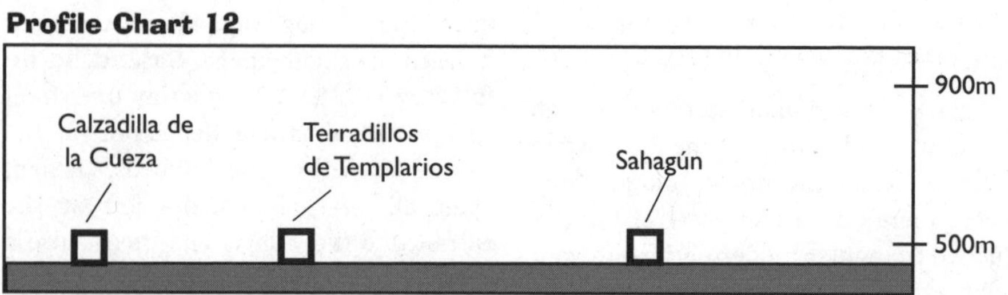

Leave the village on the unnecessarily named Calle Mayor, soon arriving at a worn map of four alternative routes to Lédigos, just before you reach the main N120 road. To follow the road route to Sahagún, turn right at the main road and take the gravel track to the left of the road. On your left, barely visible, are the ruins of the twelfth-century Monasterio de Santa María de Las Tiendas, while the small hills to your right are catacombed with wine cellars. A little further on, there's a large abandoned house with a huge cross made from old oil drums. Walk through fields and trees along an easy track, crossing the dry Río de la Cueza. To the right of the road, at the top of a slight rise, there are picnic tables and a monument; keep straight on along a stone track a few hundred metres further on.

The route shadows the road all the way to Sahagún, with slight detours into the many villages along the way. At the bottom of the hill you arrive at **Lédigos** (Ⓐ), where there's an **albergue** (52 beds, kitchen, open all year). Cross the road to walk through this small village, then cross back over the road and carry on walking on its left-hand side. About 3km later, the camino bears left to visit the hamlet of **Terradillos de Templarios** (Ⓐ). There's not much here apart from an **albergue** (55 beds, kitchen, open all year) and a distinctive church, built from brick because of the lack of nearby stone.

Over the next few kilometres, the camino passes through a couple of blink-and-you'll-miss-them hamlets along the side of the main road. The N120 is quieter here as the new A231 runs alongside it and most drivers prefer to race along the newer, bigger road. After crossing a stream called the Arroyo de Templarios, you come to a picnic area and soon arrive in **Moratinos**, with its wonderful, hobbit-looking underground cellars. Head left to walk through the village, then cross the N120 to walk along its right-hand side. In a little under 3km, arrive at the hamlet of **San Nicolás del Real Camino**, a former Templar village with a reconstructed eighteenth-century brick church.

The roadside track is to the left of the road once more. At the top of a rise, after about 4km, you'll get your first view of Sahagún ahead. Soon afterwards, there's an optional detour to the **Ermita de la Virgen del Puente**, which is characteristic of the local Mudéjar style and sits next to a Roman bridge over the Río Valderaduey. You can also look to the south to see the fifteenth-century fort at Grajal de Campos.

The approach to Sahagún is disheartening, first crammed between two major roads, then heading straight through the town's industrial zone. Eventually, after a couple of kilometres of this, you'll reach the outskirts of Sahagún. Take the first left past the big white grain silo that's dominated the skyline for a while now. Walk past the train station on the left and the bullring on the right, then turn left soon afterwards to cross the railway tracks via a bridge. The *albergue* is on the right as you enter town.

Sahagún Ⓐ Ⓗ €

Sahagún is a busy, no-nonsense town, much more attractive than the ugly approach suggests, and at its best during the hustle and bustle of the Saturday morning market.

Meseta

Sahagún was an important religious and economic centre in the eleventh and twelfth centuries, famous for its plentiful wheat fields, three-week-long markets and the **Vat of Sahagún**, a huge trough of wine. Much of the credit for the town's prosperity must go to Alfonso VI, who showered money and prestige on the town in gratitude for the help he received from the **Monasterio de San Benito** during the war with his brother, Sancho III. It became the most powerful Benedictine monastery in Spain, at its peak controlling almost 100 other monasteries, and home to a prestigious university. But the glory wasn't to last, and both the town and the monastery were in steep decline by the time a couple of eighteenth-century fires razed much of Sahagún.

Today, nothing remains of the monastery, apart from a crumbling nineteenth-century tower and the twelfth-century Romanesque Capilla de San Mancio. The arch of San Benito, which formed part of the monastery façade, is now a city gate, straddling a street at the far end of town.

Near the arch is the twelfth-century **Iglesia de San Tirso**, a splendid example of the brick Mudéjar architecture of the *meseta*. Although wheat and vines are plentiful, the region has very little stone, and local craftsmen, many of them settlers from North Africa, devised a brick-based building method as a necessary and creative response to the stone shortage. Look out for the closed, horseshoe-shaped arches and the simple, unornamented design, possibly influenced by Islam's prohibition of human and animal representation.

It's also worth looking at the decorative brickwork and the Muslim influences found in Sahagún's other main churches, the Romanesque-Gothic Iglesia de San Lorenzo and the Santuario de la Peregrina, a twelfth-century Gothic-Mudéjar church that was once part of a Franciscan monastery.

Accommodation

The **albergue** (85 beds, kitchen, open all year) is just on the right after you cross the railway bridge.

$ Pensión la Asturiana, Plaza de Lesmes Franco 2 (☎ 987 78 00 73)

$$ Hostal Alfonso VI, Calle Antonio Nicolás 6 (☎ 987 78 11 44)

$$ Hospedería Benedictina, Santa Cruz (☎ 987 78 00 78)

The walk out of Sahagún is a brief yet pleasant one, passing street lamps decorated with scallop shells, then crossing the stone, arched Puente de Canto, originally built by Alfonso VI in 1085. Cross the road and walk on the gravel track alongside it, where trees planted on either side provide some shade.

The grove of poplars next to the campsite on your right is the site of the eighth-century Legend of the Flowering Lances. Charlemagne's troops, preparing for battle with Aigolando the next day, stuck their lances into the ground. When they awoke the next day, some of the lances had grown bark and were covered in leafy branches, a sign of martyrdom. Although the lances were cut down, the omens proved true as the battle, along with some 40,000 of Charlemagne's men, was lost. The lances again took root, and a large forest grew where they had been planted.

In a couple of kilometres, you'll see the village of Calzada del Coto ahead, and soon the track ends at a maze of roads, excessive and underused even by Spanish roadbuilding standards. Cross the road here, following a faded yellow arrow, and continue on the other side of the road. At a bus stop in 100m, the route splits.

The original *camino francés* mostly follows the road to Mansilla de las Mulas, passing through Bercianos (Ⓐ, 37 beds, kitchen open all year) and El Burgo Ranero (Ⓐ, 26 beds, kitchen, open all year). More pleasant, though with fewer facilities, is the Calzada de los Peregrinos, the route we describe that heads along dry, thyme-scented tracks across the *meseta*. If you do head this way, it's a good idea to buy food in Calzada del Coto, as Calzadilla de los Hermanillos' culinary options are limited to a small shop and *bocadillos* in the bar. You'll also need to ford a thigh-deep, slow-moving stream.

To follow the camino to Calzadillo de los Hermanillos, turn right, following a yellow arrow and the road signs for Calzada del Coto. Cross the A231 on a road bridge and reach Calzada in a few hundred metres.

Calzada del Coto (Ⓐ) is a small village with a bar, grocery and a tiny **albergue** (24 beds, no kitchen, open all year) next to the football field, which can be opened by the woman who lives across the road.

Leave the village via Calle Real, which soon changes into a wide, dirt road. Take the right-hand fork in a couple of hundred metres, passing some farm buildings. It's a flat landscape of close-cropped grass and scrubland, and the yellow arrows painted on low stones can be hard to spot. In a kilometre or so, follow a short tarmac section to cross a bridge over a railway. You're walking along an old Roman road, and there are said to be a couple of Roman milestones at the Dehesa de Valdelocajos, a small hill you'll climb a few kilometres after crossing the railway.

Eventually, the village of Calzadilla de los Hermanillos comes into view as the land becomes more fertile and you pass a shaded picnic spot with a fountain and swings on your right. Although there are many wheat fields here, flowing and rustling in spring, sheep have been the region's agricultural staple since the Middle Ages, when flocks of up to 40,000 sheep were commonplace.

A couple of kilometres after the picnic area, you arrive in **Calzadilla de los Hermanillos** (Ⓐ). The small **albergue** (16 beds, kitchen, open all year) is on the left as you enter the village, and it's a lovely, little-visited place to stay. Off-season, it's so quiet that you may need to buy your own toilet paper. There's a small village shop, and a couple of bars, one of which serves *bocadillos* — but not before 9pm. It's fascinating to wander around the simple, timeless village, checking out the adobe architecture and getting lost amongst the maze-like streets.

Walk out of Calzadilla on the main street. The route for the next few hours is so straightforward that all you have to do is keep straight ahead for 20km or so. There are no villages along the stony track, and nothing to distract you on the flat, endless expanse apart from whiffs of lavender, wild thyme and a variety of birds: look out for hoopoes, with their dramatic crests, whoop-whoop call, and loping flight.

The camino crosses the occasional stream, and slowly veers towards and

Map 13 (key page 213)

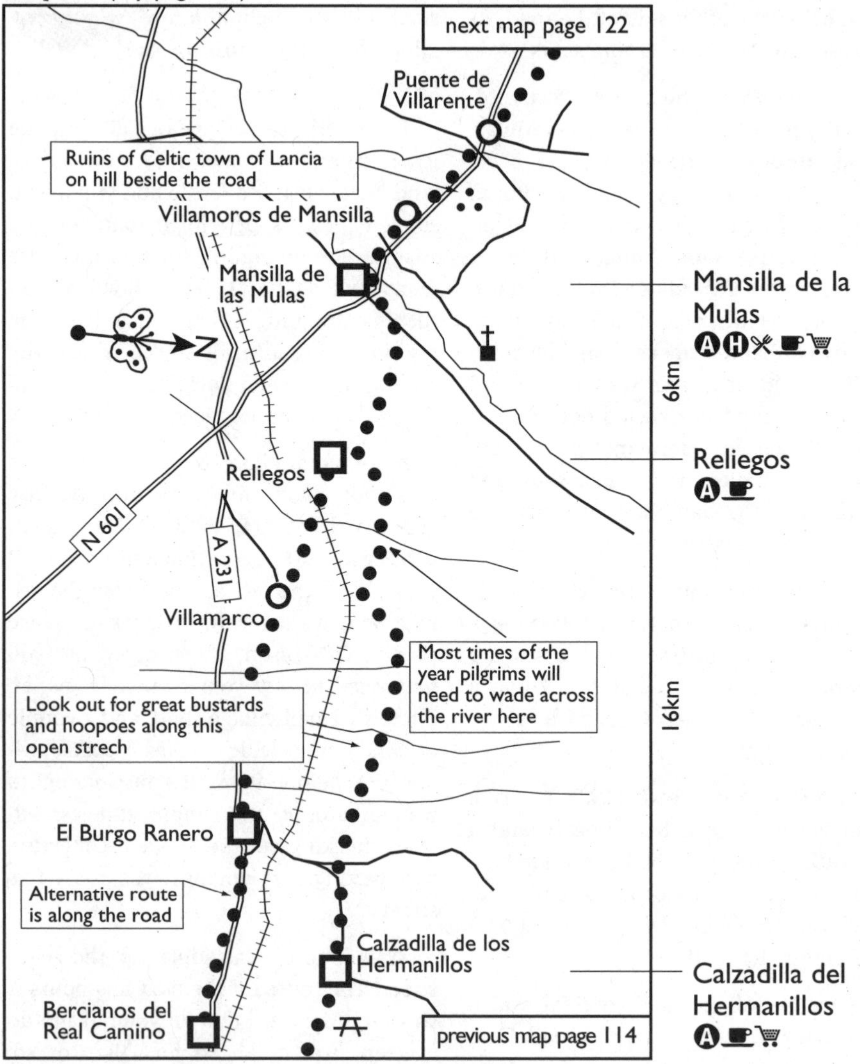

next map page 122
Puente de Villarente
Ruins of Celtic town of Lancia on hill beside the road
Villamoros de Mansilla
Mansilla de las Mulas
N
Reliegos
N 601
A 231
Villamarco
Most times of the year pilgrims will need to wade across the river here
Look out for great bustards and hoopoes along this open strech
El Burgo Ranero
Alternative route is along the road
Calzadilla de los Hermanillos
Bercianos del Real Camino
previous map page 114
6km
16km
Mansilla de la Mulas
Reliegos
Calzadilla del Hermanillos

Profile Chart 13

900m
500m
Calzadilla de los Hermanillos
Reliegos
Mansilla de las Mulas

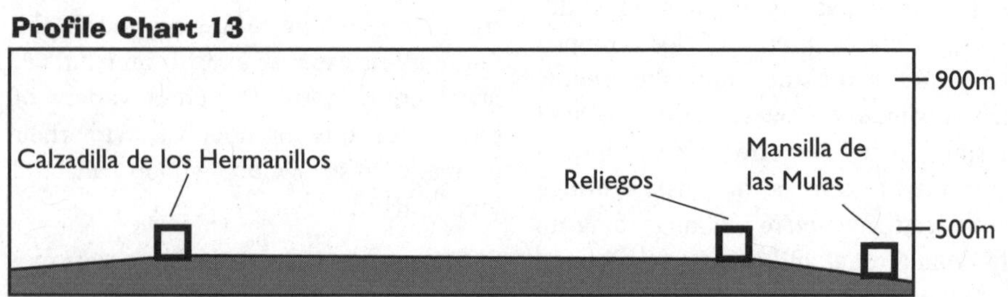

then away from the railway near Villamarco, over to your left on the *camino francés*.

Eventually, the route dips into a slight hollow where you have to ford a river, which can be anything from knee to thigh deep. It's slow-moving, and it's easy to see where to put your feet, but for safety's sake, undo the waist strap of your rucksack before crossing in case you slip. As well as providing a fleeting adrenalin rush, the crossing is an authentic taste of the kind of obstacles faced by medieval pilgrims.

Up ahead, you'll see the village of **Reliegos** (Ⓐ) where there's an *albergue* (100 beds, kitchen, open all year). The camino curves to the right, bypassing the village and heads downhill along a straight track with very few yellow arrows and views of Mansilla de las Mulas in the distance. After about 3km, turn left on reaching a narrow tarmac road, then turn left again on reaching the N625 about 1km later. Soon afterwards, cross the road and walk along its right-hand side past a modern hotel. Head under a road bridge, past a cemetery on the right, then through the Puerta de Santiago into the old walled centre of Mansilla de las Mulas. The *albergue* is on the main street, just past the square on the left.

Mansilla de las Mulas ⒶⒽ

An elegant town of pleasant plazas, Mansilla de las Mulas is circled by splendid medieval walls. The fancy *pastelarías* that line the main square might seem ostentatious after the simple adobe houses of Calzadilla de la Cueza, but their sweet, gooey offerings are sublime. *Mansilla* may derive from the Spanish for "hand" and "saddle", and the town's crest depicts a hand resting on a saddle; *Mulas* refers to the town's mule market.

The **walls**, in some places an impressive three metres thick, were successively built, destroyed and rebuilt in the Middle Ages. Much of the wall is still intact and it's worth walking all the way around town to get a closer look. Highlights include the stretch of wall along the banks of the Río Esla, and the Arco de la Concepción, the only intact gate.

Accommodation

Albergue (70 beds, kitchen open all year).
$$ Hostal Las Delicias, Calle Los Mesones 22 (☎ 987 31 00 75)
$$ Hostal Los Faroles, Avenida Picos de Europa 32 (☎ 987 31 09 49)

The long approach into León from Mansilla de las Mulas is an uninspiring one, mostly following the busy N120. To leave Mansilla, walk past the *albergue* and keep straight on across the stone bridge over the Río Esla, looking behind you for fabulous views of the city walls. There are hills ahead and mountains in the distance, a welcome break for the eyes after the flat *meseta*. At the end of the bridge, cross the road to the gravel track parallel to the road. The hill on your right was the site of Lancia, the last holdout of the Celtic Asturians before the city was captured by the Romans in 26BC.

The gravel track ends and you rejoin the road just after a sign for **Villamoros de Mansilla**, a few kilometres outside Mansilla de las Mulas. Walk through the village on the road, then rejoin the track soon after the village. In a few hundred

metres, follow a narrow path up to a side road, then turn left on joining the main road soon afterwards. Cross the Río Porma over the rickety, forlorn and much-restored 20-arch bridge that leads into Puente de Vilarente, passing a picnic area on your right.

Puente de Vilarente (🅗✕☕🛒) has shops and restaurants, although the donkey taxi that once took sick pilgrims from the old hospice at the end of the bridge into León no longer exists. If you want to stay, try **Hostal El Delfín Verde** (**$**, ☎ 987 31 20 65) or **Hostal La Montañesa** (**$$**, ☎ 987 31 21 61).

At the far side of Puente de Vilarente, cross the N120 at a petrol station, then turn right almost immediately down a gravel track. Walk under some power lines and past a few industrial buildings, heading gradually uphill. Walk through **Arcahueja**, passing a playground, and then ignore the track to the left about 1km later that detours to the village of **Valdelafuente** (☕): both the detour and the regular camino are signed. Climb uphill, passing factories and getting deceived by false summits, then about 1km after the road to Valdelafuente, turn left on reaching a minor road.

In about 300m, cross the N120 at a particularly polluted and busy stretch, then turn right to walk along the left-hand side of the road, climbing slightly. At the top of the hill there are fabulous views of León spreading out into the *meseta*, with the glorious backdrop of the often snow-tipped Montes de León and the Cordillera Cantábrica. Despite the views, this is one of the nastiest stretches of the camino, following an exhaust-choked major road.

In another few hundred metres, just as you get your first view of León's cathedral, veer left down a wide modern street as the main road curves to the right. You'll soon find yourself in **Puente Castro** (✕☕🛒), now merged into suburban León, where there are plenty of café-bars, the dilapidated Iglesia de San Pedro, and some curious subterranean houses. In a little under a kilometre, you'll reach the bridge that gives Puente Castro its name. Turn left to avoid the bridge, originally Roman but rebuilt in the eighteenth century, and instead cross the Río Torío over a pedestrianised bridge 50m further on.

At a roundabout soon afterwards, turn left for León's municipal *albergue*, but keep straight on for the second *albergue*, the city centre and the camino. The route into León is well-marked with yellow arrows and the occasional brass scallop shell embedded into the sidewalk. Walk down Calle Alcade Miguel Castaño, cross the road in about 1km, and then walk through a small park, Plaza Santa Ana. Walk up Calle Barahora, veering right to visit León's second *albergue* in the Monasterio Benedictino de las Hermanas Carbajalas, or keeping straight on to head to the cathedral. Turn right up Calle Generalismo Franco, passing through the city walls, and arrive at the cathedral in about 500m.

León 🅐🅗✕☕€🅘🛒

León is a delightful city of open squares, wide pedestrianised boulevards and narrow, café-crammed winding streets. By day, office workers stride meaningfully about town, but in the evening the city noticeably relaxes as families, couples and friends slowly promenade in their stylish finery, window-shopping and *tapas* bar crawling until the small hours.

Founded by the Romans in the first century to guard the gold mines further west, León was used as a base to subdue the pesky, dogged inhabitants of what are now Galicia and Asturias. León's heyday came about a millennium later, beginning when Ordoño II transferred the Christian capital from Oviedo to León in the tenth century, building monuments and settling on a site for the cathedral. Just 80 years later, the city was destroyed by al-Mansur's Muslim troops, but León's momentum was unstoppable, and the city that grew from the ruins became bigger and more important than ever. As León's kingdom became unwieldy and difficult to govern, the kingdom of Castilla was created, with a capital in Burgos. The two kingdoms officially united under Fernando III in 1252, but León was quickly subsumed into her younger, bigger offspring. This still rankles with *Leóneses*, and although separatism isn't as strong a movement as in the Basque Lands or Galicia, you'll see lots of *Léon sin Castilla* (León without Castilla) graffiti scrawled on road signs.

León's glorious, light-filled **cathedral** is a masterpiece of Gothic architecture, its stunning walls of **glass** stretching upwards in a riot of colour. Serene in cloudy weather and dazzling in the afternoon sun, the cathedral's open, thirteenth century, French design allows beams of light to play across the nave, leading the eye upwards to a sumptuous feast of blues and reds and greens.

You'll get a crick in your neck from wandering around and around the cathedral to take in the gorgeous, luminous whole, so it's worth bringing binoculars to get a better look at the windows' fine detail. Stained glass was popular with patrons; guild-funded windows depict craftsmen and other workers, while others place noble benefactors next to saints and religious figures.

Back at ground level, almost every surface of the wooden fifteenth-century **choir-stalls** is carved with religious imagery and personification of the vices. Look for gluttony heaving his belly in a wheelbarrow, a lusty priest spanking a naked boy, and an avaricious noble being led into hell for his gambling sins. The cathedral's **chapels** are lovely and contain some beautiful Gothic tombs, including those of Ordoño II and Bishop Martín Rodríguez el Zamorano, one of the driving forces behind the cathedral's construction.

The most interesting exhibits in the **Museo Diocesano**, reached through the Gothic cloister, are the intricate, black and white prints of the cathedral's stained glass windows, a fascinating testament to the artisanship of the glassmakers and beautiful in their own right.

Once you've had your fill of the cathedral's Gothic glory, saunter down Calle Ancha, turn right at Gaudí's **Casa Botines**, a fairytale palace tame by the architect's flamboyant standards, and arrive at the **Basílica de San Isidoro**, home to the best-preserved and most splendid Romanesque **frescoes** in Spain. The church, built on the site of a Roman temple to Mercury, was commissioned by Fernando I and constructed in the eleventh century to house the bones of San Isidoro, a Visigothic archbishop, scholar and author of the world's first encyclopaedia. It's not exactly clear why the remains of San Isidoro, who was from Seville, came to be in León, although the romantic view is that the saint's bones could not rest once he heard of the reconquista, and demanded to be moved from Muslim southern Spain to the Christian north. Another version has Fernando accepting saintly relics from the Moors as a price of surrender; the bishops of León and Astorga

Map 14 (key page 213)

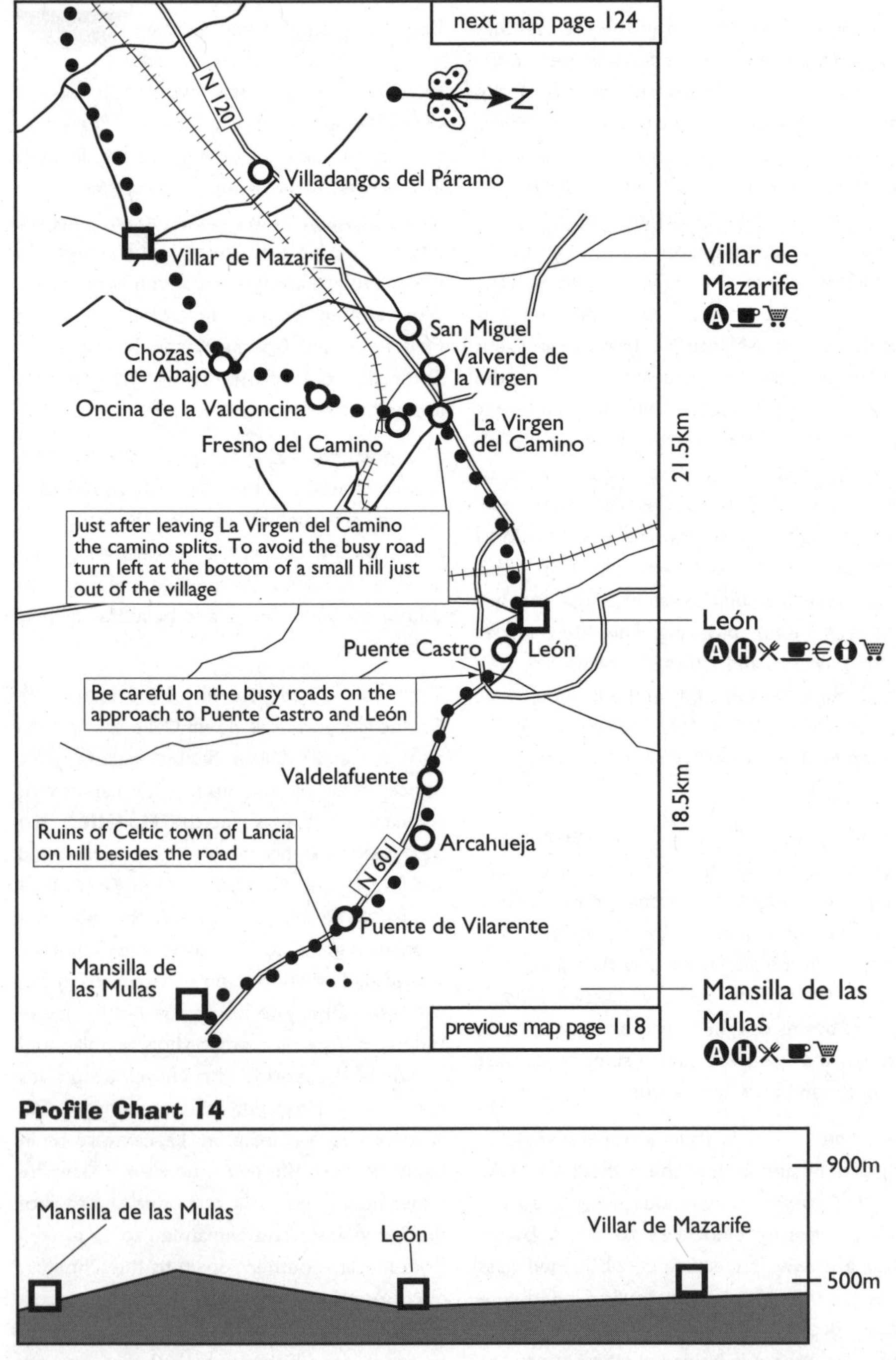

made the trek down south to collect the bones of Santa Justa, but somehow ended up with San Isidoro instead.

The church itself is worth visiting for its carved capitals and the **Puerta del Perdón**, the first Door of Pardon on the camino, through which sick pilgrims could pass and be granted the same absolution as pilgrims who reached Santiago. Next door is the **Panteón de los Reyes**, magnificent resting place of a string of monarchs from Fernando onwards until Napoleon's troops desecrated the tombs. Although the tombs are gone, the Romanesque frescoes remain, thick with intense colour and vivid imagery.

The frescoes date from the beginning of the thirteenth century and are unrestored — it's staggering to think that these painting have been in place for almost 800 years. Most of the ceiling and arches are taken up with various scenes from the life of Jesus, from the flight into Egypt to Christ in heaven. One of the frescoes shows a month-by-month representation of the farming year: in October, a man harvests acorns, a couple of pigs standing happily at his feet, but by November, one of the pigs is done for, slaughtered for food. The capitals at the far end, flanking the original entrance to the church, depict Lazarus' resurrection and the curing of a leper; this is probably the earliest example of figurative sculpture in Spain. Above the Panteón, the museum displays valuable treasures from the church, including the silver reliquary of San Isidoro, while the small library holds a collection of massive, illuminated books from as early as the tenth century.

The **Hospital de San Marcos**, along the camino on the way out of town, was a hospice from the twelfth to the fifteenth centuries, and served as a monastery and headquarters of the Knights of Santiago for even longer. The current building, fronted by a magnificent, huge Renaissance façade and topped by a Baroque Santiago Matamoros, is now a luxury *parador* with a sumptuous, antiques-filled interior. The chapterhouse contains an archaeological museum that includes Roman weapons from León and Maragato artefacts from around Astorga, and there are also medieval treasures in the church sacristy.

León is a big city with all facilities, some excellent restaurants and wonderful *tapas* bars. The **turismo** is on Plaza de Regla 4, opposite the cathedral (☎ 987 23 70 82).

Accommodation

León has two **albergues**. The municipal *albergue* (64 beds, kitchen, open all year) at the entrance into the city, and the one at the Monasterio Benedictino de las Hermanas Carbajalas (45 beds, no kitchen, open all year) closer to the centre,

$ Pensíon Puerta del Sol, Calle Puerta del Sol 1 (☎ 987 21 19 66)

$$ Hostal Guzmán el Bueno (☎ 987 23 64 12)

$$$ Hostal Boccalino, Plaza San Isidoro 9 (☎ 987 20 30 60)

$$$$ Parador San Marcos, Plaza San Marcos 7 (☎ 987 23 73 00)

It's a long exit out of Léon through suburbs and an industrial zone, but you'll eventually find yourself in a familiar landscape of red soil and endless horizons. It's clear that the *meseta* is coming to an end, though, and greener sections and undulating hills lighten the monotony.

A bus-tour-style trip past León's famous sights leads you out of town. From the cathedral, walk down Calle Ancha, turn right at the Casa Botines,

Map 15 (key page 213)

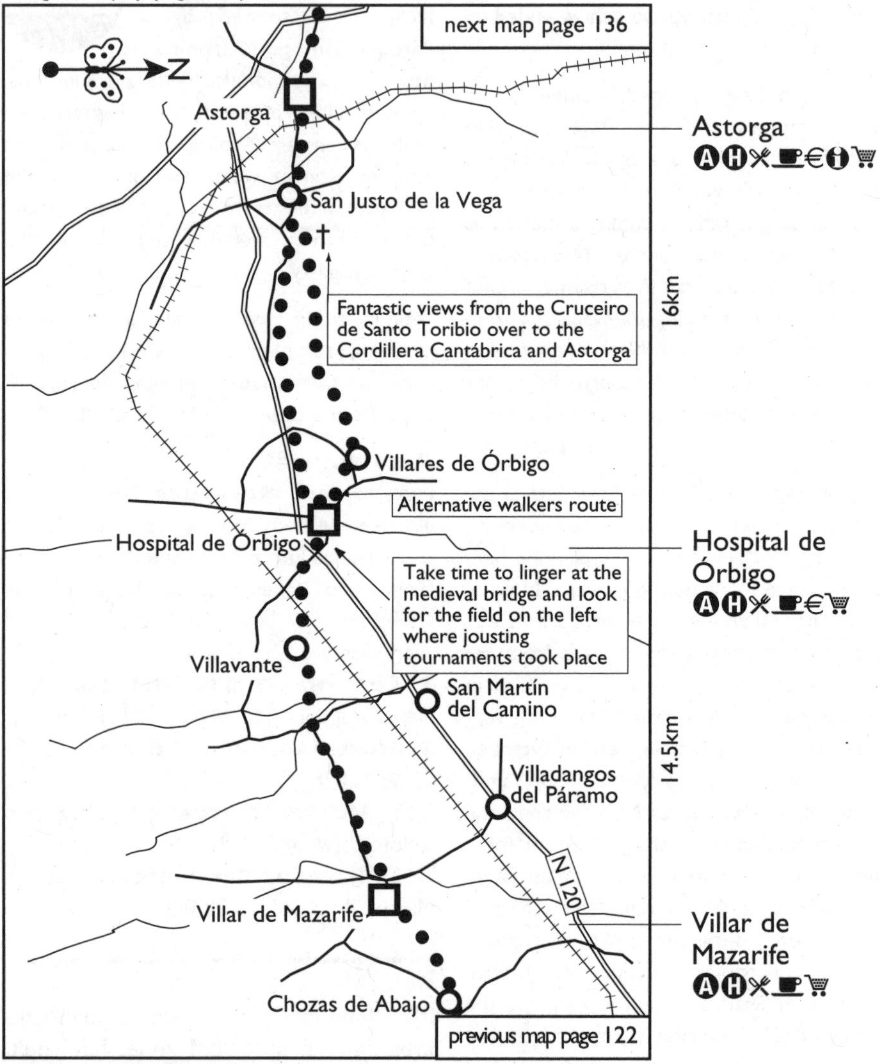

next map page 136

Z

Astorga

San Justo de la Vega

Fantastic views from the Cruceiro de Santo Toribio over to the Cordillera Cantábrica and Astorga

16km

Villares de Órbigo

Alternative walkers route

Hospital de Órbigo

Take time to linger at the medieval bridge and look for the field on the left where jousting tournaments took place

Villavante

San Martín del Camino

14.5km

Villadangos del Páramo

N 120

Villar de Mazarife

Chozas de Abajo

previous map page 122

Astorga
A H € i

Hospital de Órbigo
A H €

Villar de Mazarife
A H

Profile Chart 15

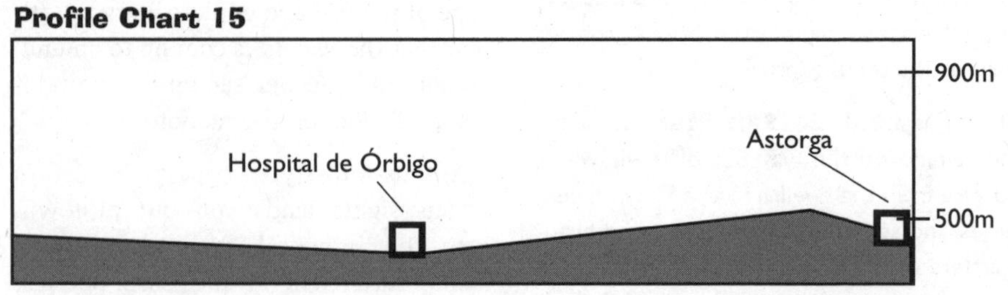

walk past San Isidoro and follow Calle Ramón y Cajal, then turn left down Calle Renueva to the Hospital de San Marcos. Walk past the *parador* and over the old Puente de San Marcos that spans the shallow Río Bernesga. Follow the main road for a while, then veer left at an old boundary cross in a little under a kilometre and take a modern footbridge up and over the train tracks.

At the other side of the bridge, the camino soon rejoins the main road at **Trobajo del Camino** (Ⓗ✕☕🛒), passing the Ermita de Santiago. If you want to stay, try **Hostal Bella ($,** ☎ 987 80 28 10) or **Hostal La Gárgola ($,** ☎ 987 80 61 80). A few hundred metres later, look out for a sharp left and then an immediate right-hand turn that takes you parallel to the road, heading uphill through a new housing estate. When the camino rejoins the main road in about 300m, cross over to walk up the Camino de la Cruz, passing some quirky underground houses like the ones you saw on the way into Léon. Turn around for great views of León as you head uphill and into an ugly industrial zone. In about 3km, turn right on meeting the N120 again and put your life into the hands of the speeding drivers who make this 400m section into La Virgen del Camino nerve-racking.

La Virgen del Camino Ⓗ✕☕🛒

In the early sixteenth century, the Virgin Mary appeared to a local shepherd and demanded that he build her a shrine. The bishop of León was unconvinced until the shepherd used his slingshot to hurl a pebble that turned into a boulder on striking the ground. The cult of the Virgin took off rapidly, spreading throughout León in a few short years. In 1522, a merchant was held captive by the Moors in North Africa, chained inside a strongbox. The Virgin, knowing of the merchant's desire to visit her shrine, miraculously transported him, chains, box and all, to La Virgen del Camino.

The façade of the modern 1961 church is dominated by a massive, modernist sculpture of the Virgin and the Apostles, with Santiago pointing towards Compostela. Inside, the merchant's box and chains are held in the sacristy. The Virgen del Camino's feast days are on September 15 and October 10.

Accommodation

$ Hostal Julio César (☎ 987 30 20 44)
$$ Hostal Soto (☎ 987 80 29 25)
$$ Hostal Central (☎ 987 30 20 41)

Just after passing the church, cross the N120 and take the small paved road downhill, parallel to the main road. In 100m, the camino splits. The authentic *camino francés* follows the main road, some 28km of cars whistling by at 100kph. The more peaceful option, and the one we describe, heads along minor country roads and farm tracks towards Hospital de Órbigo.

To follow the peaceful route, turn left where the path splits, cross a large dirt track soon afterwards and climb uphill. Once you reach the top of a small rise, bear left along a paved road, then walk under the A66 through a tunnel. Keep straight on, skirting the edge of the modern hamlet of **Fresno del Camino**, then following the road into **Oncina de la Valdoncina**. At a T-junction, turn right then first left towards a playground in a small square. Take the dirt track at the far

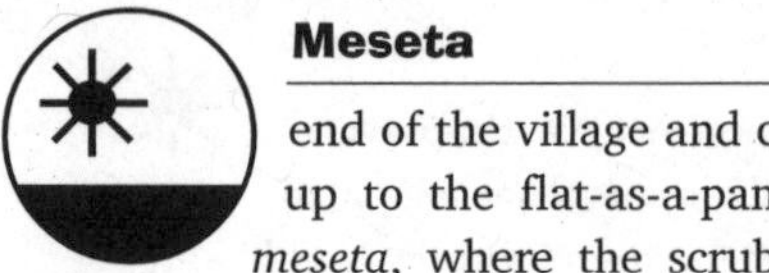

end of the village and climb up to the flat-as-a-pancake *meseta*, where the scrubland is punctuated by occasional vineyards and fields, and pilgrims are keenly watched by swallows and black kites. Keep left at a junction soon afterwards, then in a few kilometres, you'll see **Chozas de Abajo** up ahead. Cross a paved road and bear right along a minor road just before entering the village; bear left to visit the village café-bar.

Follow the flat minor road all the way to **Villar de Mazarife** (Ⓐ), a little over 4km away. On the way into Villar de Mazarife there's a splendid medieval-style mosaic on the right, showing pilgrims on their way to Santiago. There are a couple of good shops here, a bar and an **albergue** (24 beds, kitchen, open all year), a quirky museum on the right as you enter the village, and a small park as you leave, ideal for picnics.

There's nothing to do on the long, shade-free 10km stretch from Villar de Mazarife to Villavante apart from wonder why there are so many small white vans in this part of Spain. After 6km, cross over a main road to a dirt farm track and almost immediately curve to cross an aqueduct. Follow this track to Villavante, where the UFO-shaped water tower seems to hover extra-terrestrially above the church. The yellow arrows give you the option of detouring right into **Villavante** () to visit the village bar or shop, but otherwise keep straight on.

The walk is a little more pleasant here, shaded by poplar trees. You'll soon cross some train tracks — stop to wave at eastbound trains, as they'll likely be carrying pilgrims on their way home from Santiago. Look for yellow arrows, as recent roadworks have altered the camino into Hospital de Órbigo. The route leads across a bridge, past a factory, then crosses the N120 and arrives about 300m later at the foot of the fabulous medieval bridge into Hospital de Órbigo.

Hospital de Órbigo

ⒶⒽ€

Hospital de Órbigo is a strategic town, located on a bank of the Río Órbigo. The river crossing was the scene of a vicious battle between the Suevi and the Visigoths in 452, and Alfonso III defeated the Moors here in the late ninth century. Puente de Órbigo, the multi-arched Gothic bridge that's one of the most important of the camino, was built in the thirteenth century, and though it has been destroyed by floods many times since, its appearance remains resolutely medieval.

The most famous episode in the bridge's history is the quest of the lovelorn Don Suero de Quiñones. In 1434, rejected by his lady love, Suero put an iron collar around his neck as a sign that he was still shackled to her. He vowed to keep the collar on until he had broken 300 lances in fights on the bridge with the best knights in Europe.

Many knights rose to the challenge and Suero and his friends were kept busy fighting them off. The tournament took place during a Holy Year and began a couple of weeks before the Día de Santiago on July 25, the peak time of year for pilgrim traffic. Suero successfully defended the bridge against all-comers and eventually reached his 300-lance target. Taking off his iron collar, Suero journeyed to Santiago, and deposited his lady's jewelled bracelet; it now encircles the neck of the statue of Santiago Alfeo in the cathedral. It's said that Suero's story may have inspired

Cervantes' *Don Quixote*. The jousting tournament is recreated at the beginning of June each year next to the bridge.

Accommodation

Hospital de Órbigo has a couple of **albergues**; the municipal *albergue* (18 beds, kitchen, open all year) at the river is reached by turning right at the end of the bridge. The other *albergue* (60 beds, kitchen, open all year) is run by a German group, and is on the main street.

$$ Hostal El Kanguro Australiano (☎ 987 38 90 31)

$$ Hotel Paso Honroso (☎ 987 36 10 10)

$$ Hostal Suero de Quiñones (☎ 987 38 82 38)

To continue the camino, keep straight on down Hospital do Órbrigo's main street. At the end of the village, the camino splits into two; both routes are signposted. Turn right for the walkers' route, and keep straight on for the road route, which is the one we describe.

Walk along a flat stone track that soon becomes a gravel track alongside the N120, and follow this road almost all the way to Astorga. After about 2km, the gravel track changes to a little-used tarmac road. Join the main road briefly, walking along the shoulder, then veer off the road 30m later to walk on a disused tarmac road. The mountains up ahead are getting much closer, signalling the imminent end of flat *meseta* walking. In spring, look out for nesting birds in the red cliffs to your right.

In a few hundred metres, the road changes to a grassy path, then soon crosses the main road and follows the same disused road, now to the left of the N120. There's yet another new road being built further to the left, so this route will soon be unattractively sandwiched in between a couple of main roads, making for less-than-interesting, exhaust-filled walking. The road climbs slightly — the first hill for a while — giving some great views of the mountains ahead. Soon after the rise, cross the main road once more at a large camino information sign, watching out for fast-moving traffic.

You're now walking through scrubland and, as the main road starts to go downhill, the camino finally veers away from the N120 to head towards San Justo de la Vega. Pass a stone cross, walk steeply downhill, then turn right to join the road into **San Justo de la Vega** (H☕🛒). There are a few cafés and shops here, and beds at **Hostal Juli** (**$**, ☎ 987 61 76 32), but you're not too far away from Astorga by this point.

At the end of San Justo, cross a bridge over the Río Tuerto, then turn right off the road on to a stone track, which winds through factories, gardens and fields. As town entrances go, this one is very low key and non-industrial. Walk over a stone footbridge, then turn left to walk along a tarmac road.

Join the main road 50m later and turn right, then cross some train tracks and turn left 200m later to walk down a side road. You're soon in Astorga proper. Follow the yellow arrows steeply uphill, then at the top of the hill, keep straight on for the *albergue,* and turn right for the cathedral. There are in fact two *albergues*, but all pilgrims must go to the first one to register.

Regional Map (key page 213)

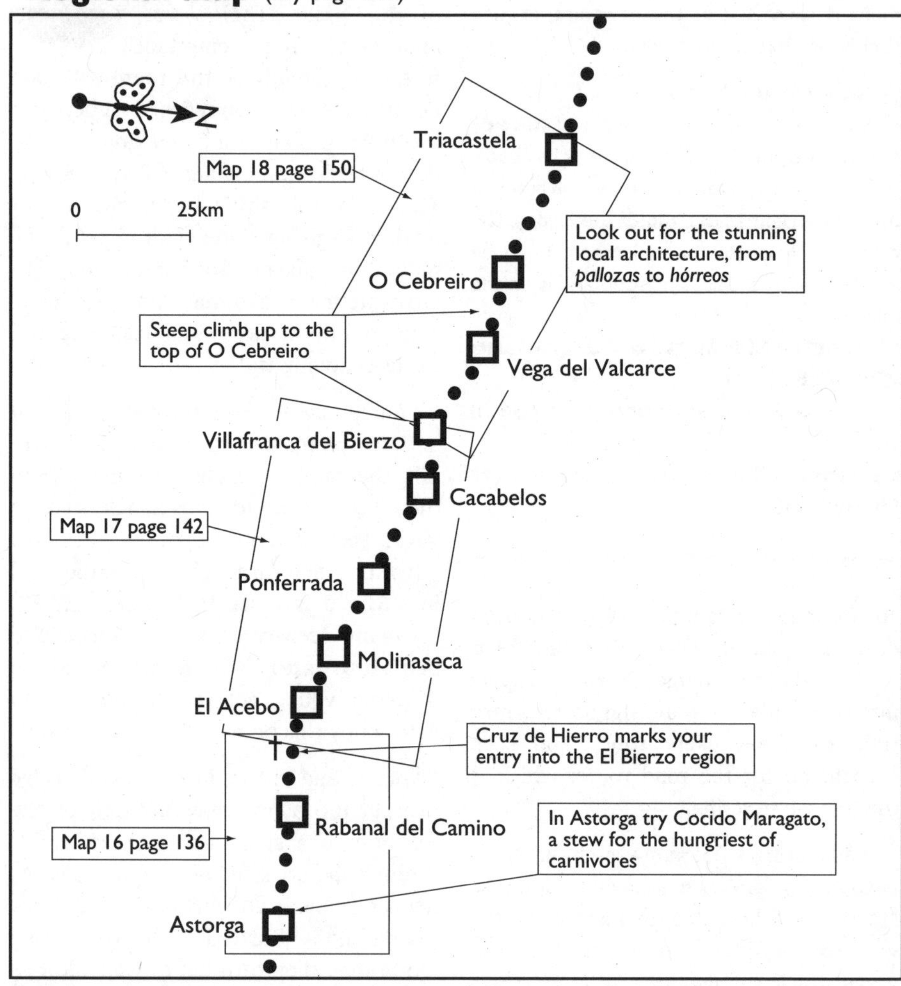

What's the weather like?

	Jan	April	July	Oct
Sun	3hrs	5hrs	7hrs	5hrs
Rainfall	30cm	19cm	6cm	19cm
Maximum Temp	6°C	13°C	24°C	14°C
Minimum Temp	-2°C	3°C	15°C	5°C

Average hours of sun, total average rainfall in cm and average temperature in degrees celsius
Figures are for the mountains; it's warmer, drier and sunnier in the Bierzo valley

Cordillera Cantábrica

Astorga to Triacastela

From Astorga to Triacastela you'll haul yourself over a couple of misty mountain passes, walking through the land of the Maragatos, Spain's ancient muleteers, and passing into Galicia. Sandwiched between these passes is the fertile El Bierzo valley, home to delicious wine, a Templar castle at Ponferrada, and the best and strangest *albergue* of the camino at Villafranca del Bierzo.

Walking

Geography

The Cordillera Cantábrica curl down from Asturias in the shape of a ram's horn, their slate, schist, quartzite and sandstone foothills jutting into the camino's way. High winds batter the mountains whatever the season, and inhibit the growth of all but the hardiest of life, while the proximity of the Atlantic means that heavy rain or even snowstorms can move in without warning at almost any time of the year.

In contrast to the mountains, the El Bierzo valley is an oasis of calm and warmth, a sunny microclimate protected by the mountains from wind and rain. It can be as much as fifteen degrees celsuis warmer at the bottom of the valley than at the top of the mountains. The climate is warm enough to grow grapes and the region is fast developing into a respected wine-growing region.

Trails

Narrow tarmac roads make up the majority of the route. The climb up and over O Cebreiro is on an old stony path, heavily used by local cattle traffic and the souvenirs they leave behind can make it slippery when wet. In whiteout conditions, snow poles along the side of the road can be followed for guidance.

When to go

It can rain at any time of year in the mountains. Summers are sunniest but the camino becomes very crowded as you get closer to Santiago, and *albergues* can be a bit of a squash. In winter, it's not uncommon for snow to cover sections of the camino and the lack of heating in *albergues* can make things a bit chilly.

Spring and autumn are a gamble, as the

weather can swing from snow to sun, and all things in between, in a few hours.

Flora & Fauna

The mountain moorland consists of hardy, low-growing plants such as heather, broom and wild thyme. Out of the wind and lower down the mountains, silver birch, sweet chestnut and oak grow in protected pockets.

The **wolf** is at the apex of the food chain here and, despite years of persecution by hunters, there are thought to be a couple of thousand animals left in Iberia. Wolves need open space to roam, as they can cover anything from 20 to 40km in a single day, smell prey or a potential mate up to 2km away and, incredibly, hear sounds from up to 10km away. While the wolf feeds mainly on wild boar and roe deer, the smaller beech marten, which looks like a large, stocky weasel, patrols mature woodlands looking for voles, shrews and mice.

In good weather, birds of prey can be seen soaring above. The pale breasted **short-toed eagle** likes to ride thermals and is often spotted hovering with its legs dangling down ready to swoop, while the **golden eagle** is able to crush a rabbit in its powerful feet. The **sparrowhawk**, which also hunts in these mountains, is often seen perched on a stump, holding its prey down with one foot and tearing at the flesh with its beak. At the edge of forests the **honey buzzard** hunts for wasps, its main prey.

Less violent birds are also commonly spotted. The **black woodpecker**'s characteristic dipping flight is seen in woodland areas, while lower down, the less elegant **grey partridge** is more likely to waddle away than fly off when surprised. The songs of whinchats, stonechats and wheatears often serenade pilgrims in the mountains, and the splendid **capercaille** makes its home in the woodlands of the western Cordillera Cantábrica.

People & Culture

The Cordillera Cantábrica have provided refuge to people for thousands of years, and although in recent times people have been leaving the mountains, the rebirth of the camino is attracting people back to remote areas. Villages such as O Cebreiro and Rabanal are slowly springing back to life as people are once more able to eke out a living here.

One of the most unique and mysterious groups of people found along the camino is the **Maragatos**, who live in the mountains west of Astorga. Their origins are shrouded in debate. Some historians believe they are related to the North African Berbers, while others point to archaeological excavations in the village of Santo Colomba de Samoza, where an ancient necropolis showed cultural links with the Phoenicians. Still others say they were slaves brought by the Romans to dig for gold in the local mountains.

Wherever the Maragatos came from, they survived to become the muleteers of medieval Spain, humping produce and other goods from the northern ports to the rest of the country. They're also a deliberately insular people. Only very recently have Maragatos started to marry outsiders, and if any strangers tried to join in traditional festivities in Astorga, the Maragatos would immediately stop dancing and refuse to continue until the interlopers left. The best example of traditional Maragato **architecture** is in the recently restored village of Castrillo de los Polvazares, just west of Astorga.

The **El Bierzo** region starkly contrasts with the land of the Maragatos. The style of architecture changes and different building materials are used: it's common to see thatched houses and slate churches in the area. Along with the grapes that thrive in the region's warm weather, you'll see local gardens mostly given over to tobacco plants.

The mountains of O Cebreiro mark the beginning of the land of the Galicians, and your entrance into **Celtic Spain**. It's not uncommon to sit in a bar in O Cebreiro and be serenaded by bagpipes, and you'll also see *hórreos* (granaries) and *pallozas* (straw-roofed stone houses), Galicia's traditional architecture. There's more about Galicia in the next chapter.

Food & Drink

Cocido Maragato is a very filling lunchtime meal and a Maragato tradition dating back thousands of years. The topsy-turvy meal's courses are eaten in a very strange order. The lunch starts with a meat course: ham, chicken, pork, *chorizo*, venison ear, pork fat (those cubes aren't potato!), and many other things with hair and skin still attached, fill a large platter on the table. It's tasty but incredibly rich, so bring along some friends to help you get through it. This orgy of flesh is followed by a second course of deliciously prepared vegetables, usually chickpeas and Gallego cabbage, then soup, and finally (and more conventionally) dessert. Don't plan on doing anything else for at least four hours after eating this meal, as you'll need all your energy for digestion!

A glass or two of red wine is sure to help slice into the richness of *cocido*. As in much of the country, the Romans can be thanked for introducing **wine** to El Bierzo. A *Denominacion de Origen* region since 1989, the best wines are made from Mencía grapes, although Prieto Picudo and Garnacha varieties are also added. Things have certainly changed since Künig von Vach wrote, "when you get there, drink wine sparingly as it burns like a candle and can scorch your very soul."

Queimada is an ancient potion said to be popular with the witches of Galicia. It is made with *orujo* (Galicia's favourite spirit, which we describe in the Galicia section on page 158), caster sugar, lemon peel, a few coffee beans and a good dose of magic. To make *queimada*, put the *orujo* and the sugar in a clay pot, then add the lemon peel and coffee beans. Then, put a small amount of sugar and *orujo* in a ladle and set the mixture on fire. Very slowly, pass the fire from the ladle to the pot and back again. When the sugar is used up, put some dry sugar in the ladle and move it above the flaming *queimada* until it melts to syrup. Pour the syrup above the flames, turning them blue. Then put out the flames, and drink.

Although you can try to recreate this in your kitchen back home, there's nothing quite like sitting in a dark room while a

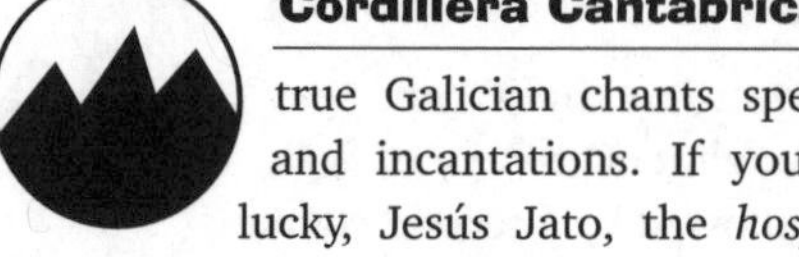

true Galician chants spells and incantations. If you're lucky, Jesús Jato, the *hospitalero* at Ave Feníx in Villafranca del Bierzo, just over the mountains from Galicia, will treat pilgrims to a *queimada* ritual.

For a more healthy option, try the delicious *reineta del bierzo* **apple**. Short-stalked, squat and chunky, it's much wider than it is high and looks a bit unappealing at first glance. The skin is pale green and dull with rusty speckles, the flesh is soft and tasty with a slightly chalky texture.

Tourist Information

Tourist Offices

There's an excellent *turismo* in Astorga, and you can also get help in Ponferrada and Villafranca del Bierzo. Contact information for the *turismos* is under individual towns.

Transport

Astorga and Ponferrada are easy to reach from all major centres in Spain. To get up and over the mountains you'll need to hire a taxi. In Villafranca del Bierzo, taxi drivers can carry your pack to O Cebreiro for a small fee, and they'll bring you along too for a few more euros. The *albergue* at Villafranca will also hump your bags up the hill.

Money

You can get cash in Astorga, Ponferrada, Cacabelos, Villafranca del Bierzo and Triacastela.

Accommodation

Albergues are plentiful, and this stretch has some of the weirdest and best on the camino. Ponferrada's modern *albergue* has comfortable, four-person dormitories, and you'll be pampered and entertained at Ave Fénix in Villafranca del Bierzo. If you're hankering for a medieval experience, head for the *albergue* at Manjarín, where you'll meet a healer and sleep with cows and fleas.

Shopping

Stock up in Astorga and Villafranca del Bierzo, as there are few shops around the mountain passes. It's always a good idea to carry a little extra food up and over the mountains in case the unpredictable weather changes suddenly.

Events & Festivals

Along with much of the rest of Spain, Astorga celebrates Carnaval and Semana Santa (Easter week) with parades and feasts. Later in the year, the **Fiestas de Santa María** in the last week of August honour the city's patron saint with a huge market, games and, of course, a massive *cocido Maragato* lunch.

Ponferrada's **Fiesta de la Virgen de la Encina** takes place at the beginning of September, closely followed by El Santísimo Cristo de la Esperanza, a festival held in Villafranca del Bierzo.

Rest Days & Detours

At **Las Médulas**, a UNESCO heritage site 20km southwest of Ponferrada, flame-red mountains hide the remains of

Roman gold mines. More than 300km of canals were built to channel water from the Río Cabrera, almost 30km away. Archaeologists guess that about 60,000 slaves worked as miners, hauling the ore out through tunnels, and then washing it in huge sluices. Today, you can visit some of the tunnels on a guided tour, and find out more in an interesting summer-only museum. Bring a torch, good shoes and clothing that you don't mind being stained by the bright red earth.

Further east, the gorgeous **Valle del Silencio** lies below the Monte Aquiana, a ghostly pale mountain revered by the Celts. At the head of the valley, you can visit the Peñalba de Santiago, a lovely, tenth-century Mozarabic church.

One of the best places to see *pallozas*, the region's traditional conical, straw-roofed houses, is north of Ponferrada in the **Ancares Leoneses**. These beautiful mountains are also home to wolves, capercaille and the occasional brown bear.

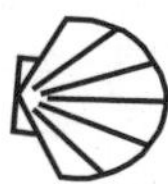

Astorga

At Astorga, the *camino francés* meets up with the *ruta de la plata*, an alternative *camino* that snakes up from Sevilla. The town's strategic location near the foothills of the Cordillera Cantábrica has long made it an important centre, and it once had over 20 pilgrim *hospitals*, more than any place apart from Burgos. From the ancient capital of the Astur tribe, it developed into Asturica Augusta, an important Roman and Christian centre that left murals, walls and other tangible remains. The gradual decline of the region in the eighteenth century has preserved much of Astorga's ancient feel and, unlike many other places of its size along the camino, it remains unblighted by industrial development.

You can easily while away an afternoon visiting Astorga's sights. The well laid-out **Museo Romano** is built over the Ergástula cave, which may have been the entrance to the old Roman forum. The intimidating city walls still stand in places and, throughout Astorga, you can peer into ongoing excavations and try to figure out the layout of this Roman frontier town. The *turismo* has a leaflet of Roman walking tours.

The town is also the capital of the **Maragatos**, a mysterious, isolated race of muleteers who preserved their culture for centuries but are now sadly losing their unique identity. Head to the Plaza de España on the hour to see traditionally dressed mechanical Maragatos banging on the **Ayuntamiento** bell. The figurines have been at it since 1748 and portray Pero Mato, the Maragato folk hero who fought at the battle of Clavijo alongside Santiago.

The jewel in Astorga's crown is undoubtedly Gaudí's **Palacio Episcopal**. Construction of a palace for the Bishop began in 1889, but once it was finished he refused to live in it,

afraid of the scandals surrounding the extravagant cost and the fantastical, whimsical architecture. It stood empty for years, briefly serving as the headquarters of Franco's *Falange* during the civil war. It finally found a more permanent tenant in the late 1960s, when the **Museo de los Caminos**, a collection of disparate images of St James and some mediocre art, was established.

The nearby **cathedral** took even longer to settle in: begun in 1471, it wasn't completed for more than three centuries. Although it's somewhat overpowered by its ostentatious neighbour, there are a few gems inside. The main *retablo* is by Gaspar Becerra, a follower of Michelangelo and Raphael, and the sweeping movement of the characters shows that he was sitting in the front row of his art class. Fill up your *credencial* with a *sello* from the ticket office at the **Museo Diocesano** next door, worth a peek for its varied exhibits.

If all this culture is making your blood sugar plummet, head for a fix at the **Museo del Chocolate**, a museum that celebrates Astorga's chocolate industry, which thrived in the eighteenth and nineteenth centuries on the back of the Maragatos' mule trains.

Astorga's **turismo** has lots of information about the region's Roman and Maragato history; it's at Calle Eduardo de Castro 5, across from Palacio Episcopal (☎ 987 61 82 22).

Accommodation

Astorga's main **albergue** (120 beds, no kitchen, open all year) is on the way into town; overflow pilgrims are led to a school about 1km away.

$ Pensión Garcia, Calle Bajada del Postigo 3 (☎ 987 61 60 46)

$$$ Hostal La Peseta, Plaza de San Bartolomé (☎ 987 61 72 75)

$$$$ Hotel Gaudí, Plaza Eduardo de Castro 6 (☎ 987 61 56 54)

The route from Astorga to Rabanal del Camino winds slowly through traditional Maragato villages on easy farm tracks and paved roads.

Follow the yellow arrows out of town, passing the modern Iglesia de San Pedro, which is decorated with a mosaic of the camino. Just after the church, cross over the NVI main road and head downhill on the quiet Calle de los Mártires, named after the Confraternity of the Martyrs who ran a pilgrim hospice in Valdeviejas. After a couple of hundred metres, pass two crosses, one on either side of the road, then head past the Residencia San Francisco on the left.

Pass a boundary sign marking the edge of Astorga, and then enter the village of **Valdeviejas**, whose parish church of San Verísimo echoes the village's Roman name, Villa Sancti Verissimi. Keep straight on, passing the Ermita del Ecce Homme on the left, and cross a bridge, veering off to the right soon afterwards to follow a purpose-built gravel track at the side of the road.

Soon afterwards, at a bend in the main road the camino splits and you have three choices.

Via Murias de Rechivaldo

Your first option is the shortest route to Rabanal de Camino, and passes through the village of Murias de Rechivaldo, where there's an *albergue*. Turn left, following one set of yellow arrows, and reach the main road almost immediately. Carry along the road for a short while, crossing a bridge over the Río Jerga. A couple of hundred metres later, at a fork in the road just before the village, take the middle of three roads, which skirts around to the left to reach the village of **Murias de Rechivaldo** (Ⓐ✕☕) via a quiet lane.

The eighteenth-century Iglesia de San Esteban has a carving of the Virgen del Pilar above the door, and the belltower stairs are exposed to the elements, a common feature of this area. At the far side of the village, the camino follows a wide track and takes you to Santa Catalina de Somoza. To reach the **albergue** (22 beds, no kitchen, open all year), turn right just as this wide track begins.

Via Castrillo de Polvazares

Your second option is to keep straight on when the camino splits, following a second set of yellow arrows towards the wonderfully restored village of Castrillo de Polvazares. This is a slightly longer route but well worth the detour.

Via Murias de Rechivaldo & Castrillo de Polvazares

The third option takes in both Murias de Rechivaldo and Castrillo de Polvazares. Follow the route to the *albergue* in Murias de Rechivaldo. Cross over the main road at the *albergue* and keep straight on until you reach the river in about 100m. Cross the river via a footbridge, turn left on the other side, then turn first right and meet up with the wide gravel track after 100m. Turn left here to head into Castrillo de Polvazares.

Keep following the gravel track then, at a picnic area at the edge of the village, turn left then take the first right into **Castrillo de Polvazares** (Ⓗ✕☕). Strolling through Castrillo, it's easy to see how the Maragato architecture captured the imagination of the writer Concha Espina, who set *The Maragato Sphinx* here. The village has been carefully and attractively restored, preserving the typical stone-walled, slate-roofed houses. You can stay at the **Hostería Cuca la Vaina** (**$$**, ☎ 987 69 10 78).

The route through Castrillo isn't marked, but it's hard to get lost. Follow the main cobbled street to the end of the village, then turn left and cross over a small bridge. Turn right at a junction just afterwards, then climb slowly uphill to meet up with the route from Murias de Rechivaldo, heading towards Santa Catalina de Somoza. On the climb up, look out not only for pilgrims walking along the ridge ahead but for a Celtic *castro* on the hill to the southwest. You are now in the heartland of the Maragatos, although the old traditions are clearly dying out here. Dilapidated thatched roofs and fields that are empty apart from stone corrals once used for cattle and resting mules attest to the lure of modern life amongst the younger Maragatos.

Once at the ridge, which offers sweeping views of Astorga and nearby valleys, turn right to join the route from Murias and head into the tiny village of **Santa Catalina de Somoza** (Ⓐ☕), about 1km away. The modern church of Santa María is said to contain a relic of San Blas, who looked after pilgrims' welfare. Tired pilgrims can stay the night at the **albergue** (38 beds, no kitchen, open all year).

Follow the well-marked route through Santa Catalina before picking up the gravel camino trail on the far side of the village. There are views of the mountains

Map 16 (key page 213)

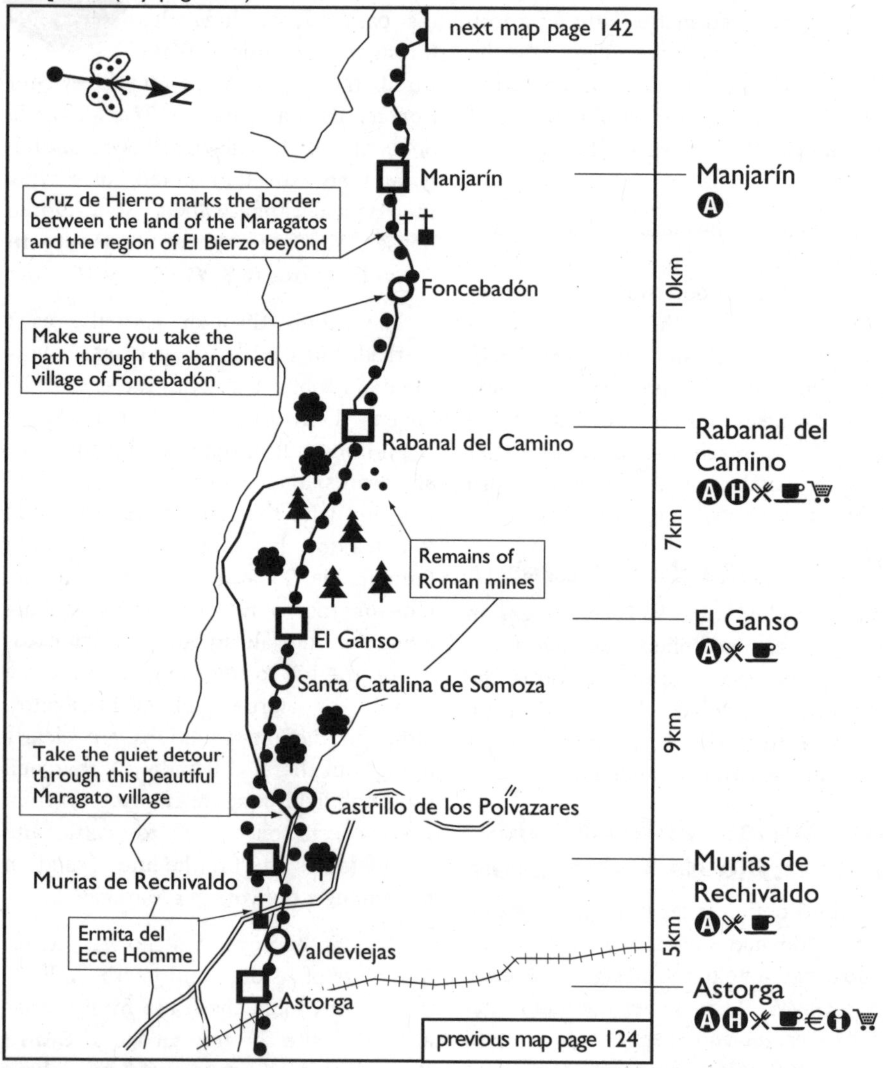

next map page 142

N

Manjarín

Cruz de Hierro marks the border between the land of the Maragatos and the region of El Bierzo beyond

Foncebadón

Make sure you take the path through the abandoned village of Foncebadón

Rabanal del Camino

Remains of Roman mines

El Ganso

Santa Catalina de Somoza

Take the quiet detour through this beautiful Maragato village

Castrillo de los Polvazares

Murias de Rechivaldo

Ermita del Ecce Homme

Valdeviejas

Astorga

previous map page 124

Manjarín

10km

Rabanal del Camino

7km

El Ganso

9km

Murias de Rechivaldo

5km

Astorga

Profile Chart 16

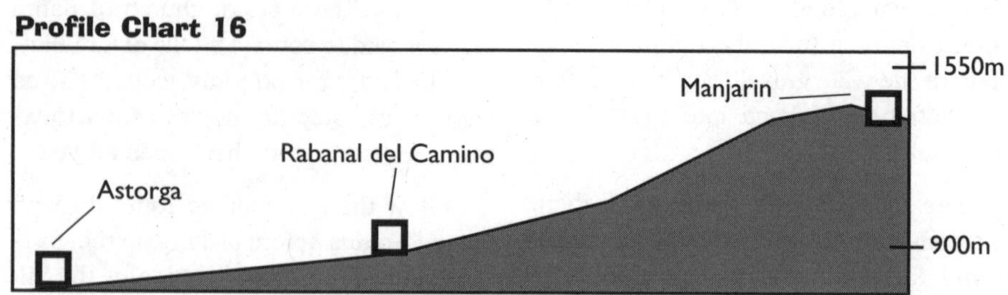

ahead as you stroll through once-cultivated land, now overgrown with pine and brambles. In spring and summer this area is a favourite habitat of the red-backed shrike, a rusty-coloured bird with a distinctive black eye strip and the gruesome habit of impaling its captured prey on thorns. After another 5km on the gravel track, you come to the village of **El Ganso** (Ⓐ✗☕).

Many houses in the village boast ancient thatched roofs made from the broom that grows all over this region, but such roofs are slowly going out of fashion, giving way to easier-to-build ones made of iron or slate. The modern **Iglesia de Santiago** hints at the camino's early popularity here; by 1142 a church and hospice were up and running to minister to the tide of pilgrims that flowed through the village. El Ganso also has an **albergue** (32 beds, no kitchen, open all year).

About 1km after leaving El Ganso, the camino joins the paved road, which you follow uphill through a young pine and oak wood. There are many new tree farms in the area, grown for fuel and construction. With fewer mouths to feed, the land is no longer needed for crops such as wheat and barley, and much of the former farmland has simply been left to go wild.

After a couple of kilometres, follow the road as it curves to the left, ignoring the right-hand turn signposted "Rabanal Viejo" and "La Malvengo". You can detour about 500m down this side road to see the site of the Roman gold mines of La Fucarona, although little remains.

Almost immediately after the side road, cross Puente de Pañote and start to climb through a young oak wood, getting your first glimpse of Rabanal del Camino just ahead. Pass a giant tree known as the Pilgrim's Oak, then shortly afterwards walk past the Ermita del Bendito Cristo. Turn right off the paved road here, and follow the dirt track into Rabanal del Camino, which soon becomes the village's Calle Mayor.

Rabanal del Camino ⒶⒽ✗☕🛒

Rabanal del Camino is slowly becoming a pilgrim bottleneck. Everyone seems to stay here, resting in one of the village's three *albergues* before tackling the mountains. Traditionally the ninth stop in the *Codex Calixtinus*, this beautiful hamlet is slowly springing back to life as the camino revival brings more pilgrims and their money. The houses are characteristically enclosed by high walls and have big courtyards in classic Maragato style.

Pass the small Ermita de San José on the way to the Iglesia de Santa María, which has Romanesque templar origins hidden under centuries of serious renovations. Legend has it that Anseis, one of Charlemagne's knights, married a Saracen bride here, although it's not clear whether the Franks' army even made it this far west.

There are a couple of bars and a summer-only shop in the village.

Accommodation

There are three **albergues** in Rabanal. **Refugio Gaucelmo** (42 beds, kitchen, open March to October, no bikes), just off Calle Mayor, was converted from the ancient Hospital de San Gregorio, where Aymeric Picaud stayed in the twelfth century. It's now run by the British Confraternity of St James. **Nuestra Señora del Pilar** (52 beds,

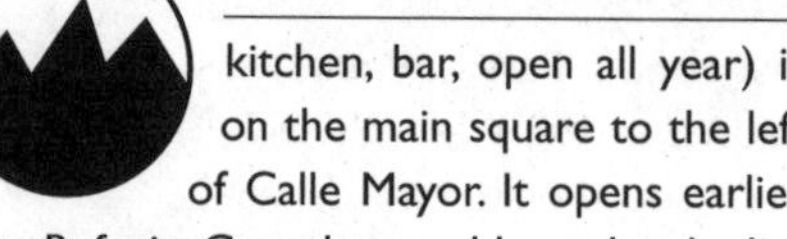

kitchen, bar, open all year) is on the main square to the left of Calle Mayor. It opens earlier than Refugio Gaucelmo and has a lovely dining room with an open fire.

The **municipal** *albergue* (100 beds, no kitchen, open May to September) is used as overflow when the other *albergues* are full.

$$ Hostal El Refugio (☎ 987 69 12 74).

After Rabanal, you'll soon encounter three highlights of the pilgrimage. The camino follows narrow paved roads uphill to Foncebadón, an eerily abandoned village, continues to Cruz de Hierro, an important pilgrim ritual stop, then passes a fascinating *albergue* in Manjarín. There's not much water for 17km, so stock up before you leave.

Walk out of Rabanal del Camino along Calle Mayor, which soon becomes a dirt track lined with gorse and heather. There are wonderful views of the mountains ahead, home to some of the few remaining wolves in Iberia. You're more likely to be struck by lightning in this treeless landscape than to see one of these shy creatures, as hunting has reduced the number of wolves in Spain to fewer than 2000 animals.

The track runs parallel to a narrow road for about 500m, and then meets the road. Keep straight on across the road to a path that's overgrown in places, although in wet or otherwise miserable weather, it's wise to simply turn right and follow the road instead, as the path joins the road in another 500m. Walk gradually uphill following an old Roman road, and pass the Fuente del Peregrino on your right, a good spot to admire the views into the valley behind you while replenishing your water.

Soon after the fountain, you'll come to **Foncedadón**, an eerie and affecting place that features heavily in modern accounts of the pilgrimage. You can keep straight on the road to avoid Foncebadón, but it's far more interesting to veer left and follow the camino through the abandoned village.

The houses are built from local slate, with thick walls to block the wind and steeply angled roofs to deflect snow. Many of the roofs are thatched with local broom, and wooden beams were often hammered into place with primitive wooden pegs rather than nails.

Nowadays, the village looks as if it's been struck by a minor earthquake; some buildings, like the church, are sturdy and complete, but others fell down long ago, and rubbish is piled up in the streets. It's often cloudy here, snow is common in winter, and when it's too warm for snow, the mountains are drenched with rain. Still, Foncebadón undergoes brief and sporadic revivals as romantically minded former pilgrims decide to settle here.

Follow the cobbled street through the village, then keep straight on at a dirt track as the houses peter out. Turn around as you leave for great views of Foncebadón, particularly in the early morning when the buildings rise ghostly and photogenically from the mist. The ruins to your left are those of a pilgrims' hospice and church built by Gaucelmo, the twelfth-century hermit who gave his name to the modern *albergue* in Rabanal del Camino. The remote stretch from Foncebadón climbs gradually, reaching the road in a kilometre or so.

Turn left here to walk along the road, and you'll soon reach the **Cruz de Hierro**. This massive, conical pile of stones marks the pass over Monte Irago and the border between La Maragatería and El Bierzo. Across Europe, Celts traditionally laid stones at peaks and passes like this one to calm the mountain gods and ask for safe passage through the mountains. Romans in the area continued the tradition, calling the stones *murias* after Mercury, their god of travellers.

Adding a stone to the pile at the Cruz de Hierro is an important camino ritual; many pilgrims bring stones from home to place here, while others pick one up along the way. If you climb to the top of the pile, you'll see scribbled messages to friends, family and spiritual beings, and pebbles painted with names and home towns from all over Europe and the Americas. The Cruz de Hierro is right next to the road, and the safety-conscious local authority is said to systematically bulldoze the pile each year.

The iron cross on the top is a later addition, placed there by Gaucelmo to make this pagan tradition more palatable to the Catholic church. The graffiti-covered Capilla de Santiago, built in 1982, makes a good windbreak and rest spot.

From here, the camino mostly follows the road, although occasional paths run parallel to it relieve the tarmac monotony. In a couple of kilometres you'll reach **Manjarín** (Ⓐ), a tiny, remote hamlet. The only soul here is Tomás, the *hospitalero*, and his unique **albergue** (20 beds, no kitchen, open all year) is a throwback to what *albergues* must have been like in earlier times. What the *albergue* lacks in basic amenities, such as beds, privacy and cleanliness, it more than makes up for in character and personality: you'll share sleeping quarters with cows and creepy crawlies, but Tomás will feed you, heal your injuries and charm you with camino stories. As you leave in the morning, he rings the large bell at the door to let Santiago know that you're on your way.

Just after Manjarín, turn left on to a track at the side of the road. It's a fairly narrow path, hemmed in on either side by tall, gorgeous heather that provides some shelter and shade. Up here, it feels like wilderness for a kilometre or so: you can't see the road for the heather, even though it's only about 50m away. Keep an eye out for alpine choughs — black, acrobatic, crow-sized birds with a vivid yellow bill and a piercing call.

Rejoin the road and climb steeply uphill, passing a heavily guarded military station on the hill to your right. At 1517m, this innocuous looking spot is the highest point of the camino, although there's still one more mountain range to cross before you reach Santiago. To your left, there are fabulous views of the steep-sided Río Meruelo. The gorgeous stone monastery of Campludo sits perched above the river, while tucked into the valley floor, a fiendishly clever medieval forge is said to be in working order.

After about 1km, take the path off to the right to cut off a chunk of road walking. Rejoin the road in a few hundred metres and turn right, passing a sign describing the attractions of El Acebo, Riego de Ambrós and Molinaseca, all places you'll pass along the camino.

The views open up ahead as the road descends to the wide and fertile El Bierzo

valley, blessed with a year-round balmy climate. The Sierra de Gristredo and the Cordillera Cantábrica, which have shadowed the camino since Navarra, tower above the outline of Ponferrada while, to the west, you can see the summits of O Courel and Los Ancares. In Visigothic times, the El Bierzo region was a major religious centre with communities of monks taking advantage of the fertile climate and remote location to farm and pray in peace.

About 100m after the tourist sign, turn left down a track. You'll get sudden, birds' eye views of El Acebo as the track descends steeply and, soon after passing a spring on the right, you enter the village.

El Acebo Ⓐ✗☕

El Acebo's importance as the gateway to the mountains was recognized in medieval times, when it was excused from paying tax for as long as the villagers maintained the hundreds of foul weather poles that guide pilgrims on this remote alpine section. Today, El Acebo is a stunning collection of slate-roofed stone houses typical of the El Bierzo region, with overhanging wooden balconies that are reached by an external stone staircase.

The Iglesia de San Miguel has an extremely large-headed statue of Santiago Peregrino. The local bar makes great fried sandwiches.

Accommodation

There are three small **albergues** in El Acebo.

Albergue de la Junta Vecinal (12 beds, no kitchen open all year).

Albergue La Taberna de José (14 beds, no kitchen, open all year).

Albergue Mesón El Acebo (24 beds, no kitchen, open all year) is linked with the town's bar-restaurant.

There are great views and lovely descents through hamlets and river valleys along the camino to Molinaseca. As you leave El Acebo on a tarmac road, you'll pass a monument to Heinrich Krause, a pilgrim cyclist who died here in 1987. It's the first of many poignant memorials between here and Santiago. You're soon able to see Riego de Ambrós ahead as you walk through a landscape of broom and wild lavender. Take the track to the left, pass a couple of posh, modern houses and enter **Riego de Ambrós** (ⒶⒽ✗☕).

The slate roofs and charming rural craftsmanship make walking through this village a delight. In Riego, you can visit the Ermita de San Fabián y San Sebastián, while the sixteenth-century Iglesia de Santa María on the edge of the village has an interesting Baroque *retablo*. Riego's **albergue** (50 beds, kitchen, open all year) is along the camino, and there are also rooms at the **Ruta de Santiago** (**$**, ☎ 987 69 51 90).

Soon after the *albergue*, turn left to keep walking through the village along the camino, then turn right near the end of the village to walk down a stony path. The cobbles here are partly washed away, and the broad, slate rocks that lie beneath the cobbles can be very slippery after rain, particularly on the initial steep section. This is one of the loveliest stretches of the whole camino, where horse chestnut trees line the route, providing shelter for songbirds like the crested tit.

The path joins the road at a modern round house. Turn right off the road

100m later up a ploughed dirt track that soon becomes a stone path, heading downhill through woodland. After 300m or so, curve around a small clearing, then descend steeply once more as you see the main road far below and the slate roofs of Molinaseca up ahead. As the path nears the road, ignore the right-angled track to the left, and instead take the left-hand fork about 200m later after a short uphill stretch.

Join the road just outside Molinaseca and turn right. Pass the **Capilla de la Virgen de las Angustias** on the right as you enter town, where Galician migrant workers once left their sickles on their way from the harvest in Castilla y León. You can peer through the iron grille to see the beautiful statue of the Virgin inside. Cross the Puente del Peregrino into town, walking down the cobbled pedestrianised main street.

Molinaseca

Ⓐ Ⓗ

Molinaseca is a mellow town that lies prettily alongside the wide Río Maruelo. The gorgeous location attracted the wealthy and the titled, who left behind houses that still bear elaborate coats of arms. It's said that Doña Urraca, an eleventh-century Queen of Castilla y León and Galicia lived here, as did the aristocratic Balboa family. Historically, the town's importance came from its strategic location on the first flat, open land this side of the mountain pass, and ancient bridges helped make it a control point along the Roman gold road. Molinaseca was a significant town in medieval times, too, and once boasted four pilgrim *hospitals*.

Today's attractions include the **Iglesia de San Nicolás**, which contains an image of San Roque Peregrino, and a weekly street market. In summer, it's a lovely overnight stop, as the Río Maruelo is dammed for swimming and becomes a focal point of the village. There are plenty of shops, restaurants and bars here.

Accommodation

Molinaseca's **albergue** is on the way out of town on the left (85 beds, kitchen, open all year).

$ Hostal El Palacio (☎ 987 45 30 94)
$ La Casa del Reloj (☎ 987 45 31 24)
$$ Casa San Nicolás (☎ 929 79 30 53)
$$$ Posada de Muriel (☎ 987 45 32 01)

At the end of Molinaseca, turn left at the main road and walk along the sidewalk of the LE42, passing the *albergue*. The few vines here mark the start of the El Bierzo grape region. After a kilometre or two, at the top of a short climb, you can see Ponferrada sprawling ahead.

The route splits just as the road starts to go downhill. You can either keep straight on along the main road into Ponferrada or turn left to follow the slightly longer but quieter route, which we describe, down to the river via Campo. In 2002, this turning was a wide dirt road, but construction of new houses was going on, and the road may be paved by the time you walk along it.

After a brief, brisk climb, you'll reach the hamlet of **Campo**, which in medieval times was Ponferrada's Jewish district. Bear left just before Campo, following the sign to **Iglesia Siglo XVII**. Beautifully restored slate and stone houses line the

Map 17 (key page 213)

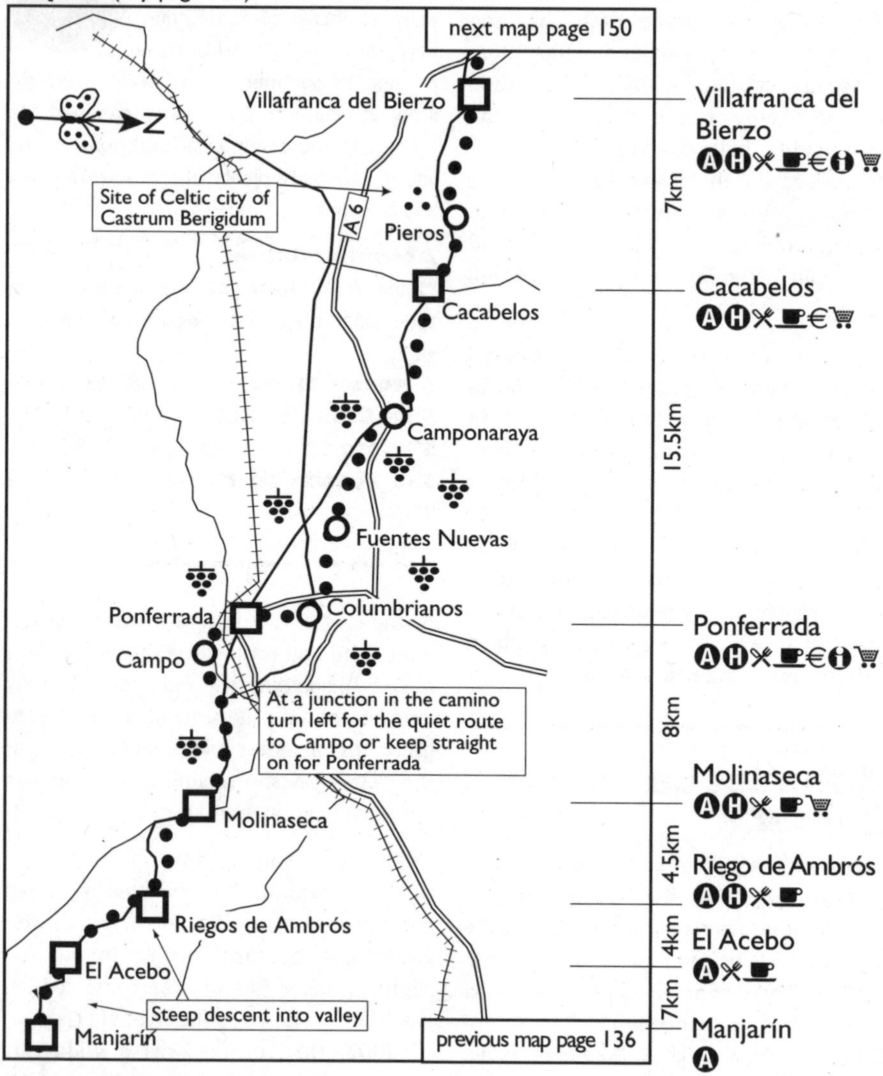

next map page 150

Villafranca del Bierzo

Site of Celtic city of Castrum Berigidum

A 6

Pieros

Cacabelos

Camponaraya

Fuentes Nuevas

Columbrianos

Ponferrada

Campo

At a junction in the camino turn left for the quiet route to Campo or keep straight on for Ponferrada

Molinaseca

Riegos de Ambrós

El Acebo

Steep descent into valley

Manjarín

previous map page 136

Villafranca del Bierzo
A H

7km

Cacabelos
A H

15.5km

Ponferrada
A H

8km

Molinaseca
A H

4.5km

Riego de Ambrós
A H

4km

El Acebo
A

7km

Manjarín
A

Profile Chart 17

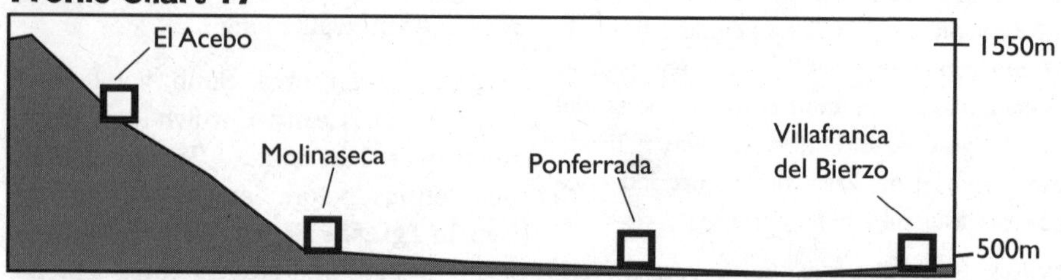

route, and there's an elaborate coat of arms on a house to the right.

At the end of the hamlet, walk along a tarmac road parallel to the Río Boeza, with good views of Ponferrada on the far bank of the river. It's easy to see how the town's castle dominates the entrance into El Bierzo as it straddles the confluence of the Río Sil and the Río Boeza.

After a couple of kilometres, turn right at a junction with a tarmac road, then walk past some houses and a winery on the left. Turn right again at a bigger tarmac road, then right once more to cross the Río Boeza over a narrow stone bridge.

Turn down Calle Camino Bajo de San Andrés, then keep straight on over the flyover into town. To reach the *albergue*, take the first road on the right, then turn right again soon afterwards on to a narrow road. The *albergue* is a modern slate and stone building in the middle of a park, about 100m down this road.

Ponferrada

Ⓐ Ⓗ ✕ ☕ € ⓘ 🛒

Once an ancient Celtic village, Ponferrada grew steadily under the Romans to become *Interamnium Flavium*, a large city in the middle of one of the Roman Empire's richest mining districts. Destroyed twice over the next 500 years, first by Visigoths in the the fifth century and then by Muslims in the ninth, its modern name comes from the long-gone iron bridge built by the bishop of Astorga in 1082. The arrival of the railway in the nineteenth century spurred Ponferrada's development, and coal mining fuelled a modern boom a few decades later. Today, the city's pretty old quarter contrasts with a mass of ugly tower blocks.

On the south bank of Río Sil is the magnificent **Castillo de los Templarios**, a must-see sight that's worth a visit even if you're not spending the night in Ponferrada. Erected by the Templars in the thirteenth century to help protect pilgrims from bandits, it's a grand, triple-ramparted, fairy-tale castle. As you crawl around the castle, up stairs and over walls, try to spot Templar crosses carved into the stone.

Excavations show that the castle was built over the remains of a Celtic *castro*, a Roman fort and a later Visigothic fort. It's looking a bit sorry for itself: having been set on fire by the French during the Peninsular War in 1811, much of the centre of the castle has now been left to weeds, although poppies are a glorious sight in early summer.

While the Templars were clearing forest to build their castle, legend says that they discovered a statue of the Virgen de la Encina in a holm oak. The statue can now be seen inside the **Basílica de Santa María de la Encina**, and the Virgin was declared Patroness of El Bierzo in 1958. The massive Templar cross on the outside of the church boldly declares the church's origins.

The **Museo del Bierzo** is fascinating, with lots of exhibits packed into the walls of the former jail. The display of weaving tools and old looms is accompanied by a video showing local women using traditional weaving methods, and the finds from local *castros* would make this museum worth a visit in themselves.

Ponferrada's **turismo** is next to the castle, on Calle Gil y Carrasco (☎ 987 42 42 36).

Accommodation

The well-equipped **albergue** (185 beds, kitchen, open all year) is below the old town; it has pleasant four-person dormitories and a

long, sociable dining table.

$ Hostal García (☎ 987 41 12 59)

$$ Hostal Santa Cruz, Calle Marcelo Macías 4 (☎ 987 42 67 00)

$$ Hostal Marán, Avenida A. López Peláez 29 (☎ 987 41 18 00)

$$$$ Hotel Del Temple, Avenida de Portugal 2 (☎ 987 41 00 58)

The popularity of the camino and the sudden jump in the numbers of pilgrims from Ponferrada onwards hasn't escaped the notice of local merchants. For the remainder of the route into Santiago, you'll pass signs luring you into shops and bars with a promise of a *sello* for your *credencial.*

When leaving Ponferrada, make sure that you follow the yellow arrows closely as the route zig-zags through the city. Cross the Río Sil at the Plaza de Las Nievas, then turn right at the Plaza San Pedro. Take the first left up Calle Río Urdiales, then turn right onto Avenida Huertas de Sacramento. On your way out of town, there's an attractive sculpture of four women cooking peppers.

On the edge of town, you'll be confronted by some unsightly reminders of Ponferrada's industrial roots: walk past a large slag heap on the left and an old disused electrical power plant on the right. At the top of a short climb, turn left at a junction, continuing to walk around the massive slag heap. Just after passing a Red Cross building on the left, turn right at a T-junction, then turn left almost immediately through an arch in a building that houses an intriguing combination of businesses: a bar and the local library. This suburb is now owned by a local coal company, and it has a strange, un-Spanish feel, with North-American-style, evenly spaced blocks and large houses.

On the far side of the arch is a modern, neo-Romanesque church with a statue of the Virgin and Child sitting on a rock in front. Keep straight on for another block and turn left, then take the first right past some tennis courts and a football pitch. Just after these, on the right-hand side, there's a *cruceiro* (cross) placed here during the 1993 Holy Year and a camino mural on the new *ermita* next to it.

Keep straight on, pass through a tunnel under the main road and then turn left 50m later to walk past the Iglesia de Santa María and into the village of **Columbrianos** (☕🛒). In front of you are the beautiful mountains of Galicia; the two flat hills to the north contain the remains of Asturi hillforts.

Cross straight over the main road, then turn right in 100m at another busy road and walk towards the Ermita San Blas y San Roque. Turn left at the *ermita*, following a lane into farmland. This paved lane leads for almost 3km to **Fuentes Nuevas** (☕🛒). At a bend in the road just before the village, keep right. Pass a small café, a whitewashed church and old houses with splendid wooden balconies.

Head out of the village, come to a main road and turn right, passing some shops and bars and taking the bridge across the Río Naraya. You're now in **Camponaraya** (🍴☕🛒), a strange mix of dreary modern houses interlaced with lovely old buildings that offer just a taste of the village's original architecture.

On the way out of town, the Co-operativa Viñas del Bierzo sells wine by the glass, industrially poured from a huge tap. You can also buy wine by the bottle here to spirit you towards Villafranca del Bierzo. There's a rest area just afterwards with picnic benches and shade for those who've drunk a little too much *vino*.

Follow the dirt road that leads uphill from the wine co-op, cross the pedestrian bridge over the main road and carry on along the dirt track on the other side. This is a lovely stretch of the camino, passing through fields of vines and with wonderful views. Most of the vines are still grown old-school style with the branches draped along the ground, but modern wire-supported vines, common in La Rioja and Navarra, are starting to surface here as El Bierzo's wine industry develops.

Cross straight over the NVI road and take the narrow paved road on the other side. After almost 1km, there's a rest area with a fountain. Keep straight on and follow the road as it heads downhill and into Cacabelos. The camino passes straight through town along the Calle de los Peregrinos, then crosses the Río Cua over a low bridge to reach the *albergue*.

Cacabelos

Ⓐ Ⓗ ✕ ☕ €

Well known for its wines, Cacabelos is a pretty little town founded by Alfonso IX in the tenth century and rebuilt after a twelfth-century earthquake. The town's archaeological museum has some interesting finds from local excavations and is worth visiting. Pilgrims can get a free drink and *tapas* at Prado a Tope, an upmarket winery at the beginning of town.

On its way through Cacabelos, the camino takes you past the market building, the Ermita de San Roque and the large Iglesia de Santa María. At the far end of town, next to the bridge over the Río Cua, there's an old mill that's been beautifully converted into a house, and an antique wooden olive press in front of an excellent *panadería*.

On the far bank, the eighteenth-century Santuario de la Quinta Angustia is on the site of a former pilgrim hospital; it's notable for a bizarre altar showing the baby Jesus playing cards with San António de Padua.

Near the bridge in January 1809, Thomas Plunkett, one of General Sir John Moore's riflemen shot the commander of Napoleon's pressuring French forces through the head. This accurate display of marksmanship saved the British army from being overrun as it attempted a shambolic winter retreat over the mountains to the safety of its navy on the coast at A Coruña.

Accommodation

Albergue (70 beds, no kitchen, open all year).
$ El Molino (☎ 987 54 68 29)
$$ Hostal Santa María (☎ 987 54 95 88).

Follow the main road uphill, passing the hamlet of Pieros. Be careful along this section as the road can be busy and there's not much of a shoulder to walk on. At the top of the hill the views across the valley to the mountains are superb.

Just to the south is the **Cerro de la Ventosa**, a large circular hill where the Asturian city of Castrum Berigidum once stood. This Celtic metropolis was conquered by the Romans and has given its name to the region of El Bierzo. The western side of the old Celtiberian defensive wall was recently excavated, and it's well worth climbing the hill for a closer look.

If you decide to visit, a path just beyond Pieros leads to this old city, and another on the west side goes through vineyards to meet the camino about 1km further along the main road.

Follow the road for a few kilometres, then at the bottom of a hill, turn right off the road down a dirt track, just after a sign for "km406". Soon afterwards, you'll pass a field of giant sculptures, part of a crazy outdoor studio belonging to a sculptor who lives in Villafranca del Bierzo.

Keep left at a fork at the top of a hill and follow the quiet track as it winds its way into Villafranca del Bierzo, a welcome relief after walking along the busy road. At a fork just on the edge of town, pilgrims who wish to spend the night here have a choice: head down and right for the municipal *albergue* or keep straight on to reach Ave Fenix, one of the most splendid *albergues* on the whole camino.

Villafranca del Bierzo Ⓐ Ⓗ ✕ ☕ € ⓘ 🛒

As a logical rest stop on the camino before the pass over O Cebreiro, Villafranca del Bierzo marked the end of the tenth stage of the *Codex Calixtinus*. It once had eight monasteries and six pilgrim *hospitals*. As its name suggests, it was settled by the Franks, who came here on the orders of King Alfonso VI to guard this strategic trading place on the banks of the Río Burbia and the Río Valcarce.

Life hasn't always been easy here. Plague killed most of the people of Villafranca in 1589, and floods destroyed the buildings nearest the river in 1715. Less than a century later, the invading French army ransacked the town in 1808 during the **Peninsula War**, but were driven out by British. The townspeople probably wished that the French had stayed when the British hooligans went on a drunken rampage as they fled from the French army in the winter of 1809. In their search for loot, the British wrecked the castle, robbed the churches and burned their priceless archives. General Sir John Moore eventually stopped the rampage by taking the drastic measure of shooting the ringleaders. More damage was done the following year as the French wrenched back control of the town.

Today, these historic scars are mostly invisible, and Villafranca is one of the loveliest towns in the whole of Spain, picturesquely set on a river and surrounded by mountains. The industrial revolution passed the town by, so it's not tainted by rampant construction and the centre of town is a maze of narrow streets and open plazas. The Calle de Agua is lined with splendid mansions, one of which was home to the nineteenth-century novelist Enrique Gil y Carrasco. In spring, there's a poetry festival in the municipal gardens.

On the way into town, next to the *albergue*, you pass the beautiful Romanesque **Iglesia de Santiago**, which has a Puerta del Perdón. Like others along the camino, if you are too ill to continue the pilgrimage you can walk through these finely carved doors and receive the same spiritual benefits as if you had made it all the way to Santiago de Compostela.

Try and visit the **Iglesia de San Francisco**, which has a groovy Mudéjar-style ceiling. This church was reputedly founded by St Francis as he made his pilgrimage, and it was heavily damaged when used as barracks in the Napoleonic wars. At the top of town, the dramatic sixteenth-century **Castillo de los Marqueses de Villafranca** is now the fortified private residence of the Álvarez de Toledo family.

Villafranca has a couple of well-equipped shops, and some good cafés and restaurants. The **turismo** is in the town hall (☎ 987 54 00 28).

Accommodation

You can stay at the comfortable **municipal albergue** (78 beds, kitchen open all year) or at the eccentric **Ave Fenix** (60 beds, kitchen, open all year), run by Jesus Jato. This impressive man has dedicated his life to helping pilgrims. His first *albergue* burnt down in 1996 and the Ave Fenix, which rose from the ashes, is slowly growing. The house rules are quirky; no getting up before 7am, and a separate room for the over 40s. Pilgrims aren't allowed to do any work around the *albergue*, and communal meals are provided for a small fee along with free coffee and tea. To top it all off, Jesús Jato takes a personal interest in the well-being of pilgrims and provides natural cures for aches and pains. On many evenings he leads pilgrims in a *queimada* ritual (see page 131 for more on this tradition) and he can even arrange for your bag to be driven to the top of O Cebreiro for a few euros.

$ Hostal Comercio, Calle Puente Nuevo 2 (☎ 987 54 00 08)

$$ Hotel San Francisco, main square (☎ 987 54 04 65)

$$ Hostal Casa Méndez, Espíritu Santo 1 (☎ 987 54 24 08)

$$$$ Parador de Villafranca de Bierzo, Avenida Calvo Sotelo (☎ 987 54 01 75)

Walk downhill through Villafranca, following the yellow arrows to the bridge over the Río Burbia. The elegant modern statue of Santiago at the foot of the bridge is the work of the sculptor whose open-air studio you passed on your way into town.

At the end of the bridge, you have two options, both marked by yellow arrows. The duller, shorter route follows the old NVI road, no longer as busy or as dangerous as it once was, now that the new motorway has taken away most of the traffic, but its narrow shoulder still makes for an unpleasant walk. The route follows the road for 10km to Trabadelo. At **Pereje** (Ⓐ), 4km along the road, there's an **albergue** (30 beds, kitchen, open Easter to October).

A beautiful but much more strenuous walk takes you over the hill to the right of the road: it's a stunning, heather-lined route with spectacular views. For this option, bear right up Calle Pradela, following the small yellow sign on the road. Climb up the narrow steep street that quickly changes to a stone track, and you'll soon have great views of the mountains and of Villafranca below. The track is lined with deciduous trees, ferns, lavender and wildflowers.

As the trail becomes less steep, the scenery opens up as heather and intense clusters of white broom replace the trees. You reach the top of the ridge after a few kilometres, from where the incredible views make it feel as though you're walking along the roof of the world.

Follow the ridge, passing under some power lines and a radio tower on the right. Descend a little through a chestnut grove, as Pradela and its vivid green meadows come into view ahead. At a stone wall, turn right to detour to **Pradela** (☕), a good option in foggy weather, or turn left to continue the camino; both routes are well marked with yellow arrows.

Keep walking through chestnut trees as the camino begins to wind through the wood, looking out for red-backed shrikes, goldcrests, bullfinches and cirl buntings. Although you're still nominally in modern Castilla y León, it's clear that you've already crossed culturally into rural, other-worldly Galicia. The yellow arrows painted on the trees can be tricky to see if visibility is poor.

Eventually, the path heads downhill along a broad track in a series of hairpin bends; smaller steeper paths cut off the corners for pilgrims in a hurry. The track and the road down from Pradela both snake downhill, but seem to avoid each other. Lots of oak trees line the track as you near the bottom of the hill and after an eerie stretch shaded by high-sided mossy walls, you enter the village of **Trabadelo** (Ⓗ☕✕).

There are no remains of the castle that once guarded the route here, but you can stay at the **Hostal Nova Ruta** (**$$**, ☎ 987 56 64 31). At a bar decorated with garishly painted gnomes, turn right up Calle Camino de Santiago. Walk to the end of the village, passing the road up to Pradela on the right, then cross an old stone bridge and walk parallel to the motorway and the old NVI. Pass a river on the left, then walk under the motorway and join up with the road route from Villafranca del Bierzo.

After the glorious peace of the high route, it's a rude shock to find yourself walking along a road with very little shoulder, fast cars and the odd truck. Bear left at the sign for **La Portela** (Ⓗ☕), which marks the start of the narrow and attractive Valcarce valley.

Walk through the hamlet, passing a bar and the **Hostal Valcarce** (**$$**, ☎ 987 54 31 80), then rejoin the road at the end of the village. About 300m later, turn left and follow the signs to Vega de Valcarce, following the old Roman road and passing through the small hamlet of **Ambasmestas**, named after the merging of the waters of the Valcarce and Valboa rivers.

The valley widens here a little, allowing farming to take place, and the region's heavy rainfall soaks the fields to a brilliant green. After a couple of kilometres, pass under an impressive, sky-high motorway bridge and arrive at the centre of Vega del Valcarce.

Vega del Valcarce

ⒶⒽ✕☕🛒

Vega del Valcarce's brief moment in the spotlight came when Carlos V stayed the night here in 1520 on his way to Santiago. The church here is dedicated to María Magdalena and the town makes a good spot for lunch before tackling the climb up to O Cebreiro.

On the hills above the village are the remains of two ruined castles. It takes about an hour to climb up to Sarracín, on the left hilltop, which was once controlled by the Marqués de Villafranca. Its defensive position offers fantastic views of the entire valley and it's clear why the castle's mysterious ninth-century founders would build a fortress here. On the right hand hilltop, Castro de Vega is little more then a pile of rubble.

Accommodation

Albergue (84 beds, kitchen, open April to October)

$$ Hospedería O Cebreiro (☎ 982 36 71 25)

$$ Hospedería San Giraldo de Aurillac (☎ 982 36 71 25)
$$ Casa Carolo (☎ 982 36 71 68)
$$ Hostal Rebollal (☎ 982 36 71 15)

Leave town on the main road, and you'll soon reach **Ruitelán** (Ⓐ☕), where there are picnic tables on the left and an **albergue** (34 beds, kitchen, open all year) on the right. A cave in the hillside above was said to be the home of San Froilán of Lugo, who became bishop of León in the ninth century.

Keep walking down the road, which has no shoulder in places. In about 1km, pass a hotel and restaurant on the left just after a sign for Las Herrerías, and veer left into the village down a minor road.

Famous in the seventeenth century for its iron forge, **Las Herrerías** (Ⓐ☕) was admired by Domenico Laffi, the sixteenth-century Italian camino chronicler who seemed overly fond of the size of local ironworkers' hammers. Today, it's a beautiful little village with the odd bar and café strung out along the camino. The original fountain was said to honour Don Suero de Quiñones of the famous jousting tournament in Hospital de Órbrigo. On the far edge of Las Herrerías, you pass through the area known as Hospital Inglés, where there are no visible remains of the former pilgrims' hospice.

Climb uphill out of Las Herrerías, catching occasional glimpses of La Faba high above. Veer left down a grassy stone track, following a camino sign that directs walkers this way; cyclists should keep to the minor road. The path leads down to the Río Valcarce, then heads steeply uphill towards the hamlet of La Faba.

This steep stretch can be mucky and slippery due to heavy use by local cattle, and you'll have to press tight against the high stone walls if a herd decides to amble past. If you manage to keep your footing, this is an enchanting section of the camino, zig-zagging uphill between stone walls with many trees acting as protection from the rain or, less likely, the sun. As you climb, there are dramatic changes in landscape and the architecture. It feels like a fast rewind through history, finally settling at some misty, magical period of conical, thatch-roofed *pallozas*, cobbled streets and a new language — *Galega*.

After a few kilometres, you'll pass the first house in **La Faba** (☕); look behind here for great views of the Iglesia de San Andrés, rebuilt in the eighteenth century, and the last parish church in Astorga. Head through the peaceful, slate-roofed hamlet, passing a sign for "O Cebreiro, 4km". There's a fountain and a café-bar in La Faba, and an **albergue** was under construction in 2002.

The views open up as the camino passes through fields and rolling hills, with alternating gentle and steep climbing. In 2km, walk through the couple of farms that make up the hamlet of **Laguna de Castilla** (Ⓐ). Although it's the last village in León, there are examples of traditional Galician architecture here: low, thatched-roofed *pallozas* and stone *hórreos*, raised granaries that you'll see in fields and farmyards all the way to Finisterre. Walk through the hamlet on Calle Santiago, which soon becomes a dirt road. There's a summer-only **albergue** here (15 beds, kitchen, open July and August).

About 100m after the last building in

Map 18 (key page 213)

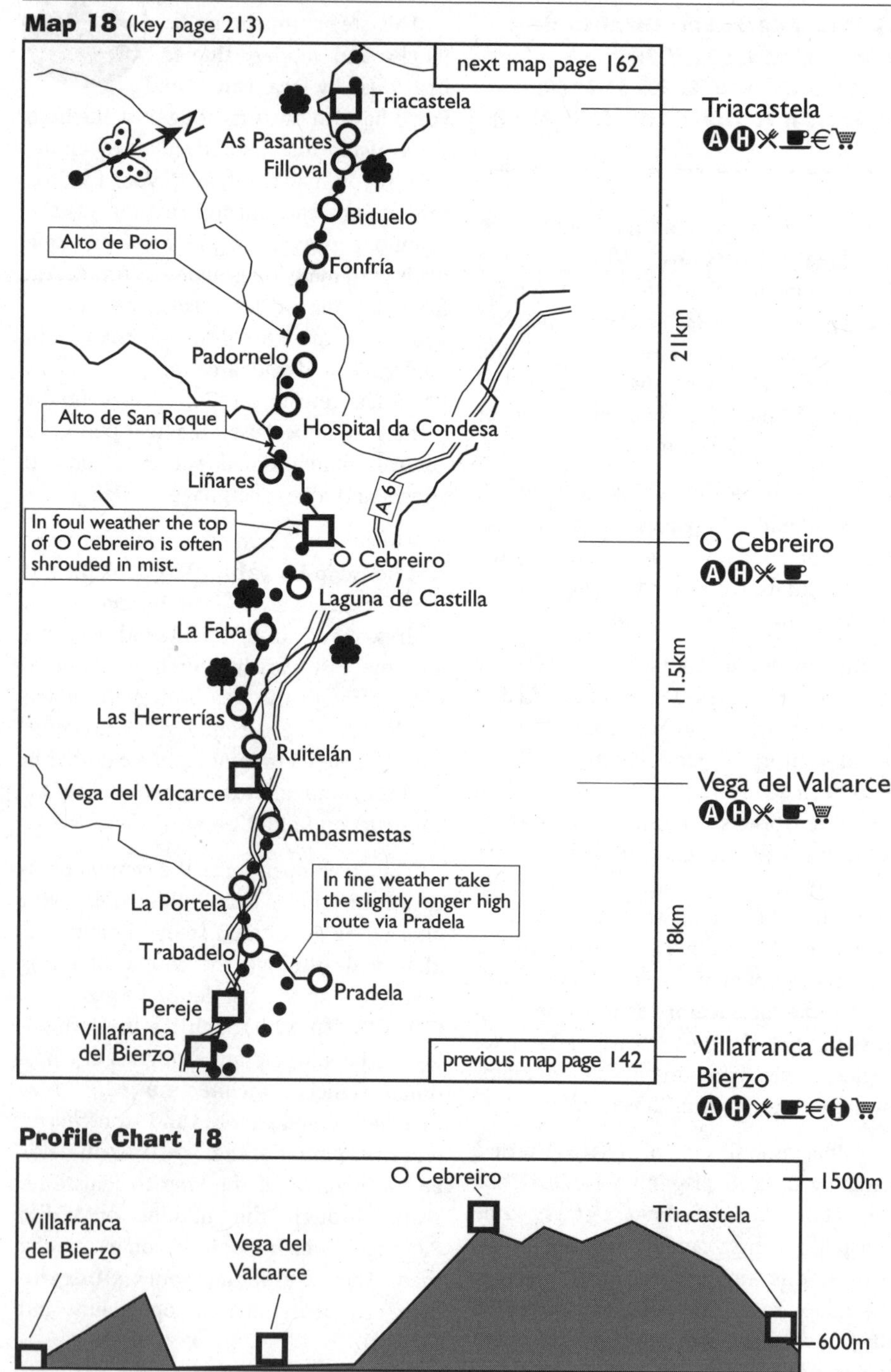

the hamlet, veer left down a grassy stone track, which soon begins to climb again, although much less steeply now. In a kilometre or two, pass a stone sign marking your entrance into Galicia. The weather is often foggy here, and can turn nasty at any minute.

During a blizzard on these mountains in the early years of the nineteenth century, Sir John Moore's retreating English army mutinied after hundreds of soldiers froze to death, throwing a heavy military chest of gold down a cliff in protest. Sir John was having a hard time of it: his soldiers had already trashed Villafranca and drunk Ponferrada dry, and it was remarkable that he managed to regain order. He almost made it home to England, but the unlucky general was shot and killed by the French in A Coruña as he oversaw the embarkation of the English troops.

The countryside is dominated by white broom, laburnum and gorse, with occasional stands of scrub oak. The area is also home to the Northern water rat, although you're more likely to see the cone of excavated earth at the entrance to the rat's small burrow, than the animal itself. The spiky green plants alongside the path are *ajenjo* (wormwood).

In another kilometre, you reach the road and turn left, neatly avoiding the viewing area on the right that tends to be chock full of bus tours. In a couple of hundred metres, turn right to walk into O Cebreiro; the *albergue* is on the far side of the village.

O Cebreiro Ⓐ Ⓗ

There are stunning pastoral views from O Cebreiro on the rare occasions that the mist clears enough to see more than three steps ahead of you. The weather can be truly awful here; summer snowstorms are not unheard of and dense fog is the norm at other times. Although it's pretty in the sunshine, murky mist seems to suit O Cebreiro's architecture perfectly.

The hamlet's round, thatch-roofed **pallozas** are a distinctive form of rural architecture once found across Celtic lands from Africa to Scotland. Their round walls and conical, straw and broom-thatched roofs aerodynamically deflect the strong mountain winds. Chimneys would interfere with the tight weather defences, so smoke escapes through the thatch itself, curing the sausages and hams that hang from the ceiling as it does so. One of these buildings houses the village's small ethnographic museum, which is well worth a look.

The focal point of the village is the modern **Iglesia de Santa María**, rebuilt in the 1960s on top of the ruins of a Romanesque church. It's believed that the Holy Grail from which Christ drank at the Last Supper was hidden here for safe-keeping in the Middle Ages. In the fourteenth century, a local farmer braved a fierce snowstorm to attend Mass at the church. The priest told the man that it was silly to come all the way just for a bit of bread and wine in such terrible weather, at which point the bread turned into flesh and the wine in the Holy Grail became blood.

The church's statue of the Virgin is said to have tilted her head to get a better look at the miracle, and she's now known as La Virgen del Milagro. Although the grail is no longer here, the remains of the flesh and blood are held in a silver reliquary donated by Queen Isabel.

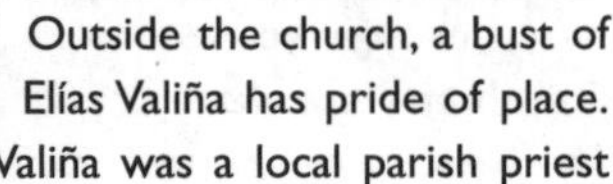

Cordillera Cantábrica

Outside the church, a bust of Elías Valiña has pride of place. Valiña was a local parish priest who wrote important books on the camino and was a driving force behind its revival during the 1960s and 1970s. He also did much to preserve O Cebreiro's *palloza* architecture, and he's buried in the village.

Accommodation

O Cebreiro has sheltered pilgrims from the mountain storms for centuries, and there were *hospitals* here from 1072 to 1854. The modern **albergue** (80 beds, kitchen, open all year) is on far side of the village.

$$ Hospedería O Cebreiro (☎ 982 36 71 25)

$$ Hospedería San Giraldo de Aurillac (☎ 982 36 71 25)

$$ Casa Carolo (☎ 982 36 71 68)

$$ Hostal Rebollal (☎ 982 36 71 15)

The route down from the mountain is exposed to the elements, but there are striking views of the surrounding mountains and valleys as you descend.

Hop down to the LU634, just below the *albergue*, and turn left along the road. Be careful here, as the road can be busy and visibility is often poor due to the weather. If the rain and fog clear, there are lovely views down over the Río Navia valley. In about 3km, the road arrives at the small hamlet of **Liñares**, set in a windy saddle of the mountains. Liñares' name comes from the local flax fields that supplied the linen for the looms in O Cebreiro's pilgrim hospice. The tiny, lovely twelfth-century village church is dedicated to San Esteban.

Climb up to the **Alto de San Roque**, where a dramatic statue of a wind-battered pilgrim (possibly Santiago) marks the pass. In good weather, you can leave the camino here to climb to the top of the nearby summit for great views over the village of Veigas de Forcas. The famous Armestos family who lived there went on to become Knights of Santiago.

Just after the statue, turn right down a dirt track and finally leave the road. Watch for harriers and short-toed eagles up high, and look down low for the pimpernel, wild garlic and blue lilies that grow on the local limestone. These wild mountains are also home to wolves: look closely for their tracks on muddy stretches. Wolves were only part of medieval pilgrims' concerns, as attacks by bandits were common along this stretch.

In a couple of kilometres, you come to **Hospital da Condesa**, which seems to be made almost entirely of slate. Follow the camino right through the hamlet, passing a sporadically open **albergue**. The tiny, beautiful church dates from the twelfth century, but was largely rebuilt in 1963.

At the end of Hospital da Condesa, carry on along the road, take a track to the right at a bend in the road, then turn left 150m later up a lane. Keep to the main track, and in another couple of kilometres come to **Padornelo**. Climb uphill on the far side of the village, gradually at first, but more steeply after passing the Iglesia de San Juan.

In a few hundred metres, you'll reach the pass at **Alto de Poio** (☕), where a cosy bar has a log fire to warm soggy pilgrims in cold weather. Although the Hospitaleros de San Juan de Jerusalen once ran the Iglesia de Santa María at this windswept pass, nowadays there are only a couple of modern houses.

Turn right at the café on to the main tarmac road, then veer right in about 500m to follow a track into **Fonfría**. The village, whose name means cold spring, is a wonderful collection of farm buildings. In medieval times, the Hospital de Santa Catalina offered healthy pilgrims heat, salt, water and a bed with two blankets, while the sick received a bonus of a quarter pound of bread, eggs and butter. Sadly, such luxuries are long gone, and you'll have to wait until Triacastela, some 10km away, for sustenance.

From Fonfría, there's a drop in altitude of 600m to Triacastela. As you descend, you may spot orange-beaked choughs that fly above this section of the camino.

On the far side of the village, rejoin the main road, then almost straight away turn right off the road down a track. In a couple of kilometres, the camino winds through the small hamlet of **Biduelo**. Keep straight on, and in another couple of kilometres you'll come to the hamlet of **Filloval**. Cross the main road next to some picnic benches, a better option than the muddy tunnel that goes under the road here. Below, there are see glimpses of Triacastela on the valley bottom.

The views as you curve down the ridge are fantastic, and the picture-perfect lush fields and farms are only slightly spoilt by a slate quarry on the valley floor. Walk along a track lined with beech trees, watching out for sparrowhawks hunting for prey in the fields on either side of the camino.

After crossing the main road once more, you pass through the wonderful hamlet of **As Pasantes**, where there's some great rural architecture. The leafy valley is dotted with ash, chestnut, hazelnut and birch, and the route becomes more of a lane, with high stone walls on either side; it can be slippery with cow dung in wet weather. Near the bottom of the mountain, you enter Triacastela; the *albergue* is in a field on your left.

Regional Map (key page 213)

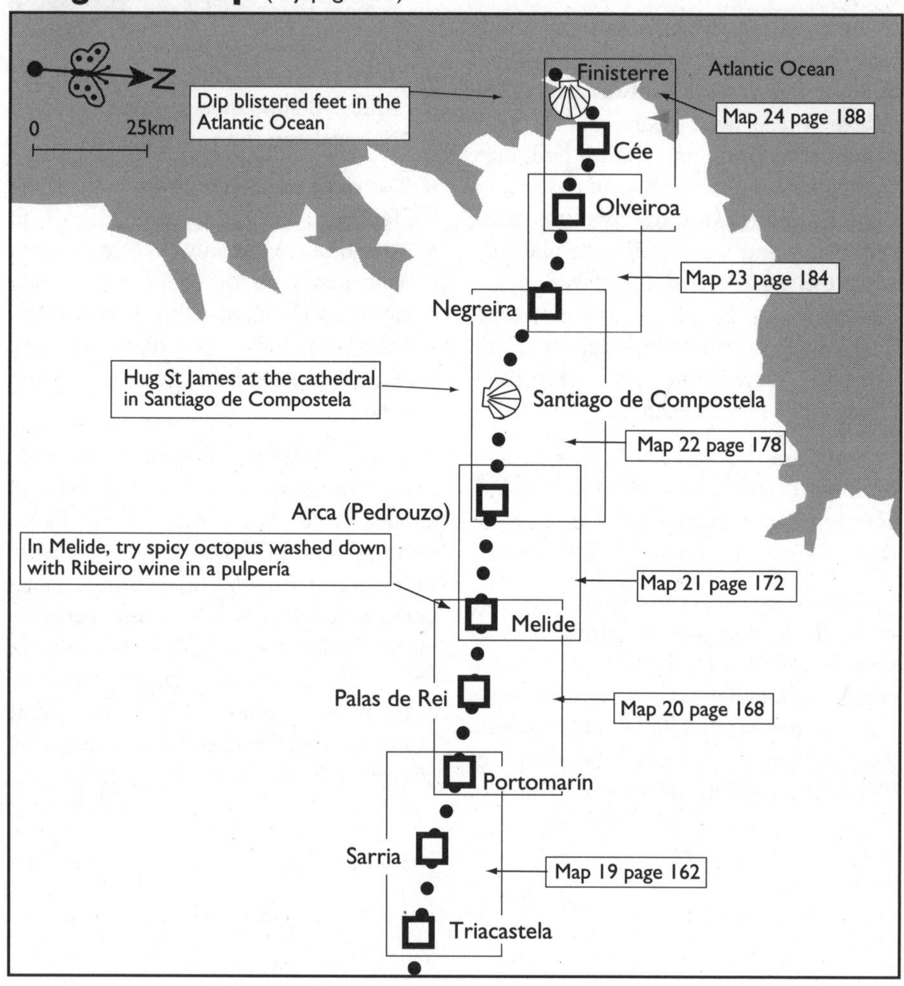

What's the weather like?

	Jan	April	July	Oct
Sun	3hrs	6hrs	8hrs	5hrs
Rainfall	27cm	15cm	3cm	19cm
Maximum Temp	11°C	15°C	22°C	17°C
Minimum Temp	3°C	6°C	12°C	7°C

Average hours of sun, total average rainfall in cm and average temperature in degrees celsius

Galicia

Triacastela to Finisterre via Santiago

Once you're in Galicia, it's a winding, up-and-down route through tiny farms and one-house hamlets and alongside rain-drenched fields and rivers. The volume of pilgrims reaches a crescendo at Santiago, where you give thanks to St James in a series of historic rituals. But don't stop there: if you follow the old Celtic route to the sea at Finisterre, you'll reach the end of the known world via the solitude of quiet lanes and ancient ways.

Walking

Geography

Soggy storms clip this corner of Iberia as they fly along the Gulf Stream, dumping bucketsful of water almost all year round. In an average year, Galicia gets rain on one day in three.

The foggy Costa da Morte is a jagged mix of cliffs and long estuaries that penetrate deep inland, and the coast is a legendary wrecker of countless ships, blown on to the rocks by storms. This maritime carnage may explain the name of the Costa da Morte (coast of death), but the coast may also be named for the nightly death of the sun as it sets on Spain's westernmost shore.

The inland landscape is one of rolling hills and steep river valleys eroded by aeons of rainfall. Lush vegetation and mild winters make Galicia stand out from other, more arid parts of Spain, but for those who know the wilder parts of Ireland, the scenery will be very familiar.

The mountains rise up the further south and east you travel. They can be dusted with snow as late as May and as early as October, and clouds seem to sit permanently around their peaks. Their proximity to the sea means that the weather here is very fickle and you can experience all the seasons on any day of the year without warning.

Trails

The Galician government has made a huge effort to promote the camino. Concrete bollards line the route every half a kilometre and are engraved with the distance to Santiago and local place names, although some rural folk say that a lot of these names are made up. Rather depressingly, the countdown to Santiago changes about 14km out of town, adding extra distance just as you're almost at

your destination. The government invested a lot of money on trail maintenance and signage in the 1993 Holy Year, and introduced Pelerín, an abstract cartoon mascot for the camino through Galicia. There's a special cycling Pelerín too, and the androgynous mascot appears on signs to show the suitability of the terrain for bikes.

The camino is much less crowded after Santiago, and the route is well-marked and wonderfully scenic. Markers give the distance to the exact metre, which seems like overkill. Confusingly, these distances vary: sometimes this distance is to Muxia, and sometimes it's to Finisterre, and it's never really clear which is which.

When to go

The old saying, "Be prepared for rain and pray for sunshine" rings true in Galicia. The winter brings almost constant storms and the sun may not shine for weeks, although it's unlikely to snow as the temperature rarely dips below freezing. In spring and autumn the weather is unpredictable, but if you're lucky you can catch a week or two of constant sunshine. Summer brings the most settled good weather but is also the most popular time of year; *albergues* will be stuffed to the gills and the camino can seem like a well-attended sponsored walk.

Flora & Fauna

Historically, the **oak** forest of Galicia was a national treasure, and its sturdy wood was used to build Spain's mighty naval armada. By the early sixteenth century, in an attempt to preserve the forest for state use, a royal decree forbade anyone from felling the huge trees without a licence.

In the nineteenth century, **eucalyptus** was brought to Spain under the mistaken belief that it would be good for construction. Eucalyptus can grow by as much as 40 feet in three years, much faster than the local oak, making it popular as a source of both pulp and firewood, but foresters soon discovered that the eucalyptus tree twists as it grows and cracks once harvested. In 1941, Franco introduced the badly misnamed State Forest Heritage Act, under which oak was widely chopped down and eucalyptus was planted in its place to feed the fledgling pulp industry, and the non-native species now accounts for almost 27% of the forest in Galicia.

When you're out walking, take a look at the undergrowth of oak and eucalyptus woods. In eucalyptus forests, there's limited plant life and very few animals; birds find little food to eat here and the tree's sticky gum can clog up a bird's throat and kill it. In stark contrast, an old oak wood is a multi-layered canopy of green. Oak forests develop slowly, the soil growing rich with decaying leaves and acorns. Ferns, foxgloves, and other small shrubs provide shelter and food for a variety of animals, and the trees themselves are covered in moss and lichen — a miniature ecosystem in their own right. Black woodpeckers nest in the hollows of old trees, while thrushes and wrens hunt for beetles and grubs among the shrubs. The stubby bullfinch with its rosy breast and black cap is often seen darting through thickets.

Galician farming practices are less intensive and pesticide-reliant than those in the more productive *meseta*. As a result, meadows burst with wildflowers in spring and early summer, and the local cows use the lush grasses to produce a rich, creamy milk that's turned into a wide variety of cheeses.

Without the region's persistent **rain**, Galicia would be devoid of damp-loving plants like the purple large-flowered butterwort and pink bog pimpernel. In the hours after a heavy rainstorm, it's common to see large green Iberian wall lizards drying themselves on slabs of rock or on walls. Fire salamanders are most easily spotted during heavy rain when they crawl out of damp crevices and go hunting: look out for their bulging eyes in wet mountain regions.

People & Culture

Picaud described Galicia as

> "a well wooded and well watered region with rivers and meadows and fine orchards, excellent fruit and clear springs, but with few towns and villages or cultivated fields. ... The Galicians are more like our French people in their customs than any other of the uncultivated races of Spain, but they have the reputation of being violent-tempered and quarrelsome."

Such quarrelsome behaviour would be understandable today, as locals cope with the tide of pilgrims that washes through their province. In fact, Galicians have a reputation of being more reserved than people in the rest of Spain, but the people are some of the kindest and most open you'll meet along the camino.

In the 1991 census, a massive 91% of inhabitants said they where able to speak **Galega**, the region's Portuguese-like language. *Galega* tends to be heard more in rural areas and it's still thought of as an old person's language. After Galicia was granted autonomous government in 1981, the study of the language took off, and modern writers like Manolo Rivas have led to a new interest in *Galega*.

The region has always been poor. The last feudal holding was only abolished in 1973, and the average worker earns about half that of workers in Germany. Since the 1950s, there's been a massive exodus of people from the countryside, initially to South America but nowadays to industrialized cities like A Coruña.

The historic poverty of the region may go some way to explaining why traditional **farming** methods remain popular. As you walk through tiny hamlets it's common to see *palleiros* (haylofts), *pallozas* (straw-covered huts), *bronas* (outdoor ovens for cooking corn bread) and beautiful *hórreos* that dry and store the corn. *Hórreo* designs and materials change from village to village, from simple, sturdy concrete blocks to intricate wood and slate designs that belie their practical function.

Galician **music** is firmly Celtic, and perhaps nothing shows the links between northern Celtic nations and Galicia better then the *gaita* (Galician bagpipe). There seems to be a type of music for every occasion. The most widespread and well-known are the *Danzas de Espadas* and *Danzas de Arcos*, which are linked to local celebrations, but more specific music includes *Alboradas,* which celebrate the rising of the sun, *Pasacorredoiras* (parade tunes) and *Pasarruas* (marching music).

If you're lucky, you might hear farmers and field workers singing traditional *jotas* (work songs) in the rural areas between Santiago and Finisterre.

Food & Drink

Galician cooking is simple, hearty and fantastic. Almost every meal begins with traditional **caldo gallego**, a thick soup made from meat, potatoes, greens and beans. *Empanada gallega de raxó* is a pie-like feast made with Galician pork and peppers.

Eat **seafood** every chance you get, as it's certain to be fresh and delicious. When in Melide, try *pulpo a la gallega*, a taste sensation washed down with white Ribeiro wine: steamed octopus is sliced up, sprinkled with paprika and placed on wooden platters, then served to diners eating communally on large wooden tables and benches. Another delight is *vieiras de Santiago*, scallops with onions and cured ham.

Those with a sweet tooth will love **torta de Santiago**, a type of almond cake dusted with sugar in the shape of the cross of Santiago. You'll see the cake all over Galicia, but particularly in the Holy City itself, where bakers tempt customers into their shops and cafés by offering a free sample.

Galicia's trademark downpours make for happy cows, and their milk is often turned into a soft and creamy teat-shaped cheese named *tetilla* (nipple).

Unlike the red-wine-producing rest of Spain, Galicia's climate is better suited to whites. **Albariño** is a straw-coloured, firm wine with a distinctive peach flavour that's slowly becoming respected outside Spain. **Ribeiro**, its lesser-known cousin, is young, fresh, cloudy and perfect with seafood. In more traditional bars it's poured straight out of the barrel into wide, shallow clay cups. Ribeiro rarely makes it outside Galicia, and EU bureaucrats insist that the bottled version is clarified, so drink your fill while you're here.

Galician beer is mostly as bland as that of the rest of Spain, but the draught version is poured from gorgeous ceramic beer taps. Galicia is also the only place along the camino where you'll regularly come across draught cider.

Made from grape skins, **orujo** is a clear firewater that'll put hairs on your chest. *Orujo* is found all across Spain, but the Galicians make the best orujo and drink far more of it than other Spaniards. *Orujo blanco* comes straight up, while *orujo con hierbas* is a green, slightly calmer version flavoured with herbs. Ask for *orujo casero* to get a meaty, homemade alternative: in true moonshine style, you'll find under-the-counter *orujo casero* in unmarked bottles in bakeries and grocers, as well as in bars and cafés.

Tourist Information

Tourist Offices

Tourist offices in Galicia are like buses; you walk all the way through the province without seeing a single one, and then you arrive in Santiago and three come along at once. For more on the Holy City's confusing array of *turismos*, see page 180.

Transport

Local buses link larger towns like Sarria, Melide and Arzúa, but services can be sporadic. It's easy to catch a train from Santiago to almost any large centre in Spain. For more information on getting home from Santiago, see Getting There & Back on page 28.

Eight buses a day connect Santiago and Finisterre, sometimes requiring a change at Vimianzo. The journey takes between two and three hours.

Money

There are banks and cash machines in Sarria, Portomarín, Palas de Rei, Melide, Arzúa, Arca, Monte do Gozo, Santiago de Compostela, Negreira, Cée and Finisterre.

Accommodation

The infrastructure of the camino in Galicia is centralized and supremely organized. Huge government investment in the 1993 Holy Year led to a flurry of new *albergues* and extensive upgrading of existing ones. You'll rarely travel more than 10km without bumping into an *albergue*; most have kitchens and decent bunk beds, and there's always a payphone outside.

The initial influx of cash hasn't been kept up, so that kitchens and bathrooms may have broken cookers, toilets or showers. The *albergues* are run by paid wardens rather than volunteer *hospitaleros*; they can be sparsely staffed, but you'll often be able to get in though an unlocked door.

Shopping

The sheer number of pilgrims in Galicia hasn't gone unnoticed by the region's budding capitalists, and many stalls and small shops are opening up to sell cold drinks and food, and lure in pilgrims with the promise of a *sello*.

Santiago is jammed full of tacky souvenir shops, and ad hoc markets spring up along its streets in summer. If you're in Finisterre early on a weekday, visit the docks for the fantastic fish market.

Events and Festivals

On July 25, the **Día de Santiago** and Galicia's national day, Santiago's Plaza do Obradoiro erupts in a sound and light display that dates back to the seventeenth century. Galicia parties for twelve months during **Holy Years**, when July 25 falls on a Sunday (2004, 2010 and 2021). Holy Year festivities begin with the opening of the Puerta del Perdón on the east side of the cathedral and end when it's firmly shut at midnight on December 31, while sandwiched in between are literally thousands of concerts, dances, exhibitions and lots of fireworks.

Galicia's other festivals seem to revolve around **food**. Arzúa's cheese festival takes place in March, Ribeiro wine festivals happen all over the province in late April and early May, there's a barnacle festival in Finisterre at the beginning of August, and many other seaside towns hold shellfish and oyster festivals throughout the year.

Some 20km north of Portomarín, the city of **Lugo** is well worth a visit. Its huge, Roman-built slate walls are some of the

best preserved in Spain, and four of the city's ancient gates remain. Lugo's monuments include the twelfth-century cathedral, the seventeenth-century Bishop's palace, and the Gothic churches in the Praza de Santo Domingo. If you're getting bored with churches, you can relax in Lugo's tranquil riverside parks or take the waters at the town's Roman baths.

About 15km northeast of Palas de Rei is the splendid underground chapel of **Santa Eulalia de Bóveda**. Built on the site of a Celtic temple and used for a time as a Roman nymphaeum, the fourth-century Visigothic chapel contains a shallow pool that may have been used to submerge the faithful in early baptisms.

From Melide, it's a 6km walk to **San Antolín de Toques**, a beautiful site with an ancient mill and the half-overgrown remains of an eleventh-century monastery and earlier church. You can turn the detour into a day trip by heading to the well-preserved *castro* of **A Graña**, about 2km away.

If you're not planning on continuing the camino to **Finisterre**, it's well worth visiting the small fishing town on a day trip, if only to dip your toes into the ocean.

A tour of the wild Galician coast can also take in important places in Santiago's life. Many pilgrims visit **Padrón**, the landing place of Santiago's stone boat some 20km southwest of Compostela, where the stone pillar to which Santiago's boat was moored is kept beneath the altar in the Iglesia de Santiago. Time your visit to take in lunch and try a plate of *pimientas de Padrón*, deliciously salty, oil-roasted green peppers.

Just up the coast from Finisterre, the Virgin Mary is said to have visited **Muxia** to hear Santiago preach, sailing here in a stone boat, which was clearly the transport of choice in the early first century. At the sanctuary of Nostra Señora de la Barca, you can see various bits of her boat. The hull moves whenever a person free of sin stands underneath it, while the keel is said to cure digestive problems.

Triacastela

Triacastela was founded in the ninth century by Count Gatón of El Bierzo after the area's reconquest from the Moors. Today, the only evidence of the three castles that Triacastela is named after is on the town's coat of arms. The Romanesque Iglesia de Santiago retains some original features, although it was rebuilt in the eighteenth century.

Triacastela has a long camino history: the area once had many pilgrim hospices, and the town marked the end of stage eleven of the *Codex Calixtinus*. When the cathedral in Santiago de Compostela was being built, twelfth-century pilgrims carried local stone from here to the ovens near Castañeda, more than 100km away.

Today, this little town is a wonderful place to relax after crossing the mountains; numerous bars and restaurants dot the streets and there are several well-stocked shops.

Accommodation

The town's **albergue** (56 beds, no kitchen, open all year) is popular and well-run, with comfortable four-bed dormitories.

$ Hostal Fernández (☎ 982 54 81 48)
$$ Hospedaje O Novo (☎ 982 54 81 05)
$$ Mesón Vilasante (☎ 982 54 81 16)

Walk straight through Triacastela until you reach a T-junction at the end of town. From here, there are two ways to reach Sarria.

Turn left to visit the **Monasterio de Samos** (Ⓐ✕▬). We don't describe this route, but it's well-marked and easy to follow to Samos and on to Sarria. The monastery was founded in the sixth century and still preserves some Visigothic stones from its original construction. The influence of the monastery was so great that at its height it controlled some 200 towns, 105 churches and 300 other monasteries. As a seat of learning, the famous library was perhaps without equal until it was tragically destroyed by fire in 1951. The Latin motto on the door reads, "A cloister without a library is like a fort without an armoury." The library's most famous patron was Padre Benito Feijóo, a luminary of the Spanish Enlightenment who wrote on such varied subjects as astronomy, medicine and religion. You can get a tour from one of monks if you ask nicely. There's an **albergue** (90 beds, no kitchen, open all year) in Samos' monastery, which can be damp and gloomy year-round.

If you don't want to visit Samos, turn right at the T-junction in Triacastela to go to Sarria via San Xil. It's a quieter, more rural route, slightly shorter than the Samos version. Soon after the junction, cross the main road and take the lane on the other side. Climb slowly, sticking to the main lane and looking out for yellow markers.

After a couple of kilometres, you arrive at the beautiful hamlet of **A Balsa**, which boasts stunning farmhouses and gorgeous verandas that overhang the road. Pass an *ermita* and climb up along the small valley of the Río Valdeoscuro. As its name, dark valley, suggests, this lovely stretch of the camino is shaded by mature oaks and chestnut trees, which offer shelter from the elements. Keep your eyes peeled along the forest edge for a glimpse of a pine marten as it hunts voles, rabbits and birds.

Join a tarmac road and turn right, passing a striking fountain with a large concrete scallop shell. The last part of the climb to the village of **San Xil** is steep but at the top you'll see wave upon wave of rolling Galician hills as you finally leave the Cordillera Cantábrica behind. The camino levels off and curves slowly to the right, before rising sharply after a few kilometres to the Alto de Riocabo. At the top of this hill, turn right on to a gravel path and begin to descend. On your left you'll get your first glimpse of Sarria in the Río Celeiro valley up ahead.

The camino slowly descends along a well-worn lane, enclosed by the beautiful dry stone walls that are a common sight along the route through Galicia. Notice the grooves in the stone made from the

Map 19 (key page 213)

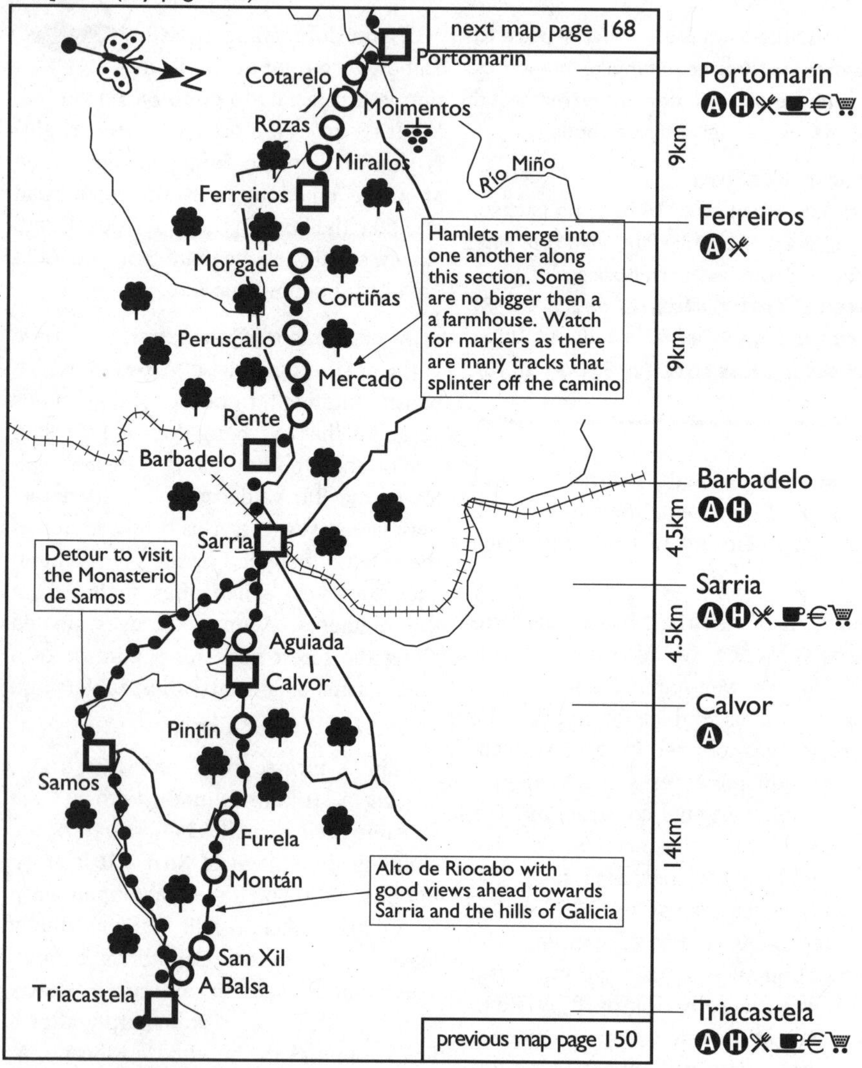

next map page 168

Portomarín
Cotarelo
Moimentos
Rozas
Mirallos
Río Miño
Ferreiros
Morgade
Cortiñas
Peruscallo
Mercado
Rente
Barbadelo
Sarria
Aguiada
Calvor
Pintín
Samos
Furela
Montán
San Xil
A Balsa
Triacastela

Hamlets merge into one another along this section. Some are no bigger then a a farmhouse. Watch for markers as there are many tracks that splinter off the camino

Detour to visit the Monasterio de Samos

Alto de Riocabo with good views ahead towards Sarria and the hills of Galicia

previous map page 150

Portomarín
Ⓐ Ⓗ

9km

Ferreiros
Ⓐ

9km

Barbadelo
Ⓐ Ⓗ

4.5km

Sarria
Ⓐ Ⓗ

4.5km

Calvor
Ⓐ

14km

Triacastela
Ⓐ Ⓗ

Profile Chart 19

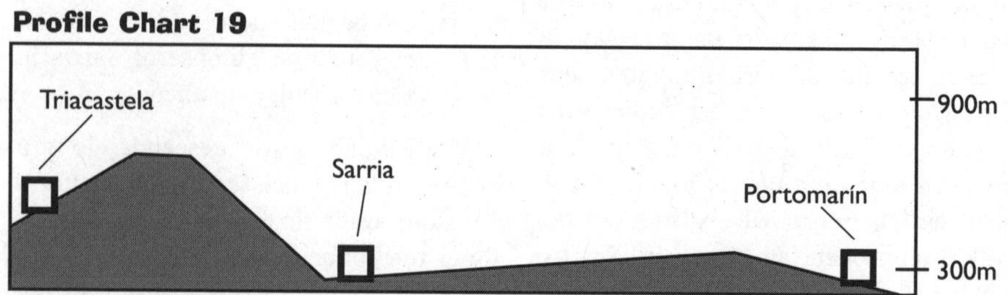

centuries of cartwheels rolling by. Pass through **Montán** with its Iglesia de Santa María, then through **Furela**.

Rejoin the paved road and keep straight on, before turning left steeply downhill on a track through a small forest. About 100m later, turn sharp right and follow the lane across the small valley and up the other side.

Meet the paved road and head into **Pintín**. Turn left and curve through the hamlet, rejoining the road on the other side, then turn right 100m later on to another dirt track that takes you through a large farm. Although corn and potatoes are grown in this region, dairy farming is the main occupation of farmers in these valleys. Most of the cows are friesians but you'll also see some *rubia gallega*, a smooth, russet-coloured cow native to Galicia.

As the paved lane veers back towards the main road, take the dirt lane on the right. Cross the main road again a short while later, and take a track that zig-zags through trees before rejoining the main road at **Calvor** (Ⓐ). Although there's a small **albergue** here (22 beds, kitchen, open all year), there are no bars or shops until you reach Sarria, some 4km away.

In a couple of hundred metres, cross the road and turn right down a lane with a sign for **Aguiada**. On the other side of the hamlet, pick up a purpose-built camino track that runs parallel to the main road, following it to the outskirts of Sarria.

Just before Sarria, the track ends. Follow the road into town, cross a main road, then take the first right at a roundabout and arrive at the Ponterribeira, a bridge decorated with modern art sculpture that spans the Río Ouribio. Turn right at the end of the bridge, then turn first left to climb up the Escalinata Mayor steps to the *albergue* and the Iglesia de Santa María.

Sarria Ⓐ Ⓗ ✕ ☕ € 🛒

The layout of Sarria's old town is based on its medieval plan, although the Celtic castle that once dominated the town's skyline was dismantled in 1860 under the banner of civic progress, so that its stone could be used to pave the town's streets. The Renaissance sculptor Gregorio Hernández, whose work graces many of the churches along the camino, was born in Sarria, while Alfonso IX, the last king of León, died here in 1230.

The camino passes the modern, undistinguished Iglesia de Santa Marina, from where there are fantastic views of the surrounding countryside. Further along, the **Iglesia de San Salvador** retains some beautiful Romanesque decorations. The **Convento de la Magdalena** is home to the Order of Mercedarians (Order of Mercy), who were less violent than contemporaries such as the Templars and Knights of St James, and simply sought to free captive Christians from the Moors. Pilgrims leaving Sarria in the early morning may be met by the ghostly figure of a monk standing in a distinctive white wool habit and offering a guided tour of the church and cloister.

There are a few stork nests around town, and these may be the last of the distinctive, untidy landmarks that you'll see on the camino. The newer, lower modern town has little soul and no real centre, but there are some interesting antique shops on its western outskirts.

Accommodation

The **albergue** (40 beds, open all year) is in a tall, narrow house with laundry facilities and a tiny, sporadically working kitchen.

$$ Hostal Londres, Calle Calvo Sotelo 13 (☎ 982 53 24 56)

$$ Hostal Roma, Calle Calvo Sotelo 2 (☎ 982 53 22 11)

$$ Hotel Villa de Sarria, Calle Benigno Quiroga 49 (☎ 982 53 19 38)

$$$ Hotel El Alfonso IX, Rúa do Peregrino 29 (☎ 982 53 00 05)

Walk past the Iglesia de Santa Marina and follow the old Rúa Maior across the top of Sarria. Turn right at a fountain, from where there are good views of Sarria and the hills behind. Approach the Convento de la Magdalena, and turn left at a cemetery just before it to walk downhill. Turn right at the bottom of the steep hill along the tarmac road, then turn left 100m later to cross the stone Ponte Áspera over the Río Celeiro. Walk along a dirt path through trees alongside the main Madrid to A Coruña railway, following the valley bottom.

Cross the railway, and you'll soon begin to climb out of the valley through a lush, mossy oak wood, a wonderful place to spot black woodpeckers as they drill into trees looking for insects. The slope begins to flatten out as you walk between fields and the camino eventually joins the road at **Vilei**. Turn left on to the road and head towards Barbadelo.

Barbadelo Ⓐ Ⓗ

Barbadelo was originally part of a large **monastery** that housed both nuns and monks, a co-habitation arrangement that didn't sit well with the powers at Samos, who staged an ecclesiastical coup in 1009. The church you see today was built soon afterwards and is the only monastery building that remains; it's dominated by a fortified tower, which has strange and fantastical animals carved into the stone blocks.

The slate-roofed stone farmhouses that dot the surrounding patchwork fields look like they should be on the western fringes of Ireland rather than in Spain. More distinctly Iberian are Barbadelos' **hórreos**, rectangular granaries built on stilts that are used to dry corn and keep it out of the reach of rodents. They usually have a cross on top for divine crop protection.

Accommodation

The **albergue** (18 beds, kitchen, open all year) is on the right about 500m after the village. You can also stay at **Casa Nova de Rente ($$, ☎ 982 18 78 54).**

From Barbadelo to Portomarín, the ancient hamlets seem to merge into each other. It's often hard to know where one ends and another begins, and some hamlets are so small that they consist of just a single slate-roofed farmhouse. Keep your eyes peeled as, although the route is well-marked, junctions and small tracks splinter off the camino in all directions. Peering into barns and farms can reveal ad hoc ethnographic museums of antique ploughs, wooden racks and ox-carts gloomily gathering dust.

About 1km out of Barbadelo, turn left down a track. You'll soon walk through **Rente**, passing a *casa rural* on the left before returning to the paved road. At **Mercado**, in about 500m, cross a tarmac road to walk on a stony dirt track that's shaded by oak and beech trees. In summer, it's common to see handsome stag beetles, which seldom stray far from the mature oak trees where they lay their eggs.

Pass a rest stop with a fountain, then turn right a few hundred metres later down another track. Cross a dammed river valley bottom on a broad, stone slab path then, at a junction with a tarmac road, keep straight on along a minor road through the modern houses that make up **Peruscallo** (✕), where there's a restaurant on the right. Carry on this tarmac road for about a kilometre, then pass through **Cortiñas**.

At the end of Cortiñas, the route changes to a stony dirt track. In less than a kilometre, walk through another hamlet, passing, in the middle of the track, perhaps the largest oak tree you'll see on the whole camino. Look out for the modern brick *hórreo* here too, less pretty than the older stone versions, but clearly showing the importance of these traditional granaries to 21st-century farming life.

Moss-covered dry stone walls line the route to **Morgade** (☕), a one-house hamlet where there's a lovely old wooden *hórreo* in front of a dairy shed and an excellent café that sells mouthwatering homemade cakes. Just past the hamlet, the tiny *ermita* on the right has been built into the natural surroundings, using the natural uneven rock as its floor.

Cross a stream, then walk up a stone path that can be flooded after rain, although wide stone slabs in the middle of the path act as stepping stones to make sure that your feet stay dry. Walk through **Ferreiros** (Ⓐ✕), then join a tarmac road. There's an **albergue** (22 beds, kitchen, open all year) and a fountain here, and the first vines since El Bierzo. Turn right at a sign for the Igrexia Romana at Mirallos, which you'll soon reach. The church has a lovely Romanesque doorway and the adjacent cemetery is home to large, ornate tombs. There's also a restaurant next door.

Turn left off the road in a further 100m and head down a dirt track, entering **Rozas** just as the track changes to tarmac. Keep straight on through the hamlet, where there's a fountain for thirsty pilgrims. About 200m later, turn right up a stone path that soon changes to a wide dirt track enclosed by mossy stone walls. Cross another road on a tarmac road, then turn left after 200m to head downhill into **Moimentos**.

At the top of a rise, there are glimpses of a reservoir and Portomarín up ahead. Turn left soon after reaching the top of the hill to walk down a dirt track, getting your first proper views of the damned Río Miño in the distance. Walk through another hamlet and turn left on to a tarmac road at a pine wood. Turn right a few hundred metres later at the end of the wood, and soon reach **Cotarelo**, where there are beautifully built stone houses.

Take the tarmac road on the other side of the village, then walk downhill and keep straight on, following the road as it veers left 100m later. From here, there are good views of the boxy fortified church that dominates Portomarín. Walk steeply downhill, then turn left at the bottom of the hill on to a newer tarmac road, and turn right soon afterwards to cross the bridge into town. As you walk over the bridge, take a moment to peer over the

rails into the gloomy waters below to spot walled lanes leading out from the submerged old town. Lots of birds call this artificial lake home, and it's common to see kingfishers, cormorants, egrets and herons.

The nicest way into Portomarín is straight up the stairs at the end of bridge. Follow the cobbled street past a fountain, then turn right for the small town centre. To avoid Portmarín, turn left at the foot of stairs and follow the road to the left.

Portomarín

ⒶⒽ✂☕€🛒

In 1956, it must have seemed to the people of Portomarín that their lucky charm had let them down. For centuries, locals believed that **La Virgen de las Nieves** protected them from drowning, and they built a shrine to her in the Middle Ages at the centre of the bridge over the Río Miño. Her statue and the town itself were threatened by Franco's plans to construct the Embalse de Belesar, a hydro-electric dam 40km downriver, creating a large lake and condemning the town to a watery grave. Maybe it was the Virgin herself who bent the dictator's ear, for a decision was eventually made to move Portomarín away from the grasp of the rising waters, although it took until 1962 to move the town's monuments to the new site above the west bank of the dammed river. A single span of the old bridge sits at the end of the new bridge, and the Iglesia de Santa María was placed on top to house the talismanic La Virgen de las Nieves.

The modern town somehow retains a lingering atmosphere of displacement and impermanence, and is perched uncomfortably and unnaturally high above the Miño.

In Portomarín, all roads lead to the chunky, fortified **Iglesia de San Juan**, built in the thirteenth century by the Knights of St John. The church, which is also known as San Nicolás, has four towers and battlements on top, and it looks more like a castle keep than a place of worship, although its militaristic outline is softened by a magnificent rose window and carved doorway.

Accommodation
Albergue (160 beds, kitchen, open all year)
$$ Posada del Camino (☎ 982 54 50 81)
$$ Hostal Mesón de Rodríguez (☎ 982 54 50 54)
$$$ Hotel Posada de Portomarín (☎ 982 54 52 00)

From Portomarín, walk down the main street, turn left at the main road, and then turn right almost immediately, doubling back on yourself to cross a rickety metal footbridge. If you missed out the town, you're already on the main road and you simply need to turn left to cross the bridge. Turn right at the end of the bridge up a road, then left in 100m up a dirt track through pine trees. As you climb, the pine trees, heather and broom thin out, giving way to more cultivated fields. According to Aymeric Picaud's twelfth-century guide, this part of the camino was famous as an open-air brothel.

The track arrives at the main C535 road, first following its left-hand side, then after about 300m switching to the other side of the road. There's less shade here, but some bushes have been planted that may provide shelter as they mature.

The camino continues to climb steadily uphill. Cross the road again at a stinky chicken factory to walk on the left-hand side of road once more. The camino veers through a pine wood and then returns back to the main road. You're soon able to see Gonzar ahead as you pass a small picnic area and fountain on the left and approach the hamlet.

There's little more to **Gonzar** (Ⓐ) than the local dairy farm, and at times the smell from the cowshed can be overpowering. The **albergue** (20 beds, kitchen, open all year) has very strange showers with half-height, wild-west-style swinging doors. If you're going to stay here, bring your own food from Portomarín as there are no shops or restaurants in Gonzar. In summer, a makeshift bar may be open, but even if it's closed, the *hospitalera* can get you a beer and a *bocadillo* if she's around. The tiny Iglesia de Santa María is usually locked.

Turn left off the road just after the *albergue*, and then right 100m later on to a dirt track that runs parallel to the main road through pine forest and fields. About a kilometre later, enter **Castromaior** (☕🛒), named after the large prehistoric *castro* that once stood north of here across the river. The ruins of a Roman camp have also been discovered on the edge of the village. Turn left along a paved road and walk through this lovely hamlet and past the small Iglesia de Santa María. There's a store and a bar here, usually open only in high season.

An ancient local legend tells of a pig herder girl who left pig snouts at Castromaior for the traditional annual sacrifice. Next day, she returned to find that the snouts had turned into lumps of coal, which she threw away, but at the last moment decided to kept a single lump. Next morning, she awoke to discover that the lump of coal had turned to a gold nugget. The girl rushed back for the rest of the coal but by the time she arrived back at the spot the lumps had vanished.

Climb uphill out of the village and meet the main road, turning left. After 200m, cross the main road and continue along the other side, admiring the views over the valley, but keeping a wary eye out for snout-shaped gold.

After a kilometre or so, cross back over the road and take the track on the left, arriving in **Hospital de la Cruz** (Ⓐ) where there's an **albergue** (22 beds, kitchen, open all year).

Curve around to cross over the newly built overpass, then turn left and then right towards **Ventas de Narón**, 1km away. Follow the paved road and enter the village, where there's a bar and a rest area with picnic benches. In 820, a few short years after the discovery of the tomb of Santiago, the Christians gained a bloody victory over the troops of the Emir of Córdoba here.

Climb out of the village and over the Serra de Ligonde, the watershed of the Río Miño and the Río Ulla, from where there are great views. Several significant Celtic settlements dot the route here, and a number of hamlets just off the camino incorporate the word *castro* (hill fort) into their name: Castro de Ligonde, Castro de Lardeiros, Castro de Gimonde and Castro de San Símon all have significant archaeological remains, and it's worth exploring these prehistoric treasures if you have time.

Head gradually downhill and through

Map 20 (key page 213)

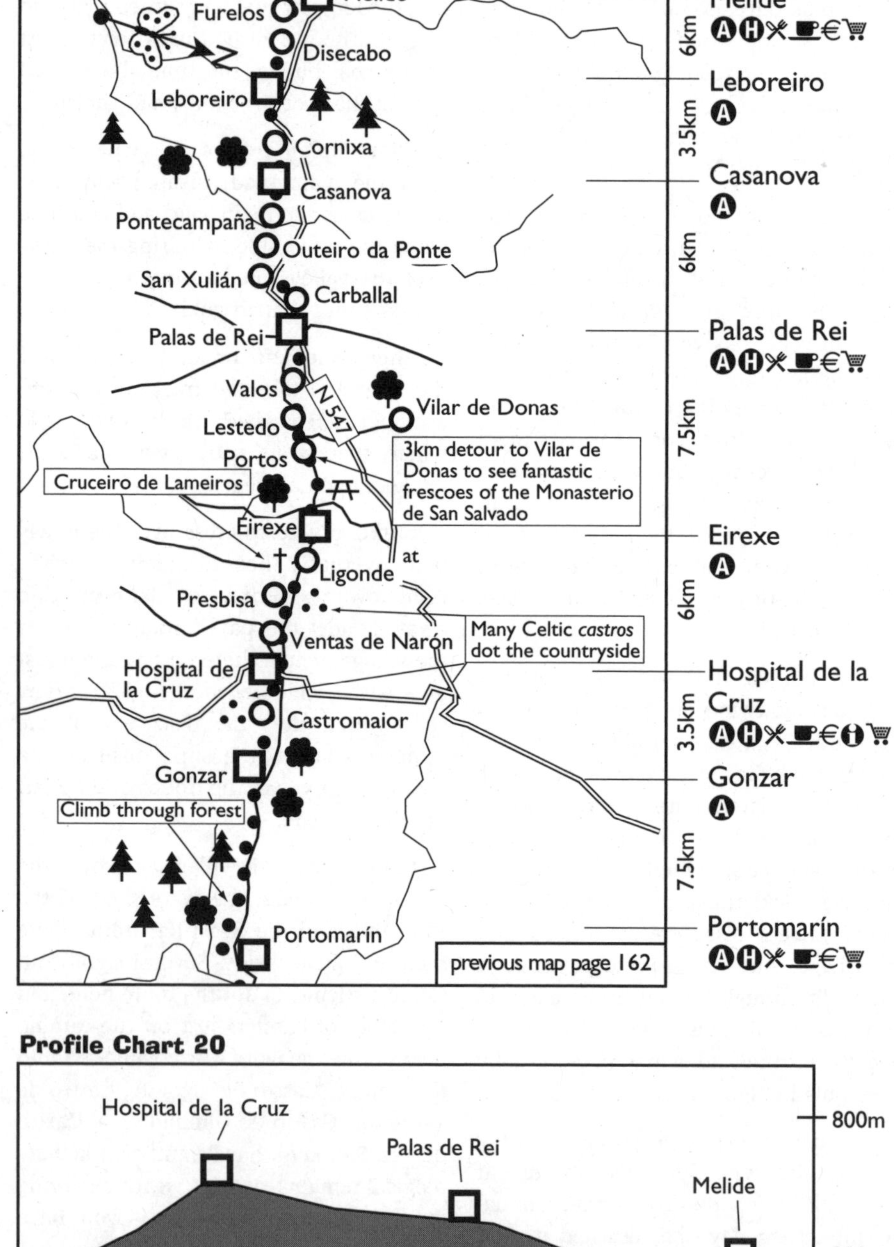

Profile Chart 20

Presbisa, then pass the small Capilla de San Marcos on the right, and walk through **Lameiros**. The lovely Cruceiro de Lameiros is on the left of the camino on the way into **Ligonde**, a hamlet stretching out along the camino for several hundred metres.

At the far end of Ligonde, zig-zag down a paved road to a bridge then climb up to **Eirexe** (Ⓐ), where there's another *cruceiro*. Keep right here, and pass the **albergue** (18 beds, kitchen, open all year) on your right, then veer left at the crossroads immediately afterwards. Just past the *albergue*, there's a picnic area and a fountain here for those in need of a drink and a rest.

At the top of a rise, five roads meet at a confusing junction. Don't panic! Simply keep straight on and head steeply downhill, admiring the views across the valley to the modern windmills perched on the far hill. Your route will eventually take you just to the left of the windmills, but for now head down into **Portos**. From here, a lane on the right detours in 3km to the Monasterio de San Salvador at Vilar de Donas. The monastery was the official burial place of the *Caballeros de Santiago* (Knights of Santiago), and its fantastic frescoes show the Parable of the Ten Virgins.

Veer right at a fountain into Lestedo, then climb up out of the hamlet. Pass a set of gateposts with two lions on top, then keep climbing past a cemetery and a *cruceiro*. Keep straight on, ignoring the tempting signs for Sucastro, and head instead into **Valos**. Walk up and over the top of the hill, passing an out-of-place eucalyptus plantation, then just before the track joins the N547 main road, keep left along a dirt track between a restaurant and a picnic area.

Skirt the one-house hamlet of **Brea** before climbing up to the top of **Alto Rosario**, the name of both a hill and the hamlet that you'll soon pass through, picking up a cobbled track at the end of the hamlet. Soon afterwards, turn left on to a dirt lane, arriving at a picnic area and sports field with fantastic views of the valley below; on a clear day, it's possible to see Monte Pico Sacro near Santiago de Compostela from here.

Keep right, walking downhill past the sports complex and wind down into Palas de Rei, turning right as you enter the town. Pass the new looking church and keep straight on through town, passing the *albergue* on your left.

Palas de Rei

Ⓐ Ⓗ ✕ ☕ € 🛒

Palas de Rei's origins are murky. No one really knows where the name comes from and it doesn't appear in historical documents until the ninth century, although there's probably been a settlement here for much longer as the surrounding area is jammed with Roman and Celtic remains. What isn't in doubt is that Palas de Rei has always been an important stop on the camino, and marked the end of the twelfth stage in Aymeric Picaud's famous guide. Predictably, Picaud didn't like it much, thinking it full of harlots who deserved, "not only be excommunicated, but stripped of everything and exposed to public ridicule, after having their noses cut off."

There's not much left from Palas de Rei's twelfth-century heyday, and the **Iglesia de San Tirso**'s Romanesque origins have been mostly obscured by later restorations.

Accommodation

Albergue (60 beds, no kitchen, open all year)

$ Hospedaje Gun Tina (☎ 982 38 00 80)

$$ Pensión Ponterroxán (☎ 982 38 01 32)

$$ Hostal Vilariño (☎ 982 38 01 52)

To leave Palas de Rei, walk down the Travesia de la Iglesia, a set of stone steps off the main street. Follow the crazy paving road out of the village and turn right as it joins the main road. Almost immediately, turn left downhill, then at the bottom of the hill, cross the road and take the bridge across the Río Ruxián.

The river is named after San Julián, the patron saint of ferrymen, innkeepers and circus performers. The legend of San Julián reads more like a Greek tragedy than the life of a Saint. One day, Julián was out hunting when a deer he killed warned him that he would murder his own parents. To avoid this fate, Julián went into self-imposed exile, but a few years later, Julián's parents discovered his whereabouts and decided to visit. Julián was out at the time, and the parents were tired, so Julián's wife offered them her own bed to rest in. On his return, Julián thought that the people in his bed were his wife and a lover, and flew into a rage, murdering his parents with his sword. Horrified by what happened, Julián and his wife made the pilgrimage to Rome to repent, and set up a hospice for poor travellers and pilgrims. After years of helping people, an angel appeared and granted them divine pardon.

On the far bank of the river, join a path that winds steeply up through **Carballal**. At the other side of the village, turn left at the main road, then take a sharp left down a short steep dirt track through trees soon afterwards. Don't be surprised if you're met by a chorus of frogs, as this section can be damp and swampy. Soon the camino joins up with a paved road, then almost straight away veers left again down a dirt track and into **San Julián** (San Xulián). The twelfth-century Romanesque **Iglesia de San Julián** is worth a short visit, and the local architecture is very different here, with roofs made from tile rather than slate. At the far end of the village, keep straight on down a dirt track.

In **Outeiro da Ponte**, rejoin the paved road and cross a bridge over the Río Pambre. Climb up the other side of the valley through the tiny hamlet of **Pontecampaña**, a lovely walk through oak trees along a stone trail grooved with many years of cart-track traffic. Rejoin the paved road and turn left into **Casanova** (Ⓐ), where there's an **albergue** (20 beds, kitchen, open all year) on the right. In a hundred metres or so, fork right and climb up through a pine and oak forest, then head down to **Porto de Bois** and the Río Villar and up the other side. Cross into the province of La Coruña, passing a large junkyard on the right, before entering **Cornixa** (✕☕), where a bar and restaurant straddle the camino. Turn left 50m later on to a dirt track and see the outskirts of Melide in the distance and Leboreiro just ahead.

Leboreiro (Ⓐ) declined sharply after its heyday in the eleventh to thirteenth centuries, when the **Iglesia de Santa María** was built to house a statue of the Virgin. Villagers following a lovely smell and a glowing light discovered the statue at a local fountain. They placed the Virgin in their church altar, but she miraculously returned to her fountain. For a few days, the villagers returned the statue to the altar, but by the following morning she had always reappeared at the fountain. Eventually, the villagers decided to honour the Virgin by carving a tympanum and dedicating the church to her. Her ego satisfied, the Virgin stayed put, although some say that she returns to the fountain each night to comb her hair. The Casa de la Enfermería, an old pilgrim hospice, is just opposite the church. Modern pilgrims can stay at the **albergue** (20 beds, kitchen, open all year).

The countryside is now much drier, with fewer trees and more thorn, broom and heather. Head downhill to **Disecabo** and cross a humpbacked bridge dedicated to María Magdalena. Keep left on a track just before the main road as the camino skirts industrial land. Two large stones in front of a factory display the names of some 250 local *amigos del camino* (friends of the camino). Soon afterwards, there's another huge stone topped by an impressive Templar cross. Follow the wide gravel track for a short while, then veer off it down a dirt track to the right, heading through shady mixed forest.

You'll soon cross the four-arched medieval Ponte Velha into the village of **Furelos**, now merged with the larger town of Melide. The Iglesia de San Juan on the other side of the bridge sometimes offers good guided tours in English. Head through Furelos, following the crazy paving road uphill and into Melide. Turn left at the main street, looking closely for yellow arrows, and walk about 200m up to a fountain and a roundabout. Turn right at the roundabout, then turn first left and walk down this street for about 400m until a yellow arrow directs you right to the *albergue* on the far side of town.

Melide

Slap bang in the middle of Galicia, archaeological evidence shows that people have lived in this area since megalithic builders erected their *dolmens* almost 4000 years ago. The **Museo da Terra de Melide** is a wonderful place to learn more about the region's history and about traditional life, customs and craftsmanship. The *camino aragónes* rejoins the *camino francés* here after detouring to Oviedo to see the Catedral de San Salvador's impressive collection of relics, including a phial of the Virgin's milk.

Melide's religious monuments, like those of many towns along the camino, are spread out along the pilgrim road. The **Iglesia de San Pedro** has a collection of fourteenth-century tombs, but they're overshadowed by the magnificently carved Cruceiro de Melide outside its doors. If it's open, the **Iglesia de Sancti Spiritus**, built with stones from the old castle and once part of a fourteenth-century Franciscan monastery, is worth visiting. Towards the western edge of town, the **Iglesia del Carmen** sits at the foot of a hill that was once the site of a castle and ancient hill fort.

Don't pass through Melide without visiting a **pulpería**. At Pulpería Ezequiel on Melide's main street, sit at long, wooden benches and sample the only thing on the menu: *pulpo* (octopus). The *pulpo* is sprinkled with Spanish paprika and drizzled with olive oil, then picked up from a rustic wooden platter with toothpicks. Mop up the tasty, spicy juice with hunks of bread, and wash the lot down with

Map 21 (key page 213)

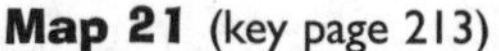

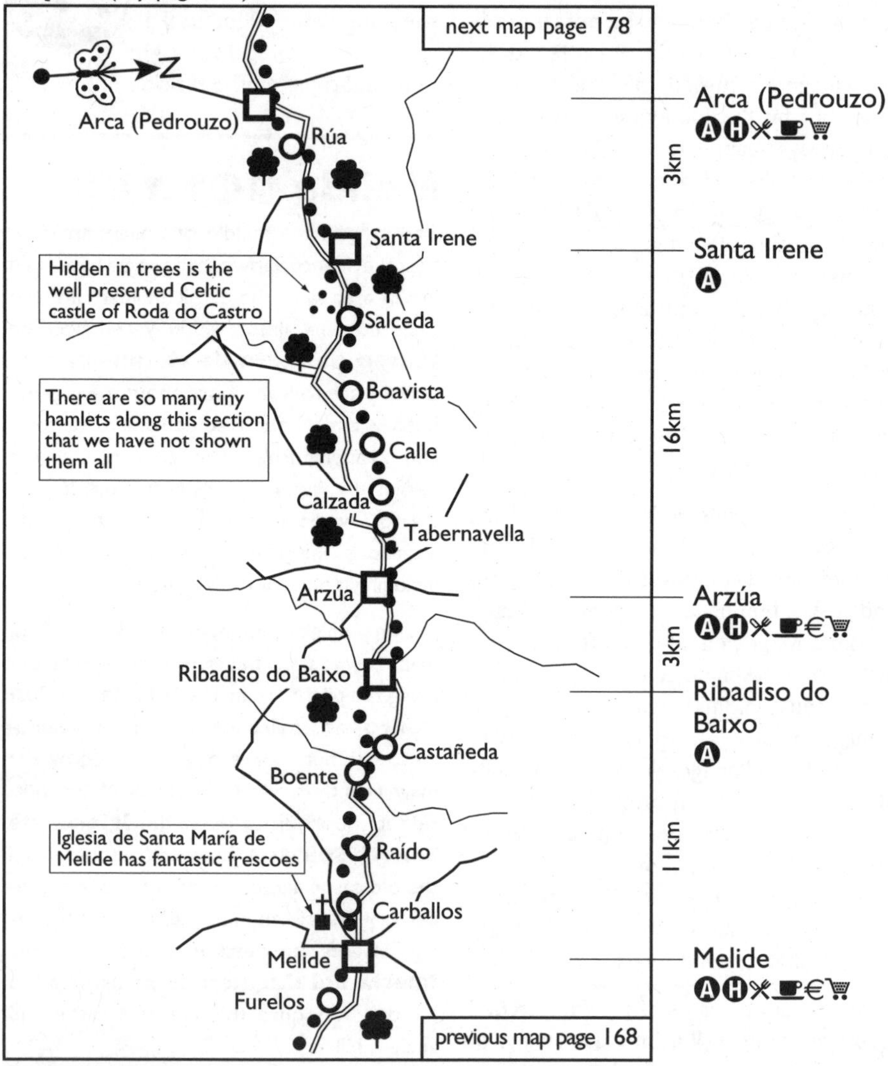

next map page 178
Z
Arca (Pedrouzo)
Rúa
Santa Irene
Hidden in trees is the well preserved Celtic castle of Roda do Castro
Salceda
Boavista
There are so many tiny hamlets along this section that we have not shown them all
Calle
Calzada
Tabernavella
Arzúa
Ribadiso do Baixo
Castañeda
Boente
Iglesia de Santa María de Melide has fantastic frescoes
Raído
Carballos
Melide
Furelos
previous map page 168
3km
16km
3km
11km
Arca (Pedrouzo)
A H
Santa Irene
A
Arzúa
A H €
Ribadiso do Baixo
A
Melide
A H €

Profile Chart 21

500m
200m
Melide
Arzúa
Santa Irene

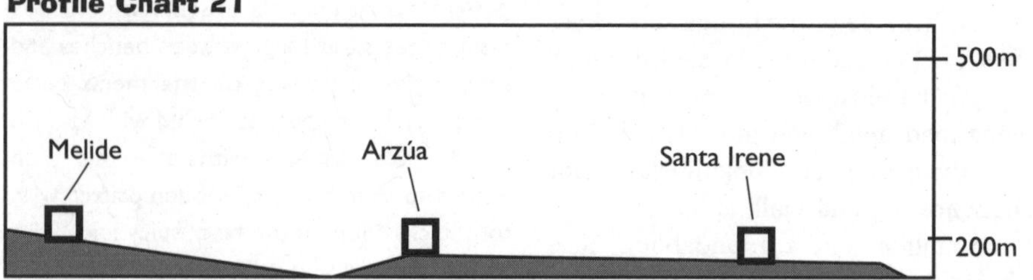

characteristically cloudy Ribeiro wine served in ceramic cups. On Sundays all over Galicia, street sellers serve *pulpo* fresh from big copper cauldrons.

Accommodation

Albergue (130 beds, kitchen, open all year)

$ Fonda Xaneiro I (☎ 981 50 50 15)

$$ Hostal Carlos (☎ 981 50 76 33)

$$ Hotel Xaneiro II (☎ 981 50 61 40)

From Melide to Arzúa, there's a lot of up-and-down climbing, and you'll start seeing more eucalyptus. To leave Melide, turn left at the *albergue* and walk down a paved road. Cross the main C547 road and keep straight on, then turn right in a couple of hundred metres down a smaller road. Pass the **Iglesia de Santa María de Melide** as the track changes to a gravel road. This lovely twelfth-century Romanesque church has some beautiful frescoes inside; try the door to see if it's open.

A little further on, pass through **Carballos**. Turn right off the road 500m after the hamlet up a gravel track, then left a couple of hundred meters later down a dirt track through eucalyptus trees, interspersed with the odd section of pine or oak. As in much of the rest of Galicia, local farmers are chopping down the native oak forest and planting fast-growing eucalyptus.

Cross a stream on broad stone slabs, then climb steeply up the other side of the valley to **Raído**. Bear right and then left to follow a dirt path at the side of the main road, walk along the road for just a couple of hundred metres, then turn left on to a broad, dirt road that heads through a mix of trees and fields. In a little under a kilometre, turn left at a tarmac road, then turn right down a dirt track through some trees. Pass a picnic area then walk past the couple of houses that make up **A Peroxa** as the road changes to tarmac. Turn left to walk through **Boente**, known for its local fountain, the Fonte da Saleta, and the Iglesia de Santiago de Boente. Reach the main road, walk on the sidewalk for 100m, then turn right at a church. The route changes to a dirt road once more, becoming a pleasant stroll through rolling countryside.

Walk downhill, cross a tarmac road then duck under the main C547 road via a tunnel. There's a picnic area on your right here at the valley bottom, a lovely spot for a rest before the steep climb up the other side. Walk past a eucalyptus wood planted in regimented lines, then turn left near the top of the steep climb to join the tarmac road at **Castañeda** (☕), where there's a café-bar just off the camino. No trace remains of the lime ovens in Castañeda where the stone blocks for Santiago's cathedral were finished. Pity the medieval pilgrims who carried the limestone from Triacastela to here!

Turn left at a sign for Río Doraña, then right 100m later. Go through **Pedrido**, a pretty hamlet in a valley bottom, then climb up the other side on a stony dirt track. The route flattens out for a while, then crosses the C547 via a bridge.

Soon, you see Arzúa on the hill opposite. At the bottom of yet another valley, cross the Río Isa as you enter the tiny hamlet of **Ribadiso do Baixo** (Ⓐ). Also known to pilgrims as Puente

Paradiso, it's a beautiful location with an excellent **albergue** (62 beds, kitchen, open all year) in the restored hospice of San Antón, which dates from the fourteenth century.

Walk uphill and turn left just before the main road, then pass under it via a tunnel. Follow a paved road past a couple of houses, then turn left to continue on a gravel track on the left-hand side of the main road. It's a long approach through Arzúa's ugly outskirts into town, but once you finally get there, veer left off the main road down a stone paved street. The *albergue* is on your left, and the main square is on the right just off the camino.

Arzúa Ⓐ Ⓗ ✕ €

Arzúa is a bustling town, renowned throughout Spain for its smooth, creamy **cheese**. This local gastronomic delight is celebrated with a statue of a cheesemaker in the main square, and if you're lucky enough to be here in March, you can celebrate alongside the locals at the town's annual cheese festival. Traditionally, Arzúa was the last stop before Santiago, although many pilgrims now opt to stop closer to their final destination.

The **Iglesia de Santiago** dates from the 1950s, and the Saint adopts his war-like Matamoros pose on top of the nineteenth-century *retablo*.

Arzúa is a large, well-equipped town with banks, restaurants and supermarkets.

Accommodation

Albergue (46 beds, kitchen, open all year)
$$ Fonda Teodora (☎ 981 50 00 83)
$$ Hostal O Retiro (☎ 981 50 05 54)
$$ Hostal Mesón de Peregrino (☎ 981 50 08 30)
$$$ Hotel Suiza (☎ 981 50 08 62)

At the end of Arzúa, the street changes to a dirt track. The valleys are gentler now, making the final approach into Santiago a lovely walk. Turn left at the road just before Preguntoño. Pass under the main road and head up a tarmac road towards **Preguntoño**. Walk out of the village on a stone track, heading uphill through an oak wood, a good spot for birdwatching.

Cross a tarmac road once the route flattens out, then about 500m later walk through **Tabernavella**. Eucalyptus plantations line the route from here to **Calzada**. Cross the tarmac road soon after the hamlet ends to walk along a dirt farm track, then keep straight on in 400m to follow a gravel track through trees.

Walk through **Calle**, past a fountain and down a wide stone slab path, then walk under an *hórreo* that attractively straddles the camino. Keep straight on down a tarmac road, then turn left in 30m down a narrower tarmac road where there's a small, makeshift café. Walk under some vines, then cross a stream via stepping stones. Cross a tarmac road and join a dirt path that changes to tarmac at the end of the village. Take a right-hand track soon afterwards, which quickly becomes paved, then turn left about 500m later down a stone track to head through farmland.

You soon come to **Boavista**, crossing the tarmac road at end of the village to walk on a dirt track. Turn left on to a narrow tarmac road at a couple of houses with vibrant, flower-filled gardens in spring and summer, then keep straight on along another dirt track. The track changes to tarmac as you enter **Alto**; keep straight on here, then turn left 200m later down a dirt track. Eventually, the camino reaches the main road at **Salceda** (Ⓐ), where there's a bar. Walk on a stone track alongside the road, which veers off to the right just before a second bar at the end of the village. You soon rejoin the road, crossing it to walk on a dirt track through eucalyptus plantations.

At **Xen**, cross a tarmac road and keep straight on. In 500m or so, walk through **Ras**, then cross the busy C547 to a dirt track on the other side. Carry on into **Brea**, turning left at a tarmac road, then right 20m later down another paved road which quickly changes to dirt. Turn left a couple of hundred metres later, then right in 50m to walk along the side of the road.

In a few hundred metres, cross the main road to walk on a stone path on the other side. There's a fountain and picnic area at the **Alto de Santa Irene** (✕☕), and a restaurant on either side of the road. Cross the road carefully here as there's poor visibility, walk on a narrow paved road, then turn left in 100m down a track. Walk downhill through eucalyptus trees and soon swing back to follow alongside the road. At the top of a hill just before Santa Irene, hidden amongst trees is the the Roda do Castro, a Celtic hill fort, whose circular defensive walls are three metres thick in places.

Santa Irene is a tiny place with little more than a picnic area, fountain, chapel and *albergues*. The eighteenth-century chapel is dedicated to the Portuguese martyr Santa Irene, a beautiful young nun who died in 653 defending her vow of chastity in the ancient town of Scalabris. There are two **albergues**: Albergue de Santa Irene (15 beds, kitchen, open all year) and Santa Irene de la Xunta de Galicia (36 beds, kitchen, open all year).

Keep walking downhill, then cross the main road to walk along a narrow tarmac road that soon changes to dirt. Pass a rustic sawmill that's hard at work processing ecologically harmful eucalyptus. Join a tarmac road at **Rúa**, a row of houses prettified with flowerpots, then walk through farmland to reach the main road in another kilometre or so.

Turn left for the *albergue* at **Arca** (Pedrouzo) (ⒶⒽ✕☕🛒), or cross the road to continue the camino towards Santiago. The **albergue** (120 beds, kitchen, open all year) in Arca is half a kilometre up the main road, next door to a supermarket. There are other shops in town, a couple of restaurants and the **Hotel O Pino** (**$$**, ☎ 981 51 11 48).

If you stayed the night in Arca, you can carry on through the village and take the first right, joining the camino at a sports centre in a few hundred metres. If you didn't stay in Arca, cross the main road and follow a dirt track through a forest, coming to the sports centre within a few hundred metres. Walk around it and turn left off the tarmac road on to a track that continues through the forest. Within a kilometre, you'll arrive at **San Antón**.

You're walking through farmland, although brash new houses are springing up and the area becomes more suburban as you approach Santiago. You'll also start to see seagulls, a sure sign that you're nearing the sea. Follow the track as it curves down to the bottom of the valley to **Amenal**.

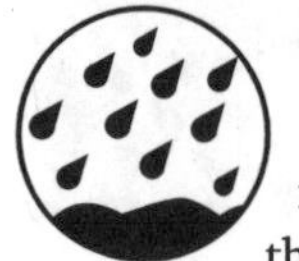

Cross straight over the main road, then climb uphill through a mostly eucalyptus forest towards **Cimadevila**. After about 2km you come to the main road at a large roundabout; turn left and follow the road past the airport. There's a large stone here, indicating that you've arrived in the district of Santiago, proof that you've just about made it.

Head downhill, past the end of the airport runway, which can be quite dramatic when planes land or take off. The trail attractively follows a small wooded ravine. After a few hundred metres cross the road to follow a path on the other side.

Take the first right down a paved road into **San Palo**, where there's a restored church, and keep left through the village, then climb up the steep paved road on its far side. At the top of a rise, turn right off the paved road on to a trail. Cross the main road and keep left at a fork 300m later, heading towards a cluster of houses, then turn right at a paved road and head downhill into Lavacolla.

Lavacolla

In the Middle Ages, Lavacolla was a ceremonial stop for pilgrims who would clean themselves up here before heading into Santiago. Although you may think that today's pilgrims are smelly, in the Middle Ages the whiff was much worse, as Christians hardly ever washed, and it was common to mock Jews and Muslims who were more concerned with personal hygiene and bathed regularly. Revoltingly, this may have been the pilgrims' first wash since they began the camino. Pilgrims would wash themselves in the small river at Lavacolla, called Lavamentula in the *Codex Calixtinus*, paying particular attention to their private parts: *mentula* means phallus, and *colla* means scrotum.

You'd be hard pressed to wash even your hands today, as the river is almost always dry and is heavily polluted, although you can get refreshments at Lavacolla's bars and cafés.

Accommodation
$$ Hostal San Paio (☎ 981 88 82 21)
$$ Hotel Garcas (☎ 981 88 82 25)

If you're in a group and hung up on pilgrim traditions, start running. The first one to reach Monte del Gozo, more than 5km away, will be declared king, a custom that seems to undo all the good work of the hosedown at Lavacolla.

The camino skirts Lavacolla's bars and passes close to the **Iglesia de Benaval**. The church, together with the Cruz de Benaval that stands in front of it, is named after the plaintive cry of a local rebel. Juán Pourón, who led an early fourteenth-century uprising, cried out to the Virgen de Belén, *Ven e valme* (come and save me), as he was sentenced to be hung for his crimes. The Virgin catapulted him to heaven instantly, denying local officials the pleasure of a hanging.

Once past the church, cross the main road and head down to the river, then cross the bridge and climb uphill to **Vilamaior**, which sits almost at the saddle of the hill. At the far side of the village, pass some picnic benches, cross a stream and climb up a little further, following the oak-tree-lined road as it makes its way towards San Marcos. Pass a radio station, turn left at a factory, then pass the militaristic San Marcos campground and turn right at a TV station.

Climb a short rise, from where you can make out the crazy hilltop sculpture at the top of Monte del Gozo. Turn right and then curve around left through the hamlet of **San Marcos** (☕🛒), where there's a small shop that also serves coffee. Keep straight on through the hamlet along the paved road, and reach the Monte del Gozo in less than a kilometre.

The **Monte del Gozo** is the Mount of Joy of camino tradition, from where pilgrims got their first, rapturous view of Santiago's cathedral spires. Today, trees and suburbs block the view, and your eyes are drawn instead to the sculpture erected to celebrate Pope John Paul II's 1993 Holy Year visit. To your left, the **albergue** (500 beds, kitchen, open all year), also part of 1993's building frenzy, does much to relieve the pressure on accommodation in Santiago during peak times. It's also soul-crushingly awful, and looks as if it was designed by a Butlins architect going through a bad bout of depression.

It'll take you about an hour to get from Monte del Gozo to the centre of Santiago, but the route is well-marked with signposts high above the sidewalk. Take the flight of stairs down to the main road, cross the A9 motorway via the bridge and follow the main road over the roundabout into town. On your left, you'll pass the Capilla de San Lázaro, which stands on the site of a twelfth-century lepers' hospital. Follow the Calle de los Concheiros through modern suburbs for a couple of kilometres, then turn left to walk down Rúa de San Pedro.

Enter Santiago proper through the Porta do Camino, the historic entry point into the old city, and one of seven gates through the former city wall. Walk down Rúa das Casas Reais and the Rúa das Animas to the small Plaza de Cervantes, then head right up Rúa da Azabachería, and cross over the Plaza de la Inmaculada. Pass under the Arco del Obispo and arrive at the Plaza de Obradoiro and your destination, the cathedral at Santiago de Compostela.

Santiago de Compostela

Ⓗ✕☕€ⓘ🛒

It's worth planning to spend at least two days in Santiago de Compostela. The city, a UNESCO World Heritage site, is one of the most beautiful in Europe and the mostly pedestrianized old centre is a maze of narrow cobbled streets and plazas that make wandering around Santiago a dreamlike, random experience. The religious zeal of the pilgrimage is tempered by a thriving university whose students drive a wicked nightlife.

The first thing most pilgrims wish to do on arrival in Santiago is visit the **cathedral**, give Santiago a hug and get their *compostela*. Medieval pilgrims would spend their first night in vigil at the cathedral and, if it was open, they would gather in front of the high altar, jostling for the best spot. This could get nasty, and in 1207 the cathedral had to be cleansed and reconsecrated because things had got so violently out of hand.

The original church was built by Alfonso II to house Santiago's tomb. Alfonso III the Greater built an even bigger church on the same spot in 899, but this was destroyed by Almanzor's Muslim army in 997. Starting from scratch, construction of the present building began in 1075 and was completed in 1211.

Map 22 (key page 213)

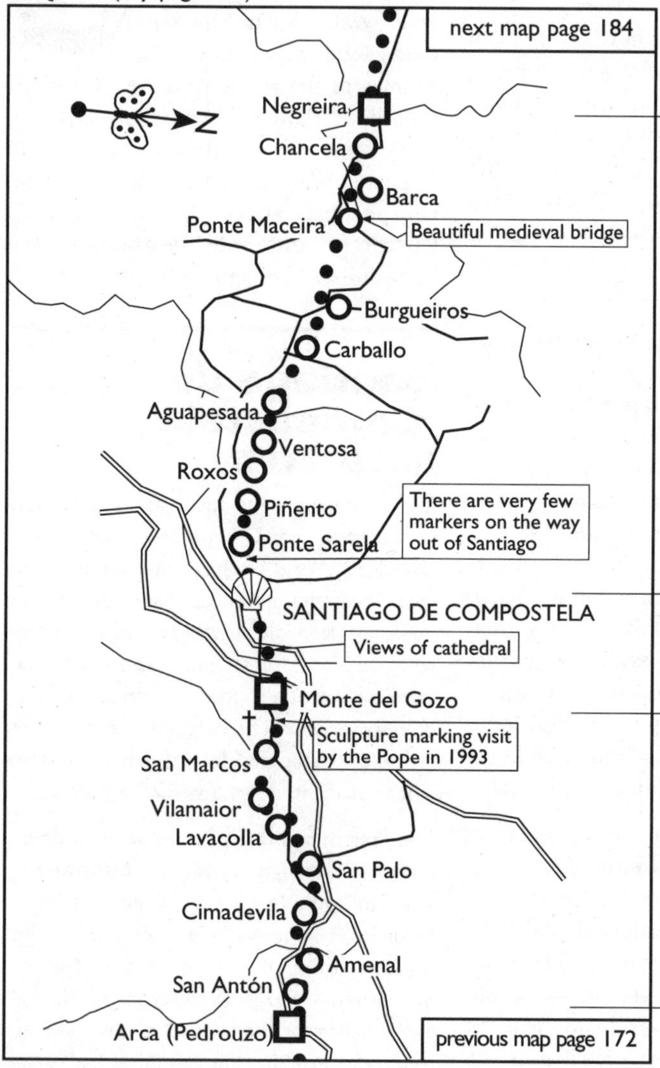
next map page 184
Negreira
Chancela
Barca
Ponte Maceira
Beautiful medieval bridge
Burgueiros
Carballo
20km
Aguapesada
Ventosa
Roxos
Piñento
Ponte Sarela
There are very few markers on the way out of Santiago
SANTIAGO DE COMPOSTELA
Views of cathedral
5.5km
Monte del Gozo
Sculpture marking visit by the Pope in 1993
San Marcos
Vilamaior
Lavacolla
San Palo
15km
Cimadevila
Amenal
San Antón
Arca (Pedrouzo)
previous map page 172
Z

Negreira

Santiago de Compostela

Monte de Gozo

Arca (Pedrouzo)

Profile Chart 22

500m
Arca (Pedrouzo)
SANTIAGO DE COMPOSTELA
Negreira
100m

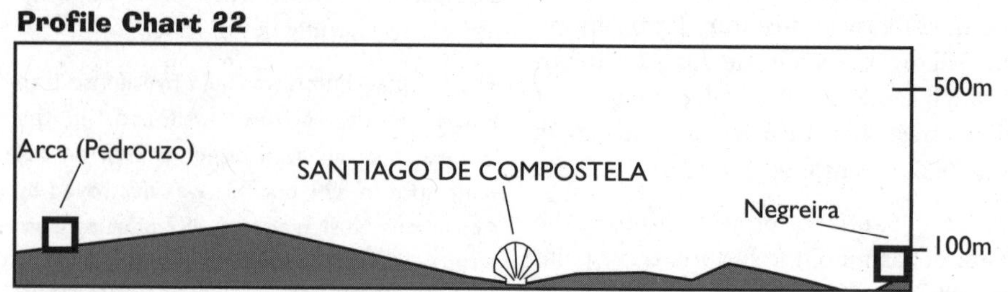

Skilled craftsmen came to Galicia from all over Europe, and hunks of limestone were hefted from Triacastela to Castañeda, where they were formed into the cathedral's stone blocks.

The cathedral is so massive and so dominates Santiago that its doors open out on to three separate city squares. The most dramatic entrance leads from the huge Plaza de Obradoiro, up the imposing double staircase to the Baroque **Obradoiro Façade**. Before you climb the stairs, walk backwards to the far side of the square so that you can take in the whole, glorious façade.

As you enter from this side, you'll suddenly reach the jaw-dropping **Pórtico de la Gloria**, built in 1168 by the Maestro Mateo, and the main entrance into the cathedral before the outer façade was built. Art historians suggest that this doorway inspired the movement from Romanesque to Gothic architecture across Europe. The pórtico is jammed with Christian symbolism and, like most things in the cathedral, it's worth visiting more than once. The middle pillar of the Pórtico de la Gloria depicts the Tree of Jesse, Santiago and the Virgin.

Over the years, a ritual for arriving pilgrims has developed. First, touch your right hand in the middle of the central column of the **Tree of Jesse** to give thanks for your safe arrival. Centuries of devoted hands have worn five finger grooves deep into the marble pillar, a humbling reminder of the tradition you're following. Around the back of the pillar is a small bust of **Maestro Mateo**, the architect of the Pórtico de la Gloria. Butting his head three times is said to impart some of his considerable intelligence to you.

Proceed up to the high altar. On top of it sits Santiago Matamoros shouldered by massive gold angels. On the right-hand side as you look at the altar you'll find a narrow set of stairs that lead behind the figure of **Santiago Peregrino**. Climb up into the shrine and embrace the thirteenth-century, jewelled statue of St James from behind. The gold crown that pilgrims could place on their heads has now sadly disappeared, along with the pilgrim tradition of placing their own hats on Santiago's head.

Next, head down into the **crypt** to see the casket that's said to contain the bones of the Saint and two of his disciples, Theodore and Athanasius. The tomb of Santiago was first discovered in the ninth century, enclosed in a stone mausoleum on this ancient necropolis. Santiago's bones were hidden several times over the centuries to keep them away from thieves and kings who wanted the relics for themselves. The bones were so well-hidden that their exact location was forgotten, but pilgrims continued to venerate an urn on the altar that was believed to hold the Saint's bones. Excavations in the late nineteenth century unearthed some bones, said to be those of Santiago when the discoverer went temporarily blind. Pope Leo XIII verified their validity a few years later, and the remains now rest in a silver coffin below the altar.

Every day at noon, there's a pilgrims' Mass. The ceremony often culminates in the swinging of the **botafumeiro** (smoke belcher), a massive silver incense burner said to be the largest in the Catholic world. It takes up to eight men in a team called a *tiraboleiros* to tie the knots and get the massive silver apparatus swinging across the cathedral. This *botafumeiro* dates from 1851, after the original was stolen by Napoleon's troops when they looted the cathedral. During Mass, the best place to sit is on either side of the main altar, so that the *botafumeiro* seems to skim the top of your head before it swings back to the roof of the cathedral.

If you're lucky enough to arrive in Santiago during a Holy Year, when the Día de Santiago, July 25, falls on a Sunday (2004, 2010, 2021), you can enter the cathedral through the **Puerta del Perdón**. The door is opened on the eve of a Holy Year, and closed on December 31.

To receive your **compostela**, final proof that you've completed the pilgrimage, present your stamped pilgrim's passport at the Oficina del Peregrino on the second floor of the Casa del Deán, just off Plaza Platerías on the south side of the cathedral. The friendly but busy staff will record your nationality and your place of departure, to be read out at the next day's pilgrims' Mass. If your motivations for the pilgrimage aren't religious or spiritual, you'll get a colourful alternative certificate instead of the traditional *compostela*.

The staff also acts as a quasi-tourist office, pointing pilgrims in the direction of accommodation and transport. You can purchase cardboard tubes to protect your document or even get your *compostela* laminated at a small trinket shop across the road from the office.

Dominating the northern side of the **Plaza de Obradoiro** and now a grand five-star hotel, the Hostal de los Reyes Católicos was originally built on the orders of Fernando and Isabel to house pilgrims and provide them with medical treatment. As part of its continuing obligation to pilgrims, the *parador* provides free meals to the first ten pilgrims to arrive at 9am, 12pm and 7pm. Arrive early as there's almost always a crowd of hungry pilgrims wanting to eat for free. To line up for your free meal, face the *parador* and turn left to walk along the front of the building to the underground parking garage and present the doorman with a photocopy of your *compostela*. You'll eat what the restaurant staff eat, washed down with a bottle or two of wine, and the food ranges from fantastic to average. Even so, it's a great experience, and you'll be led through the sumptuous, multi-courtyarded *parador* on your way to the staff dining room.

There's much more to see in Santiago. If you're here for a couple of days, invest in one of the many detailed guides to the city available from local bookshops. There are lots of trinket shops hoping to lure money from your wallet, and you can buy anything from tacky key chains decorated with a *flecha amarilla* (yellow arrow), to a life-size replica of the *botafumeiro*.

There are three **turismos** in Santiago: the municipal and the regional ones are on Rúa do Vilar, while the camino *turismo* on Avenida da Coruña (closed weekends) has information on the route to Finisterre.

Accommodation

There's no longer an *albergue* in Santiago, as it was forced to close after being constantly trashed by partying pilgrims. Pilgrims can, however, stay at the **Seminario Menor**, just outside town, for a few euros, although any celebrations will be severely curtailed by the strict curfew.

$$ Hostal La Estela, Raxoi 1 (☎ 981 58 27 96)
$$ Hostal Alameda, Rúa do San Clemente 32 (☎ 981 58 81 00)
$$$ Costa Vella, Calle Puerta da Pena 17 (☎ 981 56 95 30)
$$$$ Hostal de los Reyes Católicos, Plaza de Obradoiro (☎ 981 58 22 00)

Although most pilgrims end their journey at Santiago, it's well worth lacing up your boots and continuing to the ocean.

The camino to Finisterre predates the medieval pilgrimage by at least a millennium. Celts and other ancient peoples travelled to the solar temple of Ara Solis, on the tip of Cabo Finisterre, to worship the sun, or simply followed the Milky Way west as far as they could without getting their feet wet. Romans thought that the westernmost tip of Spain, Finis Terrae, was the end of the world, and would watch with concern as the sea engulfed the sun each night, hoping that it would rise again the next morning. Even medieval pilgrims often continued to the sea. Many visited Padrón and Muxía, places connected with Santiago's miraculous arrival in Spain, but churches dedicated to the Saint and pilgrim hospices also lined the route to Finisterre.

The easy-to-follow *Camino de Fisterra* is much quieter than the *camino francés* before Santiago. The locals along the path aren't overly burdened by throngs of pilgrims, and are often genuinely pleased to see you. Dogs are happy to see you too, but some can be vicious, so take care. If you're returning to Santiago, consider leaving some equipment at your hotel and travelling light to Finisterre.

Stand in the Plaza do Obradoiro facing the *parador*, and turn left to walk down Rúa das Hortas. In about 200m, cross a road to walk along Rúa do Cruceiro do Gaio, which changes its name, first to Rúa do Pozo de Bar and then to Rúa de San Lorenzo. Occasional faded yellow arrows are painted on the road but, apart from these, there are no signs until you reach a park in a few hundred metres. Turn right at a concrete bollard here, the first of many on a mostly well-marked trail, to head through the small park on a wide, shady, grit path. Turn left at the end of park and walk down Costa do Cano, a narrow road edged by high walls, dripping with plants and rich with the intense smell of jasmine in spring and summer. You're soon in the countryside, and the rapid exit from Santiago is a stark contrast to your arrival in the city.

Cross a stone bridge at **Ponte Sarela** and turn left past some buildings to walk down a dirt track, then at a fork in 50m, take the left-hand (lower) track, which soon narrows to a path. Cross a stream, then take the left-hand fork 50m later, down a path that can be overgrown. At a small clearing in a few hundred metres, keep straight on past a concrete camino bollard.

The trail is lined with foxgloves, ferns and blackberries, and it can be a little mucky underfoot after rain. In a few hundred metres, cross an open patch of ground and walk uphill towards some modern houses, then turn left at a wider dirt track as you reach the houses, looking behind you for great views of Santiago. Turn left at a tarmac road in 50m, then turn right up a paved track in a couple of

hundred metres. The route soon narrows to a stony dirt track after passing a house, and you're now walking through an oak wood that's a deep, startling green, intense and vibrant with ivy and moss.

Predictably, the oak is soon usurped by eucalyptus, and the change in light quality is instantly apparent, as is the sudden lack of undergrowth. The path flattens out near the top of a hill, then curves right at a concrete sign. Ignore minor tracks off to the right and left, and walk downhill, mostly through eucalyptus trees but also passing occasional and welcome stretches of oak. Turn right on to a smaller track just before walking under some power lines, then walk uphill again for short while before curving left to walk steeply downhill. Turn left 200m later and reach a narrow tarmac road in 50m; turn right here, then left at another road soon afterwards.

Reach **Piñeiro**, where the traditional architecture is overwhelmed by big, modern houses as Santiago's commuter belt stretches westwards. Keep straight on in a couple of hundred metres down a narrower tarmac road as the main road curves to the right. Follow this minor road as it curves to the right around a modern house in another 200m or so. The paved road changes to dirt as you walk along fields, then changes back to tarmac as the fields end. Turn right 100m later, then turn left to pass a huge *hórreo* and walk down a narrow tarmac road past the older village houses.

Leave Piñeiro on a narrow tarmac road. It's a lovely, pastoral scene, with great views back towards the village of meadows, stone houses and *hórreos*. Pass a few very grand houses, then turn right up a tarmac road, ignoring the yellow arrows that lead straight on. Note that new houses are being built here and the road may soon be paved. Follow the road as it curves to the left, then turn right just after the bend to walk on a stony path uphill through eucalyptus and deciduous woodland. This is a well-marked route through trees, although the track is sometimes eroded and bumpy. The terrain on the whole is a bit rougher than most of the route before Santiago but it's still easy going for the most part. Ignore side tracks and emerge on a paved road at the start of a village.

Turn left at a tarmac road in a couple of hundred metres, then turn right 20m later to walk on an old narrow road. There are lovely old houses here, and vines all around this area are strung high off the ground on parallel wires to protect the grapes from damp. Leave the village on a narrow tarmac road, then turn right in about 500m just before a small square sports centre.

Cross a bridge over the Río Roxos, then veer left 50m later, following a concrete bollard and ignoring a large white arrow painted on the road that leads right. Walk through pine and eucalyptus trees, then in about 500m, turn right to walk uphill on a tarmac road that soon changes to dirt.

Up ahead, you'll see Roxos, but turn right just before reaching it to walk along a lovely flat track through trees, passing a cluster of beehives on your right. The track soon emerges at a dirt road in **Roxos** (✕), then in about 100m reaches the main road, where there's a restaurant/bar called Meson Alto do Vento.

Turn right at the restaurant, and walk

down the road for about 500m, then at a bus stop at **Ventosa**, turn right down a narrow tarmac road. Cross another tarmac road, walk through a group of houses and past a big electricity pylon as the paved road changes to stone. Turn left in a couple of hundred metres as the stone changes back to tarmac, cross a stream, then turn left at the main road to walk along the sidewalk. Pass a shop on the left, and a lumber mill on the right. In front of you, the wide valley is speckled with red roofed hamlets. Walk gradually downhill to **Aguapesada** (✂🛒), a village of pretty stone houses with small square windows, passing the Meson O Cruceiro restaurant on the right.

At the bottom of the valley, turn left down a paved stone street next to a lovely, single-arched medieval bridge that's been recently restored. In a couple of hundred metres, cross a tarmac road and walk uphill on a narrower tarmac road that changes to a narrow dirt track as the houses end and you enter a eucalyptus and pine wood. This is a steep, tough climb with little shade, although occasional stone benches offer a place to rest. After about 2km, turn right at a tarmac road, next to a stone bench and a TV tower.

Climb for another 500m or so, then pass a fountain and soon reach the top. In a few hundred metres arrive in **Carballo** (☕), beautifully set amongst fields and trees, and dotted with the region's traditional red-roofed stone houses. There are lots of songbirds here, too, and gorgeous views across another beautiful valley of red-topped houses. The lower part of the village has two bars.

Leave Carballo on the main road, and soon enter **Burgueiros**, a wealthy hamlet with lots of big new houses. Almost immediately, you'll pass a sign for **Ponte Maceira** (✂☕) and soon see the gorgeous village ahead in a brilliant green valley. Veer left towards the village's centre once you've passed the first few houses, and soon reach an excellent bar-restaurant. The restaurant is posh and expensive, but you can get excellent sandwiches and drinks at a modest price in its café and it's idyllically set next to a weir on the wide Río Tambre.

The bridge after which Ponte Maceira is named elegantly spans the river; from its centre you may see a heron calmly standing at the edge of the river, or a kingfisher darting just above the water. Construction of the bridge began at the end of the fourteenth century, although much of what you see today dates from a sympathetic eighteenth-century restoration.

Turn right to cross the river, then turn left at the end of the bridge. On the other side of the river you'll see the **Capilla de San Brais** and a medieval *pazo*, a grand Galician country house, surrounded by beautiful gardens. Walk past a *cruceiro* on your left, gruesomely decorated with a carved skull and crossbones at its base. Turn left at the end of the village down a narrower tarmac road, walking through fields near the river in a beautiful green valley.

In a little under a kilometre, veer left off the road to walk down a dirt track towards the river through ivy-encrusted trees. Foxgloves line the route here, glorious in late spring and early summer. Pass under the arch of the "new" nineteenth-century bridge that leads to Ponte Maceira Nova, then veer away from the

Map 23 (key page 213)

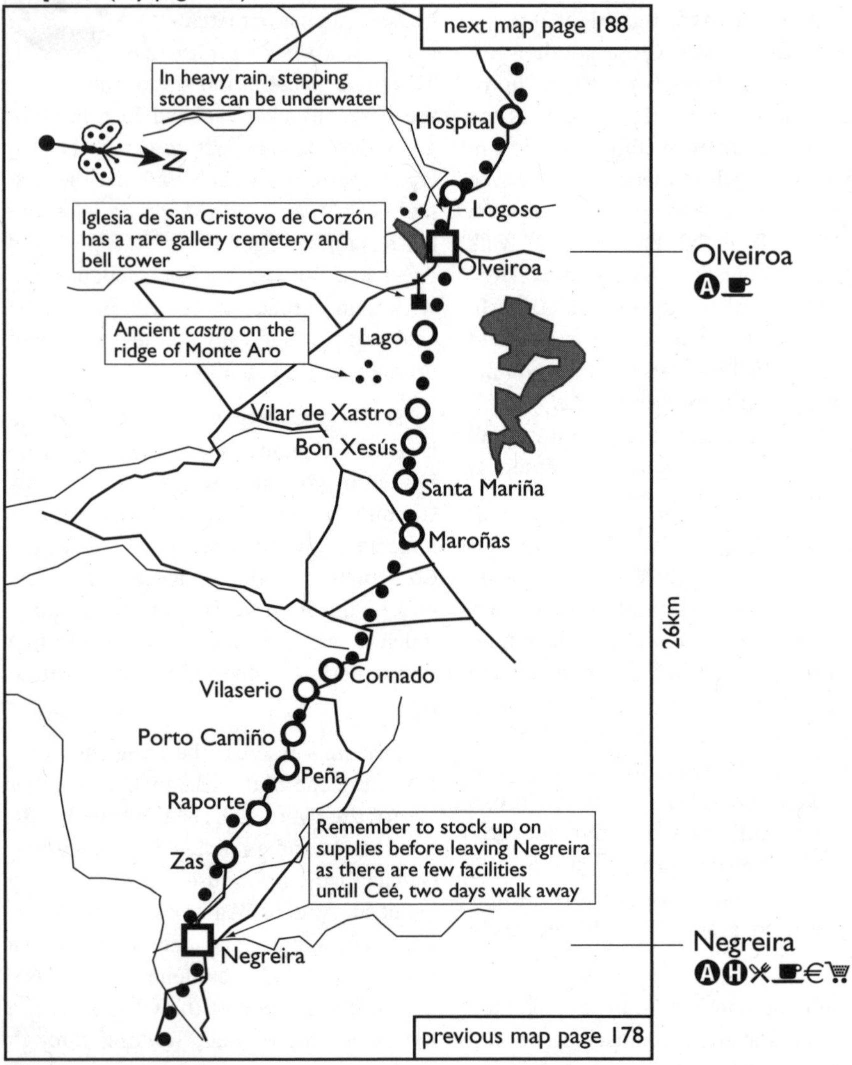

next map page 188
In heavy rain, stepping stones can be underwater
Hospital
Logoso
Iglesia de San Cristovo de Corzón has a rare gallery cemetery and bell tower
Olveiroa
Lago
Ancient *castro* on the ridge of Monte Aro
Vilar de Xastro
Bon Xesús
Santa Mariña
Maroñas
26km
Cornado
Vilaserio
Porto Camiño
Peña
Raporte
Zas
Remember to stock up on supplies before leaving Negreira as there are few facilities untill Ceé, two days walk away
Negreira
previous map page 178
Olveiroa
Negreira

Profile Chart 23

500m
100m
Negreira
Cornado
Bon Xesús
Olveiroa

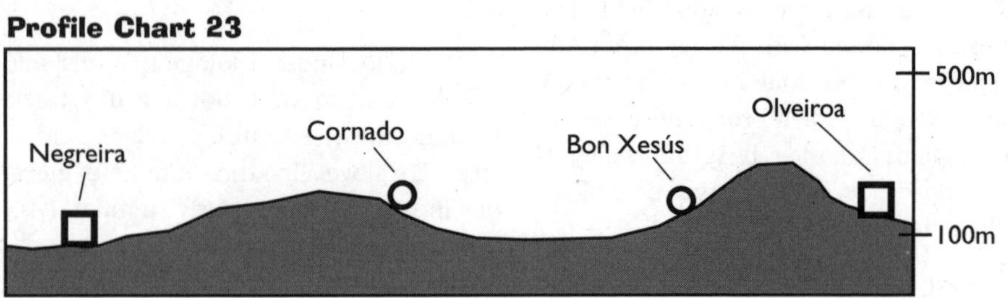

river along a farm track through fields.

Join the main road after about 500m and turn left to walk along it, mostly bypassing the modern, nondescript village of **Barca**. Turn left at the end of the village to walk down a minor road. You're still walking along the valley floor, and there are lovely glimpses of the tree-lined river from here. Walk uphill past a small factory, finally leaving the river behind. After a brief climb, the camino starts to go downhill into **Chancela**, passing a huge mansion called the Pazo de Chancela and you'll soon see Negreira ahead, encroaching on and blending into Chancela.

At the main road soon afterwards, turn left to enter Negreira. Pass some apartment buildings and a statue of a pilgrim on the main road into town. The *albergue* is just outside town, but there's limited signage and very few yellow arrows; to reach it, turn left a few hundred metres after the statue down the Rúa de San Mauro. In a few hundred metres, pass under the stone arch that links Pazo de Cotón with Capela de San Mauro. Cross a bridge over the Río Barcala, and turn left 100m later up a narrow tarmac road. You'll reach the *albergue* in about 1km.

Negreira

Negreira is a modern, well-equipped town with decadent pastry shops and excellent seafood restaurants. The town's notable monument is the fortified, medieval Pazo del Cotón. Its solid grey exterior was restored in the seventeenth century, and it's joined to the Capilla de San Mauro by an enclosed, arched walkway.

Accommodation

The modern **albergue** (16 beds, kitchen, open all year) has the twin luxuries of single beds and modern, sex-segregated bathrooms. There are extra mattresses for summer overflow.

$$ Hostal Residencial Tamara (☎ 981 88 52 01)

$$ Hostal-Restaurante La Mezquita (☎ 981 885 128)

The route from Negreira to Olveiroa passes through a mix of forest and farms. The beginning is especially lovely, heading along an old trail, with fantastic views across multiple valleys. There's almost nowhere to buy supplies, so make sure you stock up on lunch and dinner provisions before leaving Negreira.

Turn right out of the *albergue* and then turn left in 100m up the road signposted "Negreira Iglesia". After about 50m, turn right and walk towards the church. Once in front of the church, turn left up some steps, walk out of the church gate, then turn right straight away. Go past some houses and head out of the village down a lane, looking out for good views of Negreira to the right. After a few hundred metres, the lane goes downhill; at the first bend, take the left-hand track heading through the trees. The slightly overgrown old lane leads along the side of the hill, with more good views to the right. Keep straight ahead when you join the main road, and carry on into **Zas**.

After about 1km on the main road, turn right on to a side road opposite a bus shelter. Pass a small church, then at a T-junction soon afterwards (still in the village), turn left slightly uphill and keep straight on out of Zas. At the next junction, keep left uphill on a dirt track

through farmland and a eucalyptus plantation. Turn right at the next junction, then left at another junction 100m later. The camino emerges from the trees just before another hamlet, then goes right at a T-junction with a dirt track, next to the hamlet's first house and heads into trees once more. Once you reach the edge of the forest, turn left downhill to a stream and climb up the other side on a rocky track.

Cross straight over a paved road, taking the slightly overgrown trail on the far side, one of the many beautiful old walled lanes that criss-cross this part of Galicia, prettily linking fields and villages.

After about 1km, descend and emerge from the forest in an area of old fields. Climb uphill from here, winding through trees towards **Rapote** and, on the far side of the hamlet, turn left downhill on a dirt track. Cross over a stream and climb up the ridge that you've seen intermittently for the last couple of kilometres; this is a lovely stretch of oak forest with ferns, ivy and big black slugs.

After a kilometre or so, you'll arrive at **Peña** (☕). To detour to the village bar, turn left at the sign in front of the first house in the hamlet, then turn right 100m later. There's no need to retrace your steps once you've had a drink: simply continue on the main road and you'll join up with the camino in a few hundred metres. If you're avoiding the bar, carry on through the village past a church and turn left at a *cruceiro*, then left again to join the main road, where you turn right.

You're now in **Porto Camiño**, a tiny hamlet with a smattering of houses. Keep straight on past the turning for Xallas on your left, then just after the last house in Porto Camiño, turn right on to a track. There are actually four tracks here: take the second from the right, just to the left of the water tank. Fire has destroyed much of the forest that was once here, judging from the burnt stumps, and gorse and broom has grown in place of the trees. Cross a stream and then, at a T-junction, turn left towards the main road.

At the road, turn right to follow it over the top of a saddle. Pass the sign for Landeira and after walking along the road for a couple of kilometres, descend towards Vilaserio. As the descent steepens, look out for a sharp left turn on to a dirt lane that takes you through **Vilaserio** (☕). Pass behind the village bar — or stop, as this is the last refreshment for 8km — and turn left on to the main road, then walk past the sign for Pesadoira and carry on the main road until you come to **Cornado**.

Turn right into this small hamlet, then take a sharp left past the bus shelter and two stones inlaid with shells, and follow the track uphill into farmland and forest. Keep left at the next fork then, at the paved road a few hundred metres later, turn right. After about 500m, turn left at a country lane that's something of a local garbage dump. Come to a T-junction and go left uphill, then a couple of hundred metres later at the top of a rise, turn right. In another few hundred metres, keep left at a fork, heading through fields with great views of the surrounding countryside.

Keep straight on over two crossroads. The lane becomes paved and then goes up and around a small rise, then crosses a stream and leads into **Maroñas**. Turn left into the village and take a moment to notice the different style of *hórreos*: Maroñas' granaries are made of stone boulders, as the rain-drenched Galician climate rots wood quickly, and stone is plentiful locally. Once through the village, keep straight on until you come to a T-junction 500m later. Turn left here, and head into **Santa Mariña** (☕), then veer right along a lane to the main road. Turn left at the main road, passing a couple of bars on the right.

Keep straight on the road for about 500m, then turn right up a paved road into the hamlets of Bon Xesús and Vilar de Xastro. There's an old *cruceiro* on the left just before the first hamlet. Veer left into the second hamlet, then as the houses end, go right uphill and take a sharp left soon afterwards. You're now on a dirt track and climbing up **Monte Aro**, where there are some remains of an ancient *castro*. Keep climbing until you reach the shoulder of a hill. Zig-zag first right, then left 100m later, and head down the other side of the ridge. Your climb up is rewarded with fantastic views, and there are many *rubias gallega*, Galicia's typical rust-red cows, in the fields. About two-thirds of the way down, turn sharp left into the hamlet of Lago.

Once in **Lago**, turn left again and follow the road for about 500m, then turn right downhill on to a quieter road next to a bus shelter. There are fabulous views of modern windmills up ahead. From Lago, energetic pilgrims who need to buy provisions can detour to **A Picota** (🛒), almost 4km away, where there are good shops.

Otherwise, continue along the paved road lined with gorse and pine trees, ignoring dirt tracks off on either side. After a couple of kilometres, you emerge at the unusual Iglesia de San Cristovo de Corzón. The church is separate from its belltower and the arched cemetery looks like a gallery of graves around the church, while the graveyard itself contains some splendid-looking crosses. Turn left 30m after the church and follow this minor road to the main road. Turn right here and cross the much-restored sixteenth-century bridge over the Río Xallas, where locals fought Napoleon's troops during the Peninsula War.

Stick to the main road for a couple of kilometres. Pass a *farmacia* on the left, and the turning for Santiago Oliveira on the right, then take the first left into Olveiroa, reaching the pretty village in few hundred metres. Turn right in the hamlet to reach the *albergue*.

Olveiroa Ⓐ☕

Olveiroa is a tiny village with stunning examples of rural architecture. Village houses are made of thick stone walls and Olveiroa's *cruceiro* is a lovely one.

The **albergue** (35 beds, kitchen, open all year) has separate, beautifully restored stone buildings for sleeping, eating and hanging out. The hospitalera cooks fabulous *sopa de ajo* (garlic soup), and pilgrims chip in with bread, cheese and whatever else they have, then sit at a communal table in front of a roaring fire. The village bar sells *bocadillos* and bottles of wine.

The trail from Olveiroa to Finisterre is badly marked and a little confusing in places, so keep your eyes peeled, particularly around Cée, for yellow arrows. You'll also finally reach the crashing waves of

Map 24 (key page 213)

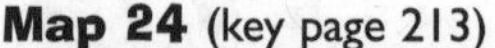

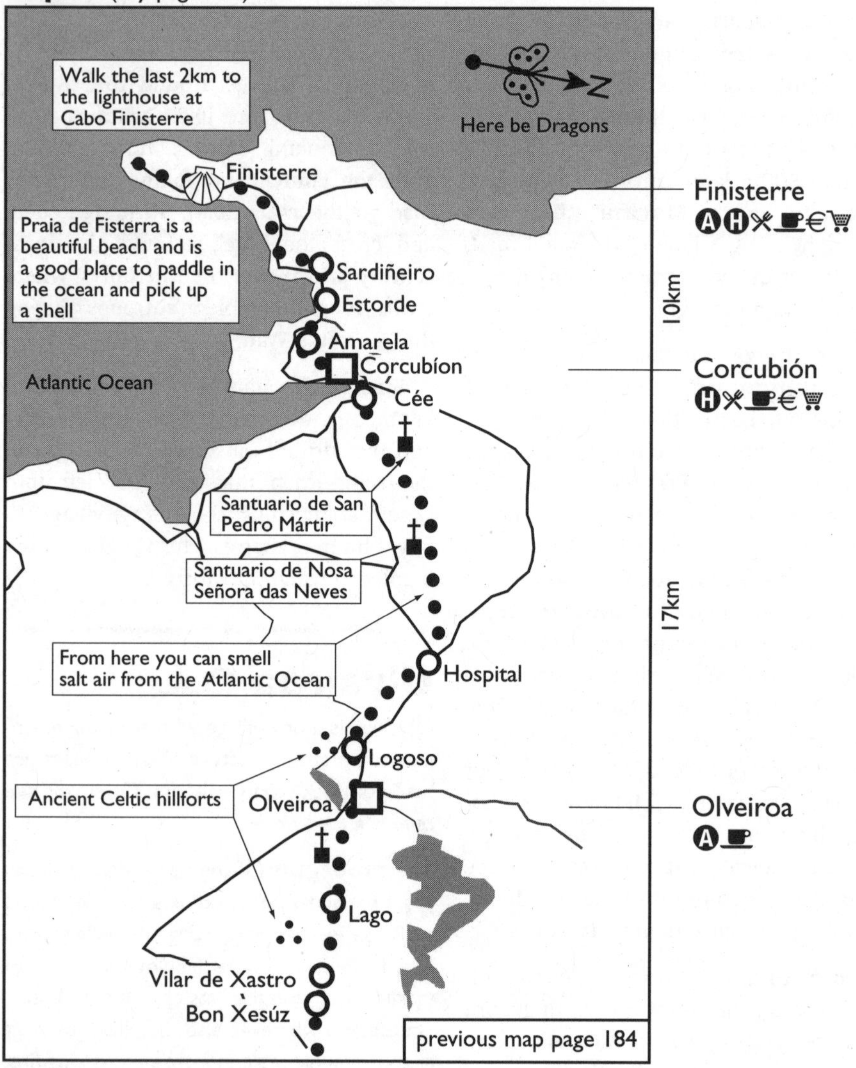

Walk the last 2km to the lighthouse at Cabo Finisterre
Here be Dragons
Finisterre
Praia de Fisterra is a beautiful beach and is a good place to paddle in the ocean and pick up a shell
Sardiñeiro
Estorde
Amarela
Corcubíon
Atlantic Ocean
Cée
10km
Santuario de San Pedro Mártir
Santuario de Nosa Señora das Neves
17km
From here you can smell salt air from the Atlantic Ocean
Hospital
Logoso
Ancient Celtic hillforts
Olveiroa
Lago
Vilar de Xastro
Bon Xesúz
previous map page 184
Finisterre
Corcubión
Olveiroa

Profile Chart 24

Hospital
300m
Corcubión
Finisterre
0m

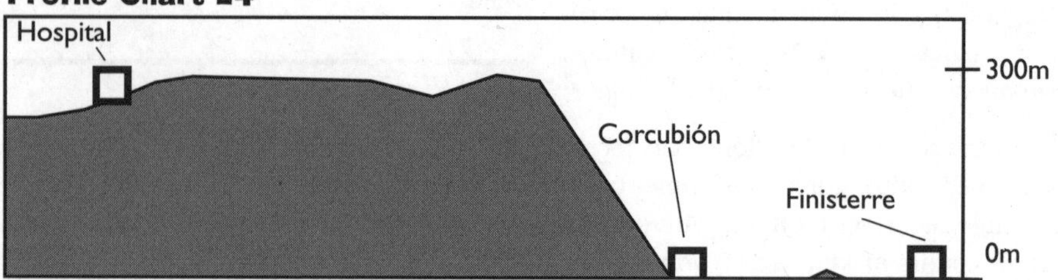

the Atlantic, a distraction that may compound your route-finding difficulties. The last stretch is along a beach, and stepping off the end of the world into the ocean is a fantastic camino finale.

Keep straight ahead through Olveiroa, retracing your steps if you stayed at the *albergue*. Head downhill, then turn left at a junction next to the village *lavadero* (wash house), and walk over a concrete bridge just before the main road. Follow a track, then fork left at a junction next to a telephone pylon, looking out for a hill fort on your left. Climb up the ridge for about 100m, then turn left to walk along the side of the hill, from where there are great views of the river in the gorge below, and of the hills and windmills that surround you. Descend to the river, and cross it via stepping stones, a hairy adventure after heavy rain, when the stepping stones can be under a fair bit of water: a walking stick can be invaluable for balance.

Climb up the other side of the valley and follow the grassy track into **Logoso**. Walk straight through the small hamlet, then at a fork on the far side, take the track going left uphill. Keep climbing until you reach **Hospital** (☕), which is dominated by a massive carbide factory then, once at the hamlet, turn right then left to join the main road. Turn left here to walk along the road, and climb up past a bar that serves great *bocadillos*.

A few hundred metres later, the camino splits. The right-hand turn takes you to Muxia, a popular pilgrim destination just north of Finisterre. Turn left to continue on your way to Finisterre, walking past the carbide factory. Soon after you leave its belching fumes behind, turn right down a dirt track. Keep straight on over open ground with few trees and lots of gorse and shrubs, then pass a *cruceiro* at a paved road and keep straight on. Not long afterwards, you come to a modern stone wall. This wall has been built directly over the track, and it's difficult to see where the camino goes, but if you keep straight on, parallel to the wall, the track will reappear in about 300m.

From here onwards, you'll start to smell the salt ocean air, although it's still another 8km or so before you reach the water. Follow the track downhill to a T-junction, turn right to head up and over a rise, then head down to the **Santuario de Nosa Señora das Neves**. Near the restored *santuario*, there's a *fonte santa* (holy fountain) said to cure all manner of ailments. Each September 8, local people arrive here for a *romería* (pilgrimage). There's a *cruceiro* in the field below.

Turn right past the *santuario*, heading downhill briefly, then begin a long, slow, eucalyptus-lined climb that lasts for almost 3km. Eventually, you'll pass the chapel of San Pedro Mártir, whose *fonte santa* is thought to cure verrucas, rheumatism and, happily for tired pilgrims, sore feet. Keep straight on, heading steadily downhill, and ignoring the very tempting cobbled path off to the right. The track gets steeper as it begins the descent into Cée, and you'll get your first views of the sea.

Just before you reach **Cée** (✕☕€🛒), turn left at a paved road, then take the first right soon afterwards. Pass a bar, the second of the day to serve tasty *bocadillos*, then turn right on to the main road. This part of the camino isn't well marked and can be confusing. The easiest way to navigate is to ignore the yellow arrows, and head instead for the waterfront road that

links the villages of Cée and Corcubión, now merged into each other.

Corcubión (Ⓗ✕☕€🛒) has some lovely manor houses, emblazoned with maritime-motif crests. There's a range of accommodation in Corcubión, including **La Cirena ($,** ☎ 981 74 50 36), **Las Hortensias ($$,** ☎ 981 74 61 25), and **El Hórreo ($$$,** ☎ 981 74 55 00). As you walk around the bay, look out for a church just off the waterfront road on the right. Just before the church, as the road rises slightly, turn sharp right uphill at a junction marked by a faint yellow arrow. At a fork not long afterwards, keep left.

Keep going until you come to the Plaza de Castelao, a small square with a taxi rank, then leave the square by the left-hand corner, and head for the **Iglesia de San Marcos**. The thirteenth-century church has neo-Gothic towers and a fifteenth-century sculpture of the church's patron Saint. At the church door, take a very sharp right up some steps, and follow the street to a small square called Campo de Rollo. Cross straight over to the tiny, high-walled lane opposite, and follow its overgrown route uphill.

Turn left once you meet another lane at the top of the hill, then turn right soon afterwards. Cross the main road, passing a basketball court and a picnic area on the left, then take the old lane that intersects two larger roads 100m later, watching for very faint yellow arrows. In 40m, turn right at a fence, and follow the boundary wall behind some houses in **Amarela**. If you pass a white house, you've gone too far, and should retrace your steps.

In about 500m, you'll arrive at the main road again. Turn left here, then turn right at a bend about 300m later, veering right soon afterwards on to a track. In a kilometre or so, turn right on rejoining the main road and follow it into the village of **Estorde**.

Keep on the main road to **Sardiñeiro** (Ⓗ✕☕), where you can stay at the **Praia de Estorde ($$$,** ☎ 981 74 55 85). Just before entering the town, look on the right for a small lane just beyond the town's name sign. Follow this lane, which recrosses the main road a few hundred metres later, then rejoin the main road in another 200m, and turn left.

In a couple of hundred metres, turn right down a narrow road, then 10m later turn left down a small lane between a house and an *hórreo*. In another 100m, just before the lane veers back towards the main road, turn right and climb slowly along the old Rúa da Finisterra.

At a T-junction just out of town, turn left along a track to walk through a beautiful pine forest. Keep straight on over the main road as the camino heads down a gully towards a tiny, dramatic cove, then climbs up the other side to meet the main road once more. Take the next left along a paved road down to the beach.

To get to Finisterre, either walk along the beach to collect your scallop shell and splash about in the sea (you'll need to wade across a couple of tidal streams), or walk along a boardwalk into town. At the far end of the beach, pass a restaurant-bar and climb up to a viewpoint. Look out for the downward pointing scallop shell here, showing that your journey is almost at an end.

Head down the street into Finisterre. The *albergue* is in the middle of town, one block up from the statue in the port, and next door to a supermarket.

Finisterre

ⒶⒽ✕☕€🛒

Finisterre is a working port with all the services of a small town. There's a fifteenth-century *cruceiro* in front of the twelfth-century Romanesque-Gothic **Iglesia de Santa María de Areas**. Domenico Laffi, the Italian camino chronicler, visited the church in the seventeenth century; the chapel next door was once a pilgrim hospice.

Finisterre shows few other signs of its camino past. Its character comes more from the sea, and it's fascinating to wander around the port, watching the primary-coloured fishing boats in the bay, or chatting with fishermen as they mend gnarled nets. The town has a couple of fancy fish restaurants, but you're better off heading down to the port and eating at one of the cluster of down-at-heel bars or at a *sardiñada*, an open air sardine grill.

Pilgrims who walk or cycle from Santiago to Finisterre are entitled to a *fisterrana*, a certificate of completion of the pilgrimage; you can get yours from the *hospitalera* at the *albergue*.

Accommodation

Finisterre's **albergue** (40 beds, kitchen, open all year) doesn't open until 7pm.

$ Hostal Cabo Finisterre (☎ 981 74 00 00)

$ Hostal Rivas (☎ 981 74 00 27)

$$ Finisterre (☎ 981 74 00 00)

From Finisterre, it's a short walk to the end of the world. To continue to the *faro* (lighthouse), walk past the *albergue*, turn right in a couple of hundred metres at Plaza Ara Solis, then turn left 50m later past the Capella de Nossa Senhora del Buensuccesso. Turn left when you reach the main road in a couple of hundred metres, soon passing the Iglesia de Santa María das Areas. Follow the road all the way to Cabo Finisterre, just over 2km away, watching out for cars as there's no shoulder. There are great views out to sea when the sun's out, but the walk is also murkily wonderful in bad weather.

You'll soon reach **Cabo Finisterre** (Ⓗ✕☕), the end of the world dramatically perched on a rocky headland. The Celts believed that the surrounding ocean was the Sea of Tenesbrosum, home to monsters and the gateway to paradise. The Romans were convinced that Finis Terrae was the end of the world where the sun was engulfed by the sea each night.

There are great views from the **Vista Monte do Facho**, high above the lighthouse. The *menhir* that once stood here was the scene of Celtic fertility rites, and couples copulated against the rock to increase their chances of conception before prudish church officials tore down the *menhir* in the eighteenth century.

There's no trace of Ara Solis, the Celts' prehistoric temple that drew sun-worshipping Iron Age pilgrims: you'll have to make do with the solid, whitewashed *faro* (lighthouse), a hotel-restaurant, and a couple of pilgrim highlights. Below the lighthouse there's a small sculpture of a pair of walking boots, where profligate pilgrims traditionally burn their shoes to celebrate their arrival at the cape. Nearby, a concrete post with a downward pointing scallop shell marks the end of the camino, a familiar and fittingly poignant symbol of your journey's end.

Pilgrim Associations

Pilgrim associations are great places to get advice and to pick up a *credencial* (pilgrim passport) before you go.

Great Britain

The **Confraternity of Saint James** (☎ 020 7928 9988; www.csj.org.uk) is the most well established and respected English-language pilgrim' association. It promotes and conducts research into the camino, publishes a newsletter, maintains a library, organizes meetings and runs the Refugio Gaucelmo in Rabanal del Camino.

US

The **Friends of the Road to Santiago** at www.geocities.com/friends_usa_santiago publish a newsletter and runs a list-serv.

Canada

The Little Company of Pilgrims (www.santiago.ca) publish a newsletter and offer helpful advice. They can also provide you with a *credencial* before you leave.

Ireland

Irish pilgrims can get useful information from the **Irish Society of the Friends of St James** at www.stjamesirl.com. The web site includes an electronic notice board for announcements.

Australia

Australian pilgrims should contact the **Australian Amigos del Camino de Santiago** at hannan@werple.net.au.

South Africa

The **Confraternity of Saint James of South Africa** has a web site with helpful tips and useful information on getting to the camino from South Africa. It's at www.geocities.com/marievanus.

Further Reading

This is a selection of our favourite books on the Camino de Santiago and about Spain in general. Visit your local independent bookshop for other suggestions, or contact one of the following (which have all given Ben a job at some point in his life):

Wanderlust, 1929 West 4th Avenue, Vancouver, BC, Canada, ☎ 604 739 2182, www.wanderlustore.com.

Stanfords, 12–14 Long Acre, London WC2E 9LP, ☎ 020 7836 1321, www.stanfords.co.uk.

The Travel Bookshop, 13–15 Blenheim Crescent, London W11 2EE, ☎ 020 7229 5260, www.thetravelbookshop.co.uk.

There's a more detailed list of retailers of *Walking the Camino de Santiago* on our web site at www.pilipalapress.com.

General

David Gitlitz and Linda Kay Davidson's *The Pilgrimage Road to Santiago: The Complete Cultural Handbook* (St Martin's Griffin, 2000) is a hefty, detailed description of all the churches, monasteries and other monuments you'll pass along the camino. Nancy Frey's *Pilgrim Stories: On and Off the Road to Santiago* (University of California Press, 1998) looks at pilgrims and the pilgrimage in a refreshing, accessible and thoughtful way; its fascinating insights into pilgrims' motivations make it one of the best books on the camino.

Pilgrim Accounts

The Confraternity of St James publish *The Pilgrim's Guide: A 12th Century Guide for the Pilgrim to St James of Compostella* (1992), a translation of Aymeric Picaud's fascinatingly misanthropic account that was one of the world's first travel guides. James Hall's translation of Domenico Laffi's seventeenth-century account is out-of-print and difficult to find, but Edwin Mullins' classic 1970s account, *The Pilgrimage to Santiago* has recently been re-issued by Interlink (2001).

Personal accounts of the camino almost inevitably reveal more about the writer than the walk itself. The most popular voyages of self-discovery are Shirley Maclaine's *The Camino: A Journey of the Spirit* (Pocket Books, 2001) and Paulo Coelho's *The Pilgrimage: A Contemporary Quest for Ancient Wisdom* (HarperCollins, 1995).

Flora & Fauna

Once in Spain, naturalists should look out for *Camino de Santiago: Guía de la Naturaleza* (Edilesa, 1999), so well-organized and illustrated that even non-Spanish speakers can use it. Both *Wild Spain* (Interlink, 2000) and *Where to Watch Birds in North & East Spain* (A&C Black, 1999) contain good general information, although there's not much specific detail on places along the camino.

People & Culture

For the best background on Spain, read John Hooper's book, *The New Spaniards* (Penguin, 1995), an erudite account of Spanish life and culture by a British journalist. Mark Kulanksy's *The Basque History of the World* (Penguin, 2001) is an opinionated, eclectic read, while Raymond Carr has collected expert historians' accounts in *Spain: A History* (Oxford University Press, 2000).

Food & Drink

If you're itching to try some Spanish cooking before you leave, Penelope Casas' *Delicioso: The Regional Cooking of Spain* (Knopf, 1996) will have you drooling.

Literature

Galicia's most famous poet is Rosalía de Castro, a huge figure in Galician culture who chronicled famine and hardship in mid-nineteenth-century Galicia; none of the English translations of her work are currently in print. Manuel Rivas, who writes in his native *Galega*, has done more than any other modern writer to revive Galician literature; his works, including *The Carpenter's Pencil*, have been widely translated.

Julián Rios' *Loves That Bind* (Vintage, 1999) is a prize-winning novel from an up-and-coming Galician writer. Born in Galicia but writing in Spanish, Nobel prize winner Camilo José Cela's works include *Boxwood* (New Directions, 2002) and *Mazurka for Two Dead Men* (New Directions, 1994).

Bernardo Atxaga is the Basque country's best modern writer; his most famous book is the dense, challenging *Obabakoak* (Vintage, 1994), but he's also written more accessible thrillers such as *The Lone Man* (Harvill Press, 1996).

Hemingway's *The Sun Also Rises* (Vintage, 2000) provides an interesting look at Pamplona and Navarra from the perspective of an American Spanophile.

Language

Castellano (Spanish)

yes	*sí*	please	*por favor*
no	*no*	thank you	*gracias*
hello	*hola* [*h* is silent]	good morning	*buenos días*
goodbye	*adios*	good afternoon	*buenas tardes*

Do you speak English/Spanish?	*¿Habla inglés/castellano?*
I don't speak Spanish	*No hablo castellano*
I (don't) understand	*(No) entiendo*
How much?	*¿Cuanto cuesta?*
Where is ...?	*¿Donde está?*
I'd like ...	*Quería*
What time does the ... open?	*¿A que hora se abre ...?*
Are there any rooms?	*¿Hay habitaciones?*

Useful walking phrases

What will the weather be like today?	*¿Qué tiempo hay hoy?*
How do I get to ...?	*¿Cómo se va a ....?*
What is this village called?	*¿Cómo se llama este pueblo?*
How many kilometres to ...?	*¿Cuantos kilómetros hay hasta ...?*
Where does this road/path lead?	*¿A dónde se va este sendero/esta carretera?*

More useful walking phrases

I'm lost	*estoy perdido*	(it's) cold	*(hace) frío*
Let's go!	*¡Vamos!*	(I'm) hot	*(estoy) calor*
right	*derecha*	rain	*lluvia*
left	*izquierdo/a*	snow	*nieve*
straight on	*todo recto*	cloudy	*nubloso*
near	*cerca*	fog	*niebla*
far	*lejos*	wind	*viento*
open	*abierto*	stormy	*tempestuoso*
closed	*cerrado*	sun	*sol*

Days, months & seasons

today	*hoy*	January	*enero*
tonight	*esta noche*	February	*febrero*
tomorrow	*mañana*	March	*marzo*
yesterday	*ayer*	April	*abril*
last night	*anoche*	May	*mayo*
weekend	*fin de semana*	June	*junio*
		July	*julio*
Monday	*lunes*	August	*agosto*
Tuesday	*martes*	September	*septiembre*
Wednesday	*miercoles*	October	*octubre*
Thursday	*jueves*	November	*noviembre*
Friday	*viernes*	December	*diciembre*
Saturday	*sábado*		
Sunday	*domingo*		
spring	*primavera*	autumn/fall	*otoño*
summer	*verano*	winter	*invierno*

Numbers

1	*uno/una*	17	*diecisiete*
2	*dos*	18	*dieciocho*
3	*tres*	19	*diecinueve*
4	*cuatro*	20	*veinte*
5	*cinco*	21	*veinte y uno*
6	*seis*	30	*treinta*
7	*siete*	40	*cuarenta*
8	*ocho*	50	*cincuenta*
9	*nueve*	60	*sesenta*
10	*diez*	70	*setenta*
11	*once*	80	*ochenta*
12	*doce*	90	*noventa*
13	*trece*	100	*cien*
14	*catorce*	200	*doscientos*
15	*quince*	300	*trescientos*
16	*dieciséis*	1000	*mil*

Euskara (Basque)

yes	*bai*	please	*arren*
no	*ez*	thank you	*eskerrik*
hello	*kaixo*	good morning	*egun on*
goodbye	*agur*	good afternoon	*arratsalde on*

Galega (Galician)

yes	*sí*	please	*por favor*
no	*non*	thank you	*gracias*
hello	*hola*	good morning	*bos días*
goodbye	*adeus*	good afternoon	*boas tardes*

Glossary

Some Spanish words used in *Walking the Camino de Santiago*, or words you're likely to see along the camino. We've also included English and other words when they may be unfamiliar.

albergue pilgrim hostel, see also *refugio*

¡Animo! Come on! (a term of encouragement amongst pilgrims)

arroyo stream

bodega wine cellar

bollard concrete post

Butlins British holiday camps of dubious architectural merit, popular around the Second World War

calle street

capilla chapel

carnaval carnival; a big festival held on Shrove Tuesday, the day before Lent

casa rural rural hotel, often a bed-and-breakfast

cashpoint bank machine

Castellano Spanish language

castro hill fort, usually Celtic

Chanson du Roland French epic describing the exploits of Charlemagne, King of France, and his knight, Roland

chorizo spicy cooked sausage

Codex Calixtinus twelfth-century pilgrim guide written by Aymeric Picaud, a French monk

cordillera range, chain of mountains

costa coast

credencial pilgrim passport, needed to stay at *albergues*

cruceiro stone crucifix

dolmen megalithic tomb

encierro running of the bulls festival in Pamplona (and also in Estella)

ermita hermitage; small chapel, usually in isolated area

euskara Basque language

euskedi Basque lands

farmacia pharmacy

faro lighthouse

fonte (santa) (holy) fountain (in *Galega*)

frontón court on which *pelota* (*jai alai*) is played

galega Galician language

gallego native of Galicia

hoover vacuum cleaner. Also used as a verb

horréo granary, usually made from stone and wood and raised on stilts; found mostly in Galicia

hospital medieval hospice, which functioned as hospital, *albergue* and hotel

hospitalero/a person who runs an *albergue*, usually a volunteer and often a returning pilgrim. Be nice to *hospitaleros*

iglesia church

Laffi, Domenico seventeenth-century Italian pilgrim who chronicled the camino

lavadero communal village wash hut

menhir prehistoric monumental stone

menú set 3-course meal, usually the cheapest way to eat out; also called *menú del día*

meseta flat plains of north-central Spain

monasterio monastery

museo museum

ossuary chapel or vessel for the bones of the dead

palloza stone building with conical thatched roof; found mostly in Galicia

palomar dovecote (building for nesting doves or pigeons)

panadería bakery

parador national chain of luxury hotels

pelota popular Basque sport, also called *jai alai*; played on a *frontón*

peregrino pilgrim

Picaud, Aymeric twelfth-century French monk who chronicled the camino in the *Codex Calixtinus*

puente bridge

pulpo octopus, a Galician delicacy served at street stalls or in a *pulpería*

reconquista Christian reconquest of Spain from the Muslims from the eighth century onwards

refugio pilgrim hostel; see also *albergue*

reliquary small box containing relics (possessions or body parts of Saints or other holy persons)

retablo altarpiece

río river

romería religious procession to a local shrine, usually made annually

Santiago St James

santuario sanctuary or shrine

sello stamp for *credencial*, received at *albergues*, churches and even cafés; *sellos* are evidence that you've walked the camino

Semana Santa Holy Week, Easter week

sidewalk US English for pavement. If we used pavement, North Americans would be walking in the road

tapas snack-sized portions of food

tarmac road asphalt road

turismo tourist office

¡Ultreia! a term of encouragement amongst pilgrims that roughly translates as Onward Ho!

Camino Log

Keep track of where you are, where you've been and where you're going.....

date	start	end	km	weather	thoughts

date	start	end	km	weather	thoughts

Keep in Touch

You'll meet a lot of people along the camino. You could scribble their addresses on a scrap of paper, but why not write them down somewhere safe?

name	address	phone	e-mail

Index

major places in **bold** type

a

b

c

d

e

f

j

k

l

m

t

u

V

W

X

Z

Keys

Map key

camino	major town or village
main road	other town or village
other road	deciduous wood
railway	coniferous wood
international border	vineyard
river	*cruceiro* (stone crucifix)
lake or sea	church
map orientation	picnic area
	historical site

Text symbols

A	*albergue*	€	bank or cashpoint
H	hotel	i	*turismo* (tourist office)
	restaurant		shop
	café-bar		phone number

Hotel prices

$	up to €30	**$$$**	€50–€75
$$	€30–€50	**$$$$**	more than €75

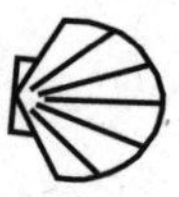

¡ultreia!